# The Orion Dimension

*Hopi Cosmology,
Earth Enigmas & Celestial Secrets*

Gary A. David

*The Orion Dimension: Hopi Cosmology, Earth Enigmas & Celestial Secrets*

**Copyright © 2020 Gary A. David**
**All rights reserved.**

No part of this publication may be reproduced, or stored in a retrieval system, or transmitted, in any form by any means, whether electronic, mechanical, photocopying, recording, or otherwise, without written permission from the author. Published by Island Hills Books and KDP.
Email: garydavid52@gmail.com.
Website: http://theorionzone.com.

**Acknowledgments**
Back cover photo: Deborah Petersen, Chaco Canyon, New Mexico, Casa Rinconada (Great Kiva), dawn June 21, 2018. Back cover photo of *katsina* (kachina) doll by the author, Arizona State Museum, Tucson. **Màasaw** [also, Masau'u], Hopi, "a spirit being, lord of the Fourth World, god of life and death, totem of the Kookop [Fire] clan... personifies the dead living in the spirit world."[1]

I would like to thank my wife Anita Descault for proofreading the manuscript and offering invaluable literary and structural suggestions.

# Contents

## Part I: The Geodetics of Mythic Memory

| | | |
|---|---|---|
| Chapter 1 | The Chakras of Ari-Zona | 7 |
| Chapter 2 | Hopi-Maori Cognation | 28 |
| Chapter 3 | Cosmopolitan Polynesia | 46 |
| Chapter 4 | Cayce and the Hopi Voyage from Mu | 62 |
| Chapter 5 | Turtle Soup—Hopi "Red City" and Mayan "Black Rocks" | 76 |
| Chapter 6 | Palatkwapi—the Case for Piedras Negras | 94 |
| Chapter 7 | Cayce's Tuaoi Stone | 110 |
| Chapter 8 | Geodesy of the Four Corners Odyssey | 120 |
| Chapter 9 | The Meridian Connection— Hopiland and Easter Island | 135 |
| Chapter 10 | Rongorongo and Mohenjo Daro | 146 |

## Part II: The Semiotics of Synchronicity

| | | |
|---|---|---|
| Chapter 11 | The ABCs of Orion—Ants, Bulls, and Copper | 163 |
| Chapter 12 | Orion's Hourglass Archetype | 179 |
| Chapter 13 | Cosmic Double Take | 193 |
| Chapter 14 | Celestial Birdman of Antiquity | 209 |
| Chapter 15 | The Orion Mind in the Cave | 221 |

## Part III: The Mudras of Immortality

| | | |
|---|---|---|
| Chapter 16 | Grasping the Hand Constellation of the Mississippians | 259 |
| Chapter 17 | The Hopi Underworld Journey | 276 |
| Chapter 18 | Grasping the Hand Constellation of the Hopi | 289 |
| Chapter 19 | A Hopi-Dogon Divagation | 308 |
| Chapter 20 | Galaxias Ophis | 322 |
| Bibliography and Endnotes | | 347 |

*This book is dedicated in loving memory of my mother
Gloria Pauline David née Armstrong
March 16, 1926 – November 23, 2018.
You encouraged and supported my work
when few others did.
May your afterlife journey fulfill your past life dreams.*

*Part I*
The Geodetics[1] of Mythic Memory

# Chapter 1
## *The Chakras of Ari-Zona*

Ari, "noble, best"– Zona, the "belt stars of Orion"

**The Road to Orion**

In the spring of 1997 I embarked on a research and writing quest that would last to this day. That fall I would turn 45, and my midlife crisis involved a change of literary partners: from poetry to nonfiction. I had been living with my family in northern Arizona for a few years, and had begun to explore the incredibly complex and intriguing Hopi culture, as well as their ancestral rock art in the region.

During a drive to the reservation in order to watch the *katsina* dancers, those bizarre, multicolored masked spirit messengers, I had an epiphany of sorts. I had recently read Robert Bauval's book *The Orion Mystery*, which basically posits that the three pyramids on the Giza Plateau corresponded to the belt stars of Orion. Up ahead on the lonely, arrow-straight road going north lay the three primary Mesas upon which the Hopi had lived, grew food, prayed and performed religious ceremonies for over a millennium. What if, I idly imagined, that triad of flat-topped mountains where the Hopi had constructed their stone and adobe villages were also an "Orion Correlation"? I put those wispy daydream clouds in the back of my mind and proceeded to experience the peaceful but pragmatic Hopi themselves.

After witnessing a number of sacred *katsina* dances of inestimable power and beauty, I returned home and got out a map of Arizona and a sky chart. What I found astounded me! There was a Hopi village or ruin site corresponding to *each* major star in the constellation—not just the belt stars. Not only that, there appeared to be an inter-relationship between the ancient villages, separated by many miles, that were aligned to sunrise and sunset points on the horizon at the summer and winter solstices. Perfectly projected upon the high desert, Orion also incorporated what I came to call a "chakra line," running down the middle of the constellation's terrestrial configuration. It stretched from southwestern Colorado to the mouth of the Colorado River and contained more that a dozen villages or ruins. In addition, the template also encompassed the spectacular Ancestral Puebloan "star city" of Chaco Canyon in New Mexico—the largest groups of ruins in the American Southwest corresponding to Sirius, the brightest stellar body in the heavens.

As we shall see, many vistas full of mystery and majesty unfold on the road to Orion.

**Hopi village of Walpi, First Mesa, Arizona, corresponding (like the Great Pyramid) to Orion's belt star Alnitak.**

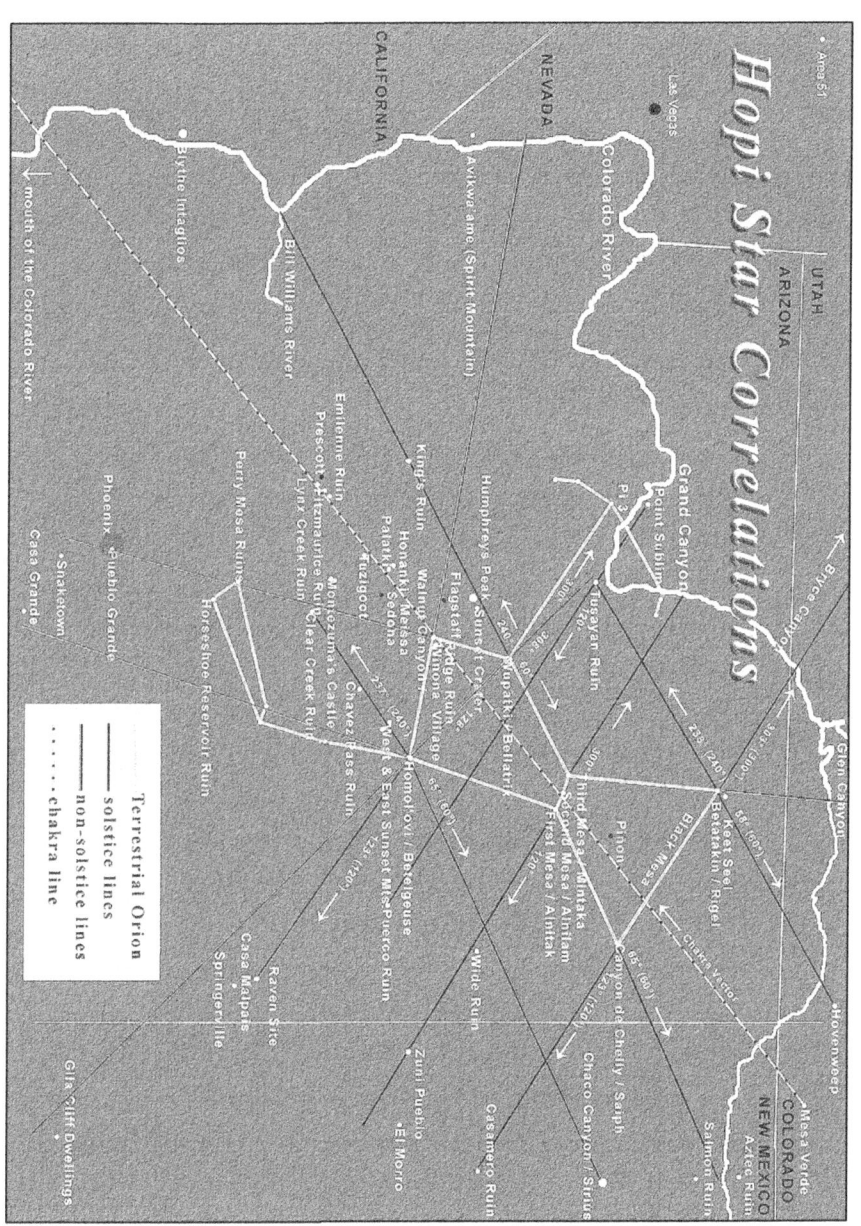

**Ley Lady Ley**

The grand chakra system mentioned above aligns a series of significant ritual and habitation sites in much the same manner as the ley lines, or the "old straight tracks," originally discovered in Britain by Alfred Watkins during the early 1920s. The scholar Janet Hizar Hansford, Ph.D., describes these ley lines in conjuction with a global grid.

> "Pioneers in theses new sciences of geodesy and the world grid are Graham Hancock, Robert Bauval, Robert Schoch, Gary A. David, Hugh Newman, Freddy Silva and others. The practice defined as geodesy is the basic conception in the study of the world grid... The worldwide pattern of ley-lines, called the world grid, is a subject being investigated in the new sciences of sacred site research and archaeostronomy. The fascination of this science is how the ancients had a deep understanding of the movements of the sun, moon, planets and constellations of our Milky Way galaxy and relied upon their priests and shamans to guide them in aligning their temples and edifices, to tap into both the telluric and stellar energies available in their regions on Earth. Rituals and ceremonies were coordinated corresponding to the time of year and stellar alignments which enhanced the power and potency of the sacred practices."[1]

As the eminent astro-archaeologist John Michell also remarks in regard to this world-wide system, "In several other parts of the world, lines linking holy centres are not only mythological paths down which the gods representing the various heavenly bodies pass at regular seasons, but have some further quality known only to native magicians. American Indians, especially the Hopi of the Southwest, appear to use them as cables of mental communication. In China they are known as *lung-mei*, the paths of the dragon, and run between astronomical mounts and high mountains."[2]

As described in *The Orion Zone*, my first book in the series, the chakra system of the Arizona Orion Correlation starts at Mesa Verde, where the "Divine Cosmic Energy" of the *kundalini* lies as a coiled serpent sleeping at the base of his terrestrial spinal column. If awakened, this "Serpent Fire" rises, passing through five chakras (literally, "wheels"), each associated with a particular element and organ of sensation: (1) Base, or Root, Chakra (*Muladhara*) = earth/smell; (2) Sacral Chakra (*Svadhisthana*) = water/taste; (3) Solar Plexus Chakra (*Manipura*) = fire/sight; (4) Heart Chakra (*Anahata*) = air/touch; and (5) Throat Chakra (*Visuddha*) = ether/sound. In addition, the (6) Third Eye, or Pineal, Chakra (*Ajna*) and the (7) Crown Chakra (*Sahasrara*) complete the lightning bolt channel of numinous serpent energy. When the feminine Serpent Fire pierces and vivifies each of the subsequent chakras, they form the liminal gates between the physical plane and the astral plane, thereby becoming etheric centers in the material realm.[3]

According to Hindu scholar and Tantric practitioner Harish Johari:

"The word *kundalini* comes from the *Sanskrit* word *kundal*, which means 'coil.' It is compared with a serpent that, while resting and sleeping, lies coiled. The comparison between a serpent and Kundalini comes because of the nature of its movement, which is spiraling and serpent-like. Kundalini is an aspect of the eternal, supreme consciousness, which is both with and without attributes. In the attributeless (*nirguna*) aspect it is the will of cosmic consciousness, and is pure consciousness. In the aspect with attributes (*saguna*), this energy is often personified as Kundalini, an aspect of the Great Goddess, just as primal energy, or shakti, is personified as Shakti. It is through the power of Kundalini that all creatures act. In individual bodies the same energy lies dormant, as a static center around which every form of existence revolves. In the phenomenal world there is always a power in and behind every activity, a static background."[4]

Author Frank Waters posited that the Hopi recognize only the upper five energy vortexes, the most important of which is located at the top of the cranium. They call the Crown Chakra the *kópavi*, or "open door," through which the soul or consciousness enters the body at birth and departs at death. It is also a portal through which humans may communicate with the Creator during their lifetime. In the Arizona Orion Correlation template, this chakra corresponds generally to the red rock country near Sedona and specifically to the Ancestral Puebloan ruin of Tuzigoot.[5]

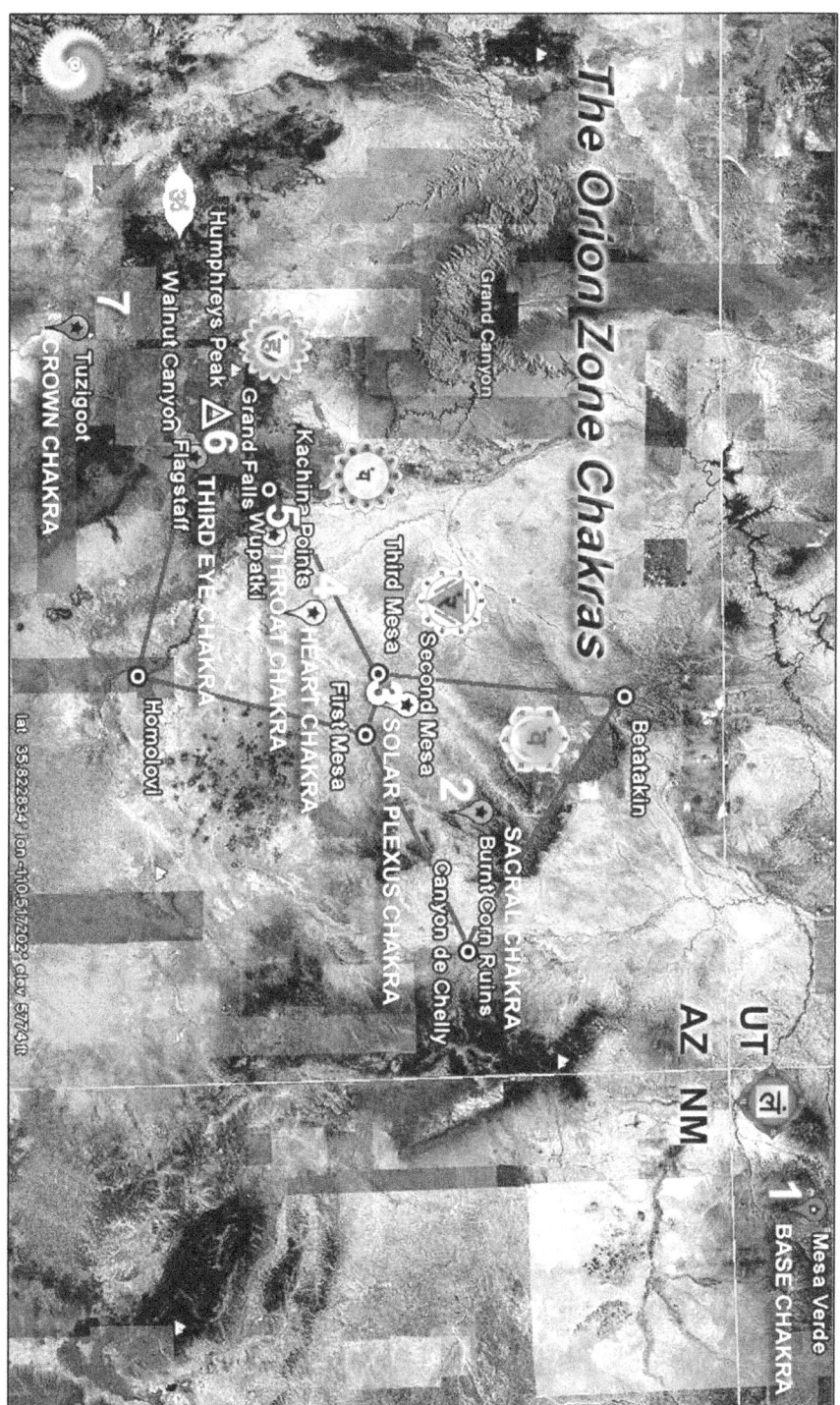

# Chakra Vector (preceding page):

*(1)* Base Chakra = Mesa Verde, the Sun (Orion) Temple in southwestern Colorado *(2)* Sacral Chakra = Burnt Corn Ruins near the village of Piñon, Arizona (corresponding to the Orion Nebula) *(3)* Solar Plexus (Navel) Chakra = Second Mesa and the Hopi village of Shongopovi *(4)* The Heart Chakra = Kachina Points, a mesa southwest of Oraibi (also called Monument Point) *(5)* Throat Chakra = Grand Falls on the Little Colorado River *(6)* Third Eye (Pineal) Chakra = Walnut Canyon Ruins in the foothills of the San Francisco Peaks *(7)* Crown Chakra = Tuzigoot Ruin and the red rock country of Sedona in the Verde Valley.

From the graphic on the preceding page, we see that the fiery Solar Plexus corresponds to the Hopi Mesas of Orion's triadic belt. Of this chakra Waters says: "The last of man's important centers lay under his navel, the organ some people now call the solar plexus. As this name signifies, it was the throne in man of the Creator himself. From it he directed all the functions of man."[6] It is fitting that the seat of Hopi culture and the matrix of their physical-cum-spiritual existence—their homestead and hearth—should be this "throne" of the three Mesas. As within, so without.

Rupestrian expert Dennis Slifer summarizes the totemic significance of the Serpent Power.

> "According to ethnography, in the Southwest snakes were regarded as powerful, sacred creatures for the same reasons as in other parts of the world. The primary attributes of the snake which make it such a potent fertility symbol include its association with water, rain/lightning, and the underworld; its ability to shed skin and appear to be immortal; its phallic form, and its power to kill or to heal. The dynamic energy of the snake as a symbol

of regeneration is probably the main reason so many snake images accompany fertility-related rock art.[7]

The 275-mile-long chakra vector of the Arizona Orion Correlation may be construed as what the Hopi might call the *Tsu' Tuuwuhi*, i.e., "Rattlesnake Line."[8]

This serpent "cable" (as Michell deemed it) that connects nearly a dozen major ancestral Hopi sites allows the *kundalini* dynamism to flow toward the southwest in a psychic algorithm—one chakra after another. Coiled in the so-called Sun Temple (a.k.a. Orion Temple, Base Chakra) and nearby Cliff Palace at Mesa Verde in southwestern Colorado, the serpent current first travels through Burnt Corn Ruins (Sacral Chakra) near the Navajo village of Piñon on Black Mesa, then intersects the Hopi mother village of Shongopovi on Second Mesa (Solar Plexus Chakra, terrestrial Alnilam), passes by a mesa called Kachina Points (Heart Chakra), proceeds over Grand Falls on the Little Colorado River (Throat Chakra), reaches the San Francisco Peaks and intersects Walnut Canyon Ruins (Pineal Chakra, terrestrial Meissa, Orion's Third Eye). Walnut Canyon in the evergreen foothills is correlated to the pineal gland, which is etymologically derived from the Latin word *pinus*, or "pine cone." The serpent power-surge finally drops into the Verde Valley and comes to rest at the hilltop pueblo of Tuzigoot (Crown Chakra). In summation, this conduit of telluric energy flows from Mesa Verde, through the Hopi Mesas, into the San Francisco Peaks, and down to the Verde Valley. Revamped and reinvigorated, the *vajra* viper blasts across northern Sonora to make a littoral exit, plying the deep blue all the way—amazingly—to the South Pacific beachhead on New Zealand's *Te Hopai*.

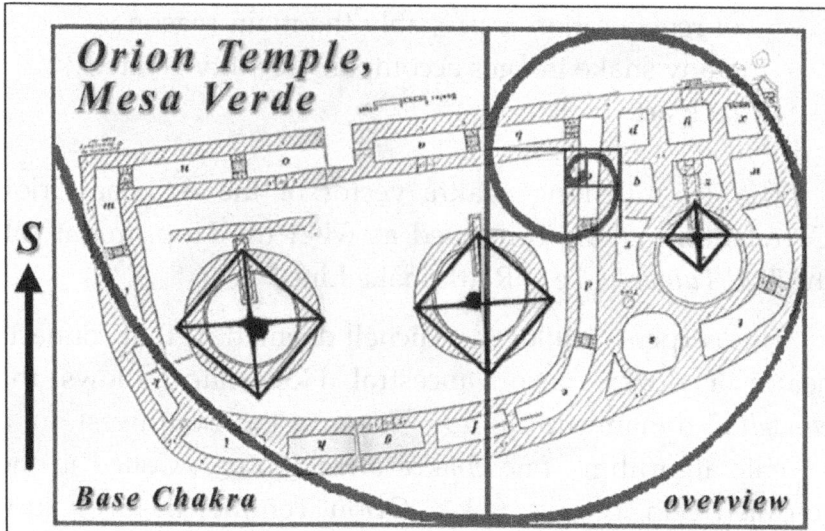

The three kivas correspond to Alnitak, Alnilam, and Mintaka (Orion's belt). Superimposed are Khufu, Khafre, and Menkaure (the Giza pyramids) as well as the Golden Mean Spiral.

1. Satellite view of the "Sun Temple," Base Chakra, Cliff Palace to the northeast, Mesa Verde National Park, Colorado. The latter is the largest cliff dwelling in the American Southwest.[9]

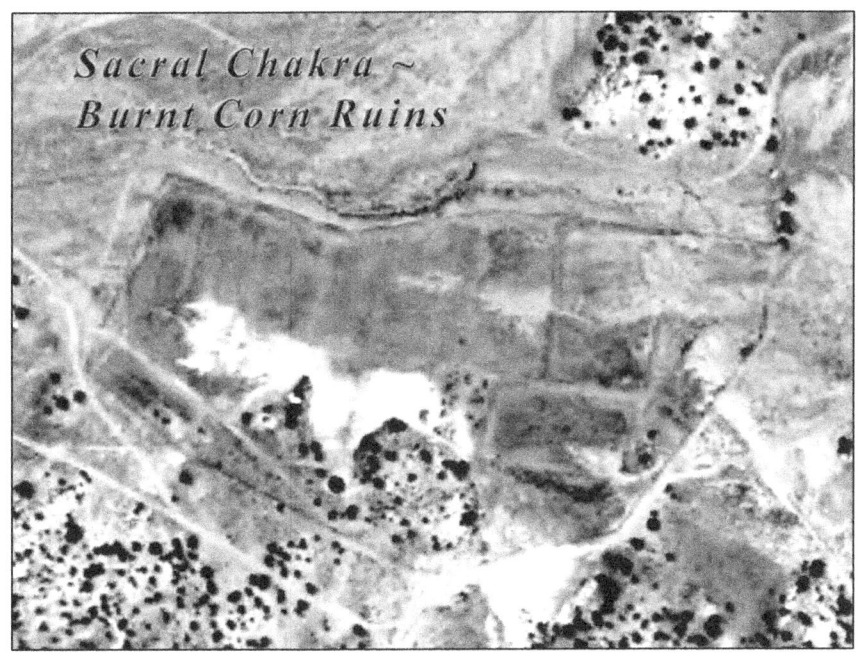

2. Google Earth satellite view of the faint outlines of the foundation of Burnt Corn Ruins, constructed circa 1100 AD, abandoned circa 1250, Sacral Chakra.

3. Mishongnovi village, Second Mesa, Solar Plexus Chakra.[10]

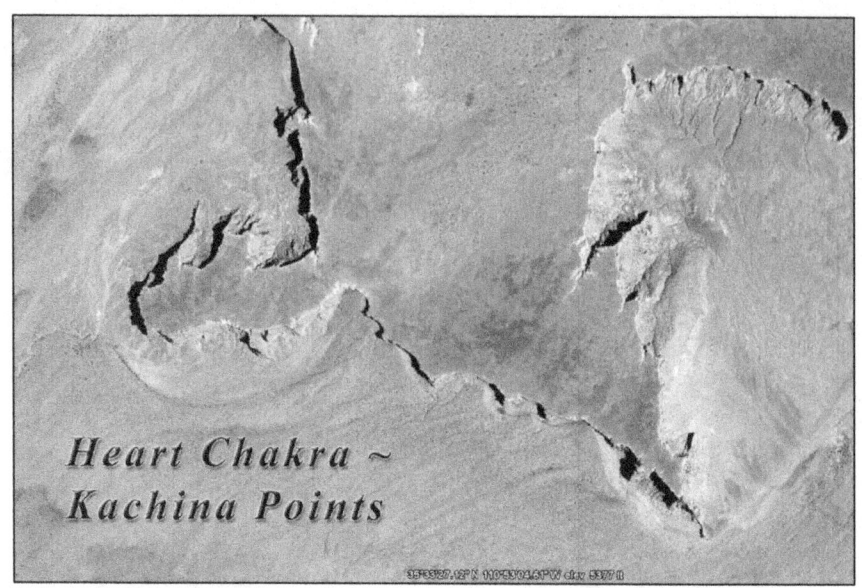

4. Monument Mountain, Google Earth photo. "In T. 3 N., R. 7 W., west side Corn or Oraibi creek, Hop Ind. Res. 'So called for a governement cairn or monument on its top.'"[11]

5. Grand Falls, Throat Chakra, photo by Fred Kovalchek.

6. Walnut Canyon cliff dwellings, 300 rooms constructed between between 1125 and 1250 AD, Pineal Chakra.[12]

7. Google Earth photo of Tuzigoot National Monument.[13]

Gary David and Graham Hancock leading a tour of Tuzigoot Nat. Mon., Clarkdale, Arizona. This 110-room hilltop pueblo built between 1125 and the late 1300s AD forms the Crown Chakra. Photo courtesy of Robert Dakota.

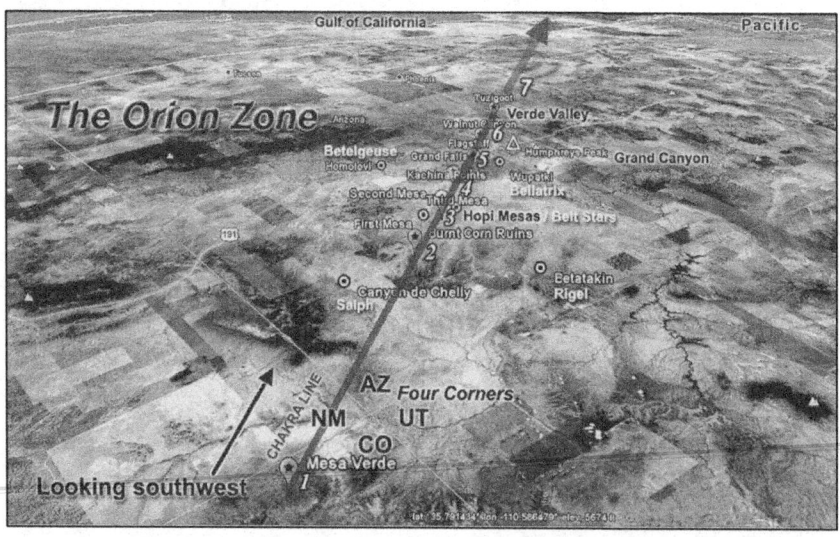

The Chakra Vector proceeds at a 231° azimuth angle into the Pacific Ocean.

## From Arizona to Aotearoa[14]

In *The Orion Zone* (2006) I first discussed the extension of the "Orion Chakra Line" across the Hopi *Tutskwa I'qatsi*, "Land and Life," over which *Kòokyangwso'wùuti* (Spider Grandmother) reigns.[15] This line runs at an angle of 231° azimuth[16] into the Pacific, which may have been the place where Mu, the submerged Mother continent, once existed.

> "The Hopi word *mu'a* means 'hit or shot' as in 'hit with an arrow.' ... the line runs from the Hopi [Second Mesa] village of Shongopovi (terrestrial Alnilam) through Walnut Canyon (terrestrial Meissa) to the mouth of the Colorado River. If this line is extended southwest across the immense distances of the Pacific Ocean, it arrives at the Somoa-Fiji-Tonga island region south of the equator. We may visualize the *kundalini*, or serpent, energy of the chakra system shooting up the terrestrial spine of Arizona Orion like an arrow, then sailing from his crown in the Verde Valley to be directed southwest across the sea, finally arriving at the possible origin or interim home of the Hisatsinom [ancestral Hopi]."[17]

I also noted that the resonant energy collected within the body of the Arizona Orion Correlation is channeled southwest across the Sonoran Desert to the mouth of the Colorado River and then into the Pacific, traversing the equator. At the time of that writing, Google Earth was in its mere infancy. I eventually found, however, that instead of the Tonga region, the line actually comes to rest in the Bay of

Plenty on NewZealand's North Island. (I had been over 500 miles off in my initial estimation over 20 years ago!)

**Standard dating of Polynesian migration in the Pacific.**

So, starting at the ancestral Hopi site of the Sun Temple (a.k.a. Orion Temple) at Mesa Verde National Park in southwestern Colorado, which is the Base Chakra of the Arizona Orion Correlation, the celestial-terrestrial *kundalini* force shoots southwest at an exact azimuthal trajectory of 231.69°. It then traverses the low desert and leaves the coastline near the mouth of the Colorado River, traveling for 7,050 miles across the Pacific into the Southern Hemisphere until it reaches the shore on the North Island of Aotearoa at a place called *Te Hopai* (37°37′ S, 175°59′ E). Mere chance? Some people believe there is no such thing as "coincidence."

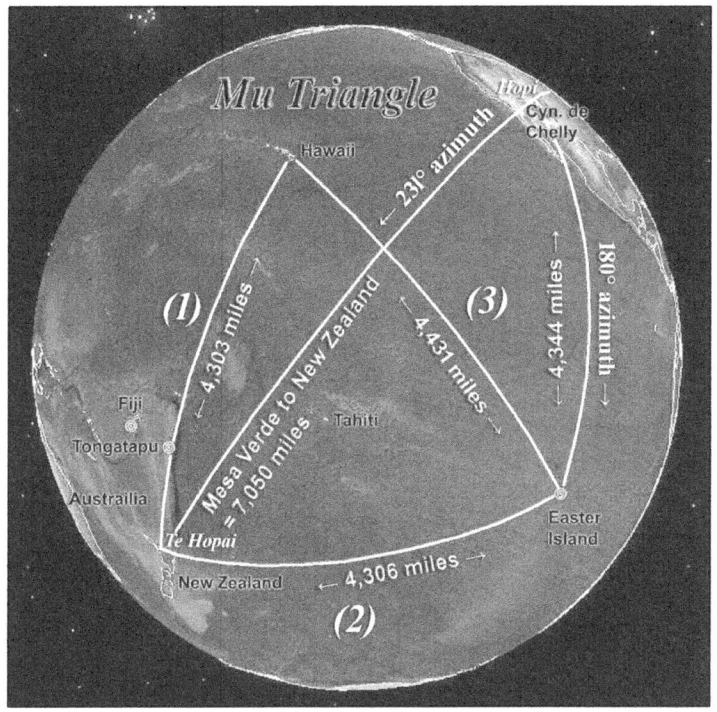

The vector of the 231.69° azimuth of the Hopi Orion Correlation ultimately ends at Te Hopai Island in northeastern New Zealand. (See pp. 25-26.) Canyon De Chelly, Arizona, and Easter Island are exactly on the same longitude: 109° 21' 01".[18] The distance between Spider Rock (see Chapter 9) located in the former and the north shore of Easter Island = 4,344 miles. The sides of the Mu Equilateral Triangle (MET) are approximately the same. Its precise distances are: *(1)* southern shore of Hawai'i to Te Hopai, New Zealand = 4,303 miles, *(2)* Te Hopai to western shore of Easter Island = 4,306 miles, and *(3)* northern shore of Easter Island to southern shore of Hawai'i = 4,431 miles. The differences between the length of the north-south longitude line (4,344 miles, 180° azimuth) and lengths of the respective sides of MET are: *(1)* 41 miles less, *(2)* 38 miles less, and *(3)* 87 miles more.

# A Couple More "Coincidences"

Te Hopai, New Zealand: <u>37° 37' S</u> latitude.

Sun Temple at Mesa Verde Nat. Mon., CO: <u>37° 10' N</u> latitude,
 31 miles south of <u>37° 37' N.</u>
Te Hopi: <u>145° (longitude) east</u> of the Great Pyramid, Egypt.

Colorado R. Delta: <u>145° (longitude) west</u> of the Great Pyramid. (445 miles southwest of Sun Temple, the point (33° 00' N latitude) at which the 231.69° vector bisects the Colorado River).

El Arenal (<u>37° 22' S</u>, 73° 37' W, 17 miles north and 5,631 miles east of Te Hopai)), Arauco Peninsula, nearly 2 miles inland from the south-central coast of Chile: chicken bones radiocarbon dated at 1321–1407 AD. Mapuche Culture area. Thus, DNA sequencing links Polynesia with South America.

"The **El Arenal** bone produced an identical sequence to chicken bones from two prehistoric archaeological sites in the Pacific: Mele Havea in **Tonga**, from upper plainware layers dating to between 2000 and 1550 B.P., which is significantly earlier than El Arenal-1; and Fatu-ma-Futi in **American Samoa**, which dates to about the same period as El Arenal-1. All ancient West Polynesian samples, early samples from **Anakena, Easter Island** and **Kualoa, Hawai'i**, and the El Arenal sample share a single unique point mutation…

"Some prehistoric contact between the Americas and Polynesia is evident from the presence of South American sweet potato (*Ipomoea batatas*) in pre-European archaeological sites in Polynesia, most notably from Mangaia, **Cook Islands**, where it is dated indirectly to ≈AD 1000. Linguistic and archaeological evidence suggest that the bottle gourd (*Lagenaria siceraria*), also from the Americas, was present in Eastern Polynesia before AD 1200. Voyaging from Polynesia to the Americas has been proposed, and debated recently in relation to linguistic and archaeological evidence for the occurrence of some watercraft, namely sewn plank canoes, and fishhook forms found in southern California which resemble Polynesian types. Sewn plank canoes have also been documented in Chile by ethnographers and claims have been made suggesting artifactual and linguistic evidence for **Polynesian influence in the Mapuche region of south central Chile**. Computer simulations suggest that voyaging eastward from Polynesia in the southern hemisphere where the mid-latitude westerlies are more accessible, is a more likely prospect than a northern route to the Americas. These southern hemisphere voyages would have brought landfalls in the central and southern regions of Chile and could have introduced the Polynesian chicken to South America. However, no securely dated pre-Columbian chicken remains or unequivocal archaeological evidence for Polynesian contact with the Americas has been reported **until now**."[19]

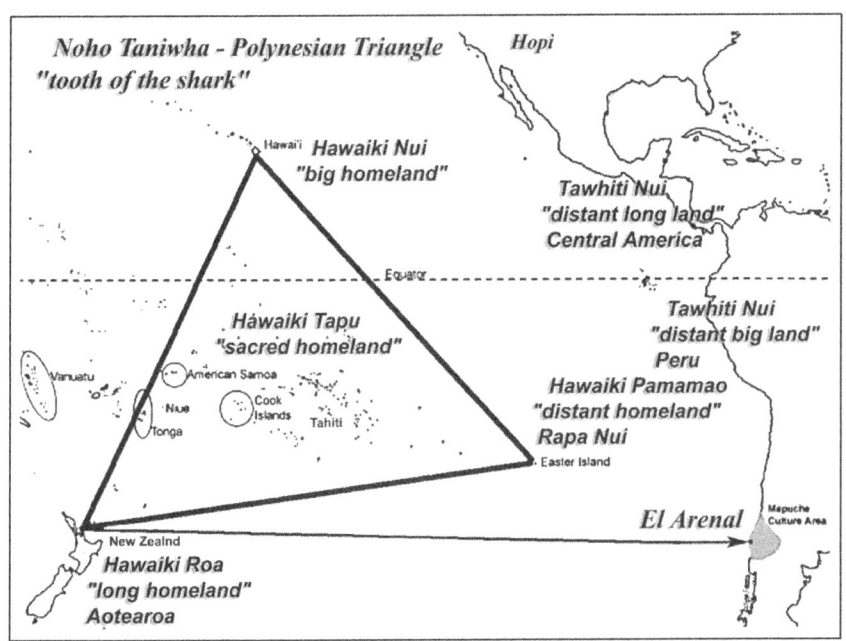

The Polynesian term *Hawaiki* means "homeland."

Tauranga Harbor in the Bay of Plenty, North Island, New Zealand. The Maori word *tauranga* means "moorings, place of anchorage." The Maori *matakana* means "vigilant, wary, watchful." *Aongatete*, means "dawn-head."[20]

The artificial-looking island is only ¼ of a mile in length. Its axis is parallel to the 231° azimuth line 7,050 miles long.

←Sunset Crater, Arizona, dormant volcano, first erupted in 1064 AD and continued for a few centuries.

Whakaari[21] → (White Island), Bay of Plenty, New Zealand, active volcano. Fire at both ends of the energy vector.

In this initial chapter we have seen the geodetic bow-shot of the serpent-fire energy of Orion's chakra tree, which has been projected upon the Arizona desert, reaches the waters of Mu—"mu'a," the Hopi word meaning to "hit with an arrow." The Hopi word *awat* means "bow," and *aw* is the "destinative postposition: to, towards, (to) there..."[22] The ultimate destination was Aotearoa, specifically New Zealand's Bay of Plenty. The Maori term *awa* denotes a "channel" (as in a river), which evokes the chakra line channeling the streaming life force called *prana* up the spine. The related Maori word *awe* (*a-weh*) means "soon" and *aweko* refers to either "old, ancient" or "knowing, understanding."[23]

Chapter 4 will discuss the Hopi inter-generational voyages from the Pacifc region of MET, the Mu Equilateral Triangle (or the "tooth of the shark") to the western shores of America. In the following chapter, however, other linguistic continuities between the Hopi and the Maori will be explored.

# Chapter 2
# Hopi-Maori Cognation

**Philological peregrination**[1]

The term "cognate," in reference to a word or morpheme, is defined as "related by derivation, borrowing, or descent."[2] In my previous book *Journey of the Serpent People*, I discussed legends of the Hopi trans-Pacific navigation from the previous Third World (or cyclic Era) to the current Fourth World.[3] Island-hopping eastward on reed rafts, these Hopi ancient mariners most likely plied the waters for generations rather than merely for years. Thus, a considerable interaction with sailors of other native groups certainly occurred, with its concomitant borrowing of both language and culture. For instance, the Hopi word for "boat" is *paki*, and the Polynesian word for "canoe" is *pahi*.[4] It is also certain that the Polynesian navigational skills were nonpareil. New Zealand ethnographer Elsdon Best (1856 – 1931) describes the maritime acumen thusly:

> "Polynesian methods of navigation are of surpassing interest, for here we have a neolithic folk who attained a remarkable skill in that science. Possessing but rude forms of stone implements, ignorant alike of compass and charts, the ancestors of the Maori far surpassed Europeans of a much more advanced culture status in sea voyaging. They steered their primitive craft by the heavenly bodies, and by the regular roll of the waves

before the trade-winds. With marvelous courage they explored vast areas of the Pacific Ocean; they settled and resettled many far-sundered isles; they carried with them cultivated food products and practiced agriculture in all suitable places."[5]

If Hopi legends of the continent of Mu and their escape during its last cataclysm brought on by a deluge have any credence at all, we could expect that the Hopi and various Polynesian groups encountered each other during their mutual, extensive exploration of the Pacific. Evidence of linguistic borrowing is rife.

Let's start with the name of geographic end-point of the vector (azimuth 231.69°) that began in southwestern Colorado and traversed the Pacific, crossing into the Southern Hemiphere and terminating in the Bay of Plenty on the North Island of New Zealand. The Maori word *Te* is a definite article, and the term *Hopai* refers to the biblical Shobai, or "captors" (Ezra 2:42).[6] Google Translate inexplicably defines the Maori word *hopai* as either "find out" or "pick up." The Maori verb *hopī* means "to be terrified, alarmed, frightened, intimidated, panic-stricken, scared, dismayed"; also, "lacking courage, timid."[7] The term *hopi* refers to "a native oven," perhaps similar to the traditional beehive oven of the ancestral Hopi.[8]

In the late 19th century the Hopi were alternatively referred to as the Moki, which literally means "die of, suffer from, be afflicted by."[9] "The name 'Moqui,' or 'Moki,' by which they have been popularly known, means 'dead' in their own language, but as a tribal name it is seemingly of alien origin and of undetermined signification—perhaps from the Keresan language [of New Mexico]…"[10] The Maori term *moki* refers to a canoe-shaped raft made of bulrushes, whereas the word *mokihi* means "raft of dry flax stalks," and *mokai* denotes "captive."[11]

So, both *hopai* and *mokai* connote "captors." Hopi long-distance sailors with their boats made of bamboo may have simply been scared to death when they were found and captured by intimidating Maori warriors on the beach at Te Hopai. Oceanic origins are hard to fathom.

In this philological foray, we come to the phoneme *ka*, the initial syllable in the name of the Hopi benevolent spirit messengers called *katsinam* (kachinas).[12] "The washing of the dead person's head [with yucca suds], and the bestowing on him of a new name, indicate that the Hopi regard death as a change of status analogous to other changes that take place in life; the covering of the face of the corpse with a cotton mask prior to burial – that they equate the dead, to some degree at least, with the katçinas and with the clouds."[13] Although it is interesting to note in passing that the Maori loan word *hopi* means "soap,"[14] their term *Ká* is significantly defined as "a rising flame, rising or burning element, such as fire" and "animating, enlivening, vigorous."[15]

These semantics are very much in keeping with a culture I have frequently revisited in my previous books. Scholar Jeremy Naydler, Ph.D., discusses this simple syllable.

> "For the ancient Egyptians, the vital energy that is associated with the *ka* was felt to emanate from the ancestors. Thus an opening of contact with the ancestors, and hence with the spirit world in general, was necessary for

the *ka* energy to become individualized or 'owned' by the living king. The event of Unas [in the *Pyramid Texts*] meeting his *ka* and it becoming integral to his self-consciousness follows naturally from his encounter with the spirits of the dead and his celestial ascent… As a result of the king's union with his *ka*, he becomes suffused with a new daimonic power, a superhuman potency…"[16]

E. A. Wallis Budge defines *ka* as "image, genius, person, double, character, disposition, the vital strength of the Ba-soul," while the word *kaka* means both "serpent, worm" and "darkness, night."[17] The term *ba* means "soul" but its homonym refers onomatopoetically to "ram."[18]

For the Tohono O'odham of southern Arizona, the noun *ka* or *kai* denotes "semen" and "seed or pit," whereas *ka'a* refers to "one's paternal grandmother or great-aunt." The verb *kah* means "to hear, understand," and the verb *kuh* means "scorch," semantically similar to the Maori word *Ká*. The O'odham noun *koh* means "rattlesnake."[19]

The Hopi term *katsina* (*ka-tsina*) is perhaps etymologically derived from the word *kátci*, "spread out," "horizontal," or "surface of the earth" and *náa*, "father," thus giving to the term a literal meaning of "surface-of-the-land father."[20] In the course of its migrations, the paternal Snake Clan had certainly spread out across the surface of the Earth. Ultimately, however, the term *katsina* is an enigma. According to archaeologist Charles E. Adams, "There is no translation for katsina. It is certainly a borrowed word. (Emory Sekaquaptewa: personal communication.) Foremost, there is no initial syllable *ka-* in Hopi. Evidence to suggest it is a borrowed term from outside the Pueblo area, rather than being indigenous, lies in the similarity of its pronunciation in the Zuni language and in Keresan spoken in Acoma."[21] From this evidence we can deduce that the *katsinam* and their correlatives in other Ancestral Puebloan groups were derived from a universal, monolithic source.

My friend, the independent researcher Laird Scranton comments on the Maori term *tua*.

> "The Maori word *tua* also refers to 'religious ceremonies taking place at the naming of a child,' comparable to the modern-day Jewish tradition of a child-naming ceremony. [Edward] Tregear roughly equates these ceremonies to a baptism, and so the suggestion is that there may be an underlying symbolic relationship to water. Appropriate to the intermediate nature of the creative processes of the Second World of matter, the Maori word *tuao* means 'transient' or not permanent.'"[22]

The Hopi word *tungwa* (pronounced *tu-ngwa*) means "name, to give a name to," while *tu'alangw* is "an evil apparition, specter, evil sorcerer," and *tuam* denotes "grave."[23] The Maori *tuakai* denotes "an ancient burial place."[24] The Hopi *tuu'awta* means "to have a vision, mystical experience of seeing something extrasensory in nature or of déjà vu."[25] In the context of the Scranton quote above, it is noteworthy that the Hopi also have a cyclic view of time, First World, Second World, etc. Furthermore, the word *hopi* in Maori, Hawaiian, Samoan, and Tahitian additionally carries the sense of "to sprinkle with water,"[26] i.e., baptism. The Maori word *atua* means "god, demon, or supernatural being."[27] This nexus of cognates has a decidedly spiritual or ritual connotation.

The simple Maori word *po* means "night" but also "primeval darkness" and even "place of departed spirits."[28] The Hopi word *pa* refers both to "water" and to "wonder, awe, surprise, doubt."[29] According to Laird Scranton, "[Elsdon] Best tells us that the Maori word *po* refers to an unseen, intangible, unknowable concept that underlies the heavenly bodies of the universe. He also says that, for the Maori, the word *po* connotes: The period of time prior to the existence of the universe. The period of labour of the Earth Mother. The period of time after death. The spirit-world or the underworld."[30]

Many cultures, including ancient Egypt, conceptualize the cosmogony as a materialization from the dark waters of the abyss. For instance, "In the beginning God created the heaven and the earth. And the earth was without form, and void; and darkness was upon the face of the deep. And the Spirit of God moved upon the face of the waters." (Genesis 1:1-2, KJV) Tregear's dictionary describes the mythic connotations of the Maori word *po* as "…the Cosmic Darkness out of which all forms of life and light were afterwards *evolved* [italics added] or procreated."[31] Incidentally, the Maori word *pa* means "to touch" or "to have sexual connection."[32]

Author Frank Waters (no pun intended) describes the Hopi Creation story:

> "The first world was Tokpela [Endless Space]. But first, they say, there was only the Creator, Taiowa [Tawa]. All else was endless space. There was no beginning and no end, no time, no shape, no life. Just an immeasurable void

that had its beginning and end, time, shape, and life in the mind of Taiowa the Creator... So Sotuknang [the Sky god, nephew of Taiowa, or *Taawa*] gathered from endless space that which was to be manifest as the *waters* [italics added] and placed them on the universes so that each would be half solid and half water."[33]

In his book *The Maori Race*, New Zealand scholar Edward Tregear states: "The cause of all things was the generative power existing in the primeval Chaos or Nothingness (*Kore*). Thence came the yawning immeasureable Darkness (*Po*), blank and unformed, yet holding within itself the potency and essence of all future life."[34] The Hopi terms *kori* and *koro* mean "cavity, cave hole"[35] — thus, a blank space. The Hopi word *qölötapi* denotes "digging stick," whereas the Maori term *ko* is "a wooden implement used for digging or planting; sometimes used as a weapon."[36] In the context of cosmogony, it is interesting to note that the ancient Egyptian word *pa* means "to be, to exist" while its homonym means "cup, pot" — that which holds liquid — and *pa-t* means "liquor, drink." In addition, *pau* and *pa-t* denote "primeval time."[37]

The Maori version of cosmogony emphasizes primal evolution rather than creation. Elsdon Best explains:

> "In place of a creation by that [Supreme] Being we have an evolutionary process arranged in genealogical form, showing the development of mind, of matter, earth and sky, of light, and finally of man, from primordial chaos, nothingness, and darkness. These remarkable allegorical myths embody some extraordinary concepts illustrating the powers of the

34

ancestors of the Polynesians in the line of abstract thought... In one of these curious evolutionary formulae Conception is given as the forbear of Growth, who produced Energy; then follow Thought, Mind, Desire, &c. Then come various phases of Po and other conditions of chaos, until the last one in conjuction with Atea (space), produces the heavens. The sky is personified by Rangi, who takes Papa, the Earth Mother, to wife, and this twain begets seventy offspring, all males, and all supernatural beings."[38]

The Maori concept of *Atea*, "space," is similar to the Hopi word *àatö*, or "underneath, below (in a general sense), underground."[39]—i.e., "down under," as in, for Hopi argonauts, the Southern Hemisphere. Specifically, *Atea* is "the last of the Ages or Time-spaces to be counted in the existence of the Universe. It is the eighteenth upward from Te Kore ('nothingness,' the Void)."[40]

One wonders if the Maori "Void," enshrouded in *Po* (Darkness), echoes the Greek queen of the underworld, Kore. The name of *Atea*, the personified Giver of Light, also carries the sense of not only "distant, far off" but also "beforehand."[41] *Kore* and *Atea*, the chthonic and the telluric, are two sides of the same coin: reverse and obverse. Mythologist Jane Harrison more eloquently makes the same point, albeit flipped: "It was mainly in connection with agriculture, it would seem, that the Earth-goddess developed her double form as Mother and Maid. The ancient 'Lady of the Wild Things' is both in one or perhaps not consciously either, but at Eleusis the two figures are clearly outlined; Demeter and Kore are two persons though one god."[42] The horizontal goddess of far spaces (objective and extroverted) and the vertical goddess of infernal restrictions (subjective and introverted) are opposite poles of the same continuum. Harrison continues: "But it is not surprising that... a religion like Orphism, which concerned itself with the abnegation of the world and the life of the soul hereafter, laid hold rather of the figure of the underworld Kore, and left the prosperous, genial Corn-Mother to make her way alone into Olympus."[43]

The word *Atea* brings up the actual name of New Zealand itself, *Aotea*, or, sometimes, *Aotearoa*. "The ususal meaning given to the Maori name for New Zealand is Land of the long white cloud. *ao:* cloud; *tea:* white; *roa:* long."[44] Again, the Hopi near-homophone agrees: *àatöqa*, "the bottom part or underpart of"[45]—that is, the bottom portion of the world. "It is an apparent allusion to the land being pulled up from the depths by Maui. All Polynesian islands were thus hauled up by deities from the realms of the Dark Night to the 'White Day.'"[46]

Maui was the pan-Polynesian god or demigod of Light and Life.[47] The epigrapher Barry Fell opined that the legends of Maui were based on a Libyan explorer of Oceania, who sailed east from the Indian Ocean across the Pacific in 232 BC, the fifteenth year of the pharaoh Ptolemy III's reign, notable for a solar eclipse visible in New Guinea in November of that year. "The word *mawi* in Egyptian means a guide or navigator, but it also sounds very like the Polynesian name Maui. In Polynesian legend Maui was a great sailor who, in the figurative speech of Polynesian tradition, was said to have 'fished up new lands' from the sea...—a poetic way of recording his discovery of lands hidden beneath the horizon."[48] The Hopi word *maawi* means "to pick from a tree, vine or plant."[49] This suggests pulling up food from the soil in the same manner that Maui pulled up islands from the bottom of the sea.

**Turns and Twists**

I realize that all these linguistic twists and turns might be starting to make you dizzy, but stay with me here. We all know that the double helix is encoded within the DNA molecules of every living organism on the planet and perhaps even beyond. However, in addition to the seven chakras of the *kundalini* system—those psycho-spiritual energy wheels positioned along the spinal column—two subtle nerves (*nadis*) called the *Pingala* and the *Ida* form a dual spiral that interlaces it. They in essence channel energy up and down the backbone that is twofold: the solar *Pingala* (i.e., right side, masculine, electrical, verbal, rational, "left brain") and the lunar *Ida* (i.e., left side, feminine, magnetic, visual, emotional, "right brain").[50]

From his online book *Living In Truth: Archaeology and the Patriarchs*, Charles N. Pope has observed that the double helix is also the "fundamental literary structure of the Torah," the body of Jewish religious literature contained in the Pentateuch (literally, "five scrolls," the first five books of the Old Testament).[51] The Hebrew word *torah* literally means "teaching" (noun) or "direction, instruction, doctrine, law,"[52] and DNA metaphorically could be considered the genetic "law." The term itself is related to the English words torsion and torque, both literally meaning "to twist."

The Hopi word *tori* also means "twisted, wrenched, distorted," and *torikuyi* refers to a pigtail hairstyle worn by married women.[53] The Maori cognate *tari* denotes "a mode of plaiting with eight strands."[54] The concept of plaiting applies symbolically to both cultures in terms of the marriage ceremony. "The Snake Maiden's hair is taken down from her customary hair whirls [i.e., whorls] and washed by her female attendant while the Antelope Youth's hair is washed by his [male] attendant. The attendants then trade places. The wedding of the couple is done by the wetting and uniting of their hair as it is twisted together in the suds. In a Hopi marriage this act in effect binds the marriage contract as is said, 'Now you are untied, ever to go apart.'"[55] This Hopi mystical marriage takes place during the Snake Dance in August. As for the Maori: "In the darkness of evening the young pair were set together in the centre of a house that had been swept and garnished, and their friends formed a circle about them, holding a thin rope of plaited grass, which was placed round the shoulders of the wedding pair and knotted into a ring (*henga*) binding them together."[56] In both cases we see a *hierogamos*, or an alchemical wedding of *Pingala* and *Ida*, the braiding of hair or grass symbolizing a caduceus.

Of relevance here is the Maori *haka*, "…a posture dance that involves the entire body in vigorous rhythmic movements, which may include swaying, slapping of the chest and thighs, stamping, and gestures of stylized violence. It is accompanied by a chant and, in some cases, by fierce facial expressions meant to intimidate, such as bulging eyes and the sticking out of the tongue. Though often associated with the traditional battle preparations of male warriors, *haka* may be performed by both men and women, and several varieties of the dance fulfill social functions within Maori culture."[57] These include the welcoming of guests, and, conversely, a warrior dance/song to provoke an enemy, as well as a mourning ritual and a wedding celebration. One key feature of the performance (other than the protruding of the tongue, like the obnoxious Gene

Simmons, co-founder of the rock group Kiss) is hyperventilation or panting. We are not surprised, then, that the Hopi word *hekwe* refers to "panting," and *haqti* means "far away, distant."[58] Incidentally, the ancient Egyptian term *heka* denotes "magic, the power of working magic, sorcery, spell, incantation, charm, word of power," and all aspects of the root *hek* are connected to a sense of singing or chanting.[59]

A few other cognates are worth attention. For instance, the Maori word *mata* means "face (countenance) or eye" but also the face of inanimate objects, such as the "face of the ocean." It alternately refers to "the medium of communication with a spirit" and "a charm, a spell."[60] Scranton adds, "Among other meanings, the Maori word *mata* can imply the notions of observing objects (such as the stars) and acquiring knowledge."[61] The Hopi word *mata* means "to show, demonstrate, exhibit" but is also refers to a small, rectangular stone bin for grinding corn (i.e., metate).[62]

I'm cognizant that this transnational cognation section is a philological farrago. But I'd like to add just a few more terms before terminating it. The meaning of the Maori word *tapu*, whence derives our word taboo, is twofold: 1. "sacred, holy, hedged with religious sanctity, devoted, to consecrate, to respect, to adjure" and 2. "under restriction, prohibited, to be defiled."[63] The Hopi homonym *tapu* denotes "bridge," or literally, "cradleboard."[64] In both senses of the word, there is an implied restriction, either of the projected pathway or bodily movements of an infant. Laird Scranton provides both the Dogon (Malian) and the Egyptian semantics of *tapu*.

> "The Dogon word *ta* can mean 'gate' or 'doorway,' and the word *pu* refers to the concept of 'totality.' Taken together, the Dogon term *tapu* would refer to a body of knowledge

> that might be seen as 'the gateway to totality, the same knowledge that was restricted to trusted initiates. From an Egyptian perspective, and knowing that the precise pronunciation of Egyptian words was uncertain, we see a likely reference to this same body of restricted knowledge reflected in the ancient Egyptian term *tepa*, which Budge defines to mean 'to overstep' or 'to transgress.'"[65]

Regarding Laird's comment on pronunciation, ancient Egyptian is called an abjad, or a language written with just consonants, the vowels being merely approximated.

Finally, patient reader, we come to the Maori words *puhana*, which means "to glow, to shine, blushing" and *pahanahana*, which denotes "to daub with red ochre and oil."[66] The Hopi term *pahana* means "Anglo; anyone of European extraction (English, Friench, German, Russian, etc.) other than those identified as Spanish/Mexican," i.e., Caucasian.[67] One might simply identify him/her as a white person with blushing red cheeks. (Or is that politically incorrect?)

*Pahan* is also the name of the Hindu snake-priests from the Oraon tribe of Jharkhand, India, and adjacent states, who supposedly migrated from Dravidian south India circa 100 BC. Their religion is a mixture of shamanistic animism, ancestor worship, and Hinduism. "The origins of the name 'Oraon' are unclear. Some Oraons say that the name is derived from *Ur* (chest), because they believe they were born of the blood from the chest of a holy man... Oraons are, as a rule, short of stature and dark-complexioned, broad-nosed, and thick-lipped. They are considered to be of Proto-Australoid stock, descended from a race that influenced the peoples and cultures of a wide area of South Asia, Southeast Asia, and the islands of Polynesia."[68]

Late 19th century scholar J. F. Hewitt compares the rituals of the *Pahans* with those of the Hopi, which he identifies as "Mexican."

> "The Mexican villagers live in long houses [i.e., pueblos] large enough to hold several generations of a family, like those of the Fiji islanders and other cognate people in Polynesia and of the Nāga villages in Assam [India]. Their ritual seems also to date from the Kushika age when the priest formed guilds which, after passing through the stages indicated by the village clans of Oraon Pahans and the barber-priests of India, developed into the caste of the Brahmans... The Kushika priest-guilds of northern India who worshipped the grain soul and the Nāga snake, and who correspond to the Mexican antelope and snake-priest, are called in the Rigveda Varshagiras, or praisers of rain, which infused the soul of life into plants and animals, and Nahasha, or sons of the ploughing-snake Nagur, whose name seems to be reproduced in that of the Mexican Nahuatl."[69]

As previously mentioned, the Hopi word *pa* means "water" and *hana* means "to bring down." If you combine these two words, they form *pa-hana*—"to bring down water," or rain.[70] So *pahana* may have had something to do with precipitation as well. Incidentally, the related Sanskrit noun *pAyana* denotes "causing or giving to drink."[71] Pahana is also the name of the "Elder White Brother," who, legends claim, was present when the Hopi emerged into the current Fourth World, but who thence migrated eastward with a promise to return at the end of the age (à la the Maya deity Kukulkán or the Aztec Quetzalcóatl).

Hearkening back to our previous discussions of the word *ka* (pp. 30-31) and the word *tari* (pp. 37-38), we find a "meaningful" cognate ("coincidence," i.e., pyschologist C. G. Jung's shorthand definition of synchronicity) in the *Pahan* priesthood of Oraon, which was known to handle a sacred artifact called "...the Dali-ka-tari, the basket (*dali*) of Ka the great snake goddess (*tari*), the rain-mother, whose dwelling-place was unknown, and who ruled both heaven and earth..." Known by Buddhists as Tara, Ka was also a star goddess in the worship of Praja-pati, the Hindu name for Orion.[72] Both the name of the tribe and the name of the constellation bear a striking resemblance to the name of the Hopi village of Oraibi, or Orayvi, on Third Mesa in Arizona.

In the third section of the previous chapter, I stated that the Hopi word *mu'a* signifies "hit or shot," as in "hit with an arrow," and metaphorically implies the vector of the azimuth (231.69°) that reaches from Four Corners of the U.S. to the eastern shore of North Island in New Zealand. The serpertine *kundalini* energy of the Arizona Orion Correlation surges forth across the desert, soars over the Pacific waters that the Hopi ancestors once plied, then transits the ghost of the Mother-continent Mu to arrive ultimately at Te Hopai in Aotearoa.

According to the 20th century esotericist James Churchward, Mu or Mu'a, the "Motherland of Mankind," reputedly measured 5,000 miles in length from east to west and 3,000 miles in width from north to south. Its northern boundary was the Hawaiian Islands while its southern boundary was a line running roughly between Easter Island

and New Zealand. (See the Mu Triangle, p. 23.) With a population of sixty-four million, Mu supposedly had a highly civilized and enlightened society, and until about 12,500 years ago it functioned as the world's center for trade, commerce, and education. At that time cataclysmic earthquakes, volcanoes, and tsunamis destroyed this great continent, leaving only the remnants of those archipelagos we see today—or so goes the legend.[73]

If Mu, or Mu'a, truly had a global influence, then one clue reinforcing this is the palindrome for "M-U-A," which is A-U-M, the divisible form of OM. This Sanskrit syllable represents the divine principle of Brahman, or God. In this regard the *Taittiriya Upanishad* states: "Thou art Brahman, one with the syllable OM, which is in all scriptures—the supreme syllable, the mother of all sound..."[74] Hence, both the mother of all sound and the mother of all people are referred to by the same letters, albeit reversed.

The Maori word *mua* carries the semantics of both "front, forepart" and "former time," as in the past.[75] In Western culture we generally think in linear terms of the past being behind us as we, in the present, proceed forward toward a blank future. Laird Scranton explains the alternate viewpoint of many traditional indigenous peoples:

> "Another symbolic concept that has importance for the cosmological tradition is that of an *ancestor*. This same concept arguably lies at the heart of Maori outlook that conceptualizes the processes of creation in relation to genealogies. We have said that in the mind-set of many ancient traditions, an ancestor was conceptualized as having preceded you and so would stand 'before' or

'ahead' of you. From that perspective, the Tamil [of southern India] word *mu* expresses the notion of 'that which was before,' while the Maori words *mu* and *mua* refer to an 'ancestor' and to 'the front or forepart' of something."[76]

Thus, the ancestors, or deceased "elders," are not sequestered far off in some vague notion of heaven or misty afterlife but are everpresent in the mundane lives of their descendents. In other words, ancestral spirits are not behind us, but we are facing them.

The Maori term *mua* also denotes "an altar as representiave of the deity Mua... a god worshipped in the temple of Wharekura."[77] In addition, "The Mua was the holy enclosure surrounding the Whare-kura and its most sacred centre was the place where stood an image of Kahukura, the rainbow god." The *Wharekura* was a temple where religious ceremonies as well as human sacrifices were held, but it also functioned as a sort of parliamentary or council chamber. It furthermore served as a college where the sons of priest-chiefs (*ariki*) were taught "mythology, history, astronomy, and the mysteries of life and death."[78] *Kahukura* was a beneficent deity (*atua*) of travelers (i.e., mariners), life, death, and disease.[79]

If Hopi myths of trans-oceanic voyaging on reed rafts from the previous Third World to the current Fourth World have any validity, New Zealand may have been their territorial "extremity," which is the literal meaning of the Maori term *Mú*.[80] The Hopi word *mun* means "flow (of liquid)" and the prefix *mus-* means "sexually aroused."[81] The Egyptian *Mu* refers to "the Water-god, the personification of the celestial waters" and "the divine essence of Osiris," namely, Orion; futhermore, Mui-t was the goddess of the primeval waters.⁸² In fact, in this Nilotic land all the permutations of the monosyllable *mu* were semantically related to water or liquid. For instance, the word *mu āa* meant "great water, flood," which was the agent of the Mother-continent Mu's demise.

The Egyptian *mut* also refers to "mother," and Mu-t was "the 'Mother'-goddess of all Egypt" as well as "Mut in the horizon of heaven." In their bizarre, polymorphous pantheon, Mu-t was also the name of "a goddess with three heads (one of a lioness, one of a woman, and one of a vulture) and a pair of wings and a phallus."⁸³ Ironically, the word *mut* also denoted "to die, dead, death."⁸⁴ At Thebes the goddess Mut included many aspects of Isis (Sirius). "The great temple of Mut at Thebes was built by Amen-hetep III, about B.C. 1450, and was approached from the temple of Amen-Rā by an avenue of sphinxes; the southern half of the building overlooked a semi-circular lake on which the sacred procession of boats took place…"⁸⁵

The next chapter will deal with the maritime mélange of the Pacific.

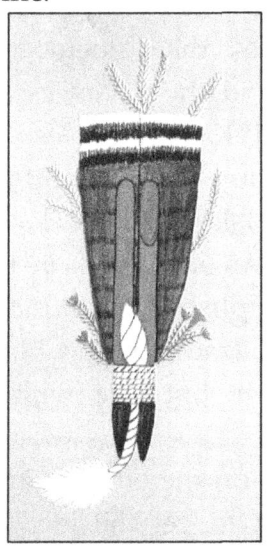

←**Hopi** *paaho, paho,* "prayer stick, prayer feather," literally, "water-arrow."⁸⁶

**Maori** *paho,* "soaring, to flutter in the air, as a bird, to float in the air without flapping the wings." **Hawaiian,**" to swim, to slide away."⁸⁷

# Chapter 3
## *Cosmopolitan Polynesia*

**Transnation Navigation**

The term "cosmopolitan" derives from the Greek *kosmopolitês*, literally "citizen of the world." It is defined as "composed of persons, constituents, or elements from all or many parts of the world," and "having worldwide rather than limited or provincial scope or bearing," or even "having wide international sophistication."[1] In this case it basically refers to a multi-ethnic, multi-cultural population that was a maritime aggregate of polities exploring and/or colonizing much of Oceania.

David Hatcher Childress in his recent book *The Lost World of the Cham* presents the concept of thalassocracy. "A thalassocratic empire is essentially a maritime empire that maintains naval supremacy through the use of a huge fleet (or fleets) of ships. A country that is a thalassocracy is a maritime trading empire with many port cities in far-flung islands and coastlines."[2] He cites the Phoenicians as a Mediterranean example of this, and the Cham as a Pacific example. "The Cham (pronounced 'Kom') peoples inhabited much of central Vietnam and a group of islands off the coast called Cu Lao Cham, or Cham Islands. I think that this island base, as well as cities up several rivers in the area, were once the center of an accomplished maritime trading empire—and empire that not only traded with China to the north and Indonesia to the south, but also with nations across the vast Pacific!"[3]

Childress goes on to comment on the ethnic salmagundi of such navigators. "So, we start to get the idea that the

Cham were a mixture of races, much like the Olmecs and the Egyptians, with some blacks and whites mixed in with oriental races. Seafarers on large ships are often a mix of races, and sailors are a group who tend to treat each other equally. It does not matter about one's racial makeup on a ship, what matters is the sailor's ability to do his job and keep the ship moving. It is the kind of comraderie that only a crew can really know."[4]

According to the late 19th-early 20th century British geographer and anthropologist W. J. Perry, "The vast region of Oceania contains two distinct peoples. In Melanesia, which comprises the western part, the Solomons, the New Hebrides and Fiji, the population is dark-skinned and negroid in type. In Polynesia, which comprises the rest of the Pacific with the exception of Micronesia, the population consists of light-skinned people somewhat akin to the inhabitants of countries west of the Pacific."[5] Early 20th century Scottish occult scholar Lewis Spence comments on these anomalous light-skinned sailors.

> "Practically throughout the entire length and breadth of the Pacific Ocean, but more especially in its more easterly latitudes, there exist the clearest and most astonishing traces of a white, fair-haired race *which owes nothing to European admixture.* [italics added] The legends of Hawaii, the New Hebrides and New Zealand are all eloquent of the past traditions of such a race, and numerous examples of it are still to be found in white and fair-haired natives who have not a drop of European blood in their veins."[6]

If not Europe, then whence? Maybe Mu? Preemptive nota bene to the hyperskeptics and anti-diffusionists: I am clearly not broaching the notion of racial superiority that contemporary white (i.e., Nordic) supremacists are wont to spew ad nauseum.

The late 19th century New Zealand scholar John Macmillan Brown observes the "European-*like* [again, italics added] features and colour" of the Oceanic inhabitants:

> "There are also many indications of a blond race having penetrated into Polynesia. There is the story, in at least all the larger areas in which there were refuges for a defeated people, of a golden or red-haired race that crossing with some of the conquering immigrants have left *urukehu*, or light-haired families and children. In New Zealand the Turehu, a light-haired aboriginal race away up in the mountains of Urewera country, crossed with the immigrants and so left numbers of *urukehu* in that region. But it is the *Patupaiarehe* that are especially referred to as the purest of the blond-haired race..."[7]

The name *Patupaiarehe*, a member of the group who lived in the mountains east and south of the Bay of Plenty, was defined as "a fairy, an elf... They were a tiny, fair-haired, fair-skinned race, bright and joyous, always singing."[8] (Echoes of *Homo floresiensis*, the 3½-feet tall "Hobbit," the skeletal remains of which were found in 2004 on the island of Flores in Indonesia. They were estimated to have lived between 100,000 and 60,000 years ago.)[9]

Anthropologist Susan B. Martinez, Ph.D., remarks on these so-called little people: "New Zealand lore has the long-sunken Hawaiki peopled over by a Caucasian race with fair skin and hazel eyes. One such group was the Mori-ori; they were in New Zealand long before the Maori and built great monuments, hill forts, and irrigated terraces."[10] (In this context, I believe the term "Caucasian" is technically a misnomer.) Martinez suggests that the term *mori* means "anointed," and indeed, the Maori word *mori* denotes "coconut oil."[11]

Late 19th-early 20th century ethnologist S. Percy Smith tries to extricate the term "Hawaiki" from its geographical and metaphysical entanglements.

> "The universality of this name points to the fact that it is extremely ancient and that it was under that form the Fatherland was originally known. With many branches, it has now become synonymous with 'Spirit-land': the place to which the spirits of the dead pass as their final resting-place. In some parts it is said to be the 'under world'; that is, beneath the present world of life... In all cases the spirit, whilst always passing to the westward, is said to go downwards, i.e., to dive into the sea, and then pass along to the sunset. It is in this manner that Hawaiki has come to be used for the place of departed spirits located underneath the earth."[12]

The spirit's afterlife journey to the west will be dealt with in Chapter 16. In regard to Hawaiki, Edward Tregear explores complexities of the mythical-cum-material realms.

> "These migration legends assert that the cradle-land of the Maori was named Hawaiki.

It is over this name and its locality that the wordy war most rages... One of these theories, however, may be mentioned as deserving special reference, and that is, that as Avaiki in Rarotonga and Mangaia means 'the Spirit World,' it is possible that it has no earthly locality, but that it has existence only in the land of dreams. Even in New Zealand we have glimpses of such meaning, thus, a tradition says, 'the boy went quickly below to the Lower World (*Reinga*) to observe and look about at the steep cliffs of Hawaiki.' It is not impossible, however, that a place which once may have had real existence could in the passing of many centuries fade from human memory so far into the realm of legend as to become eventually the Land of Shadows, the dim region of the Under World. Wherever the locality of the primal Hawaiki, it is certain (so far as oral tradition can be trusted)[13] that in coming to New Zealand from one of the latter named Hawaiki, the Maoris had experiences different from any they could picture in New Zealand surroundings. They affirm that in the place they came from there were *large animals*; that *the sun was exceedingly hot*; that some of the *tribes of people (enemies of their own fair race) were black, with hair standing out* [italics added] all round their heads, and not fastened in a knot, Polynesian fashion."[14]

Although excessive heat and bushy hair may refer to Melanesia, megafauna clearly points to Africa.

A Samoan, Polynesian type.

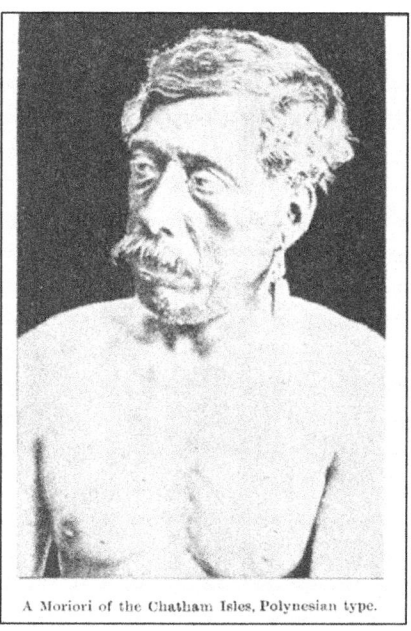

A Moriori of the Chatham Isles, Polynesian type.

Note: The Chatham Islands are an archipelago located about 500 miles east of South Island, New Zealand.

A Solomon Islander, Melanesian type.

A Maori girl, Polynesian type.

These photos show the range of racial diversity of Oceania.

A Samoan girl. Polynesian type.  A Fijian, Polynesia-Melanesian type.

John MacMillan Brown states that the primeval "fatherland" (really, the Motherland) of Polynesia called Hawaiki was "...not merely Po, or darkness, or night underground, but under the sea. The spirits of the dead have to plunge in order to get to it."[15] The Hopi word *haawi* means "climb down, go down, or descend," and the word *ki* means "house, home."[16] For the Hopi, *Hawa-i-ki* could be designated as the "home-down-under," or the aqueous underworld located in the Southern Hemisphere.

**The Time of the Hopi Mariner**

In the passage quoted below, Albert Yava, a 20th century Hopi-Tewa man from Arizona, describes the *Patki* (Water) Clan's journey over the ocean. Today this clan is in charge of sky-watching in order to regulate the agricultural and ceremonial calendar. In particular, the *taawa mongwimu'yta*[17] ("sun-chiefs") calibrate sunrise and sunset points on the horizon for the purpose of determining the summer and winter solstices. In fact, the Water People imported to Hopiland the important winter solstice ceremony called *Soyal*.[18] Perhaps the skills crucial in navigating upon the ocean were eventually adapted to an agrarian existence in the desert after the Hopi made it to their final homeland— the *Tuuwanasavi*, "a sandy place about four miles southwest of Oraibi," literally "sand-middle," the Hopi Center of the World.[19]

> "In Hopi the Water Clan is called Patkiwoema. That can be traslated as Dwelling on Water, or Houseboat, Clan... and this refers to their tradition that sometime after they left the place of emergence they made a long journey across a large expanse of water in boats with dwellings constructed on them. The body of water is believed to be the ocean, but just what part of the ocean it was we do not know. It seems that the Water Clan had a big village somewhere before Palatkwa [Palatkwapi], but corruption and evil set in and they had to leave. That is when they made the ocean voyage. Palatkwa was their next big village. One thing you hear from the Patki people is that in ancient times they were white, not Indian color. They say, 'My ancestors had white skins, but because of evil things that happened, we lost all that.' They also say, 'The Patki people are the ones who are supposed to

teach the Hopis good moral values, how to lead good lives.'"[20]

The Tewa are a Pueblo group that currently lives along the Rio Grande in New Mexico, but some of its members also live in a village called Hano on First Mesa in Arizona. The Hopi name for spiritual chief is *kikmongwi*, but the similar Tewa term is *poa'atoyong*, which literally means "leader-after-the-flood." —namely, the flood that destroyed the Third World (Era).[21] Directly adjacent to Hano is the Hopi village of Sichomovi (Sitsom'ovi), which was established by the *Patki* Clan.[22]

**Albert Yava (1888 – 1980), Tewa-Hopi, a member of the Tewa Stick (Spruce) Clan and an inducted member of the Hopi One Horn Society. (See Chapter 17.) Yava's mother was a Tewa and his father was a member of the Hopi *Pakti* Clan.**

In my book *Journey of the Serpent People*, I provide genetic evidence linking the Hopi and other tribes of the American Southwest to indigenous groups of Oceania, including the trait of albinism.[23] Another germane marker is called the human lymphocyte antigen (HLA). These alleles are basically proteins on white blood cells that produce antibodies. (An allele is an alternative form of a gene—one member of a pair—that is located at a specific position on a specific chromosome.) The distribution of HLAs differs among world populations and may thus be used in tracing ancient migrations. Canadian genetic researcher Bede Fahey states the following fact in a lengthy monograph: "The phylogenetic relationships for the HLA system show the Pima population of North America to have the closest relationship with the Maori..."[24]

The Hopi were known to incorporate members of the Pima (Akimel O'odham), who now live in central Arizona.[25] Albert Yava relates the fact that the Hopi clans originated from different directions, ultimately to merge at the *Tuuwanasavi*. "We had Pimas coming in from the south. And there's an Apache strain too. Those clans that came here from Palatkwa [*Palatkwapi*—see Chapter 6, current volume], such as the Water Clan, Sand Clan and the Tobacco Clan, brought Pimas and Apaches with them."[26] (A genetic analysis by Lisa A. Mills, Ph.D., also revealed that the Ohio Hopewell culture (circa 100 BC to 500 AD) had the same nucleotide point mutations as the modern Pima, Apache, and Navajo.[27])

Oceania is essentially a "water world," and the aquatic supercedes the terrestrial in pragmatic and pyschological importance. As I have shown, diverse racial and tribal groups amicably interacted or vied for supremacy as they plied the sea-lanes. As Dr. David Lewis, nautical scholar and navigator explains: "The Polynesians' and Micronesians' habitat is a primarily aquatic one, the proportion of dry land, exclusive of New Zealand, in the third of the Pacific where they dwell being of the order of two units of land for every thousand of water. It is understandable that few aspects of the history and culture of Oceania can be separated from sea-going. Ocean space can inhibit contact (through terrestrial features like mountain ranges may do so equally) but they become highways rather than barriers as maritime technology—especially navigation—becomes effective."[28]

Carl L. Johannessen, Professor Emeritus at the Univerisity of Oregon, describes the maritime mélange.

> "At early times, the Polynesians were sailing huge wooden ships carrying families, warriors, pigs, chickens, dogs, food, and trade goods for colonization of new-found lands, or simply for visits to known islands. Rats were commonly present in these cargoes and they were eaten as protein on the trips... In modern times, Thor Heyerdahl, a respected archaeologist and anthropologist, created rafts in an indigenous style from sketches and plans as recorded in illustrations by Spanish conquistadores. He proved that balsa or reed rafts could be used to cross any ocean and to carry chemicals, plants, and animals in those crossings. If Heyerdahl could travel such distances on rafts, surely the sleek, fast Polynesian ships could have made the trip to the Americas and back even more easily. The abundance of American crop plants and weeds found in the eastern islands of the Pacific... indicates that maritime folk had

traversed these eastern stretches of the Pacific Ocean many times."[29]

Evidence for trans-Pacific voyages in pre-Columbian times includes flora, fauna, parasites, and pathogens that are found both in Southeast Asia and the Pacific archipelagoes as well as on the North and South American continents. The list is too extensive to delve into here, but the most well known plant example is, of course, the sweet potato (*kumara*), found both in South America and western Pacific islands. However, according to studies done by French researcher Charles Nicolle in 1932 and Brazilan researcher Olympio da Fonseca in 1970, one disease-causing organism, endemic typhus (*Rickettsia typhi*), is found both in Mexico, Guatemala, and the southern U.S. as well as in the Pacific islands and the Far East. "The Typhus of Mexico and Guatemala was murine typhus, the same as in New Zealand, Australia, and Southeast Asia. Typhus murine might have come from the Vikings, but that is not very logical. Nicolle supposes that it reached the Americas via rats on Polynesian vessels."[30]

Elsdon Best describes the Maori relationship between the celestial realm and the pelagic realm in terms of their calendric system.

> "The year began with the first new moon after the heliacal rising of Matariki (the Pleiades), about the middle of June, among the East Coast tribes. Quite possibly the Pleiades year was brought into the Pacific area from southern Asia in past centuries. In some areas, as the far north and the Chatham Islands, the rising of Puanga (Rigel [the left foot of Orion]) seems to have marked the advent of the new

year. The Maori of former times had a remarkable knowledge of the stars, and had assigned names to many of them. At the time when he was making deep-sea voyages his study of the heavenly bodies was his salvation... Those stars he believed to possess much influence over his food-supplies; they wer personified and spoken of as ancestors; their warning often preserved him from danger. Above all, those stars had looked down upon his remote ancestors in the lost fatherland, and had watched the gallant old sea-rovers explore the vast Pacific in times long passed away. Some of the star-names are known over a wide area, as from New Zealand to the Hawaiian Isles."[31]

Mr. Best goes on to relate how the agricultural system was synchronized with the stars. "The Maori tells us that the planting season was marked by the star Puanga (Rigel), Atutahi (Canopus), Tautoru (Orion's Belt), and Whakaahu. According to place and season, the time differed, but we may say that crops were planted from September to November. An old folk-tale has it that Mahuru (personified form of spring) sends the cuckoo hither from Hawaiki to tell the Maori people when to plant the *kumara*." He also states that the heliacal rising of the star Vega in the constellation Lyra, which the Maori identify with the ancestral tutelary being named Whanui, commences the harvest season.[32]

Many contemporary elders from the Hopi, the Zuni, and many other tribes refer to their "star ancestors," who, they say, brought their people knowledge of how to live a righteous life. According to Nancy Red Star, a Cherokee "runner": ("I am a runner between generations, sexes, cultures, and worlds.") "Our history with extraterrestrial life (or, as an elder corrected me, 'ultraterrestrial' life) is of global significance at this time. Spiritual wisdomkeepers around the world have recognized signs that were predicted by the ancient prophecies. These signs have signified the Time Keepers that they must now speak their closely held sacred knowledge concerning our origin from the stars; the influence of visitation on the formation of culture, tradition, and ceremony; and the imminent return of our Star Guardians."[33]

In the next few chapters we will explore Palatkwapi, the legendary "Red City of the South" mentioned by Albert Yava. We will also consider the possibility that this location is actually a Mayan ruin in Guatemala. In fact, some scholars believe one of Edgar Cayce's lost Halls of Records lies hidden there.

*From Cook's Voyages.*
Double Canoe of Ra'iatea in 1769.

Maori *waka*, "war canoe," Otago Museum, Dunedin, New Zealand.

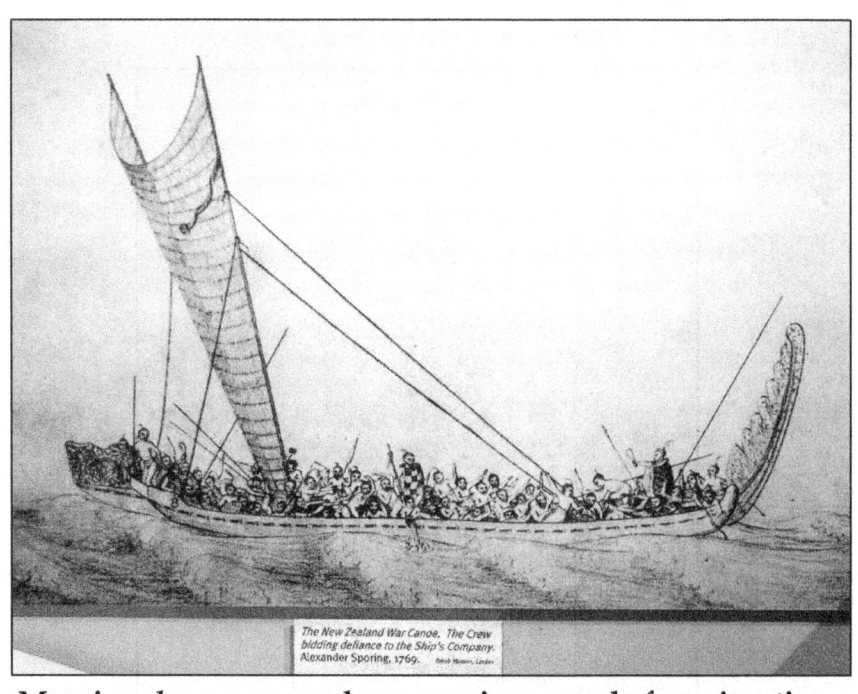

Maori *wakas* were used as oceaning vessels for migration.

←Cover of French 2005 translation of Don C. Talayesva's book *Sun Chief: The Autobiography of a Hopi Indian*, 1942.

Maori Chief, Polynesian type.

# Chapter 4
# Cayce and the Hopi Voyage from Mu

**The Case of the Cliff Dwellers**

The lost continent of Mu in the Pacific Ocean was frequently mentioned in the life readings of Edgar Cayce. Known as the "sleeping prophet," this 20th century psychic was renowned for his abilities to find physical cures for his clients, describe past lives in Atlantis, Egypt, or other locales, and prognosticate about future world-events. In one instance a woman in her former life (whom Cayce routinely describes as the "entity") apparently migrated from Mu to the American Southwest during the beginning of the deluge. "...we find the entity was in that land now known as American, during those periods when changes that had brought about the sinking of Mu or Lemuria, or those peoples in the periods who had changed to what is now a portion of the Rocky Mountain area; Arizona, New Mexico, portions of Nevada and Utah."[1]

The Hopi refer to their ancestors as *Hisatsimom*, whereas for the same group archaeologists use the term Ancestral Puebloans—those who constructed the ancient stone "apartment complexes" called pueblos. (These people were formerly called the Anasazi, which is actually a Navajo term meaning "ancient enemy.") If these structures are located underneath the Southwest's many natural alcoves or rock shelters, they are known as cliff dwellings. In one life reading, Cayce even mentions these denizens of the high desert by name. "The entity was among the first that have become known as the cave or cliff dwellers, in the portions now known as Utah, Arizona, Colorado and New Mexico. In those environs and places did the entity make for its activities, in the name, Uramm."[2] Another past life reading describes the role that the individual played in the development of the Pueblo culture. "The entity was in that land now known as the American during the periods when there were sojournings of those from the Land of Mu, or Lemuria. The entity was then among the first of those that were born in what is now portions of Arizona and Utah, and among those who established the lands there for the building up or growing of that civilization in those experiences; and was in the name Uuluoou. The entity led many to a greater understanding of how there might be made the closer relationships with the material things and the spiritual thoughts of the people."[3]

**Edgar Cayce (March 18, 1877 – January 3, 1945)**

Edgar Cayce's desk in "the Vault," headquarters of the Cayce Foundation, Virginia Beach. Photo by Gary A. David.

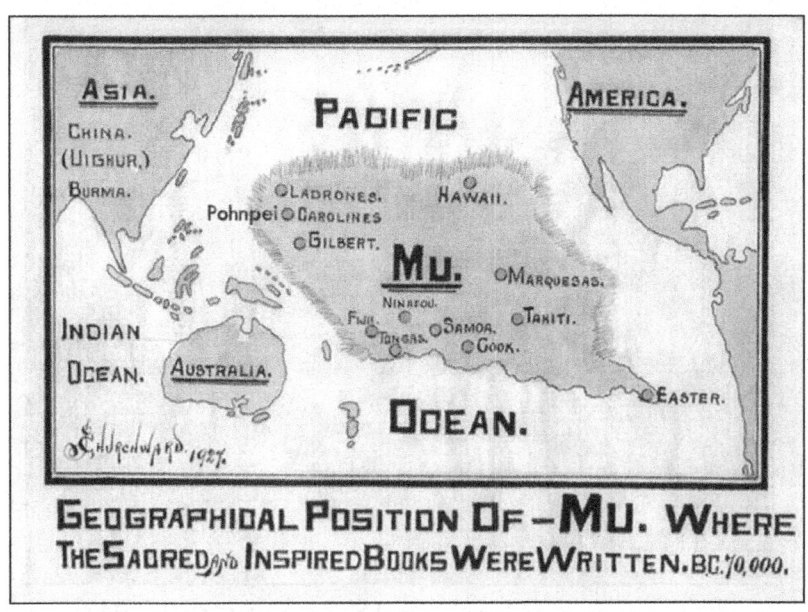

James Churchward's map of the "Lost Continent of Mu."

64

**Cliff dwelling, White House Ruin,
Canyon de Chelly, Arizona. Photo by the author.**

Cayce in yet another reading refers to the "Lost Tribes" and gives a specific migration date from Mu that is much earlier than the conventional 8th century BC date for the Ten Lost Tribes of Israel.

> "With the injection of those of greater power in their activity in the land, during that period as would be called 3,000 years before the Prince of Peace came, those peoples that were of the Lost Tribes, a portion came into the land; infusing their activities upon the peoples from Mu in the southernmost portion of that called America or United States, and then moved on to the activities in Mexico, Yucatan, centralizing that now about the spots where the central [portion] of Mexico now stands, or Mexico City. Hence there arose through the age a different civilization, a MIXTURE again."[4]

Despite his idiosyncratic mode of expression, Cayce presents a consistent picture of a migration from Mu to the western coast of Central or North America and the Desert Southwest. In one interesting Cayce reading we even envisage a woman who had migrated from India to Arizona, there to become an influential individual.

> "172-3 12. In the one before this we find in that land now know as America, in that land known as that of the West. The entity then among those that were come into the land as immigrants from the far east, now, or from the now known as India land, settling with those peoples in the plains now known as Arizona. The entity among those, then, that set up this

combination of cults that built in the land the temples and the dwellings in the rocks. The entity then gained much through that experience, becoming the priestess to those peoples... and giving much to the aborigines of the land, and understanding, and of [the] same came those that made of the land, or of the metals and the clays, much of that that was later taken in the Yucatan land, in the Mexico land, into the southern land, being driven down by the heavy men from the north."[5]

The entity apparently migrated to Arizona, bringing her knowledge of metallurgy and pottery production, which was taught to the people and later exported to Mesoamerica. Archaeologists have found evidence in southern Arizona and northern Mexico of the smelting of copper artifacts, including tiny bells. Ceramic production, of course, achieved a cultural acme in the American Southwest.

The "heavy men of the north" is possibly a reference to the nomadic Chichimecs, literally "Sons of the Dog." This barbaric tribe originally inhabited the so-called *Gran Chichimeca*, a vast territory north of Mexico. Instead of being a unified tribe, they were a loose aggregate of diverse bands whose character has been compared to that of the Germanic tribes that swept down from the north in the 5th century AD to attack Rome. The Chichimecs are frequently contrasted with the Toltecs, whose primary urban center was Tula (north of Mexico City in the State of Hidalgo) and who in that specific region and time period were considered the epitome of refined civilization. "'Chichimec,' on the other hand, literally means 'descendants of the dog,' and was used in one sense to refer to the hungry nomads who inhabited the wide-open spaces north of the cultivated fields, the hunters and gatherers who used the bow and arrow, dressed in deer skins, and ate raw meat."[6] As the bellicose group from which the Aztecs are believed to have later descended, the Chichimec hordes migrated down from the north, eventually reaching the Valley of Mexico sometime between the 11th and the beginning of the 14th century.[7] Cayce's time-frame, however, is much earlier than the 12th century AD historical migration.

**Codex Boturini, 16th century. The glyph of the Ancestors, *Colhuaca*, rests atop the pyramid on the island-continent of Mu. A paddler departs from the island and reaches the shore at the 1 Flint, or 1168 AD. He goes to a grotto inside of the bent hill Colhua, where the Aztec war god Huitzilopochtli is declaiming. The migration (see footprints) is shown going west to east, ultimately to arrive at Tenochtitlán (Mexico City).**

# Structural Similarities Between Temple and Kiva

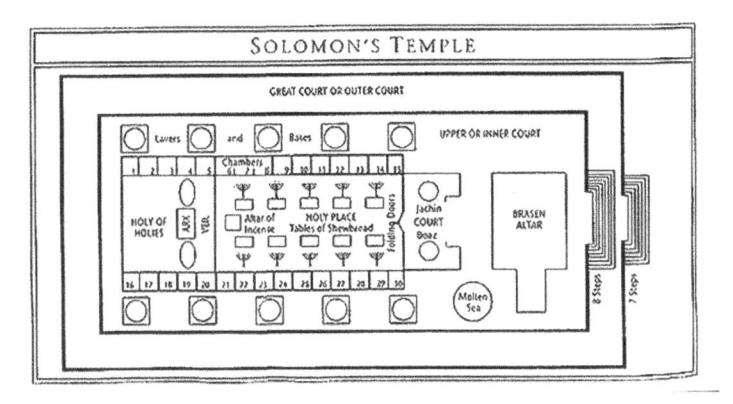

**SOLOMON'S TEMPLE**

**TYPICAL RECTANGULAR HOPI KIVA**
Ground plan for chief kiva, Shipaulovi, Arizona

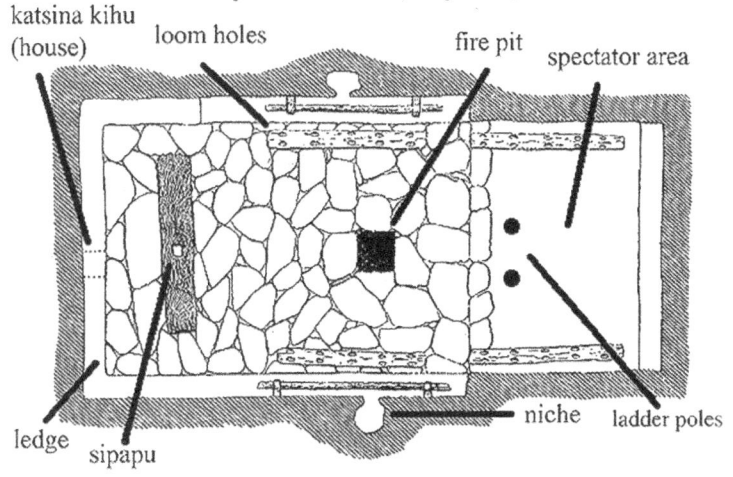

katsina kihu (house), loom holes, fire pit, spectator area, ledge, sipapu, niche, ladder poles

The sipapu is the Hopi "Holy of Holies," and represents the First World.
The flagstone area in the middle represents the Second World.
The raised platform on the right for spectators represents the Third World.
The overhead hatchway via a ladder represents the current Fourth World.

*"In the beginning... we started from Jerusalem."* -Louis Numkena, Sr., Moenkopi, Arizona

*"...the original* sipapuni *(earth navel) was in Egypt, India, or Jerusalem..."*
-Jasper Poola. First Mesa, Arizona

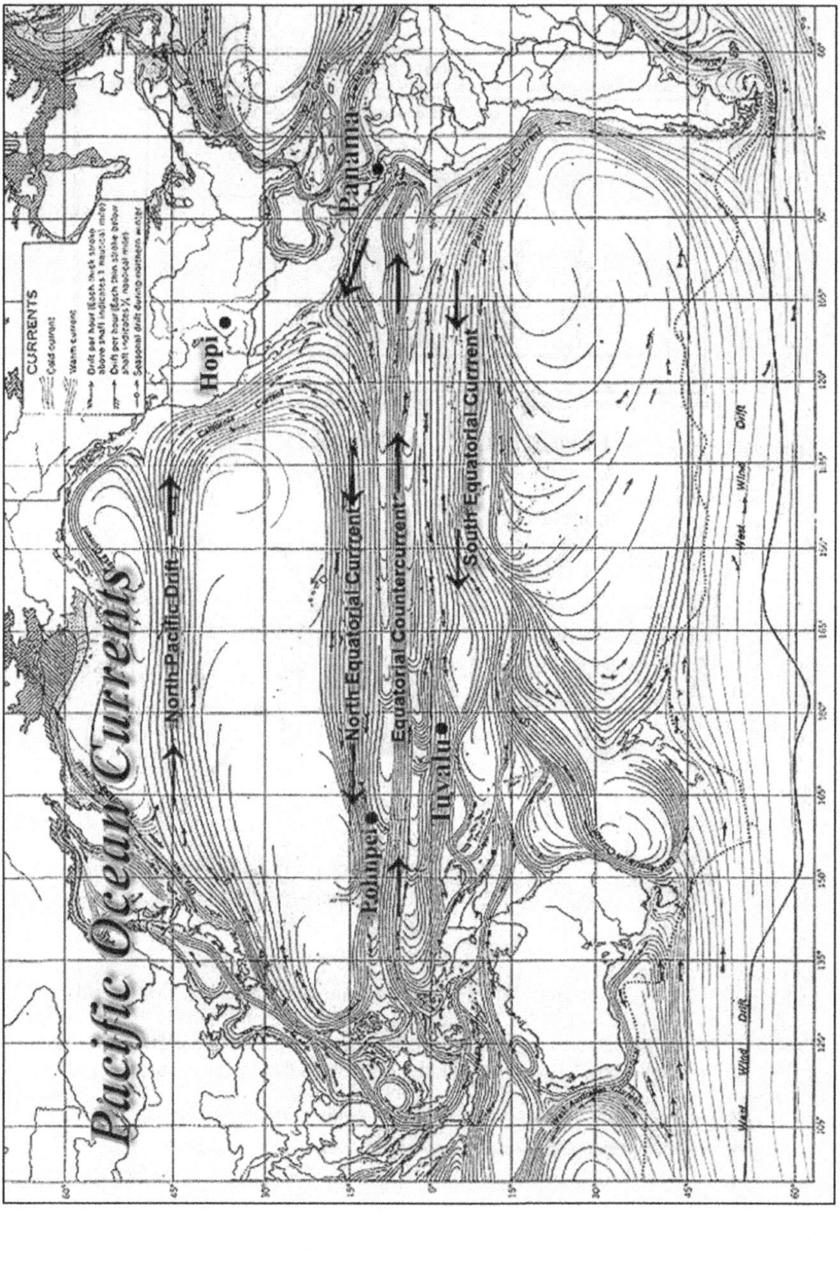
Pacific Ocean Currents
North Pacific Drift
Hopi
Panama
North Equatorial Current
Equatorial Countercurrent
South Equatorial Current
Pohnpei
Tuvalu
CURRENTS

## The Journey to Palatkwapi

Harold Courlander, scholar of Hopi culture, comments on ubiquitous tales of the tribe's trans-Pacific migration. "The myth of the arrival by an ocean voyage persists in various clan traditions. The name Water Clan in Hopi is Patkinyamu, literally meaning Dwelling-on-Water (that is, Houseboat) Clan. The belief is that before these people arrived at ancient Palatkwapi they reached the present world after a long water crossing." Apparently, "…they had escaped from a place of wickedness by floating in houseboats across a great sea."[8] The ancestral Hopi's various voyages on reed rafts to the western coast of Central and North America are detailed in my previous book *Journey of the Serpent People*.

For both the ancestral Hopi and the modern Hopi, the "Patkinyamu," or *Patki* Clan, is in charge of sky-watching in order to regulate the agricultural and ceremonial calendar. In particular, the *taawa mongwimu'yta* ("sun-chiefs")[9] calibrate sunrise and sunset points on the horizon for the purpose of determining the summer and winter solstices. After the Hopi made it to their final homeland, perhaps the skills of the mariner were converted to those neccesary for desert farming. The *Patki* Clan is also associated with both the Reed Clan and the Corn Clan.

Palatkwapi was commonly known as the Red City of the South. It can be defined as "a mythical city in the migration legends, the Red-Walled City, 'red-masonry: wall.'"[10] Its name is derived from the words *paala*, which denotes both "red" and "moisture, liquid" and *kwap'iw*, "stacked up" (i.e., stones, literally "neck bones").[11] The early 20th century ethnographer Alexander Stephen describes this idyllic landscape.

"Many days [years?] ago the Hopitu lived in the south where the rocks and the earth are red and they lived happily there for many days, owning many sheep and horses and having many beautiful women. Also the art of making blankets, silver and gold ornaments, working the turquoise and many beautiful shells was far better understood than today. They manufactured many kinds of colored cloths from wool and cotton, using different kinds of dyes. Flowers were highly cultivated and used in many feasts and dances. It was while living in that country that the handsome cotton robe used by the high priest in the sacred duties of his office was made. It was highly figured by the weaving in of silver or copper threads; flowers, birds, vines of many kinds and the horned water serpent were to be found in the pattern."[12]

The artifacts and rituals in this passage clearly indicate a Mesoamerican culture, and not a lifeway associated with the Desert Southwest. The mention of the domesticated animals of the post-Spanish incursion (i.e., after circa 1540 AD) may, of course, merely be a fanciful embellishment. It should be noted that the horned water serpent Palulukang, an analogue of the Mayan Kukulkán and the Aztecan Quetzalcóatl, was the agent of Palatkwapi's destruction due to social chaos, sexual promiscuity, materialistic avarice, gambling, and the general iniquities of its citizens.

In his *Hopi Journal*, A. M. Stephen remarks on Hopi cosmology and its directional symbolism: "On the [sun-chief's] altar the nadir is represented in the south. Inferably

Pala'tkwabi is the Underworld, i.e. the world before the Emergence."[13] From this we may infer that the proto-Hopi existence in the Red City of the South was part of the Third World, which was essentially destroyed along with the continent of Mu by a global deluge. In the aftermath of this devastation, subsequent migrations northward to the Four Corners region of the U.S. were by necessity undertaken. The Hopi eventually found their ultimate homeland in the Fourth World.

## The Destruction of Palatkwapi

As noted, the Third World (Era) was destroyed by a flood of biblical proportions, and the devastation of Palatkwapi was accomplished by the same means. Here we see the result of this upheaval in the domestic realm. "...now the Bálölöokongs [water serpents] were shooting forth from the ground with streams of water in all parts of the village, from the fireplaces in the kivas, in the houses from the water vessels, and in fact everywhere. Water began to fill the houses in the village. Soon the houses began to fall, burying many of the inhabitants under falling walls."[14]

The early 20th century ethnographer and archaeologist Jesse Walter Fewkes claims that the One Horn (*Kwan*, literally "agave") Society brought the legendary Plumed Serpent cult from Palatkwapi to Arizona.[15] The analogous Hopi creature named Palulukang is a horned water serpent similar to the Mayan Kukulkán or the Aztecan Quetzalcóatl. Acting as the spirit-protector of the *Patki* Clan, this terrifying creature inhabits bodies of water such as lakes, subterranean springs, or cenotes, but also has the power to bring rainfall.

Incidentally, the fierce paramilitary One Horns function to this day in Arizona as a sort of village police force.

> "There was a rumbling in the distance. The sound grew louder as it came closer. The earth began to shake. Large stones slid from their foundations and the walls of the houses cracked. The buildings began to crumble and fall. Out of the gray cloudless sky rain poured down, and a cold wind swept through the plaza. The people of Palatkwapi fled to their houses seeking refuge, but even as they did this, water began to flood out of their fireplaces, washing through their rooms and the doorways. In the plaza the floodwaters rose. The violent shaking of the earth caused more walls to collapse. Where once the people had danced in the plaza there was now a deep pond. From the earth underneath this spot, where the kikmongwi's [chief's] nephew had been buried, the head of the great water serpent Balolokong [Palulukang] appeared. Balolokong's head reared higher and higher as his body emerged out of the earth. On the back of his head was a single horn like the one worn by the young man who had been interred there. Balolokong's eyes turned this way and that, surveying the crumbling walls of Palatkwapi. The people fled in terror, but there was no more sanctuary in the village, which by now was submerged in the surging water. In the flight to the safety of higher ground outside the village some children were lost or swept

away, and some of the old and the crippled were left behind."[16]

We can see parallels to the destruction of the Hopi city of Palatkwapi in the K'iche Mayan mythological and historical narrative named the *Popol Vuh*.

> "Again there comes a humiliation, destruction, and demolition. The manikins [wooden people], woodcarvings were killed when Heart of the Sky devised a flood for them. A great flood was made; it came down on the heads of the manikins, woodcarvings… There came a rain of resin from the sky… They were pounded down to the bones. Their faces were smashed because they were incompetent before their mother and their father, the Heart of the Sky, named Hurricane. The earth was blackened because of this; the black rainstorm began, rain all day and rain all night… The stones, their hearthstones were shooting out, coming right out of the fire, going for their heads, causing them pain. Now they run for it, helter-skelter. They want to climb up on the houses, but they fall as the houses collapse."[17]

# Chapter 5
## *Turtle Soup—Hopi "Red City" and Mayan "Black Rocks"*

Although some scholars (myself included) have posited at one point or another that the sacred city of Palatkwapi described above was possibly the Mayan site of Palenque, further evidence may point to another location in Mayaland. Strategically located on the north bank of the Middle Usumacinta River in northwestern Guatemala, Piedras Negras was once one of the primary centers of influence and power in the Lacandon Maya region. Its Spanish name means "black rocks," referring to the dark limestone outcroppings of this hilly, karst topography along the river. Traditional dating for this site is as early as 1000 BC, but the kingdom reached its cultural apex circa 450 – 800 AD in the Late Classic period.[1] Population of the city itself is estimated at 2,500, while 50,000 people may have lived in the surrounding area. The site contained at least a dozen pyramids, numerous palaces and sweat baths, and two ballcourts.

Piedras Negras has three principle groups of architectural structures: South Group, East Group, and West Group. The oldest buildings are in the south nearest the river, and they are the lowest in elevation. One can imagine a procession from lowest to highest, starting at the South, proceeding to the East, and terminating at the Acropolis in the West. "These main architectural groups are bounded to the northwest and southeast by *small natural valleys that, though usually dry, sometimes carry water during periods of great rain or even flood when the river rises to its highest levels in the wet season* [italics added]. The small beach formed where the southern barranca meets the river is the natural landing for river traffic floating downstream, and it was certainly a significant point of access in ancient times as well."²

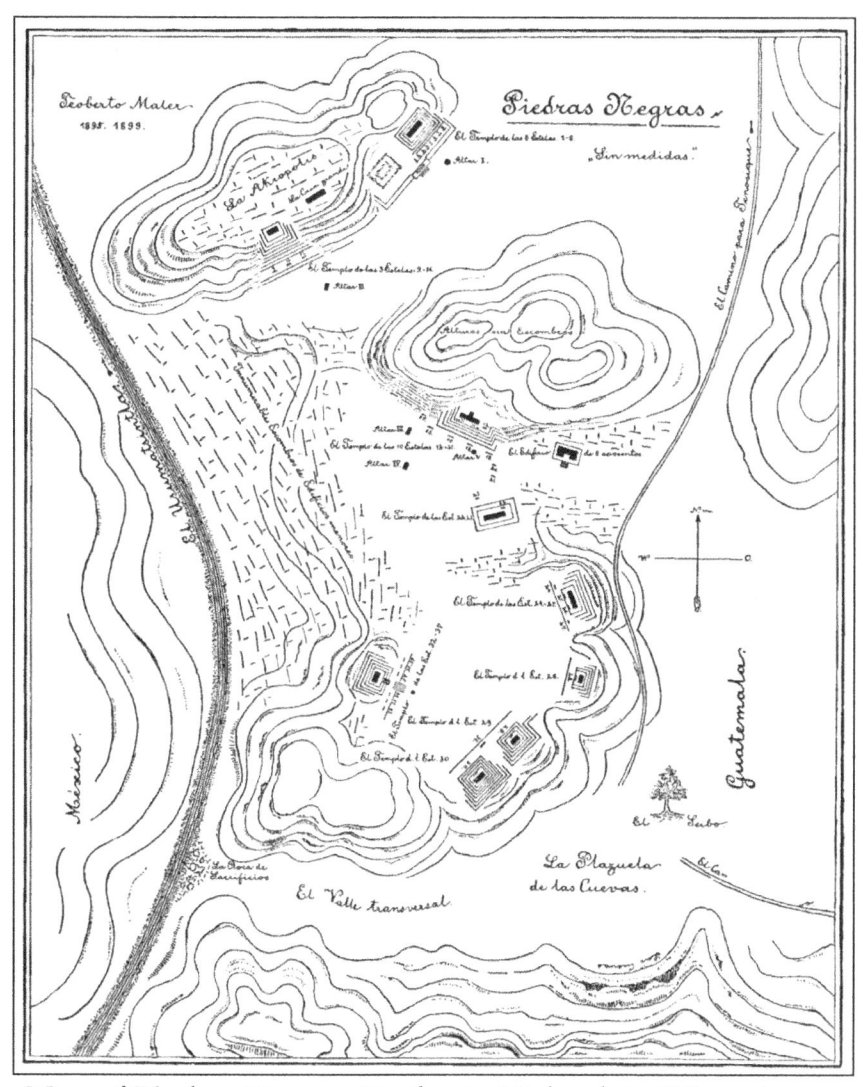

Map of Piedras Negras, Teoberto Maler, late 19ᵗʰ century.

The Maya refer to the site as *Yokib*, or "Entrance" (to a cave or canyon?). It is located near an erstwhile cenote hundreds of yards wide, perhaps once filled with water.[3] In this context it is significant that the Hopi prefix *yok-* means "rain," and the word *ki* means "house, place." Thus, House of Rain—that is, the jungle.[4] According to Dr. Gregory Little and Dr. Lora Little of the A.R.E. (Association for Research and Enlightenment, which Edgar Cayce founded), Piedras Negras is linked in mythological tradition and symbology to a cosmological Turtle.

> "Interestingly, the hieroglyphic symbol that the Maya used to identify Piedras Negras includes a logograph [i.e., ideogram] meaning *cave* and a burial symbol called a *quincunx*. This latter symbol is also connected to the emergence of the Father God Itzamna from the back of the turtle at the time of Creation. Mayan researcher James Brady has recently concluded that tunneling was common under the structures of the Mayan center cities. In addition, Piedras Negras is very near the largest cenote (a sink-hole caused by the collapse of underground rivers) ever found in Guatemala."[5]

**Emblem Glyph for Piedras Negras, Classic Maya.**

The morphology of the turtle's carapace is cave-like. Is something mysterious buried at Piedras Negras? Let's look further.

**The Acropolis at Pedras Negras, painting by Russian archaeologist Tatiana Proskouriakoff.**

The dynasty that ruled Piedras Negras was made up of members from the Turtle Clan—the Turtle Lords. Ruler 2 (as archaeologists designate him) was Itzamna, named after the culture-bringing Creator God associated with the priesthood, divination, calendrics, agriculture, esoteric lore, and writing . Legends tell of the latter's journey by boat from the east, along with two so-called Paddler Gods—nocturnal Jaguar and diurnal Stingray.[6] David Stuart, premier epigrapher of Mayan glyphs, remarks on this dynamic duo's relationship with cyclic time.

"The Paddlers' deep involvement with Period Ending rites build on their documented roles as primordial actors in calendrical ritual. On Quirigua Stela C, they play a key role in the famous narrative of the foundational bak'tun-ending 13.0.0.0.0 4 Ahau 8 Cumku, when 'thrice the stones were raised.' The first of these dedications was overseen by the Paddlers, establishing their prime importance in setting the mythological example that later kings would follow. It's maybe relevant that the cyclical movement of time was symbolically encoded in the opposed night-day name of the two gods."[7]

Maize god One Hunahpu emerges from the cosmic Turtle shell at the Creation, assisted by his twin sons Hunahpu (Jr.?) and Xbalanque. Painted bowl, El Petén, Guatemala, 680–750 AD. This central figure may also represent Itzamna.

Mark Pitts, another contemporary epigrapher, comments on the glyphs found on a circular slab that had been placed in front of the Acropolis and supported by tripod stones.

> "Piedras Negras Altar 1 is unusual because it tells of rulers in the prior era. The text begins in the year 4691 BC and then moves forward 4 baktuns to the beginning of the current era, or 13.00.00.00.00 in the Maya calendar. According to the ancient Maya when the current era began on the Calendar Round date of 4 Ajaw 8 Kumk'u, the 'Paddler Gods' changed the Hearth Stones at a place called the 'First Three Stone Place.' As in many Maya homes of today, the fire and hearth, generally surrounded by the three stones for cooking are the center of life's activities. In the cosmic sense as well, the three stones are the center of the universe. In fact, we are told that creation happens 'at the edge of the sky.'… Rough Translation: *"On September 7, 4691 B.C. 9 baktuns were completed. He (name unreadable) witnessed it, the Holy Piedras Negras Lord. It happened at (name unreadable), the holy place. Four baktuns later on 4 Ajaw 8 Kumk'u the 13th baktun ended. The Paddler Gods changed the hearth stones. It happened at the edge of the sky, at the First Three Stone Place. Turtleshell witnessed it, the Holy Piedras Negras Lord. It happened at the Five Flower Place."*[8]

Inscribed Altar 1. "The stones that are circular, that were of the magnetized influence upon which the Spirit of the One spoke to those peoples as they gathered in their service, are of the earliest Atlantean activities in religious service, we would be called today." Edgar Cayce (reading 5750-1, # 14)

Jaguar Paddler     Stingray Paddler

Mayan glyphs. Note mouthpiece of Jaguar Paddler.

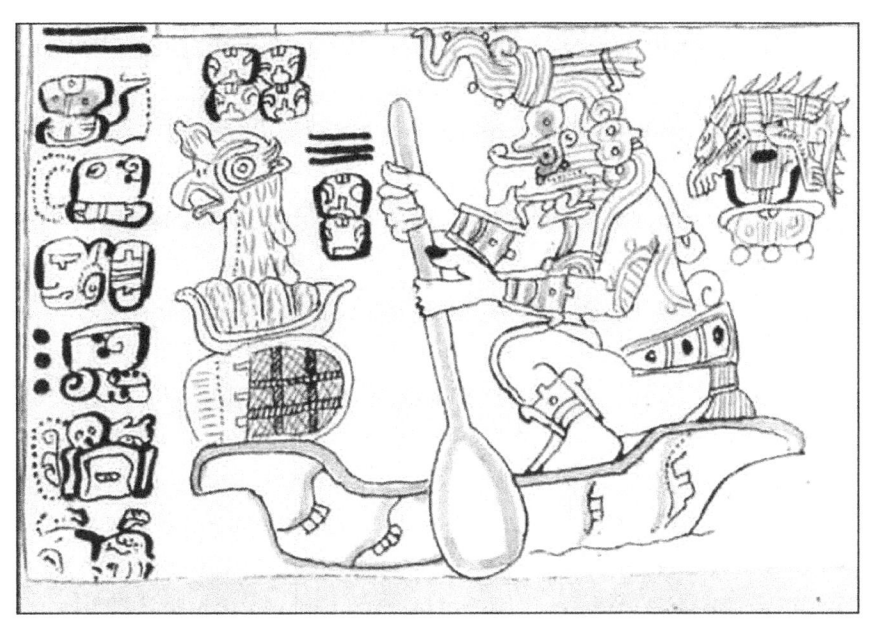

Paddler God in turtle-shell boat, Dresden Codex.
Note three circles on belt (stars of Orion?) and mouthpiece.

Participant in the *Theyyam* Dance of Kerala, India.

Thousands of years old, the *theyyam* cult displays various aspects of Mother Goddess-worship, spirit-worship, ancestor-worship, serpent-worship, and animal- and tree-worship. In Hindi the silver fangs (seen in the photo on the preceding page) are called *ekali*, which resemble the same Mayan mouthpieces. We recall from the previous chapter Cayce's reference to an ancient immigrant from India.[9]

A Mayan fresco mural painted circa 800 AD on the north wall of Room 1 at Bonampak in Chiapas near the Guatemalan border depicts Orion's belt on a turtle's back. The Quiché Maya of the Guatemalan highlands use the term *cahuleu* to describe the dual nature of what we call the world. It literally means "sky-earth."[10] The turtle may in fact be a precise anagogue or hieratic analogue for this Mayan concept. The upper shell, or carapace, would correspond to the dome of the sky, while the lower shell, or plastron, would correspond to what appears to be relatively flat ground—the plain of the earth plane. The late scholar of the Maya John Major Jenkins sums up the cosmology of the Maya in regard to the celestial realm.

> "Astro-mythology, astro-theology, archaeo-astronomy, mytho-astronomical ideation—however you phrase it, the connection between celestial cycles and cultural ideas on earth defines the highest insight of Mesoamerican religion, which can best be described with the Hermetic principle "as above, so below." Sky and earth, subjective and objective realities, are interrelated, two sides of the same coin. We see this tangibly in astronomically timed rites of Maya kingship. We also see it in city names and city planning, in which cities were

oriented to astronomically significant horizons and reflected the structure of the cosmos."[11]

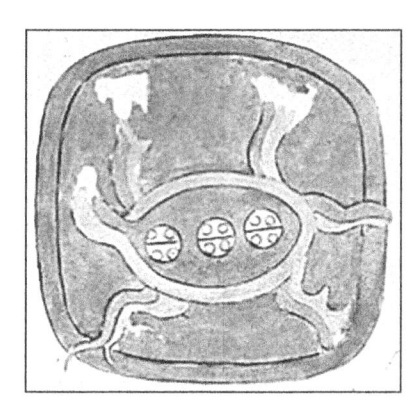

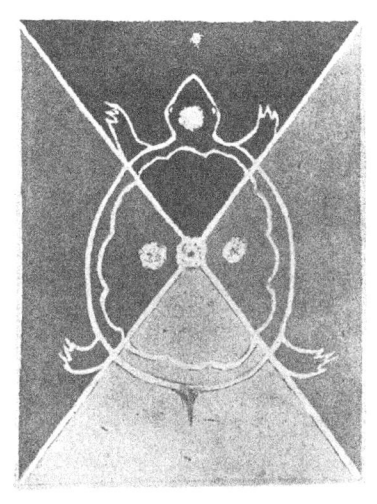

**Left: Fresco mural at Bonampak, Chiapas, Mexico. The three stones on its shell represent the belt stars of Orion. Right: Sand painting for child-naming ceremony, Acoma Pueblo, New Mexico. Four triangles are painted with directional colors, and the hourglass shape (see Chapter 12) as well as the turtle's head suggests the constellation.**

Most archaic societies, it appears, maintained a complex inter-relationship between the terrestrial and the celestial, which not only determined where and how their temples and cities were to be placed but also regulated the rhythms of their daily lives, both in their mundane and spiritual aspects.

In addition to the aforementioned connection of the turtle with Orion's belt, the Maya knew this aquatic reptile as the patroness of childbirth named Mayauel (Maya-uel). She was also the goddess of pulque, the intoxicating milky drink made from the agave, a large cactus that was considered by the Nahua people to be the Tree of Life.[12] This corresponds in Maya cosmology to the celestial Maize Tree, or the *Wakah-Kan* ("Raised-up sky"), that sprouts from the Turtle's carapace at the point where the Milky Way crosses the ecliptic at nearly a right angle.[13]

The Tewa-speaking tribes of northern New Mexico perform a sacred Turtle Dance at the winter solstice or shortly thereafter. Like the Hopi *Soyal* ceremony, this Puebloan dance is synchronized by the appearance of Orion in the overhead hatchway of the Winter People's *kiva*.[14] (The Tewa have a moiety system of Winter People and Summer People, each group assuming the ceremonial duties of the particular season.[15]) The Mayan word for turtle is *ak*, very similar to the Tewa prefix *Ok-*, suggesting this creature whose dorsal shell mirrors the sky. *Oku share* is the name for the Turtle Dance. *'Oku* means "turtle" but it also means "hill," the latter perhaps suggesting the shape of the turtle's shell. *O'ke* is the Tewa word for San Juan Pueblo, located at the confluence of the Rio Chama and the Rio Grande. The Mayan word for star is the near homonym *ek*.[16] The native name of Acoma Pueblo is *Ako*. The words *O'ke*, *Oku*, *ak*, *ek*, *Ako*... Are all these similar syllables connected with the turtle and Orion's belt merely a coincidence? I think not.

The Maya were known to use turtle shells ceremonially as musical instruments, beating them with antlers.[17] Even today the Hopi put dried antelope hooves inside turtle shells to make eerily sounding rattles which are affixed to their right knees during *katsina* dances. The Hopi Turtle Kachina (*Káhayla*) is also known as the Hunter Kachina (*Maak̠*, or *Mahk*), considered a guardian or warrior figure—all attributes of the archetypal Orion.[18] Incidentally, the Hopi word for turtle is *yöngösona*, literally, "prickly pear [cactus]-craver"[19]

*Tewa Turtle Dance*

↑ turtle shell rattle      ↑ white mask and red eyes ↑

Glyphs of the Palenque Temple XIX platform. On the left is the glyph for *Ahau* (or *Ajaw*), "Lord," the last and most important logograph in the Mayan 20-day calendar. On the right is the glyph for *Mak*, both "turtle-shell" and the Mayan Classic 13th month. The name of this glyph is also a homonymn for the Hopi Hunter/Turtle Kachina mentioned above. *Ak* (or *ahk*) = "turtle." At the center of the naturalistic shell, note the St. Andrew's Cross, which may refer to the cardinal directions. The three circles above the rectangle (firmament?) possibly connotes Orion's belt.[20]

Masau'u (Màasaw), Hopi *katsina* doll, Left: Arizona State Museum. Right: Heard Museum, Phoenix, Arizona. Photos by the author. Looking at the Mayan glyph of *Ahau* (preceding page), most Hopis would identify their deity of death, fire, the underworld, and lord of the earth.

It comes as no surprise, then, that another word for the Egyptian *Duat* (or *Tuat,* i.e., the Afterlife realm) is <u>Ak</u>ert.[21] In this context it is interesting to note that the Hopi word *atkya(q)* means "down, down there, down below" and refers to the underworld.[22] Paradoxically this realm is conceptualized in the heavens. Re-enforcing the *ak* phoneme in connection with the turtle, the Egyptian word *paqit* means "tortoise or turtle shell," and one turtle-god is named *Qeq-ha*.[23]

Incidentally, the ancient Egyptian word *Abesh* referred to "one of the seven stars of Orion" (which one, we are not sure), as well as to "a benevolent serpent-god." On the other hand, Āpesh was the name of the Turtle-god.[24] "The Tortoise-god Āpesh... was associated with the powers of darkness, and night, and evil, and a place was assigned to him in the heavens with their representatives. In the clxist Chapter of the *Book of the Dead* mention is made of the Tortoise, or Turtle, in such a way as to suggest that he was an enemy of Rā, and the formula 'Rā liveth, the Tortoise dieth,' is given four times, once in connexion with each of the four winds of heaven."[25] Thus, the cyclical struggle between the Sun and Orion, both diurnally and seasonally.

This Turtle-Orion parallel is continued on the North American continent in the Lakota (Sioux) cosmology, where Alnitak in the belt is perceived as *Keyapiya*, the soft-shelled turtle, whose terrestrial correspondence is Gillette Prairie, a grassy area located within the ponderosa pine forests of South Dakota's Black Hills.[26]

Some tribes claim that the North American continent was called Turtle Island. The *Walam Olum*, purportedly a series of translations of pictographs made by the Lenni Lenape (or the Delaware Indians), states the following: "In that ancient country, in that northern country, in that turtle country, the best of the Lenape were the Turtle men."[27]

The Akimel O'odham (Pima—again, *ak*) of southern Arizona have a song that in part goes: "The Black Turtle approaches us, / Wearing and shaking his belt of night."[28] This may refer to the Milky Way, the ecliptic, or perhaps even Orion's belt. The turtle reputedly causes sores, and the singing of this song with a turtle shell rattle is a remedy.

The Zuni (native name *A'shiwi*) of New Mexico gather turtles from the sacred lake named *Kothluwalawa* around the time of the summer solstice. It is here that the departed souls are thought to reside. The turtles are brought back to the village, where they are tenderly and reverently treated as if they were relatives. Then they are ritually killed, their flesh and bones placed in nearby a stream and their shells carefully saved for use as dance rattles. The apparent purpose of this ceremony is to send the souls of the ancestors that inhabit the turtles' bodies back to the spirit land.[29] Like the Tewa, the Zuni also have a Turtle Clan.

**Cosmic Turtle of the Maya carrying three hearthstones, Madrid Codex. The three crosses on the stones are universal symbols referring to stars. The two cords suspending the turtle represent the ecliptic.**

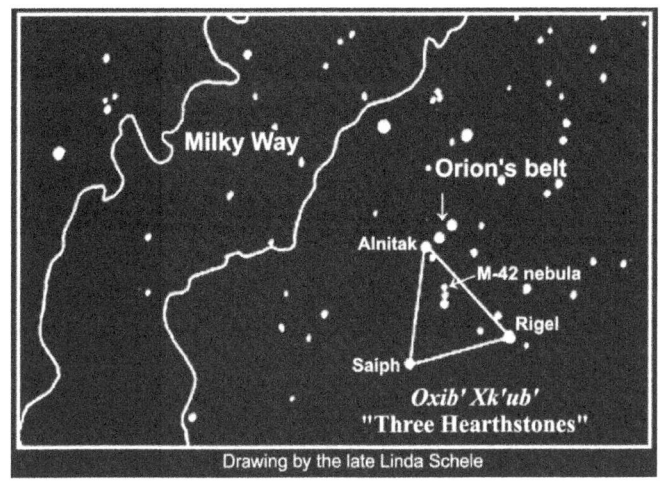

Triangular celestial hearthstones, Maya star knowledge.

Mimbres turtle bowl, circa 1000 AD, southwestern New Mexico. In Ancestral Puebloan rock art and ceramic painting, the checkerboard symbol signifies the Milky Way. The 12 points possibly represent the zodiacal constellations.

The legendary Chintamani Stone is represented by three circles arranged in an equilateral triangle. Posessing it allowed one to see into the past or predict the future. Similar to the dark green, meteoric mineral moldavite, it was reputedly brought to Earth by emissaries from a planet orbiting the star Sirius. This artifact is variously referred to as Lucifer's Stone of Heaven, the Treasure of the World, the alchemists' Philosopher's Stone, and even the Holy Grail itself! Upon the collapse of the League of Nations at the onset of World World II, the Russian artist and mystic Nicholas Roerich transported this stone to Tibet where it was relayed to Shambala, mythical Land of the Immortals. According to author Mark Amaru Pinkham, "Roerich maintains that the stone or fragments of it have been in the possession of King Solomon,as well as the chiefs of the conquering Mongol tribes, including Tamurlane, Ghengis Khan, and Akbar the Great."[30] Note the tautological name of the tolerant 16th century Mogul emperor of India: Akbar.[31]

**Oil painting by Nicholas Roerich, "White Stone – Sign of Cintamani or the Horse of Happiness," 1933. Note the fire element of the Mayan hearthstones and the Tibetan letters.**

The following chapter will delinate the correspondences between the mythical Hopi "Red City of the South" called Palatkwapi and the historical Mayan site of Piedras Negras.

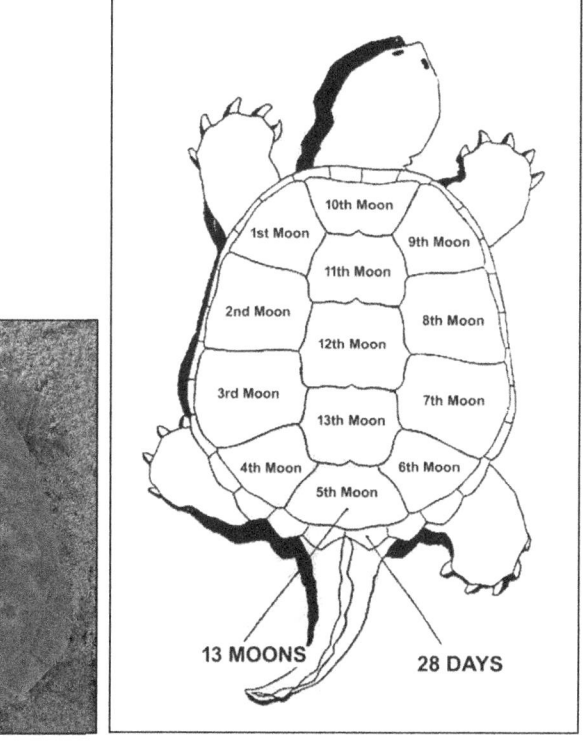

Left: Desert tortoise, which recently lumbered through the author's back yard in southern Arizona. Right: Calendar shell, we can readily see why the ancient Maya conceptualized Orion as a turtle shell. The three *hexagonal* scutes (keratin plates) in the middle of the carapace correspond to the belt stars. (We shall explore the importance of the six-sided figure in Chapter 7.) 10 scutes surround these central plates and total 13—one of two sacred numbers in the Maya calendar. The 28 plates on the edge of the shell correspond to the lunar cycle. 13 X 28 = 364, with an additional day conceptualized as being outside of time.

# Chapter 6
# *Palatkwapi — the Case for Piedras Negras*

Given the Mayan association of terrapins with the primary winter constellation, we must ask: Were the Turtle Kings of Piedras Negras also the sovereign Lords of Orion? The first ruler (namely, Ruler A) of this ancient city was known to be Itzam K'an Ahk, "Precious/Yellow Turtle," or Turtleshell, who reigned about 460 AD. A series of turtle monarchs ruled intermittently between the mid-5th and the early 9th centuries AD.[1]

**So-called God N, Dresden Codex. He shows distinctive elements of the first Piedras Negras king, including a turtle shell on his back, upon which is a quincunx symbol. He also carries a ritual shaman's bag in his right hand.**

Model of the Acropolis in the West Group, Piedras Negras.

In their book *The Lost Hall of Records*, John Van Auken and Lora Little adduce various architecture orientations that either mirror or line up with the constellation Orion. For instance, on the Acropolis three major pyramids may correspond to the belt stars (J-4, J-6/Court, and J-3: Alnitak, Alnilam, and Mintaka, respectively). Like the Giza-Nile relationship, they propose the Rio Usumacinta as an analogue to the Milky Way. They also discuss a few potential Orion correlations or alignments in the South group (too numerous to detail here).

Also in the latter section of Piedras Negras is one of only two ballcourts found there. This is located at the center of a lozenge-shaped quincunx formed by the cave burial of a holy man as well as a number of significant petroglyphs that are possibly much older than the rest of the site. (See graphic on p. 97.) Three round stone markers had been embedded at the center of the playing field. They had once been inscribed but are eroded beyond decipherment. "From information provided by hieroglyphic inscriptions, researchers have determined that the ballcourt was a sacred site. It appears to have been used to replay the creation story and for ritual human sacrifice. The Maya believed that the ballcourts actually opened into the supernatural world. Interestingly, different ballcourts provided access to different locations in this other world. Some ballcourts were believed to provide transport to the time and space of the last creation."[2]

This chthonic concept greatly resembles the architectural feature found in every Hopi *kiva*, or subterranean prayer chamber: the *sipapu*, which serves as an inter-dimensional gateway to the underworld as well as a link to the previous Third World (or Era). (See graphic on p. 115.) In addition, the ancestral Hopi also once played the sacred ball game, and archaeologists have discovered many courts in the Four Corner region.

**Ballcourt, Wupatki National Monument, Arizona— farthest north on the continent. The great Mayan tradition ends here, nearly 1,800 miles northwest of Piedras Negras.**

*Piedras Negras*

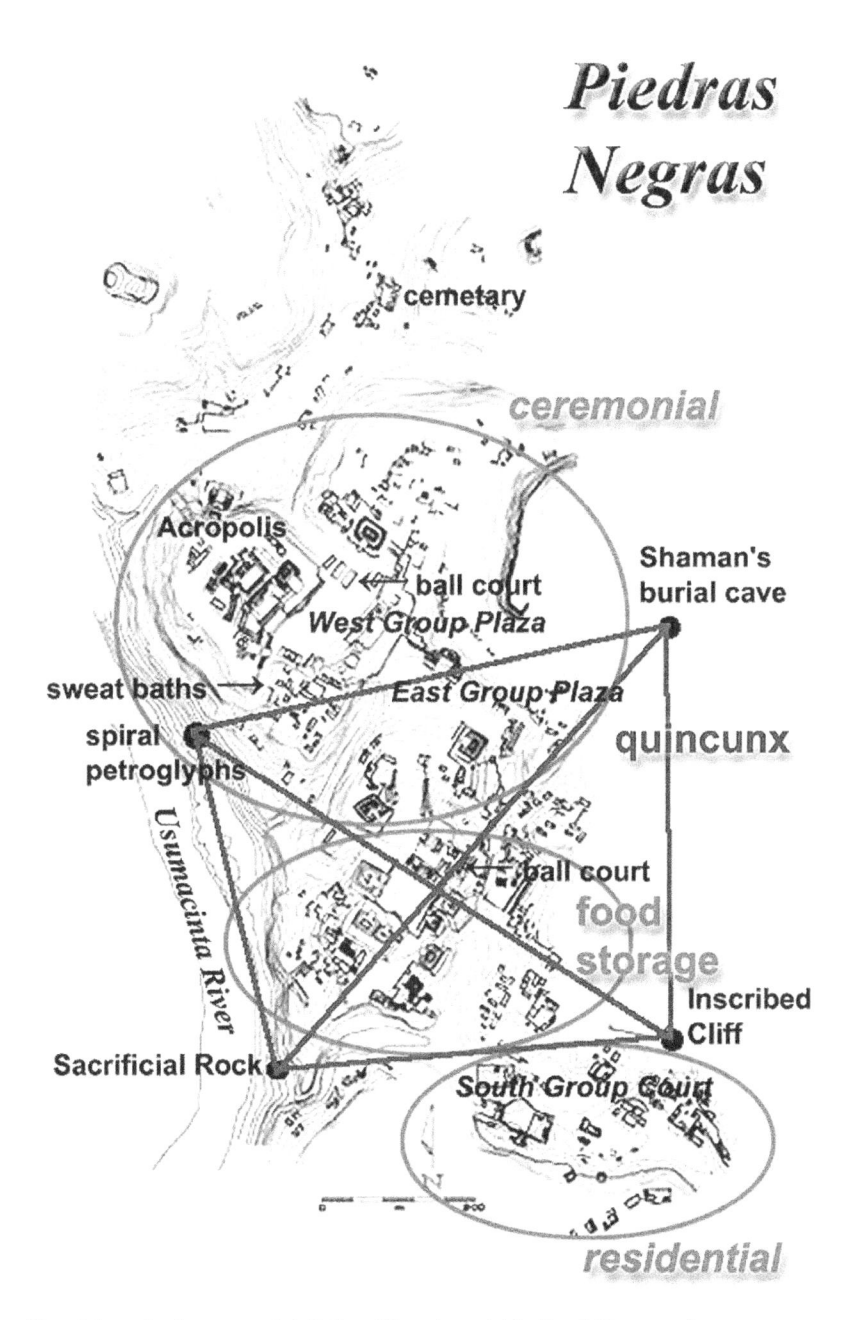

after Van Auken and Little, *The Lost Hall of Records*

Spiral petroglyphs are found all over the globe and were carved in all ages, but those found on the rocks of the riverbank at Piedras Negras appear to be pre-Maya due to their style—cruder than that of the elegant Mayan sculptures. These inscriptions even include double spirals, which copiously occur as well in the ancestral Hopi territory. "About 425 m down stream from the Sacrificial Rock are some interesting geometrical patterns cut in broad shallow lines on the tilted flat surface of a rock-ledge in the stream bed. The designs are badly weathered and identifiable with difficulty. They cover several square meters of rock. The designs seem to be limited to spirals."[3]

In rock art the single spiral can alternately represent swirling water, a whirlwind, migration, or an interdimensional portal. According to J. E. Cirlot's *Dictionary of Symbols*, "The double spiral represents the completion of the sigmoid line, and the ability of the sigmoid line to express the intercommunication between two opposing principles is clearly shown in the Chinese Yang-Yin symbol."[4] As Van Auken and Little remark:

> "...perhaps the spirals are an ancient symbol of the Atlantean records buried nearby. Double spirals or scrolls symbolize both evolution (unwinding) and involution (winding in) and can represent the cycles of life or of the cosmos. This would be a fitting emblem to mark the location of the records since, from Cayce's readings, we are given to understand that they contain a history of civilization possibly going back to the time of creation. In addition, the double spirals at Piedras Negras are reminiscent of the scroll form and could have

been carved to represent written documents. Since Cayce indicated a Hebrew connection to the Maya, it should be noted that the Hebrew *Torah* originated in written scroll form around 900-600 B.C."[5]

Both the English words "tornado" and "torsion" and the title of the *Torah* share the same root. The former words etymologically denote "to twist." As mentioned in Chapter 2, historical scholar Charles Pope likens the double helix (double spirals) with the structure of the Torah.[6] We also saw that the Hopi verb *tori* means "get twisted."[7] In addition, the Hopi traditionally conceptualize eddies in water as indicating the "gate of Maasaw's house," who is the god of the underworld and death.[8] (See photo on p. 88 of his *katsina* doll representations.)

**The blowhole vents cool, non-toxic radioactive air from the "underworld"—merely one of many interconnected, labyrinthine passageways in a subterranean cavern system extending to within a 50-mile radius. It must have been a welcome relief for the ball players. Photo by the author.**

Double spiral with trident staff, Homolovi State Park, northern Arizona. Photo by the author. We probably do not need to be reminded that the trident was the weapon of the sea god Poseidon, whom Plato claimed to be the ruler of Atlantis.

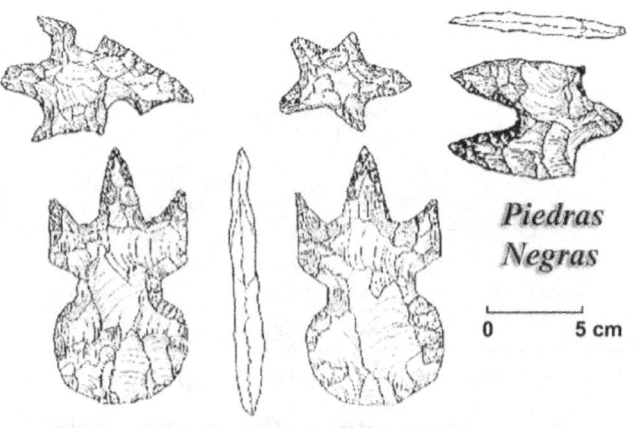

*Piedras Negras*

Selection of eccentrics from Cache 57, Pyramid 0-13

Note trident-shaped flints, and the five-pointed star similar to the Egyptian version.

100

Outside the central portion of Piedras Negras southeast of the Acropolis is the so-called Inscribed Cliff. (See map above.) About 15 feet above ground level is a petroglyph depicting the side view of a turtle with an *Ahau* glyph on it. Van Auken and Little comment in this regard on a 1997 Brigham Young University archaeological report:

> "They concluded that the inscription was 'highly suggestive of maize-god emergence scenes connected to such turtles.' This means that the site was most likely used for ceremonial activities that included the reenactment of the sacred creation story related to the turtle shell. In one of the Maya creation myths, the First Father, Itzamna, (also called the Maize-god) paddles with two companions in a canoe to the place of the three stones of creation which become a turtle's shell through which 'he can be reborn and create a new universe.' The Maya date this creation event as occurring on August 13, 3114 B.C., a date that brings us closer to the chronology in Cayce's story. In addition, there is evidence that, for the Maya, the three stones of the turtle's shell may have been represented by the movement of the three stars in the belt of Orion."[9]

In Chapter 4, I discussed the ancestral Hopi's journey to, and the destruction of, Palatkwapi. According to the 20th century Hopi chief Tawákwaptiwa, this "Red City of the South" possessed characteristics that included the following:

***1.*** The proto-Hopi clans first migrated southward into South America and then returned northward to settle at Palatkwapi, the red-earth place.[10] One early archaeologist of the site, Linton Satterthwaite, comments on the geology of the region: "...the soil immediately over bedrock is *red clay* [italics added]..."[11]

**Hol ceramics, 500-300 BC, red and orange monochrome.**[12]

In the Nahuatl language of Mesoamerica, *atl* means "water."[13] In the Quechua language of South American, *anti* means "east." One of the groups of the Inca Empire, for instance, was called the <u>Anti</u>*suyu,* which lived northwest of Cusco in the Andes (*Antis*).[14] Ergo, *Atl-antis*. In his book *Atlantis: the Andes Solution*, J. M. Allen claims that Atlantis was in fact located on the Bolivian Altiplano south of Lake Titicaca. He posits that *antis* instead means "copper," a red metal.[15] Red is the Mayan directional color for east, whereas for the Hopi red refers to southeast. The Hopi word for copper is *sivapala* (*Siva-pala*), literally "metal-red."[16] According to author Frank Waters, the previous Hopi Third World (Era), which they call *Kuskurza*, has east or southeast as its symbolic direction, red as its color, and copper as its metal.[17] Orichalcum (Greek, *orei-chalkos*, literally "mountain copper") was a copper-gold alloy that reputedly covered the walls of Atlantis. The name Orion, or Oarion, may derive from the Greek word *oros*, "mountain." The English word "ore" comes from a conflation of numerous older words meaning brass, copper, bronze, or brazen. In Homer's epic The Odyssey, Orion in the underworld holds "a brazen club."[18] Cayce, of course, stated in one of his readings that Atlantis was inhabited by the red race. "Those in the Gobi, the yellow. The white - rather in the Carpathians than India, though this is the change to which they are made. The red, of course, in the Atlantean and in the American. The brown in the Andean. The black in the plain and the Sudan, or in African." (364-13)[19]

**Artist's conception of Atlantis with red concentric rings.**

Continuing with the Hopi characteristics of their Red City of the South:

2. Palatkwapi was built in three sections: (1) ceremonial—the most important (2) food storage (3) living quarters for the clans—residential. (See map on p. 97.)
3. The ceremonial section was a terraced architectural structure four stories high: (1) On the ground floor, the *katsinam* (spirit messengers) taught the initiates the meaning of the previous three Worlds (Eras) and of the current Fourth World. (2) On the next higher level were taught the structure and functions of the human body, and that the highest purpose was to find the One Spirit within matter. (3) On the third story were instructions on the workings of nature and healing power of plants. (4) On the fourth floor (which was smaller, making the structure appear like a pyramid) only initiates who had attained high consciousness and a deep knowledge of the laws of nature were allowed. "Here they were taught the workings of the planetary system, how stars affected climate, the crops, and man himself. Here too they learned about the 'open door' on the top of the head [in Hopi *kópavi*, the Crown Chakra], how to keep it open, and so converse with their Creator." The main door faced east, as two smaller doors faced north and south.[20] (See drawing on next page.)
4. A river ran underneath all three sections. A. M. Stephen, 19th century ethnographer of the Hopi, claimed that in the geography that encompassed Palatkwapi, one river flowed from northwest to southeast, and another from east to west. Below the juncture in a low land lay the city.[21] Of course, the Rio Usumacinta flows in the opposite direction: southeast to northwest, emptying into the Gulf of Mexico.

However, upstream from both Piedras Negras and its rival city Yaxchilán, the Rio Pasión flows from the east to conjoin with the Usumacinta near the ancient site of Altar de Sacrificios.

**The four levels of the Acropolis described by the Hopi as Palatkwapi, Red City of the South.**

5. Palatkwapi was surrounded by a high wall. Although no high walls of a defensive nature have been found at Piedras Negras per se, archaeologists have recently discovered a series of stone walls up to six feet high demarcating the boundary about two-thirds of the way between Piedras Negras and Yaxchilán to the southeast. These walls were constructed about 1,300 years ago along a four-mile-long stretch between the small hills of this rough terrain. At the same time a

number of settlements were built on the Yaxchilán side of the border. Watch towers were placed atop these hills, and paths through the rain forest led to the walls; thus, the barriers served as control points.[22]

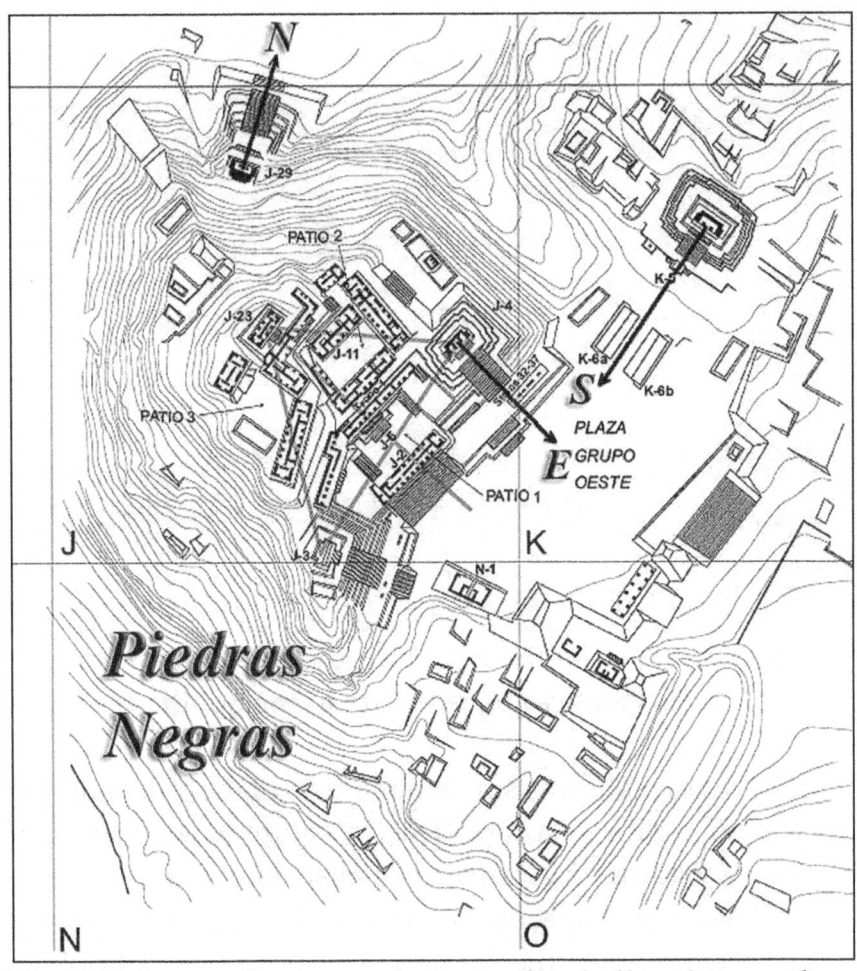

The Hopi sometimes use inter-cardinal directions rather than cardinal ones. The "main door" may refer to the structures on the Acropolis (J-3, J-4, and J-23) facing southeast. J-29 roughly faces north, and K-5 faces south.

6. In their April, 2004 expedition of Piegras Negras, Drs. Greg and Lora Little suggest that there may be a tunnel system under the city, particularly on the north side of the mountain where the Acropolis is located. Built into the base of mountainside, the J-29 pyramid has many layers of construction, the oldest and lowest apparently having the most advanced architecture. An earlier expedition had unearthed a cache of iron and crystalline stone. In addition, Greg Little encountered a large stone with a hole bored through it, which resembles the "*yoni* stones" found in India as well as the "stones of the ancestors" that the *sangoma* Creda Mutwa of South Africa uses in his shamanic practices. Archaeologists have found Hopi burial artifacts of doughnut-shaped stones with the hole possibly allowing for the soul's escape.[23] The Littles also speculate that a tunnel may exist beneath the dominate pyramid in the East Group (O-13), because they found cool air rushing out from under it (much like the Arizona "blowhole" mentioned above).[24]

7. A Brigham Young expedition in 1998 had found on the back side of the O-13 pyramid "…a continuous face of plastered, *red-painted masonry* [italics added], with considerable modifications and additions, along with evidence of intrusive burials." In the front of the pyramid the archaeologists also discovered "…one of the largest known caches in the Maya Lowlands, consisting of approximately 129 eccentrics (54 chert, 75 of obsidian, most in groupings of nine equivalent shapes [see drawing above]), 1 bird skeleton, 1 vessel with 8 jade beads and 9 pyrites (interspersed with jade, *Spondylus* [spiny mollusks], and hematite flecks),

and a marine spiral shell, all placed in a prepared cist. The cache certainly marked the axis of the pyramid."[25]

8. Hopi chief Tawákwaptiwa's version of Palatkwapi's demise involves an invading group from the north. The Spider Clan was denied access to the city so they attacked. The Palatkwapians were driven out of the first two sections of the city, and they made a last stand in the ceremonial area, "across one corner of which ran a small river." Then the Spider Clan (*Kòokyangwngyam*) cut off the water flow from the river, so the Palatkwapians dug a tunnel under the river and escaped. However the *katsinam* (kachinas, or spirit messengers) remained behind to protect the spiritual essence of the city.

> "'Now we, the *kachina* people, will remain here to defend the city, while you make your escape in the darkness. The time for us to go to our far-off planets and stars has not come yet. But it is time for us to leave you. We will go by our powers to a certain high mountain, which you will know, where we will await your messages of need. So whenever you need us or our help, just make your *páhos* [prayer feathers]. Now another thing. We are spirit people, and we will not be seen again by you or your people. But you must remember us by wearing our masks and our costumes at the proper ceremonial times. Those who do so must be only those persons who have acquired the knowledge and the wisdom we have taught you. And these persons of flesh and blood will then bear our names and be known as the

Kachina Clan. Now it is dark. The time has come. Go quickly.'"[26]

**Hopi drawing of *Sohu katsina* (Star kachina). The stars on his crest represent Orion's "belt"; the cross and crescent represent Venus and the Moon respectively.**

**The ghosts of Piedras Negras' night.**

# Chapter 7
## Cayce's Tuaoi Stone

According to Edgar Cayce's readings, in the early days of Atlantis the "Tuaoi Stone" was an instrument by which inter-dimensional communication was achieved. The Littles and Van Auken explain:

> "Cayce's story of how the destructive forces were unleashed is entwined with the mysterious crystal. The story begins with the 'White Stone,' a stone 'in the form of a six-sided figure,' which was also referred to as the 'Tuaoi stone.' Initially this stone was used for communication with the divine, in a way that appears similar to how Native American shamans utilize crystals. A priestess of the Law of One would gather together a group and concentrate on the stone, eventually entering an altered state of consciousness. From the stone would come a form of speech interpreted by the priestess. The speech came from what Cayce referred to as the 'saint realm,' which imparted 'understanding and knowledge' to the group."[1]

In later times the Atlantean segment of society known as "Children of the Law of One" with their reliance on higher powers was superseded by the "Sons of Belial." (Cf. 1 Samuel 2:12 "Now the sons of Eli were sons of Belial; they knew not the LORD.") This latter group was materialistic, morally corrupt, bellicose, and avaricious. Much like many politicians today, they became ego-centric rather than focused on communitarian welfare and spiritual enlightenment. Focused upon technological manipulation, they converted the Tuaoi Stone into a Tesla-like zero point energy device that could power aircraft and submarines at a distance; however, it could also be used for more nefarious purposes. "The Tuaoi Stone, once a conduit to God, had now become a 'terrible crystal' or a 'firestone'—an energy source that could be easily utilized as a powerful weapon. Cayce related that Atlantis had several crystals set up into power stations located at various places. For unclear reasons, the crystals were accidentally tuned too high, causing a violent destruction."[2]

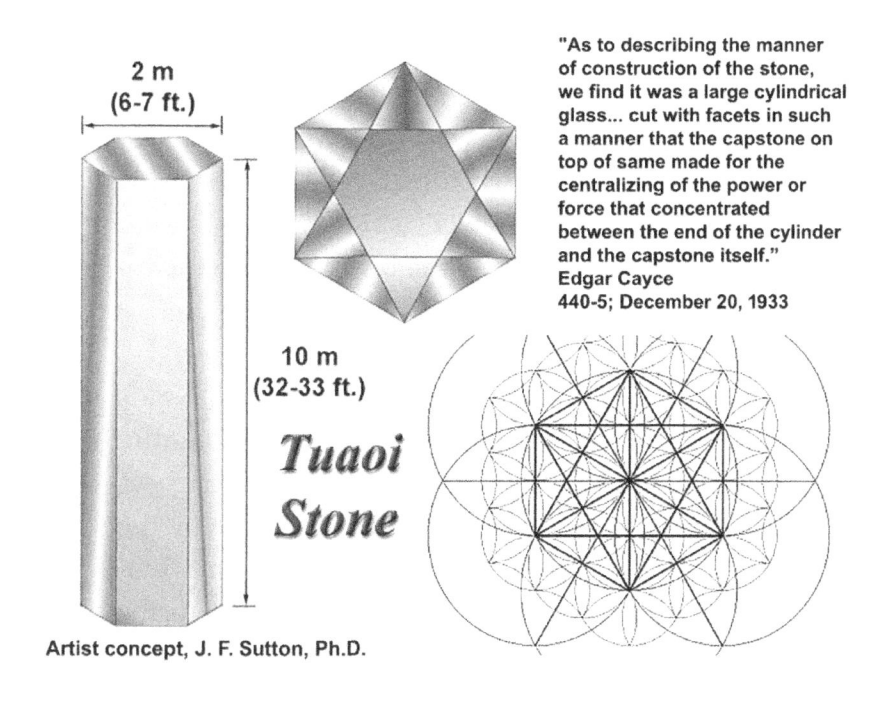

*Tuaoi Stone*

2 m (6-7 ft.)
10 m (32-33 ft.)

"As to describing the manner of construction of the stone, we find it was a large cylindrical glass... cut with facets in such a manner that the capstone on top of same made for the centralizing of the power or force that concentrated between the end of the cylinder and the capstone itself."
Edgar Cayce
440-5; December 20, 1933

Artist concept, J. F. Sutton, Ph.D.

The following are two of Edgar Cayce's readings that discuss this enigmatic stone.

> "(Q) Going back to the Atlantean incarnation - what was the TUAOI STONE? Of what shape or form was it?
> (A) It was in the form of a six-sided figure, in which the light appeared as the means of communication between infinity and the finite; or the means whereby there were the communications with those forces from the outside… It was set as a crystal, though in quite a different form from that used there. Do not confuse these two, then, for there were many generations of difference. It was in those periods when there was the directing of aeroplanes, or means of travel; though these in that time would travel in the air, or on the water, or under the water, just the same. Yet the force from which these were directed was in this central power station, or TUAOI STONE; which was as the beam upon which it acted." 2072-10; July 22, 1942

> "The preparation of this stone was in the hands only of the **initiates** at the time, and the entity was among those that directed the influences of the radiation that arose in the form of the rays that were invisible to the eye but that acted upon the stones themselves as set in the motivating forces - whether the aircraft that were lifted by the gases in the period or whether guiding the more pleasure vehicles

that might pass along close to the earth, or what would be termed the crafts on the water or under the water. These, then, were impelled by the concentrating of the rays from the stone that was centered in the middle of the power station, or power house (that would be termed in the present)."[3]  440-5; December 20, 1933

John Van Auken and Lora Little claim that Piedras Negras was possibly the site of one of three "halls of records" buried just prior to the destruction of Atlantis. Its purpose was to store all the wisdom of the ages, or Akashic records—a sort of metaphysical Library of Alexandria. The other two repositories were reputedly located under the right front paw of the Sphinx at Giza and in the vicinity of Bimini. The co-authors point to evidence that the quincunx, the Emblem Glyph for the city (see graphic on p. 78), was generally used in inscriptions associated with burial.[4] In his readings Cayce also mentioned another type of emblem. As Van Auken and Little summarize, "Several Yucatan records contain information regarding the construction of the Atlantean firestone. Cayce even specified that certain stones which contained the emblem of the firestone were uncovered in Yucatan and may have been place in museums in Pennsylvania, Chicago, and Washington during the 1930s." A November, 1933 reading states in particular: "Also the records that were carried to what is now Yucatan in America, where the stones (that they know so little about) are now – during the last few months – being uncovered."[5] Although northwestern Guatemala is not considered today as Yucatan, it is close enough in a general sense. The Satterthwaite expedition from the University of

Pennsylvania just happened to be excavating Piedras Negras *in 1933!*

The word "Tuaoi" has some interesting cognates in the Hopi language. The noun *tu'a* refers to "spirit, evil apparition, specter, evil sorcerer, harbinger of death." The word *tu'àm* means "grave," and *tu'awi'y* is a "sign, representational meaning, or significance."[6] The word *tu'awi* means "message, communication," and the word *owa* is "stone."[7] Thus, all these connotations have to do with the spirit world, shamanism, signs or portents, communication with spirits, and grave burial. Combining the Hopi words, we find *tu'a-owa* ("spirit-stone") sounds very much like the name "Tuaoi" from Atlantis. In addition, a cognate to the name of the Atlantean firestone is the Hopi word *uw*, "ignite," or "fire." If the "t" is dropped, the phoneme *úwi-owa*, "fire-stone," is similar to Tuaoi.[8]

Although I do not intend to dwell upon the technical aspects of this putative instrument, retired NASA research scientist J. F. Sutton, Ph.D., has speculated on its possible functionality in light of the Cayce readings.

> "This huge machine is excited by an external laser directed at a facet near one end in a direction such that the beam inside the prism orbits around the axis of the prism, reflecting from each facet in turn, six reflections per revolution, and many thousands of revolutions, following a helical path... This is analogous to a right-circular, cylindrical helical coil of copper wire carrying an electric current. When the orbiting laser beam reaches the end of the last facet at the far end of the crystal, a final reflection at the appropriate angle

redirects the beam so that it continues orbiting in the same sense or direction, but the helical path now progresses back to the starting end of the prism. At the starting end of the prism, a similar reflection once again redirects the beam back toward the far end, and so forth, ad infinitum."[9]

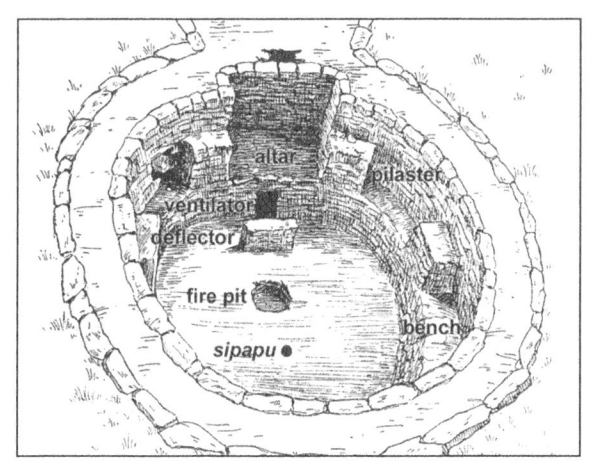

**Round, hexagonal, *kiva* of the Ancestral Puebloans. Like the Tuaoi Stone, The *sipapu* is the symbolic tunnel to both the underworld and the previous Third World.**

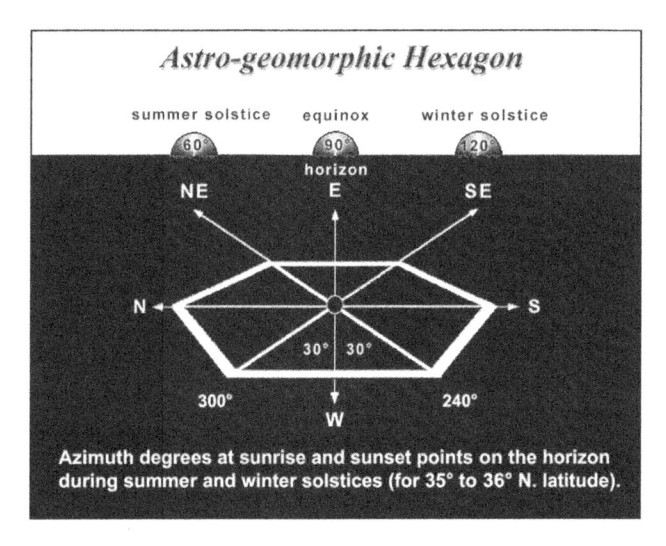

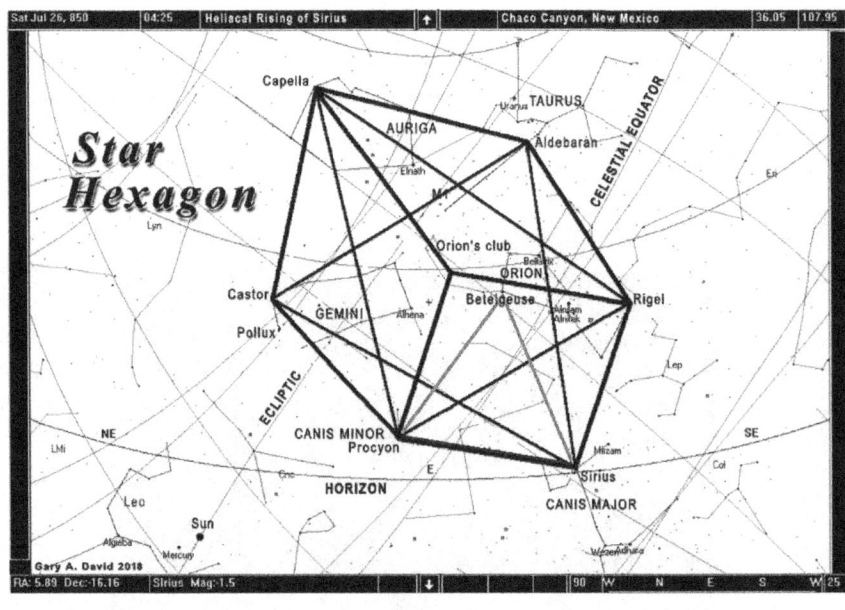

**Overview of Great Kiva at Chetro Ketl in Chaco Canyon, New Mexico**

- 0° N
- 60° summer solstice sunrise
- 120° winter solstice sunrise
- 180° S
- 240° winter solstice sunset
- 300° summer solstice sunset
- W equinox sunset
- E equinox sunrise
- roof supports
- vault
- firebox

astro-geographic hexagon formed only at 35° to 36° latitude

azimuth angles measured in degrees

---

*Sat Jul 26, 850  04:25  Heliacal Rising of Sirius  Chaco Canyon, New Mexico  36.05  107.95*

**Star Hexagon**

Capella, Uranus, TAURUS, AURIGA, Aldebaran, Elnath, CELESTIAL EQUATOR, Orion's club, ORION, Betelgeuse, Castor, GEMINI, Athena, Pollux, Rigel, Alnitam, Alnitak, Lep, ECLIPTIC, CANIS MINOR, Procyon, Mizam, HORIZON, Sirius, CANIS MAJOR, Col, Leo, Algieba, Sun, Mercury

Gary A. David 2018
RA: 5.89  Dec: -16.16  Sirius Mag: -1.5

116

Preceding page: Except in the very southern portions of the southern hemisphere, the so-called Winter Hexagon is visible not only in winter but in any season when the following constellations can be viewed: Canis Major, Canis Minor, Gemini, Auriga, and Taurus—all surrounding the figure of Orion. The polygon's six vertices are comprised of the following respective stars: Sirius, Procyon, Castor, Capella, Aldebaran, and Rigel. Connecting the alternate vertices of a hexagon will give you a hexagram—that is, a Star of David or Solomon's Seal. In addition, an equilateral triangle (outlined in gray) is formed with Betelgeuse at the apex and Procyon and Sirius at the base. The apex of one triangle resting on the horizon is Sirius, the brightest star in the heavens. It achieved its heliacal rising in the predawn hours of July 26th (New Years Day in the Maya Calendar, by the way), 850 AD. The Hopi know this star in the Greater Dog as *Ponótsona*, literally "sucks from the belly," or mammal.[10] This triangle's base formed by Castor and Aldebaran is very near M1 (Crab Nebula). The base of the other triangle making up the Star of David is formed by Procyon and Rigel, while its apex is Capella. The Greeks knew this star as Amaltheia, the she-goat who suckled Zeus. Orion's club forms one corner of this sky cube. (Technically, it is a rhombohedron, or stretched cube.) In my book *The Orion Zone*, I made the case that Orion served as the celestial version of the Hopi god Masau'u (Màasaw), who rules the earth plane as well as the underworld and death. He also wields a short club called a *maawiki*.[11]

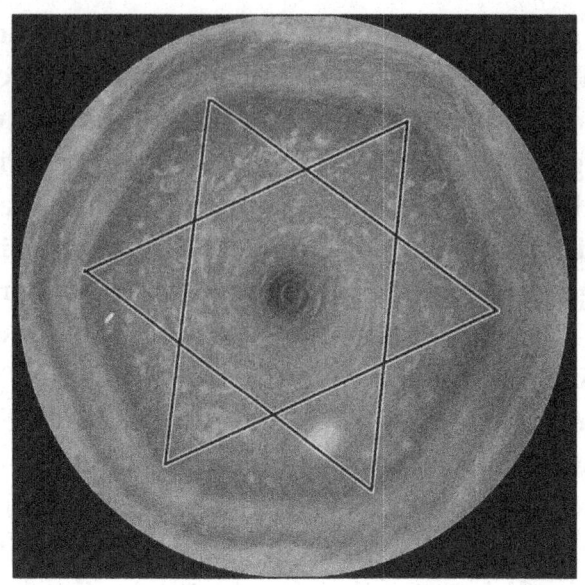

Star of David superimposed on an infrared image from NASA's Cassini spacecraft that shows a counterclockwise-rotating, hexagonal wave pattern in the atmosphere above the North Pole of the planet Saturn. This enigmatic cloud-hexagon measuring 8,575 miles on each side is surrounded by a number of concentric circles. For the direct correlation between Saturn and Orion, see pp. 180-181.

**Coda: Red City at "Black Rocks"**

Archaeologists have long known about the Hopi-Maya connection as evidenced by a vibrant trade network between the two regions. Among other things this social and commercial interaction provided the brilliant feathers of scarlet macaws (and even live birds!) to the American Southwest. In addition, theobromine, a cacao marker (i.e., chocolate), has been found on cylindrical, ceramic drinking vessels in Chaco Canyon, New Mexico. The nearest cacao trees are about 1,200 miles away, and Piedras Negras is over

1,600 miles from the 11th century Metro-Pueblo Center, so a concerted effort must have been made to transport the precious beans.[12] In Chapter 6, I had argued that Piedras Negras may have been the historical embodiment of the legendary Patlatkwapi. Here the Turtle Lords of the Maya once reigned, their culture and cosmology imbued with the veneration of the constellation Orion.

One of Edgar Cayce's readings (specifically, 5750-1) claims that during the final stages of Atlantis' demise in 10,600 BC, an entity named Iltar along with ten devotees migrated in boats from the province of Poseidia toward the setting sun. They eventually landed somewhere on the Yucatan peninsula, making their way past the Laguna de Términos to the mouth of the Usumacinta River, a major passageway inland.[13] These ancient mariners may have actually been the mythological Paddler Gods of the Maya referred to above. Guided by divine light of the Law of One, they ultimately came ashore at Black Rocks, whereupon they constructed their first temples. Like pagan sanctuaries worldwide that provide the sacred loci for subsequent synagogues, mosques, and cathedrals, the initial settlement at Piedras Negras would impart to the later Maya a legacy of peace and a palpable spirit of enlightenment. This particular influence on the southward-migrating Hopi clans temporarily living amongst the Maya may have tempered the former's character as well. The word *hopi* literally means "behaving one, one who is mannered, civilized, peaceable, polite, who adheres to the Hopi way."[14] Perhaps the Children of the Law of One, originally from Atlantis, and the Hopi "People of Peace," originally from Mu, came together in order to share a common spiritual destiny.

The next chapter focuses upon the sacred geometry of the American Southwest.

# Chapter 8
## *Geodesy of the Four Corners Odyssey*

### Gimme Three Steps

> "The sacredness of the triad and its symbol—the triangle—is derived from the fact that it is made up of the monad and the duad. The monad is the symbol of the Divine Father and the duad of the Great Mother."[1]  –Manly P. Hall

All across the globe many holy mountains or sacred structures mysteriously occur in a triangular configuration. Author Freddy Silva has found examples of such in Egypt, India, China, Japan, Peru/Bolivia, Great Britain/Ireland, and even Arizona/New Mexico. He correlates this to the *Rig Veda*'s triadic steps of Vishnu, who according to legend measured out the earthly realms. "By now it was becoming clear that the triple steps of Vishnu in 'widely stepped paces' measuring out the earthly region referred to a geometric-geodetic blueprint of power points. True to his attribute, Vishnu brings order to the world. And this arrangement doesn't just apply to the placement of sites, it is also the order that comes from a balanced mind when interacting with them, which it was hoped would lead to a balanced society."[2] Note that the Hopi (and presumably their ancestors) are/were all about the concept of balance, as demonstrated and achieved by their ceremonial cycle.

Three major Ancestral Puebloan (ancient Hopi et al.) sites had also been arranged in a near-equilateral triangle pattern: Pueblo Bonito in Chaco Canyon National Historic Park, the Sun (Orion) Temple at Mesa Verde National Monument, and Mummy Cave in Canyon del Muerto (Canyon de Chelly National Monument). (1) Chaco Canyon to Mesa Verde:

81.32 miles (2) Canyon del Muerto to Mesa Verde: 80.85 miles (3) Chaco Canyon to Canyon del Muerto: 79.01 miles. Chaco Canyon is the largest group of ancient pueblo ruins in the American Southwest. Mesa Verde is home to the largest cliff dwellings in the Southwest. Wrapped in yucca fiber, two naturally mummified corpses found below Mummy Cave Ruin provided the name of the pueblo, which contained about 75 rooms dating from the late 13th century AD, although one wooden beam was radiocarbon-dated at 306 AD.[3] (See p. 138.)

A similar triangular pattern is seen to the south, with Zuni Pueblo being the apex of the equilateral triangle and Chaco to Canyon del Muerto the base. (1) Chaco Canyon to Zuni: 84.74 miles (2) Canyon del Muerto to Zuni: 85.26 miles (3) Chaco Canyon to Canyon del Muerto: 79.01 miles

In the northern example, the exact center of the triangle happens to be a trident-shaped mesa. On the left "tine" a pair of tire tracks proceeds from the north and terminates at what appears to be a low stone structure.

**The tripartite mesa at the center of an equilateral triangle in northern New Mexico. (More fieldwork needed.)**

*Sacred Geometry of the Orion Zone*

In addition, a right triangle is formed by the following three sites in Arizona: Canyon del Muerto, Wupatki National Monument, and the *Sipapuni* (Hopi "Place of Emergence"), natural travertine dome on the Little Colorado River in Grand Canyon. The latter site is perhaps the most importance locus in Hopi cosmology because legends describe the ancestral Hopi (*Hisatsinom*) ascending a giant reed from the subterranean Third World (Era) to the current Fourth World. After they climbed out of Grand Canyon they began to populate the Colorado Plateau. Mummy Cave in Canyon del Muerto is due east of the *Sipapuni*. Wupatki National Monument encompasses a number of 12th century Ancestral Puebloan ruins north of Sunset Crater, a dormant volcano that erupted about 1064 AD and continued to belch lava and smoke for centuries. The main ruin of Wupatki ("tall house") contained approximately 200 rooms constructed of red sandstone slabs, as well as an open, circular amphitheater, and an oval ball court in which was played a game similar to that of the ancient Maya.[4]

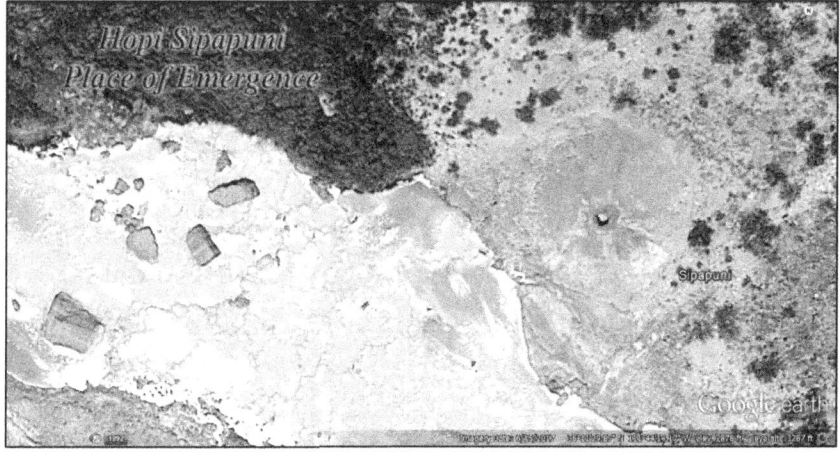

**Hopi and Zuni *Sipapuni*, sacred "Place of Emergence," a natural limestone dome on the Little Colorado River.**

Above: Una Vida in Chaco Canyon with Fajada Butte. Below: winter solstice sunset window in Pueblo Bonito. Next page below: summer solstice sunrise streams through window on right and falls as a small golden rectangle in the niche at left.

Above: Pueblo Bonito. Below: Casa Rinconada, Great Kiva.
Dawn, summer solstice, June 21, 2018. Photos by author.

Left: Mummy Cave Ruin, Canyon del Muerto, Canyon de Chelly National Park. Photo by Adam Clark Vroman, 1904.
Below: Cliff Palace at Mesa Verde, Colorado.[5] Photo by G. Edward Johnson (Lorax), 2003.

Above: Wupatki Ruin. Below: amphitheater at Wupatki.

The previously mentioned right triangle formed by Canyon del Muerto, Wupatki, and the Hopi *Sipapuni* is essentially a Pythagorean triangle whose sides have ratios of 5: 12: 13. (See graphic on p. 133.) In his book *Sun, Moon and Earth*, British author Robin Heath calls this sort of polygon a "lunation triangle." The term "lunation," or lunar month, is the period between one new moon and the next, which is approximately 29.5 days. The shortest side of the right triangle (5-side) can be divided into 3 and 2, a harmonic point at which the hypotenuse of a smaller right triangle is formed. Whereas the diagonal of the larger triangle measures 13, that of the smaller one measures 12.369—the exact number of lunations in a year. Heath conceives (no pun intended) of this interaction of 12 and 13 to be a sort of *hierogamos* (as we recall the "Manly" quote that commenced this chapter).

> "The true number of months in the year falls between 12 and 13, and in order to define a true soli-lunar calendar, this figure, 12.368, must be determined. The lunation triangle is defined as a 5:12:13 right triangle, the second Pythangorean triangle, with the '5' side divided as 3 : 2. A new hypotenuse to this point measures 12.369. The Moon, 13, thereby becomes married to the Sun, 12, where the female, 2, joins the male, 3. The sacred marriage of Sun and Moon, made in heaven, is witnessed on Earth, and occurs at the musical fifth, the most harmonious interval (3 : 2). Musical allegories abound… and Solomon's throne is wisely placed at the 3 : 2 point in the Temple."[6]

Heath goes on to mention the "fishy story" found in John 21:1-11, when Jesus reappears a third time after the resurrection and tells the disciples to cast the net on the starboard side, whereupon they pulled up 153 fishes. The square root of 153 = 12.369.

In 1992 while living near Carnac in Brittany, Heath received a spontaneous revelation of the sacred landscape of the Ancients that incorporated Stonehenge, the Preseli Hills and two islands in the Bristol Channel. He saw "in a flash" that Lundy Island, three miles long and about one mile wide, was situated along a north-south line that reached due north over 50 miles to the source of the Stonehenge bluestones in Pembrokeshire, Wales. Stonehenge itself lies over 120 miles due east of Lundy on the Salisbury Plain.[7] These sites formed a Pythagorean triangle, the starting point of which was Lundy, which in Welsh is known as *Elen*, which means "elbow, bend, right-angle"—clearly a geographic descriptor. (See Google Earth photo on p. 132.)

The Celts conceptualized Lundy Island as the Isle of the Dead, an Otherworld where souls were ferried to join their ancestors in the land of the setting sun. We are not surprised, then, to find a "Templar Hill" there, or the site of the "Giants' Graves," from which skeletons eight feet in length were once unearthed. Citing historian Geoffrey Ashe, Heath suggests that Celtic traditions esteemed Lundy Island as a portal to the paradisiacal *Annwn*, the "abyss," or the underworld, mystical realm of spirits and fairies.[8] The Welsh term *Annwn*, or *Annwfyn*, is pronounced "Anu-n."[9] It is interesting to note that the most sacred precinct of ancient Egypt was Heliopolis, called *An*, (biblical On).[10] However, some scholars believe it was pronounced *Āwanu*.[11] In addition, the supreme sky god of Sumer was known as Anu.

> "In Mesopotamia the assembly of gods in the sky constituted the highest authority in the universe, determining the course of events on earth. Under the leadership of Anu, the god of heaven, whose name means 'sky', 'shining', 'bright', the cosmic order was established out of primeval chaos as an organized whole. He was, in fact, the personification of the sky and the most potent force in the cosmos, older than all the other gods, and the ultimate source of existence... In his celestial abode he kept the bread and water of immortal life, and it was he who gave the divine authority exercised by kings on earth."[12]

Co-author John Michell, esoteric expert on astro-archaeology and Earth Mysteries, sums up Heath's achievements.

> "One effect of the scheme is that the site of Stonehenge is precisely and ideally related to a spot at the centre of Lundy Island in the Bristol Channel. The discovery of this relationship was made by Robin Heath and first published in his *A Key to Stonehenge* (1993). He noticed that Lundy is on the same latitude as Stonehenge, and about 123.4 miles to the west. A right angle at Lundy generates a line due north that passes over the sacred island of Caldey near Tenby in South Wales and continues to the Preseli district where the Stonehenge bluestones came from. A line from

there to Stonehenge completes a Pythagorean triangle with sides of 5, 12 & 13."[13]

Caldey Island falls precisely on the 3:2 point of the shorter 5-side line. This smaller island hosts St. Illtud's church, reputedly the oldest in Wales, which oddly contains a square menhir rising from within a round well. Heath wryly comments:

> "Nearby, in the ancient monastery grounds, may be found a circular well, overgrown and neglected, in the centre of which has been placed a large square-section megalith. This coming together of prime male and female symbols is a pagan arrangement unlikely to be other than an embarrassment to the present order, perhaps one reason for the neglected state of these ancient gardens. The more esoteric numerological meaning of the numbers 2 and 3, espoused in all the traditions from the Rig Veda through to Pythagoras and later texts, offers some confirmation that the geodetic meaning was understood, for where else may one find a megalith sited with a circular holy well?"[14]

The British example of the lunation triangle just *happens* to have nearly the same dimensions as the Arizona triangle. In the former case: $a^2 = 54$ miles, $b^2 = 123$ miles, and $c^2 = 135$ miles. In the latter case: $a^2 = 50.6$ miles, $b^2 = 123$ miles, and $c^2 = 133$ miles. Is this merely a coincidence, or evidence of intercontinental contact in ancient times?

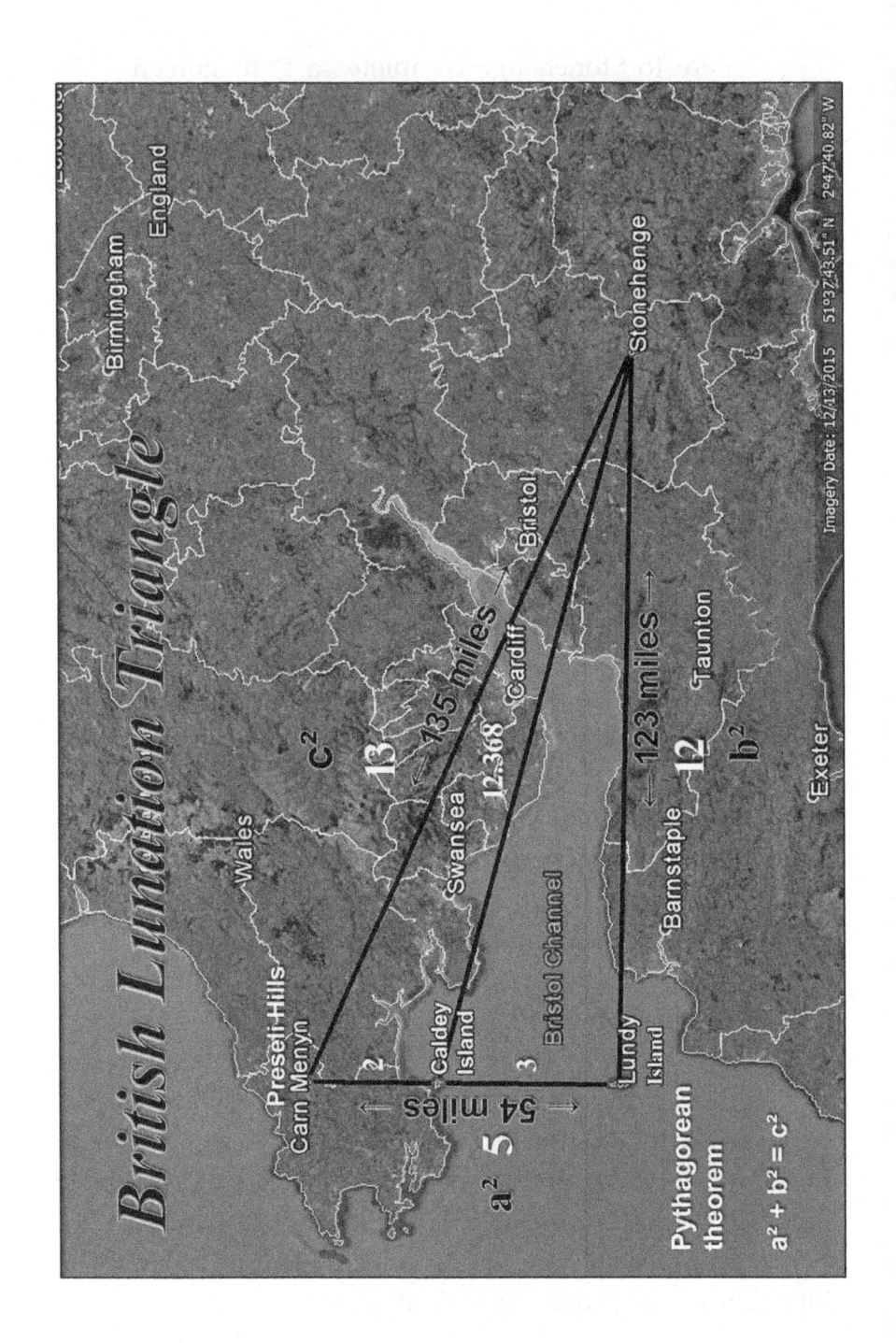

## British Lunation Triangle

Carn Menyn — 54 miles — Lundy Island
$a^2$ 5
2 Caldey Island
3 Bristol Channel
$c^2$ 13 ← 135 miles
12.368
Swansea — Cardiff — Bristol
← 123 miles → Stonehenge
Barnstaple 12 Taunton
$b^2$

Pythagorean theorem
$a^2 + b^2 = c^2$

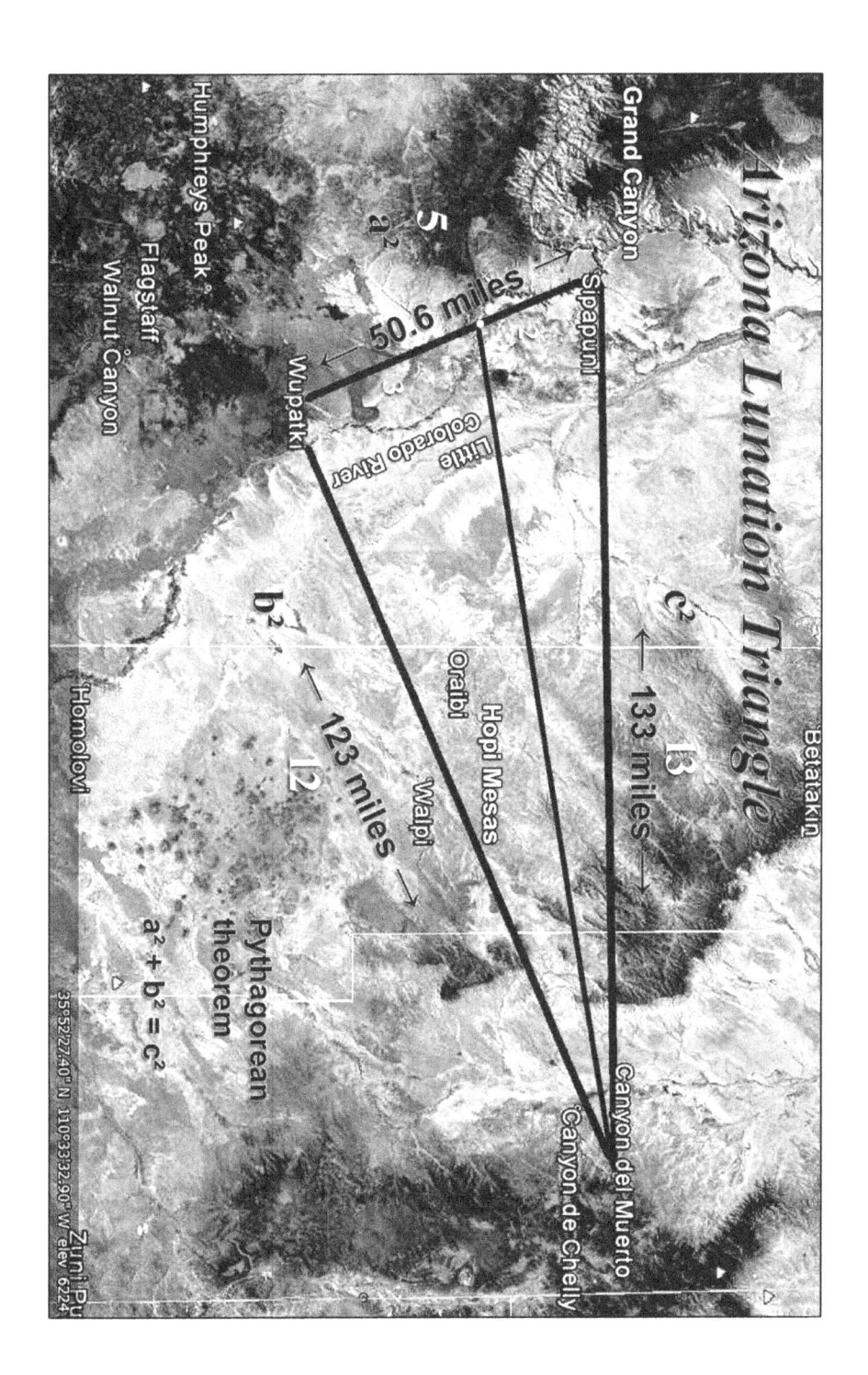

*Arizona Lunation Triangle*

Grand Canyon

Humphreys Peak
Flagstaff
Walnut Canyon

$a^2$
5
Sipapuni
← 50.6 miles
Wupatki
Little Colorado River

$b^2$
← 123 miles →

Homolovi

Oraibi
Hopi Mesas
Walpi

Pythagorean theorem
$a^2 + b^2 = c^2$

Betatakin

$c^2$
13
← 133 miles →

Canyon del Muerto
Canyon de Chelly

35°52'27.40" N  110°33'32.90" W  elev 6224

Zuni Pu

We remember that one of the angles of the British right triangle was Lundy Island, a purported gateway to the underworld. In the Arizona example this subterranean passageway is fulfilled by the *Sipapuni*, whence the Hopi emerged from the previous Third World (Era), and to which the souls of the dead migrate. 30 miles due west of the *Sipapuni* lies Point Sublime on the North Rim of Grand Canyon. This spectacular eagle's eyrie is a locus held sacred by the Hopi.

Considering the opposite angle, we find that most of the Preseli bluestones erected at Stonehenge circa 2900 BC are metamorphic spotted dolerite. (Only 43 of an estimated 80 of these bluestones remain.) However, four of these stones are rhyolite (ash flow tuffs).[15] This igneous element conceptually corresponds to the Wupatki ruins of northern Arizona, located near the base of 1,000-foot-tall Sunset Crater, which, as previously mentioned, began to erupt pyroclastically in the 11th century. If one travels 31 miles north-northwest along the shortest side of the triangle, one arrives at the 3 : 2 point where the line crosses the Little Colorado River. From this vantage the summer solstice sun sets over Point Sublime over 40 miles to the northwest.

Whether Canyon del Muerto was named for the pair of mummies retrieved from one of its cliff dwellings or due to the Spanish military expedition's massacre of 115 Navajo men, women, and children seeking refuge in a cave on a winter day in 1805, the canyon provides a focal point for a meridian that extends thousands of miles to the south. As we shall see in the next chapter, the longitude line forms a significant global axis created by an ancient system of geodesy.

# Chapter 9
# *The Meridian Connection— Hopiland and Easter Island*

**"Just Ask the Axis (He Knows Everything)"**[1]

The meridianal nexus of sacred sites is a geo-odyssey stretching inscrutably far into the twilight of our past. However, the conundrum of global longitude flummoxed Western civilization until 1761, when an English clockmaker named John Harrison finally invented a chronometer precise enough for navigators to correctly determine meridian lines—though the device was not regularly in use until the following decade. In his groundbreaking book *Fingerprints of the Gods*, Graham Hancock discusses evidence of a much earlier longitudinal legacy. "The Piri Reis Map of 1513, for example, places South America and Africa in *the correct relative longitudes*, theoretically an impossible feat for the science of the time. But Piri Reis was candid in admitting that his map was based on far earlier sources. Could it have been from one of these sources that he derived his accurate longitudes?"[2]

Since the Pueblo People were for the most part ceremonially, psychologically, and pragmatically oriented to the four solstice sunrise and sunset points on the horizon, the cardinal directions nonetheless held great power in their minds—especially the non-equinoxial North and South. For an agricultural society such as this, the concept of a straight north-south line must have been an abstraction with awesome—in the old sense of the word—spiritual implications: North, the direction of immutable circumpolar stars sweeping around their axis; and South, the way the sun god Taawa journeys in winter, a spirit road beyond this life. In this context we are reminded of Rudolf Otto's phrase describing the numinous: *Mysterium tremendum et fascinans* ("fearful and fascinating mystery").[3] The eastern and western horizons with their solstitial points were both related to the mundane world of planning and planting, but the north-south road conceived of as a vertical axis would ultimately lead to the timeless realm of the spirits. To put it briefly so as not to get side-tracked, in Puebloan cosmology, North was the direction of the underworld, whereas South was the direction of the celestial realm.

In my previous books I have referred to Southwestern archaeologist Stephen H. Lekson as a maverick of the mainstream, if only because his prose, unlike that of most other archaeologists, is actually lively and fun to read. His 1999 book titled *The Chaco Meridian* ponders the cognitive shift that ancient peoples experienced when confronted with the concept of north-south alignments. His hypothesis states that a number of significant pueblos were located on 107° 57' 25" W longitude. These include: (1) the massive pueblos in Chaco Canyon at the center, (2) Aztec Ruins to the north (both in northwestern New Mexico), and (3) the adobe pueblo of Paquimé (a.k.a. Casas Grandes) to the south (in Chihuahua, Mexico). Incidentally, the latter site is nearly on the same *latitude* as the Great Pyramid. Specifically, Paquimé is only 26.73 miles north but 7,488 miles west of that fabled Egyptian monument. These pueblos were also constructed in a chronological series: Chaco, 850 – 1150 AD; Aztec, 1100 – 1300 AD; and Paquimé 1250 – 1450 AD.

Lekson comments on the conceptual ramifications for the Ancestral Puebloans of the Chaco Meridian:

"For cognitive issues, 'landscape' may be as appropriate to early societies as 'space' is appropriate to later societies, like ours. That's an interesting if simple model, and a place to start: People thought about what they could see—effective, experienced space. The Chaco Merdian signaled a shift—a point-of-change, a transition—from a landscape world to a spatial world: thinking beyond the seeable. Not thinking *about*—any primate can think about what's over the next hill—but thinking *with*: abstract geometry in that term's very literal translation. The meridian is a peculiarly human, *spatial* interest. It is both fixed and arbitrary: fixed as the only real direction, yet arbitrary in its economic uselessness. The Chaco-Aztec-Paquime alignment imposed a remarkable spatial geometry, referenced to that fixed direction, over a series of unrelated landscapes—regions so large and diverse that today we label them the Colorado Plateau, the Mogollon Uplands, and the Chihuahuan Desert; and we consider their archaeologies to represent altogether different cultures."[4]

If we travel west from Chaco Canyon a distance of 78 miles, we come to 109° 21' 32" W longitude, which might be called the Rapa Nui Meridian. It extends southward from Mummy Cave, transects the hoodoo spire of Spider Rock in Canyon de Chelly, cuts through Arizona and the inhospitable Sonoran Desert of Mexico, grazes the tip of the Baja peninsula, shoots across the Eastern Pacific, crosses the Equator, finally traveling more than 4,300 miles to a tiny speck of windswept rock in a vast ocean. The name of this triangular island less than 15 miles on its base and 10 miles on each side is, of course, Easter Island. It is the epitome of isolation, lying 2,600 miles due east of Tahiti and 2,500 miles due west of the Chilean coast.

**Cliff dwelling of Mummy Cave Ruin, Canyon del Muerto in Canyon de Chelly National Park, Arizona.**

Spider Rock, 800 ft. high, rises as an *axis mundi* at the juncture of Canyon de Chelly and Monument Canyon. The Diné (Navajo) legend of Spider Rock goes something like this: Spider Woman was the first weaver and the top of this monolith is her home. Disobedient or nasty kids are warned that if they persist in their misdeeds, she will descend, abduct and carry them back up, then proceed to boil them alive and devour them. The white things you see at the top are the bones of these unfortunate children.

*The Rapa Nui Meridian*

longitude 109° 21' 32" W

180° azimuth

4,358 miles

Canyon del Muerto

Easter Island

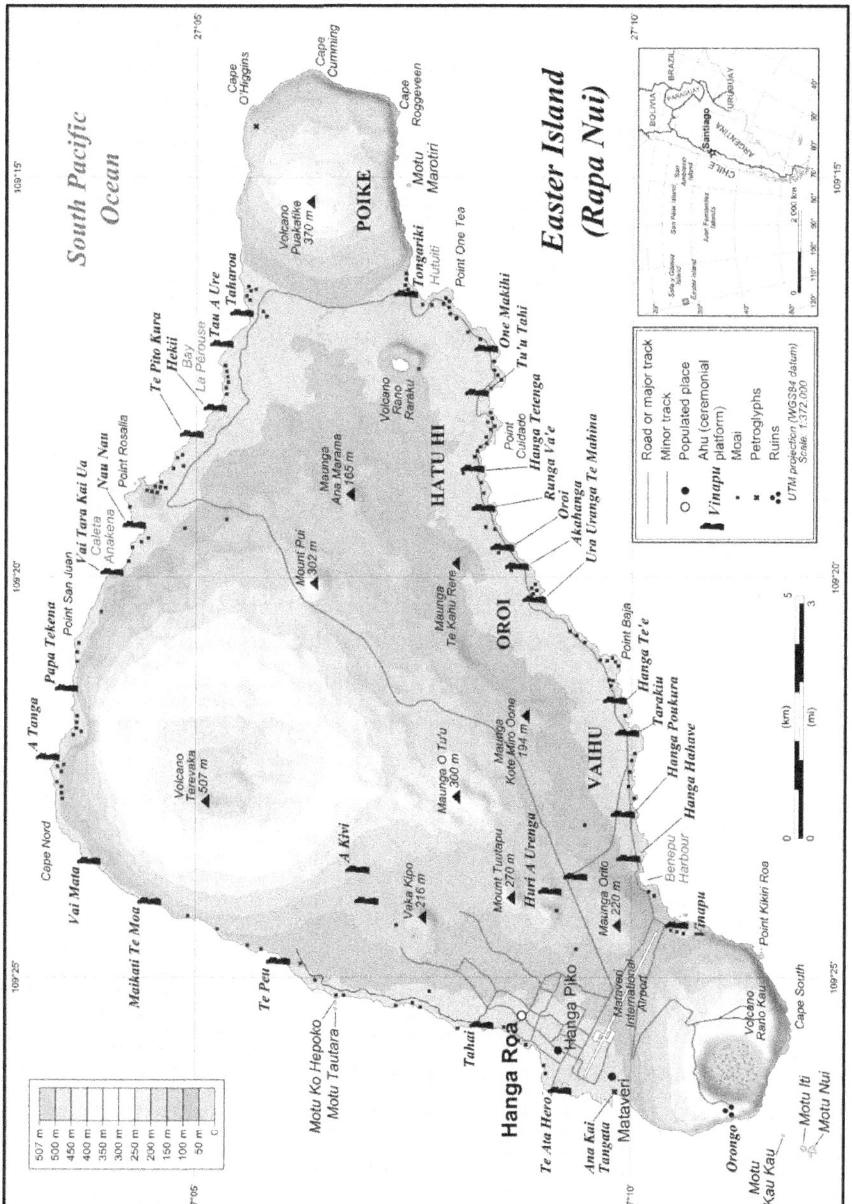

Easter Island
(Rapa Nui)
South Pacific
Ocean
POIKE
HATU HI
OROI
VAIHU
Hanga Roa
Hanga Piko
Mataveri
Mataveri International Airport
Volcano Terevaka 507 m
Volcano Puakatike 370 m
Volcano Rano Raraku
Volcano Rano Kau
Mount Pui 302 m
Maunga Ana Marama 165 m
Maunga Te Kahu Rere
Maunga O Tu'u 300 m
Maunga Kote Miro Oone 194 m
Mount Tuutapu 270 m
Vaka Kipo 216 m
Maunga Orito 220 m
Cape O'Higgins
Cape Cumming
Cape Roggeveen
Motu Marotiri
Point One Tea
Tongariki
Hutuiti
One Makihi
Tu'u Tahi
Point Cuidado
Hanga Tetenga
Runga Va'e
Oroi
Akahanga
Ura Uranga Te Mahina
Point Baja
Hanga Te'e
Tarakiu
Hanga Poukura
Hanga Hahave
Hangapu Harbour
Vinapu
Point Kikiri Roa
Cape South
Orongo
Motu Iti
Motu Nui
Motu Kau Kau
Ana Kai Tangata
Te Ata Hero
Tahai
Motu Ko Hepoko
Motu Tautara
Te Peu
Maikai Te Moa
Vai Mata
Cape Nord
A Kivi
Huri A Urenga
A Tanga
Papa Tekena
Point San Juan
Vai Tara Kai Ua
Caleta Anakena
Nau Nau
Point Rosalia
Te Pito Kura
Hekii
La Pérouse Bay
Tau A Ure
Taharoa
Road or major track
Minor track
Populated place
Ahu (ceremonial platform)
Moai
Petroglyphs
Ruins
UTM projection (WGS84 datum)
Scale: 1:372,000
(km)
(mi)
507 m
500 m
450 m
400 m
350 m
300 m
250 m
200 m
150 m
100 m
50 m
0
27°05'
27°10'
109°15'
109°20'
109°25'
BRAZIL
BOLIVIA
PARAGUAY
URUGUAY
ARGENTINA
CHILE
Santiago
Easter Island

Hanging down like a plumb bob, the long line comes ashore at the northern apex of the island near a site designated as *A Tanga* or *Ahu Tanga* (see map above). According to Russian archaeoastronomer and Polynesia researcher Sergei Rjabchikov:

> "The name *A Tanga* means (The deity) *Tanga* (*Taanga, Tama, Tangaroa, Tamaroa*). It is well known that this platform is located at the almost most northern rim of Easter Island. Moreover, the *ahu* points to north very precisely. Notice that the sun moved (and moves) from east via north to west each day. Hence, the *ahu* was a solar observatory. Since the god *Tangaroa* was the sun deity in the Society Islands and in the Western Polynesia, the remnants of that cult could be retained in the Rapanui astronomical notations. Thus, the platform oriented on the midday sun was named after the sun deity. It is common knowledge that the Miru tribe and the neighbours believed in the supreme deity *Tangaroa*."[5]

Taking into account a coincidental possibility in this context, I would nonetheless like to note that the Hopi word for sun god is *Tawa*.[6]

It is not my intention (or bailiwick) to engage in a full discussion of the archaeology of Rapa Nui and its famous *moai* statues. However, one site deserves attention vis-à-vis the Hopi and astronomical orientation of monuments. *Ahu Akivi* is located about a mile-and-half inland on the west-central part of the island. Unlike all the other statues on

Rapa Nui, the seven *moai* arranged in an east-west line on their platform (*ahu*) face outward toward the ocean. These *moai* were constructed of a uniform height and weight, averaging 16 feet tall and 18 tons. Archaeologists found a crematorium behind the platform, so the site may have been associated with death rituals. Folklore suggests that the *moai* represent the seven scouts that Hotu Matu'a, the future supreme ruler of Rapa Nui, had sent out from his homeland Hiva to find this new island paradise he had seen in a dream. (It should be noted that Hotu Matu'a finally landed at Anakena, near the northern tip of the island heretofore mentioned.)[7]

The row of statues faces the equinoxial setting sun, vernal and autumnal. More importantly, the *moai* direct their gaze (once carved from coral but now missing) toward the setting of Orion's belt in late autumn (in the Southern Hemisphere, late May), shortly before he disappears into the underworld for a period of 70 days. This astronomical phenomemon is known as the constellation's heliacal setting—the last time for a certain period that these stars can be seen before they are lost in the sun's glare.[8]

**The *moai* of *Ahu Akivi* face westward toward the sea. Photo by Arian Zwegers.**

The backs of the *moai* as they watch the heliacal setting of Orion's belt (*Tautoru*) in 1300 AD. The seven *moai* correspond to the seven brightest stars of the constellation.

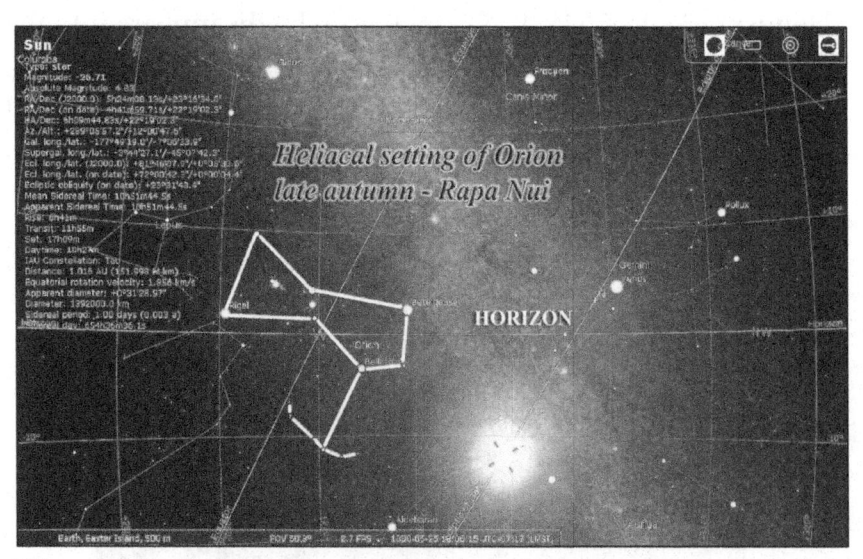

May 25, 1300 AD, Easter Island, heliacal setting of Orion. Sun is 12° below the horizon.

As previously noted, the natives of Rapa Nui refer to their legendary homeland as *Hiva*. In this regard Graham Hancock writes: "We learn that it was once a proud island of enormous size, but it too suffered in the 'great cataclysm' and was 'submerged in the sea.' Afterwards, a group of 300 survivors set out in two very large ocean-going canoes to sail to Te-Pito-O-Te-Henua ["the Navel of the World"], having magically obtained foreknowledge of the existence of the island and of how to steer a course using the stars."[9]

The reader will recall that the Hopi term *kiva* is a sunken or subterranean ceremonial lodge. When descending into this structure via the ladder that extends through its roof, one is symbolically entering the previous era known as the Third World, which is conceptualized as antediluvian. In addition, the overhead hatchway of a *kiva* is the frame through which Orion is sighted shortly after midnight on the winter solstice, thereby commencing the ceremony. In other words, Orion synchronizes this most important of Hopi rituals called the *Soyal*. It may be significant, then, that the name of this Rapa Nui platform focused upon the setting of Orion is named *Ahu Akivi*.

Hancock goes on to describe the ancient astronomers of Easter Island: "Traditions state...that ages ago there existed on the island a brotherhood of 'learned men who studied the sky.' These Tangata Rani were instantly recognized because they were 'tattooed on their faces with coloured spots'— somewhat like the astronomer priests of Heliopolis in ancient Egypt, who wore distinctive leopard-skin cloaks with coloured spots."[10] We should note here that the Hopi god Màasaw (Masau'u) is also conceptualized as having multicolored spots or splotches on his head, especially in his *katsina* form. (See photos of Hopi dolls on p. 88.)

The next chapter undertakes a Passage to India, of sorts.

# Chapter 10
## *Rongorongo and Mohenjo Daro*

Coincidences come in two ilks: insignificant and meaningful, the latter of which psychologist C. G. Jung called synchronicity. In this case you decide: Easter Island is located at 27° 09′ 28″ south latitude; the ancient Indus River city of Mohenjo Daro is at 27° 19′ 27″ north latitude.

Geodetically less significant but still noteworthy is the fact that the longitude lines of of the two sites are located about halfway around the world from each other—specifically 177.5°, or two-and-a-half degrees shy of 180. In other words, the respective longitude lines are between 153.75 and 154 miles apart. (At the latitude of Mohenjo Daro, 1 degree of longitude = 61.5 statute miles; at the latitude of Easter Island, 1 degree of longitude = 61.6 statute miles.)[1]

Another numerical "coincidence" draws our attention. From Easter Island to the aforementioned Mummy Cave is 4,358 miles.[2] From Mummy Cave over the North Pole to Mohenjo Daro is 8,055.57 miles; the sum of these two numbers is 12,413.57 miles. The Earth's polar circumference is 24,860 miles (as opposed to the equatorial circumference, or 24,901 miles). This means that the distance from Easter Island to Mohenjo Daro is .499—almost half—the meridian circumference of the globe.

A line drawn longitudinally from the Hopi *Sipapuni* over the North Pole to Mohenjo Daro is 8,061.4 miles and is .13 of a degree east of a True North/South line, or about 7.5 miles. (We remember that an eastward line from the *Sipapuni* to Mummy Cave in Canyon del Muerto is 133 miles in length and is 88° azimuth—or two degrees north of an exact west-to-east line.)

*Meridian Passage to India*

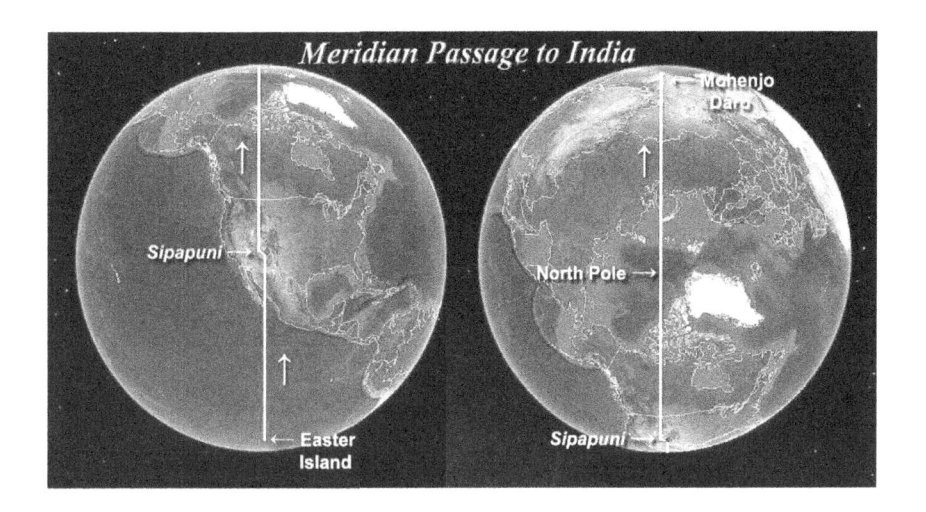

Sipapuni — Easter Island — North Pole — Mohenjo Daro — Sipapuni

Polish author Igor Witkowski comments on the geodetics of the Easter Island-Indus River connection.

> "In light of the facts we may therefore rule out coincidence, especially if we take into account that it's the only such case on our planet. The straight line connecting these two points we may name an 'axis of the world.' By the way, it is also questionable to consider the inaccuracy as an error. After all, the city of Mohenjo Daro was certainly established earlier than the 'messengers' of the super-civilization reached Easter Island — it was just the closest piece of land to the place where 'the axis' passed through the surface of our globe. Exactly — globe! The authors of this undertaking must have realized that Earth is a sphere, have precisely known its dimensions, the location of its equator, and so on!"[3]

You may be asking how Easter Island and Mohenjo Daro are related. After all, the latter was once a major metropolis of 40,000 or so inhabitants located along the central Indus River (now in Pakistan). Beginning circa 2900 BC, it flourished between 2500 BC and 1900 BC. The city, which was laid out on a grid system and constructed of fired bricks, contained a water suppy and sewage system, with a plethora of wells and public baths. Its streets fell silent for 3,000 years before Rapa Nui was first settled, according to mainstream archaeologists. So, what is the connection between two sites located literally on opposite sides of the globe? Surprisingly, the link might be linguistic.

A number of wooden boards discovered on Rapa Nui during the 19th century contained a series of uniformily sized pictographs or ideograms, inscribed in rows using a shark's tooth or obsidian flake. Although basically undeciphered, this glyphic "script" known as *rongorongo* has been considered by some to be a form of proto-writing. The term *rongorongo* is Rapanui for "recite, declaim, or chant," so these may have been used as a mnemonic device for oral recitations. The tablets employ a system called reverse boustrophedon, like the "ploughing of an ox." That is, the glyphs are read to one direction; then the tablet is turned upside down and read in the opposite direction.[4]

The glyphs themselves feature representations of humans, birds, bird-men, fish, crustaceans, plants, and geometric designs. Early 20th century Swiss anthropologist Alfred Métraux describes the island's bizarre form of commuication. "A strange and disturbing symbolism is manifest in a number of figures combining the most disparate elements: human bodies ending in geometric patterns or partially animal in form, triangles and lozenges embellished with ears, hands clinging to bars, and designs based other parts of the human body.... A whole fantastic world seethes before our eyes as they run along these alternating rows of signs." Despite its uncanny appearance, Métraux adds: "Graphic art has rarely reached such a level of perfection in any primitive culture."[5]

Rongorongo tablet, Mamari tablet, late 19th century photograph. 12 inches long and 8.25 inches wide. Note the three linked-lozenges glyph (especially in the third, fourth, and fifth full lines from the top). This represents Orion's belt *(Tautoru)*, which is associated with the female puberty ceremony held during the vernal equinox (September).[6]

Now for the antipodes. The so-called Indus script was a pictographic method of communication used in Mohenjo Daro and another city in the Indus River Valley named Harappa. The symbols were incised mostly on small, rectangular stamp seals but sometimes on pottery and sundry ornaments. In addition to the abstract glyphs, which number about 450 different signs, various animals were depicted, including elephants, bulls, water buffalo, rhinos, tigers, and even unicorns! Archaeologists have found approximately 3,500 different specimens produced by the Indus Valley civilization.[7] According to contemporary German freelance writer Egbert Richter-Ushanas:

> "The Indus Script and the Rongorongo Script have several things in common, apart from the fact that both are still regarded as undeciphered. The most striking parallel is that some pictograms look identical, as was pointed out already by G. de Hevesy, though he relied on insufficient renderings of the signs. Moreover, signs that look identical or nearly identical in its form must not have the same meaning. It cannot be denied, however, that both writing systems make use of a similar method of rendering words by pictograms and word sequences by ligatures and fusions. Moreover, the number of basic signs in both scripts is about 100. It is known that the Rongorongo script was not used for ornamental purposes, but that the inscribed tablets called kohau rongorongo were recited publicly on special occasions with a religious purport. Many of the inscriptions of the Indus seals and tablets look too short for a recitation, but since they have amulet function they served for a religious purpose, too. This is also evident from the motifs."[8]

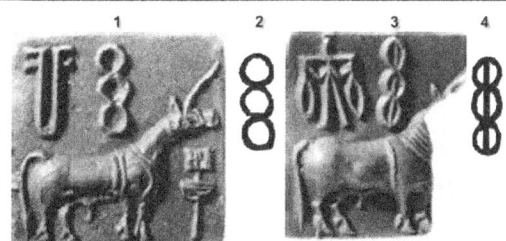

Columns I, III, V, and VII are Indus script.
Columns II, IV, VI, and VIII are rongorongo.

1 & 3: Indus script. 2 & 4: *rongorongo* script

#1: Unicorn and ritual fire post (bottom-right corner). In addition to the linked lozenges noted above, three circles vertically stacked represent Orion's belt. The line through #4 may genealogically refer to Rapui Nui founder Hotu Matua and his two sons. It may also represent a caduceus.[9]

In his recent book on the relationship between the Dravidian Tamil (Thamizh) language and the Indus River script, my friend and colleague Shree Subash Chandira Bose states that the ideogram in the upper-lefthand corner of #1 (previous page) is the the letter *Pa* and corresponds to both the 5th note of the musical scale (in the Italian solfeggio, *Sol*—a dominant 5th) and the *Vishuddi* (throat) chakra.[10] The Sankrit word *pa* denotes "drinking,"[11] so it is perhaps more than mere coincidence that the Hopi word *pa* denotes "water."[12]

Subash Bose identifies the #3 glyph (preceding page) as a devotee of Lord Shiva who carries an *annakkaavadi*, which is a pole with two bags at each end for holding the food he collects from various households to be distributed to other devotees. Some ideograms that Bose cites also have a *Pa* glyph instead of a head, which connotes water.[13]

Shiva (or Siva) also incarnated as Prajapati (or Pasupathi), god of Creation and procreation. Mr. Bose states: "The 'Paasupatha Brahmno Upanishad' is a Saiva Upanishad which envisions Lord Shiva as the Supreme Brahman, the witness of everything and the impelling force behind all movements and actions. **He is Pasupathi, 'Lord of the Souls.'**"[14] As master of all created beings, Prajapati took the form of the stag Mriga, which in Sanskrit literature denotes the constellation Orion.[15] Pursuing his own daughter named Rohini in the form of a doe (Aldebaran in Taurus), he was shot by an anonymous hunter (Sirius in Canis Major) who was trying to avenge this incestuous impulse. The belt stars represent the arrow still sticking in the stag's body.[16]

Book X, Hymn 7, of the *Atharva Veda*, composed during the latter half of the second millennium BC, discusses what is deemed the *Skambha*, the Sanskrit word for a "prop, support, pillar, buttress, fulcrum, the Fulcrum of the Universe, and identified with the Supreme Being..."[17] It is essentially the personified *Axis Mundi*. (Remember what Jimi Hendrix sang? "Just ask the Axis. He knows everything.") He is the World Tree with its shamanistic, tripartite levels: the fiery celestial realm of the gods, the tangible terrestrial realm of the living, and the aqueous nether realm of the dead.[18] His round trunk sprouts forth gods like branches in the air. He forever holds up heaven and earth. He is where the four compass points converge. He is the golden egg thrown into the still pool of the Universal Mind. He pervades all of Existence, and owns both the surging oceans and the arteries pulsing within Man. In him are the cosmic Law and Faith united. In him both Death and Immortality merge within humanity.

> "Tell of that Skambha, who may he be?
> In him there is no darkness, no evil exists in him.
> In him are all the *three lights* [italics added]
>     that are in Prajnapati, the Lord of creation.
> He knows the golden reed standing in the waters,
> He truly knows the mysterious Prajnapati.
> It is by the Skambha that these two, heaven and earth,
>     remain established in space.
> In Skambha abides all things that have a soul,
>     and all that which winks and closes its eyes."[19]

The "three lights that are in Prajnapati" quite possibily refer to the belt stars of Orion. The "golden reed" rising from the waters of the abyss is symbolic of the cosmogony. Regarding the *skambha*, the eminent scholars Giorgio de Santillana and Hertha von Dechend have stated:

"As *radius* automatically calls *circle* to mind, so *axis* must invoke the two determining great circles on the surface of the sphere, the equinoctial and solstitial colures.[20] Pictured this way, the axis resembles a complete armillary sphere. It stands for the system of coordinates of the sphere and represents the frame of the world-age. Actually the frame defines a world-age. Because the polar axis and the colures form an individual whole, the entire frame is thrown out of kilter if one part is moved. When that happens, a new Pole star with appropriate colures of its own must replace the obsolete apparatus."[21]

Indeed, the *Atharva Veda* itself refers to a great circle of 360° and the 12 signs of the zodiac.

"One is the wheel, twelve are the bands,
  three are the hubs—who understands it?
Therein are fixed three-hundered and sixty pins,
  and pegs that are firmly fixed....
Though manifest, yet it is hidden, mysterious,
  by name the ancient, the great mode of being.
There in the Skambha are set this all,
  Therein are established all that stirs and breathes.
Up eastward, downward in the west, it rolls,
  with countless elements, one-wheeled,
  single-fellied [-rimmed].
With a half of itself it created all existence,
  What has become of the other half that remained?...
A bowl is there with aperture sideways
  and the bottom upturned.
In it is deposited glory of all forms,
  thereon sit together the seven Rishis,
  the keepers of it, the great sphere."[22]

The upturned "bowl' may refer to the dome of heaven with its seven sages—either the seven major stars of Orion or the seven major stars of Ursus Major. The great "sphere" is the frame constructed from the great circles of the ecliptic and the colures of the equinoxes and solstices.

Prajnapati is the focus of the well known Proto-Shiva terracotta seal from Mohenjo Daro (M-34A, National Museum, New Delhi). The vignette shows a clearly ithyphallic yogi who sits upon a throne supported by hourglass-shaped drums (see Chapter 12) as he meditates in a lotus posture. We can see three of his faces, but presumably he has four, or perhaps five—one gazing in each direction as proof of his omniscience. His headdress is comprised of massive, curving horns and a fountain-shaped crest. He wears a brocaded shirt embossed with chevrons on his chest. As Lord of all Beasts, he is surrounded by a curious totemic or heraldic menagerie: a rhinoceros, a water buffalo, an antelope or goat, a tiger ridden by a humanoid stick figure, and an elephant. The lower-right corner of this square seal is broken off. The top portion has a row of five glyphs, plus an attached stick figure. Subash Bose has interpreted these glyphs as the Tamil phrase *Pasu itta pathiyogan*.

"(Pa + Su+ it +ta + Pa + thi + Yo (ga) + an)

**Pasu itta pathi Yogan**
**Pasu**–means 'Soul or life' of all living beings,
**Itta**–means giving birth,
**Pathi**–means 'Father/Lord',
**Yogan**–the letter 'Yo' and the suffixed symbol 'an',
reads as Yogan–means Yogi/saint.

[quote continued on next page]

"Meaning: The five-faced human with crown seated on a throne in yogic posture called *Moola Pandha Aasanam*. The Yogi is the Father/Lord who gave birth to all living beings, so he is called '*Pasu itta pathi*', and he is a Yogi/Yogan."[23]

*Proto-Shiva, Mohenjo Daro seal*

**Indus River Script, from top of seal above.**

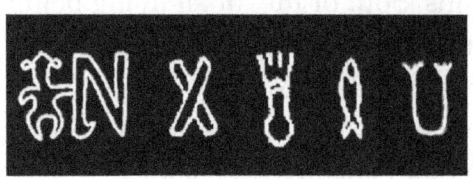

**Random *rongorongo* glyphs, undeciphered, Rapa Nui.**[24]

If, as the Vedic text says, the "three lights" in Prajapati represent Orion's belt, then he is the ever-turning Axis, the axle of the cosmic mill (i.e., "Hamlet's Mill"), around which the firmament revolves. His head—the small pyramid of stars made of Meissa (a.k.a. Heka)[25] and Phi1 and Phi2— points toward the North Star, which in 2830 BC, around the time of the inception of Mohenjo Daro, was not Polaris but instead Thuban.[26]

The glyphs on the seal (preceding page) correspond to various major constellations.[27] However, they are configured not in the way these constellations appear as we gaze up from the earth (in the Northern Hemisphere, of course). The actual positions of the stars depicted on this artifact are instead seen from an opposite vantage—namely, that of the gods. Imagine a deific viewpoint from beyond the stars focused upon the Earth. It is as if we are looking through a translucent, two-dimensional plane of the constellations where the star patterns are horizontally flipped from their terrestrial orientation. (See Hevelius' drawng on p. 300.)

In the row of glyphs on the seal the water symbol is followed by a fish symbol, which also appears frequently in the *rongorongo* script. (The Indus Script is generally read from right to left.) The contemporary Finnish Sindhologist Asko Parpola explains the significance of the latter glyph: "In most Dravidian languages the usual word for 'fish' is *meen*. This phonetic shape can also be reconstructed for the mother language, Proto-Dravidian. A homonym *meen* denoting 'star' has also existed in Proto-Dravidian. Both words refer to a glittering object, and appear to be derivatives from the Proto-Dravidian root *meen*, 'to glitter, to sparkle'. The 'fish' pictograms of the Indus script, then, can be interpreted as denoting gods, if stars were used as symbols of deities."[28]

**The three stars on the fish's side may represent Orion's belt. Drawing of a Pre-Harappan potsherd from Amri, south of Mohenjo Daro, circa 3600 – 3300 BC.**[29]

Revelant to this discussion are German researcher Michael H. Dietrich's observations on *rongorongo*. "The big shark is one of the signs of the Milky Way in Rongorongo. The fish sign is another one for our galaxy. But in the sky over the Pacific in the night, there were a lot of different fish as single stars or constellations..." (via Google Translator)[30]

So, how can we explain the spatial and temporal disparity between these two similar scripts? (Is it actually Mehenjo Rongo and Rongo Daro?) Are both parallel pictographic or ideogrammic systems our inheritance from a long-lost super-civilization? My friend and traveling companion, British author Graham Hancock has suggested this scenario throughout the quarter century arc of his research and writing. Witness this from his most recent book, *America Before*:

> "What's tantalizing, however, is that the influence of the lost civilization declares itself repeatedly in the commonalities shared by

supposedly unconnected cultures all around the ancient world. The deeper you dig, the more obvious it becomes that they did not get these shared features from one another but from a remote common ancestor of them all. We see only the effects and modes of expression of that inheritiance, not its source, and all searches for the key to the mystery have thus far been in vain."[31]

Graham writes that the earnest search for Earth's lost civilization has been something like tracking the Invisible Man. Traces of his prior presence are found all over the planet—in our mythology, beliefs, customs, languages, texts, arts, mathematics, architectures, etc. He has left us a legacy of indelible clues for his erstwhile existence, yet he remains elusive.

Passage *from* India to Rapa Nui? Just ask the Axis. He knows everything.

**Graham Hancock and Gary, Chevelon Canyon, Arizona, 2017. Photo by Santha Faiia (taken on my iPhone).**

*Part II*
The Semiotics[1] of Synchronicity

# Chapter 11
## *The ABCs of Orion—Ants, Bulls, and Copper*

### Orion and the Ant People

One of the oldest, and at one time the largest, Hopi villages was named Oraibi, which shares the *Or-* prefix with the constellation Orion. *Orai* means "Place of the Rock," "Round Rock," or "Rock on High."[1] This village is located atop one of the three primary Mesas where the Hopi had finally settled circa 1100 AD after centuries of migration. My series of nonfiction books, beginning with *The Orion Zone*, have put forth the theory of an Arizona Star Correlation, in which these three Mesas correspond to the belt stars of Orion, similar to the three major pyramids on the Giza plateau.[2]

Orion's actual Indo-European linguistic root is frankly astonishing. The name Orion is formed by dropping the initial 'm' in the stem *morui*, which supposedly means "ant."[3] The constellation's narrow waist perhaps suggests this insect. Hopi legends from the American Southwest describe "Ant People" and how they provided refuge in subterranean caverns ("ant *kivas*") for the Hopi during the destruction of the first two Worlds (Ages). A *kiva* is "an underground or partially underground ceremonial chamber."[4] Morphologically round in prehistoric times, the Hopi *kiva* for almost a millennium has been constructed in a rectangular shape as the quintessential Ancestral Puebloan communal structure. The Hopi prefix *ki-* means "house, home"[5] and *-va* means "at, on."[6] Incidentally, the Sanskrit word *ki* means "ant hill," and *va* means "dwelling."[7] In

Sumerian mythology the goddess Ki was the "Earth-mother of the land."[8] In the Zoroastrian tradition a *var* was defined as "a subterranean fortress or city"—*ergo*, a chthonic stronghold.[9] The Iranian term *var* might be a cognate of the Hopi word *warànta*, which means "save, reserve for future use"[10]—something which ants do extraordinarily well. In Sanskrit, *var* or *vara* means "protector, defender, encirclement, cover, or fortune," all of which could refer to an underground fastness and storage facility. The Sanskrit *var* can also mean "ocean" or a "receptacle of water,"[11] which is confusing until we recall that the underworld as well as the sky were frequently conceptualized as a vast ocean.

**Petroglyphs at Cottonwood Creek Ruin, northern Arizona. Note central figure's antennae and insect-like eyes. The large figure in the inset also has an insectoid head. "Crows-feet" at the right symbolize warfare.**

Referring to Hopi lore, we see that only the virtuous members of the tribe following a certain cloud by day and a certain star by night were able to find the sky god Sótuknang, who elected to save these "chosen people" by leading them to the Ant People for protection. In these legends the ants are portrayed as generous and industrious, teaching the Hopi the merits of food storage and giving them aliment when supplies ran short. In fact, the reason why the ants have such thin waists today is because they once deprived themselves of provisions.[12] Another account of the earliest times describes the Hopi themselves as actually being ants. "When they were way underneath, they were ants."[13] The word "underneath" refers alternately to the Ant Kiva and the First and Second Worlds, the latter of which are conceptualized as being subterranean, i.e., beneath both the previous Third World and the current Fourth World. According to another rather brutal myth entitled "Why the Ants Are So Thin," a great number of Ants were living east of Toko'navi, or Navajo Mountain near the Arizona-Utah border, the prehistoric home of the Hopi Snake Clan and Sand Clan. During an initiation into the Katsina Society two of these Ants dressed up as fierce, giant-like Hu *katsinam* (kachinas) and flogged the Ant children so hard that they were almost cut through in the middle of their bodies, hence their slenderness.[14] In this case the insects are described not in the allegorical manner of an Aesop fable but in an almost anthropomorphic way.

Each February the Hopi perform the *Powamu*, or Bean Sprouting Ceremony, inside the *kivas*. "The central part of the Powamu is the germination of beans. To keep the symbolism straight some corn is planted, but beans have two advantages: they grow faster at this time of year and the results are edible. The *kivas* make excellent hot houses in which all sorts of containers full of dirt and bean seeds are placed, while the fires are kept up day and night."[15] This ritual may commemorate a time when the Hopi sprouted beans inside caverns in order to survive. It is significant that the Hu *katsinam* in the myth mentioned above are an integral part of *Powamu* ceremony that initiates children into the Katsina Society.[16]

It is suffice to say that the Hopi word *anu* means "ant," and the Hopi word *naki* or *nakwats-* means "friend."[17] The Anu-naki = "ant friend"—the Sumerian Annunaki. It comes as no surprise to find that the Sumerian god of the sky is named Anu. According to the late University of London history and philosophy of religion professor E. O. James,

> "In Mesopotamia the assembly of gods in the sky constituted the highest authority in the universe, determining the course of events on earth. Under the leadership of Anu, the god of heaven, whose name means 'sky', 'shining', 'bright', the cosmic order was established out of primeval chaos as an organized whole. He was, in fact, the personification of the sky and the most potent force in the cosmos, older than all the other gods, and the ultimate source of all existence... In his celestial abode he kept the bread and water of immortal life, and it was he who gave the divine authority exercised by kings on earth."[18]

## Ant Antecedents

- In the Bible the Nephilim are the "giants in the earth."
- Ancient Hebrews, Arabians, and Syrians
  all referred to Orion as "the Giant."
- The Sumerian term NFL (not football but Nefilim, Nephilim)
  means "those who came from Heaven to Earth."
- But... the Aramaic word *nephîliâ* is the name for Orion.
- And... the Hebrew word *nemalim* means "ants."
- The name Orion originally comes from the Indo-European
  word *morui*, which means "ant."
- The Hopi word *anu* means "ant."
- The Hopi word *naki* means "friend."
- On Sumerian seals the Anunnaki are seen as wingéd sky gods.
- Mature ant colonies produce winged ants.

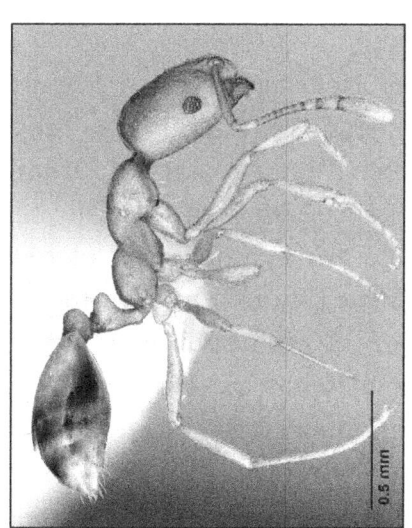

Left: Pharaoh Ant (*Momomorium pharaonis*), West Africa. Elongated head, reddish body, dark abdomen with stinger. Right: Akhenaten, 18th Dynasty, 1351–1334 BC, with his child, shown with elongated skull. Cobra on uraeus resembles the ant's mandibles. Spindly neck, arms, and legs. His body resembles the ant's thorax and abdomen.

Anu was also the appellation of the Celtic mother goddess, who influenced human fertility, the Earth's fecundity, bountiful harvests, and cattle. She was also the wife of the sun god Belenos.[19] In addition, Anu was another name for the Egyptian ceremonial and religious site of Heliopolis (City of the Sun, the biblical On) since early Dynastic times or even before. It was here in the Temple of the Phoenix that the *Benben* stone of meteoric iron was kept—an *omphalos* whereon the Bennu, or mythical firebird of temporal cycles, perched. During the Middle Kingdom the Bennu bird was equated with the "soul" of Osiris, i.e., Orion.[20] Furthermore, the Egyptian word *anu* meant "gift, tribute, offerings, products, revenues, income, increase, wages, something brought in."[21] These denotations refer to both the ants' ability to store provisions and the reverence given to the Ant People.

The Hopi term for Orion is *Hotòmqam*, which literally means either "to string up" (as beads on a string) or "trey" (three).[22] This could refer to either the three stars of Orion's belt or perhaps the stars Betelgeuse, Alnilam (middle belt star), and Rigel. However, it could also symbolically relate to the tripartite form of the ant: head, thorax, and abdomen. These shiny, bead-like sections of the ant's body may indeed have their celestial counterpart in what the Hopi consider the most important constellation in the heavens. The appearance of Orion through the overhead hatchways of Hopi *kivas* still synchronizes many annual sacred rituals, especially the *Soyal*, the paramount winter solstice ceremony.[23]

The above-mentioned *morui* is the root-word of Orion associated with ants, which in southern Africa also happens to mean "one who is rich in cattle."

"In the Sesotho language of Lesotho, a person who is wealthy is called a 'morui.' However, not all forms of wealth are equally respected. One who is rich in cattle is more highly respected than one who keeps his wealth in a bank account or household property. The reason for this is that cattle can benefit not only the owner but the whole community. The true morui will place some of his cattle in the care of others in the village so they, too, can benefit from them, loan them to others for use during the plowing season and sell them to those in need, with the price depending on the circumstances of the one in need. Money in the bank or household property is considered a selfish form of wealth, whereas cattle can help transform the whole community. A man with money 'only helps himself'; a true morui 'knows the poor.' A morui is a vital part of village life and productivity, not someone detached and separated from it."[24]

This spirit of generosity is in keeping with the aforementioned Ant People.

## Orion and the Bull

In the 1960s a bronze statue of a bull dedicated to Orion was found on Younan Mountain (elevation 7,500 feet) located 20 miles north of Damascus, Syria. It bore Greek inscriptions describing an offering made by a warrior named Tamanaius to the legendary celestial giant.

In 2009 archaeologists excavated the ruins of a Roman temple on the northwest slopes of the peak. They uncovered a pedestal thought to be either a sacrificial altar or a beacon guarding the site, which consisted of three structures. The easternmost one was a Byzantine monastery constructed from stones of the other two (perhaps mirroring Orion's belt). In this later structure they found 4th and 5th century AD coins as well as bronze or iron spearheads and arrowheads, along with nails and other metal artifacts. Local lore indicates that this was in fact Orion's birthplace. "Archaeological finds in a Roman temple found in 2009 suggest that the legend may have originated somewhere around the mountains of Bloudan, particularly Younan Mountain, and later the myth reached Greece and was incorporated into the Greek myth cycle."[25]

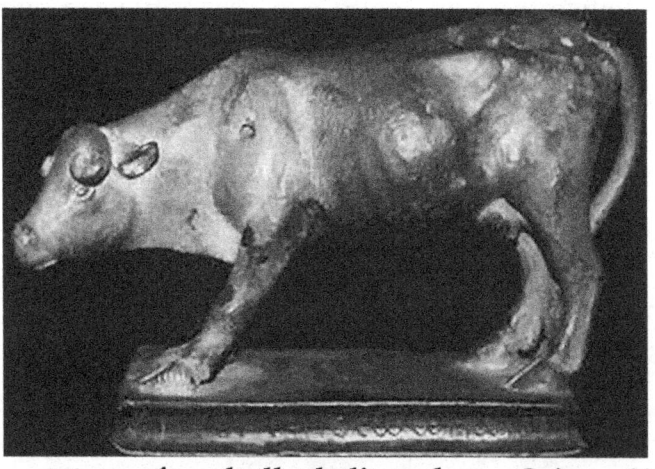

**Bronze statue of a bull dedicated to Orion, Younan Mountain, southern Syria. On its base are the words of a Roman soldier: "Thamanios the veteran piously set (me) up to the god Orion."**

In this context we may recall the Greek myth of Orion's birth. Zeus, Hermes, and Poseidon were traveling on Earth, when they encountered Hyrieus, King of Boeotia, which was the oldest city in Greece. This childless widower desired to have a son. The gods then urinated on the hide of a bull and buried it in the ground. Nine months later Orion emerged. The hide possibly represents the adjacent constellation Taurus. In this case Orion's name alternately derives from *urina*, or "urine."[26]

Picking up the theme of ants again, we note one particular type. "The name *pissant* arises from the urine-like odor produced by their nesting material—needles and straw from pine trees—and the formic acid that constitutes their venom. *Formica rufa* is one such ant, but there are others with similar characteristics. It may be derived from the term pismire."[27] The Hopi name for this small, black "piss ant" is *sisiw'anu*.[28]

**Orion's birth from a bull-hide, assisted by Jupiter, Neptune, and Mercury (Zeus, Poseidon, and Hermes), Michael Maier, *Atlanta fugiens*. At the far left the alchemical artist looks on; at the far right is Mars (Aries).**

One version of the Greek myth says that an ox-hide rather than a bull-hide was used, so this might be related to the hide-shaped copper ingots that were smelted during the Bronze Age. A Cypriot incense burner from circa 1200 BC shows a member of the so-called Sea People carrying a large copper ingot ox-hide across his shoulders. Some scholars claim that this group, which ruled the Mediterranean and perhaps the world during this time, was actually comprised of the mariner-invader Anatolians in alliance with the mariner-trader Phoenicians.[29] Author Frank Joseph, however, believes that the Sea People were from Atlantis, though his interpretation of the myth uses a much later timeframe than do most. "According to Plato, the Atlanteans were the foremost copper barons of the Bronze Age."[30]

More importantly, the six-sided ingots resemble the morphology of the Orion constellation, with their narrower portion in the middle. Copper ingots formed like an hourglass have been found in as diverse regions as Zimbabwe and Crete. I personally have found ancient oxhide-shaped petroglyphs in the Northern Cape province of South Africa.[31] (See photo on p. 177.)

Considering the connotations of gold and wealth, one is not surprised at the origin of the term "bullion." It derives from the Latin *bullio*, which means "boiling," referring to the melted mass of ore—but also, boiling mad, as a bull. Or in the immortal words of Mick Jagger: "Ooh, see the fire is sweepin'/ Our very street today / Burns like a red coal carpet / Mad bull lost its way." Is all of this just BS, or does it in fact carry the weight of a papal bull? Probably somewhere in between.

## Orion and the Copper Trade

In addition to the "urine" etymology, the name Orion might possibly derive from the Greek word *oros*, or "mountain." The English word "ore" comes from a conflation of number of older words meaning brass, copper, bronze, or brazen. Orichalcum (Greek *Orei-chalkos*, or "mountain copper) was a copper-gold alloy that Plato said covered the walls of Atlantis. In *Critias* he remarks on King Poseidon's opulent temple: "In the interior of the temple the roof was of ivory, curiously wrought everywhere with gold and silver and orichalcum; and all the other parts, the walls and pillars and floor, they coated with orichalcum."[32]

Orion was also known as a skilled smith, or worker in metals. "It is said that Orion was an excellent workman in iron; and that he fabricated a subterranean palace for Vulcan."[33] During the Bronze Age, Orion may have excelled as well in the forging of copper and tin. This world-era corresponds in Hopi legends to Kuskurza, the Third World, which, like Atlantis, was destroyed by a deluge. This age was symbolized by the color red and the metal copper—in Hopi called *sivapala*.[34] (Many Hopi elders now say we are at the end of the Fourth World.)

In southern Arizona the Akimel O'odham (Pima) and the Tohono O'odham (Papago) refer to the ancestral Hohokam as *Sivanyi*, literally "Metal Ones."[35] This name comes from the fact that they had forged a great quantity of tinklers and small bells from copper mined locally. The Hokokam had inhabited the Phoenix Basin (i.e., "Valley of the Sun") for about a thousand years beginning in 300 BC and had built the major villages of Casa Grande, Pueblo Grande, and Snaketown—all near the modern metropolis of Phoenix. (Recall the ancient Egyptian Temple of the Phoenix at

Heliopolis.) Inhabitants of this city, by the way, are called Phoenicians. Incidentally, the root *zona* in Ari-zona literally means "The girdle [belt] of Orion."[36]

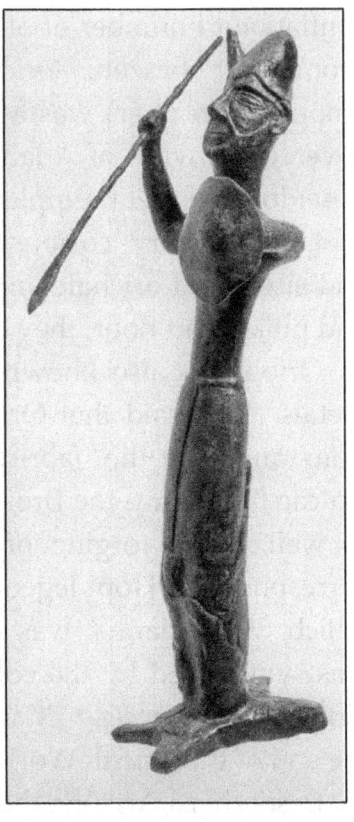

Left: ox-hide-shaped copper ingots from Crete and Mycenae, Numismatic Museum, Athens.
Right: Bovine-horned warrior demigod standing on ingot, bronze statuette with conical hat, javelin and shield, 30 cm., 1150 BC, Cyprus.

The Hindu god Siva (or Shiva) once assumed the form of a hunter and shot one of Brahman's heads with an arrow—thus creating Orion.[37] Siva was a less violent aspect of the ruddy Rudra, lord of storms and cattle. Siva's Third Eye *chakra*, or pineal gland, is reputedly made of copper, and is represented on his phallic-stone shrine called a *lingam*.³⁸

**Left: copper ingot, Crete. Right: Cognates in ancient Egypt and Hopi Arizona. The morphology of the ingot and constellation are the same.**

S. Kalyanaraman of the Sarasvati Research Center claims that copper ingots originated in the Indus River Valley.

> "Who invented the oxhide ingot shape? I suggest Meluhhan artisans did in Mohenjo-daro/Harappa/Chanhudaro/Dholavira, ca. 3rd millennium BCE, using the tin ore brought in as cargo, by seafaring merchants from Ancient Far East, from the largest Tin Belt of the globe in Irrawaddy-Salween-Mekong Himalayan

river basins—along the Ancient Maritime Tin Route which linked Hanoi (Vietnam) and Haifa (Israel), predating the Silk Road, by about two millennia. Evidence is provided by a deciphered prism tablet showing a boat carrying oxhide ingots and with Indus Script inscription which is dateable to ca. 2500 BCE (Mature Harappan phase). This could be the earliest recorded evidence for an oxhide ingot."[39]

Tablet from Mohenjo Daro of a boat with two ox-hide ingots as cargo, flanked by two palm trees. The boat contains two water fowl; on the left is possibly another, and on the right the rudders. (See previous chapter.)

Following up on metallurgic aspects of the *ur-* prefix, we find that *urruru* is the Sumerian word for "to smelt," and Oruru was an ancient mining center in Bolivia near Tiawanaku.[40] In addition, *uradu* is the Sumerian word for "copper," and Eridu was the oldest and most sacred city in Sumer.[41] In turn, Eri was the name of the Igbo (Nigerian) equivalent of the Egyptian Thoth, who taught the science and art of metallurgy, but he is sometimes conflated with Osiris (i.e., Orion), god of the underworld and resurrection.[42]

Again, the *eri-* prefix reminds us of the river at the foot of Orion: Eridanus. The major star Epsilon Eridanus may be what the ancients called the *zalos*—i.e., some sort of celestial portal or stargate to the underworld.

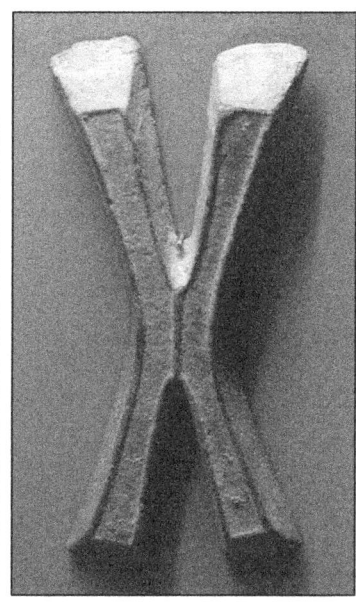

Left: Petroglyph of ox-hide ingot engraved into horizontal "pavement" of glaciated andesite, 150 yards by 75 yards, containing over 3,500 petroglyphs. Driekops Eiland ("three hills island"), San culture, 8000 – 1200 BC (?), near Kimberley, Northern Cape, South Africa. Right: Orion-shaped copper ingot from Zimbabwe, National Museum, Bloemfontein, South Africa. Photos by the author.

According to the eminent scholars Giorgio Santillana and Hertha Von Dechend:

> "That there is a whirlpool in the sky is well known; it is most probably the essential one, and it is precisely placed. It is a group of stars so named (**zalos**) at the foot of Orion, close to

Rigel (beta Orionis, Rigel being the Arabic word for 'foot'), the degree of which was called 'death,' according to Hermes Trismegistos, whereas the Maori claim outright that Rigel marked the way to Hades (Castor indicating the primordial homeland). Antiochus the astrologer enumerates the whirl among the stars as Taurus. Franz Boll takes sharp exception to the adequacy of his description, but he concludes that the **zalos** must, indeed, be **Eridanus** 'which flows from the foot of Orion.'"[43]

Now we know our ABCs: They are more than mere letters used as colorful building blocks for concepts. Instead they function as disparate yet essential elements of the Orion Zone. And we discover that XYZ is not a termination but the ineffable and ineluctable Matrix of the *Mysterium tremendum et fascinans* ("fearful and fascinating mystery").

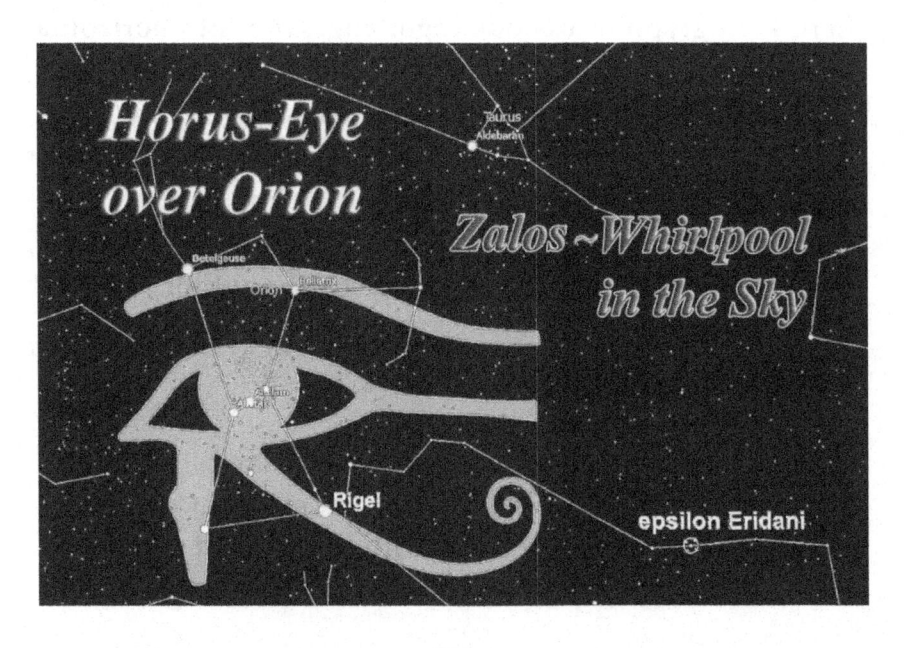

# Chapter 12
## *Orion's Hourglass Archetype*

**When Worlds Collide**

Microsoft's Windows used to pass the download time by showing us a flipping hourglass icon. (Now it uses a clockwise-pulsing circle.) We often think of the clichéd "sands of time" slipping from the upper glass chamber to the lower one. Ephemerality. Temporality. Causality. Mortality. Chronos, bringer of old age. Father Time wielding a scythe. Or even gloomier, the Grim Reaper. J. E. Cirlot defines the hourglass as: "A symbol denoting the inversion of the relations between the Upper and Lower Worlds—an inversion encompassed periodically by Shiva (or Siva), the lord of creation and destruction. Connected with it are the drum—similar in shape—and the cross of St. Andrew; the symbolic significance of all three is identical."[1] If we take a down-turned equilateral triangle and a similar up-turned triangle with two of their apexes nearly touching, by interpenetrating them we produce the Star of David (Solomon's Seal). Thus, we have the world of Above colliding with the world of Below.

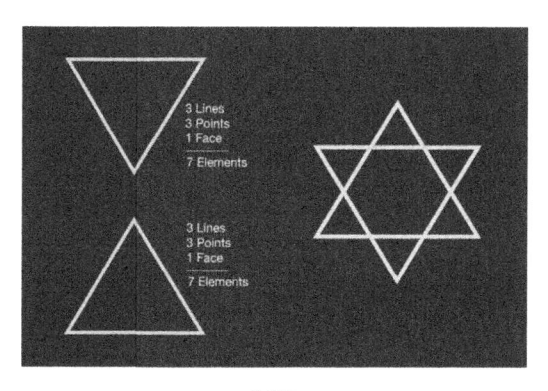

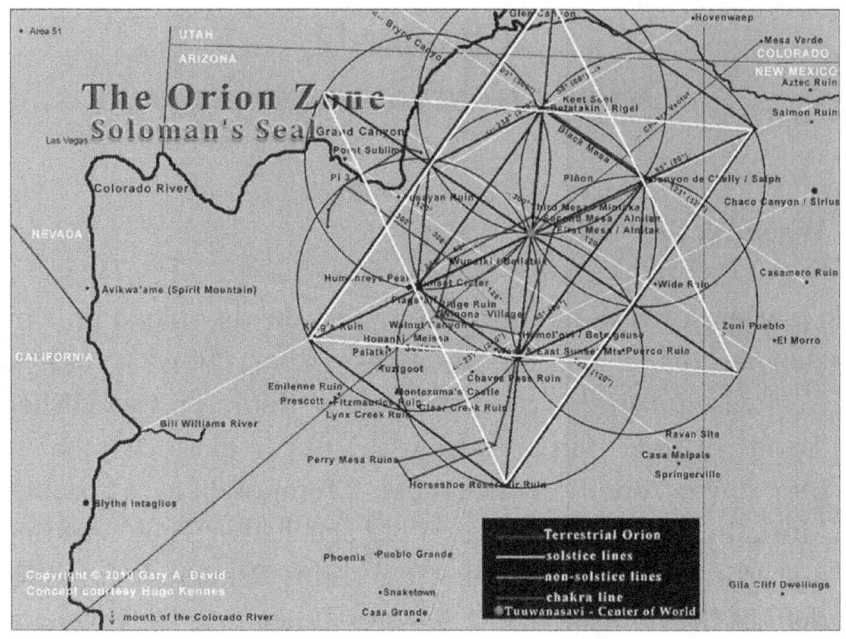

Overlaid on the hexagon/cube and the "Flower of Life" is Star of David, composed of two interlocking equilateral triangles. Orion is projected upon the Arizona high desert. The dot is the Hopi *Tuuwanasavi*, "center of the world."

The Greek god Cronus, or *Kronos*, was the titan who devoured his own children. The term *chronos*, or "time," literally means "to grind," "to erode," or "to wear down" — as the process of material existence entropically grinds everything to dust. A crony (literally, "long-lasting") is a contemporary, a fast friend, a word that sometimes implies ill-gotten political or social favors, or cronyism. The adjective "chronic" refers to a disease of lengthy duration.

The Roman equivalent of Cronus was Saturnus, or Saturn. As Lord of the World and temporal cycles, Saturn rules the domain of sensory perception and physical manifestation. As Lord of Time, Saturn controls spiritual causation; as a planet, Saturn astrologically controls karmic dispensation. Both the Roman god Saturnus and the planet Saturn historically corresponded to Orion. Anthropologist Francis Huxley explains the direct correlation.

> "He [Saturn] is also to be found in the constellation Orion, who wields that sickle-shaped sword called a falchion and which farmers call a billhook.... For the Egyptians Orion was associated with Horus and the soul of Osiris; in the Hindu Brahmanas he is seen as Prajapati in the form of a stag; several nations in the Middle East refer to him as the Giant, or the hunter Nimrod mighty before the Lord; and he was Saturnus to the Romans."[2]

Among the Hindu legends compiled in the *Rigveda*, Prajapati (Praja-pa-ti) is associated with Orion. According to the Indian Nationalist Bal Gangadhar Tilak (1856 – 1920), "Prajapati, as represented by Orion, may also be naturally supposed to commence the year when the vernal equinox was in Orion [4000 – 2500 BC]."[3] In addition to the Hindu term *Prajapati* denoting Orion, this constellation is also known as *Kal-Purush*, or the "Time-Man."[4]

Astronomer, mathematician, and mystic Johannes Kepler (1571-1630) claimed that each of the Platonic solids corresponds to one of the classical elements as well as to one of then-known planets. To the six-faced cube, which is a three-dimensional hexagon, he assigned the element earth and the planet Saturn, located farthest from the Sun of the originally known planets. Orion can be conceptualized as a variation of the hexagon with two opposite angles collapsed inward. In other words, the constellation is conceptualized as a six-sided figure shaped like an hourglass.

## Our Hourglass and *Cuprum*

This geometric shape is found in the rock art and ceramics of many cultures around the globe. As an anthropomorph, the torso consists of two opposing triangles with their apexes touching. Native American rock art expert LaVan Martineau suggests that the universal symbol of conflict or war is "two arrowheads meeting head on."[5] The same hourglass symbolism is associated with the younger Navajo War Twin named "Born-for-Water."[6]

**Hourglass torsos of ceremonial dancers, looking backward and holding hands, circling clockwise. Energy lines on faces of alternating figures. Sacaton red-on-buff ceramic cauldron, Snaketown, 950 – 1150 AD. Photo by the author.**

In the previous chapter I discussed hourglass iconography in terms of six-sided copper ingots shaped like bovine hides, which in turn reflect the morphology of Orion. I also suggested that the constellation's name may derive from either *urina* ("urine"[7]) or from the Greek word *oros*, ("mountain"), from which the English word "ore" derives.

We also saw that the oldest continuously inhabited village on the North American continent was constructed on Third Mesa in Arizona about 1120 AD by the Hopi and is named Oraibi (OR-RYE-BEE), also spelled Orayvi). The term *orai*—like the first two syllables in the name Orion—means "Rock on High" or "Round Rock." "[Oraibi] is named after a prominent point at the drop on the southwest side of the village."[8] The Tamil word *Orai* is an ancient unit of time measurement equivalent to one hour, which is significant when we recall the Tamil name of Orion is *Kalapurusha*, or "Time-man."[9] However, Orion's actual Indo-European root is, in a word, astounding. To repeat, the name "Orion" is formed by dropping the initial 'm' in the stem *morui*, which supposedly means "ant."[10] These hourglass anthropomorphs could be seen as ant-like.

On a macro-level Orion was known by the Arabians as *Al Jabbar* and by the Syrians as *Gabārrā*, or the Giant. In a similar vein, this stellar configuration was recognized by the Hebrews as *cesil*, which means "a fool" or "an impious, godless man." His terrestrial counterpart was Nimrod, the giant Hunter who ruled the Mesopotamian city of Babel.[11]

> "Some suppose that the fable respecting Orion was a copy of the story of Abraham entertaining the three angels, who came and foretold to him the birth of a son, though his wife was superannuated. Others assert that it

has a great resemblance to the story of Jacob, especially as the name of Jacob's staff is given to the three brightest stars in the constellation of Orion, and the name of Jacob, which signifies *strong against the Lord*, (upon account of the mysterious combat he had with an angel), may have given rise to it."[12]

Now the associated *oros* (ore): The word "copper" is derived from the Latin *cuprum*. In Hopi, "copper" is *palasiva* (*pala-siva*), literally "red metal."[13] The Hindu god Siva (Shiva) once assumed the form of a hunter and shot one of Brahman's heads with an arrow, thus creating Orion. The Sanskrit word for "copper" is *ambaka*, which was also called Siva's Eye—corresponding to his Third Eye, or pineal gland.[14] In temples dedicated to Siva, a copper or bronze pot hangs over a *lingam* (phallus), upon which water constantly pours—stressing the metal's procreative aspect.

As previously noted, the hourglass figure in North America signifies warfare between Native American tribes. For the Igbo tribe of Nigeria, however, it signifies the Great Mother Goddess called Mbari.[15] In India this double-triangle may represent the female-male complex (Siva-Sakti). It may also symbolize the hourglass drum, or *damaru*, the two-headed sacred drum of Lord Siva.

*Damaru* attached to a *trisula* (trident). Lord Siva carries both, who incarnates as Prajapati (Orion). (See pp. 143-148.) Note similarity of the trident to the hieroglyphic for copper, p. 180.

Lower-left: face-centered cube, the crystal structure of copper. Right: Platonic solids model of the solar system, from Kepler's *Mysterium Cosmographicum*.

Astrological symbol for Saturn combines cross and scythe.

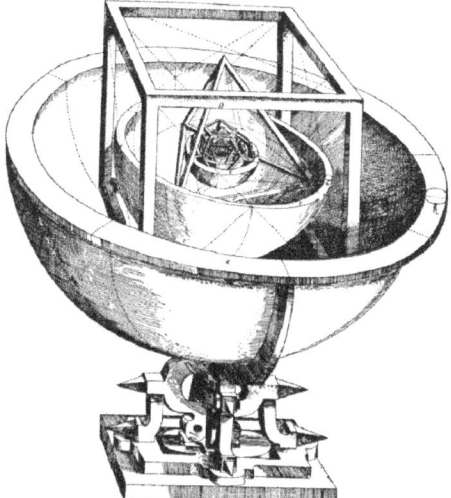

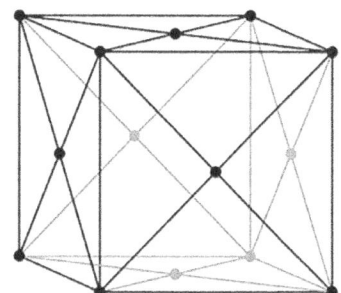

Mural of Siva *lingam* with suspended copper pot holding water, Fort Meherangarh, Jodhpur, India.

We have solid evidence of an "Orion archetype" as seen by the pictographs (rock paintings) at Narthamalai, Tamil Nadu in India dated to 1500 BC or earlier. Painted in white (kaolin), a human figure is seen with the typical upraised right arm, as well as the left arm holding a shield or club or spear. Associated with this figure is a representation of two triangles with their apexes touching.

My friend and colleague, Shree T. L. Subash Chandira Bose, describes the pertinent rock art of his native Tamil Nadu. "The human form with his raised right hand and stretched left hand holds something like a club and a shield respectively. The shape of his head looks like bird's head. This rock art may be denoting the Orion or Hunter constellation. The ancient name of the Orion or Hunter is Kalapurusha, or Mariman and Ekadasa Rudra." The Tamil word *mariman* means "death, dying,"[16] whereas Mr. Bose explains that "Ekadasa Rudra" refers to the divine form of Lord Siva in his 11 manifestations.[17]

Partially due to his Tamil heritage, Shree Subash stresses the metaphysical aspects of Indian rock art.

> "The ancient people living in the soil of Satyaputra—son of truth—were masters of coding sacred information secretly in the form of Rock Arts. One such secret script is 'Om'. Om is truth (satyam), truth of universal nature. Om is also known in various languages and cultures as 'Aum, Hum, Aman, and Ameen'. The minor variations in its forms may be due to the pronunciation of the alphabets (phonetics) in different languages. Truth (Satyam) is the seed of the universal tree."[18]

Rock painting at Onake Hills, Rampur, Raichur Dt., Karnataka State, India, courtesy of Shree. Subash Chandira Bose.

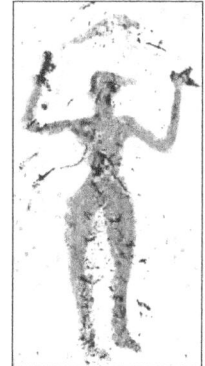

Upper-right: T. L. Subash Chandira Bose, Tuzigoot Ruin, Arizona, 2007. Middle: bird-headed Orion, Tamil Nadu.

Upper: Orion pictograph, Tamil Nadu. Right: Bird-heads with hourglass torsos, rock art, Tamil Nadu.

One example of the globally sown seed-syllable of *Om* is the Hopi word for cloud: *Omau*. Clouds not only bring life-giving moisture to the desert but also are conceptualized in Hopi cosmology as the spirits of deceased ancestors.[19] In addition, we can assume that the Hindu *Om* served as the ur-syllable for the Dogon Amma (see pp. 310-312), the Libyan Ammon, and the Egyptian Amun. Thus, English speakers also conclude prayers with "Amen."

Some Vedic scholars claim that Betelgeuse (a "red giant," the right shoulder of Orion) is the abode of the third deity of the Hindu Trinity: Brahma, Vishnu, and Siva—the latter a later and less violent form of Rudra, referred to above. One of the many aspects of Rudra is "Lord of Cattle." It is curious to note that in a blood-sacrifice of cattle to this storm god, the "armies of Rudra," i.e., serpents, are invoked.[20]

Egyptologist Robert Bauval opines that the astro-theological cow and bull symbolism of the Pre-Dynastic Cattle Herders of North Africa was focused upon the Big Dipper, Sirius, and Orion.

> "Indeed, according to most Egyptologists and archaeoastronomers, it is only these three stellar asterisms that can be identified with any certainty from ancient Egyptian texts and drawings. The pharaohs knew the Big Dipper as Mesekhtyw, the thigh (of a bull or cow), and Sirius as Spdt, which was linked to the well-known goddesses Hathor and Isis. Orion was known as Sah, and this constellation was associated with Osiris and the pharaoh who, in turn, was also symbolized as a celestial bull and the celebrated Apis Bull of Memphis. Further, all of these clues involving cattle and

megalithic astronomy specifically involving Sirius, Orion, and the Big Dipper strongly suggest a link across the centuries of religious ideologies between the prehistoric society of the Sahara and that of pharaonic Egypt."[21]

According to Masonic scholar Robert Hewitt Brown, the hourglass was a preeminent Egyptian symbol.

> "The hour-glass was one of the sacred astronomical emblems of the Egyptians. Clement of Alexandria, who gives a description of one of their religious processions, informs us that the *singer* went first, bearing the symbol of music, and that he was followed by the *horoscopus*, bearing in his hand an hour-glass, as the measure of time, together with a palm-branch, these being the symbols of astrology or astronomy. It was the duty of the *horoscopus* to be versed in and able to recite the four books of Hermes which treat of that science. One of these books describes the position of the fixed stars; another the conjunctions, eclipses, and illuminations of the sun and moon; and the others their risings and settings. The hour-glass is, therefore, peculiarly an astronomical emblem of great antiquity."[22]

The petroglyph figures on the following page are holding a large, leaf-shaped spear, possibly copper. To the right of the right-hand figure is a bovine, perhaps an auroch, the extinct European wild ox *Bos primigenius*—also called "urus" (Orion?)—ancestor of domestic cattle. Also shown is a smaller hourglass-shaped anthropoid with a staff in its right hand. Of course, no tulips grow naturally in that region, so the heads look more like the Egyptian hieroglyphic for "copper ingot" (*hemt*) shown here at the lower-right. Triad of circles may represent Orion's belt. They also resemble a Hopi squash bud or blossom icon, which symbolizes their germination god Alosaka.

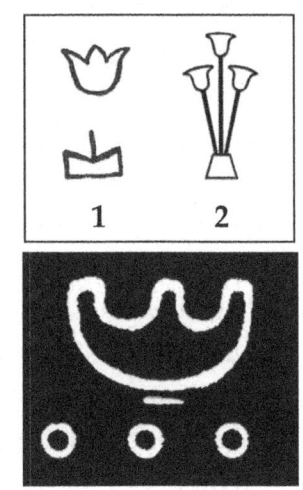

Left: Petroglyphs of two males with hourglass torsos and "tulip heads," Aïr Mountains, northern Niger, circa 500 BC. Upper-right: 1. Two Hopi iconographic forms of the squash bud or blossom (*patangsi*), which symbolizes rain. 2. Hieroglyph *mhw*, "papyrus." Egyptian *Mehuiu* = "the Great Flood," *mehu* means "drowned man," and *Mehi* is a "serpent-deity." Lower-right: hieroglyph, "copper ingot."[23]

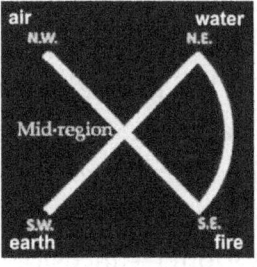

Preceding page: Left: Pictographs, red ocher, Kishvalai rock art site, Tamil Nadu, India. Local residents identify the rock shelter, which is shaped like a bird's head, as "Blood Rocks." We see a double ax, an hourglass, two so-called Celtic crosses, and a few other symbols, including an open-ended hourglass (*Niradharayogam*), which refers to the five elements: sky, air, earth, fire, and water. Right: Symbol represents the zenith (mid-region) plus the four intercardinal directions (or four solstice sunrise/sunset points: northwest = air; southwest = earth; southeast = fire; northeast = water. The arc between northeast and southeast indicates that water extinguishes fire.

Bronze torus, interconnected hexagons and cubes of the Flower of Life, Igbo Ukwu, Anambra State, Nigeria.

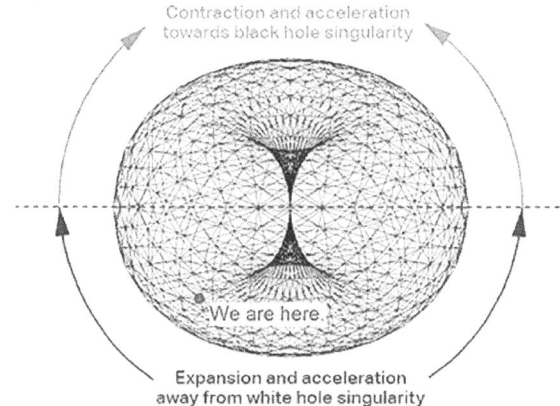

*Galaxias torus*, singularity at the center.

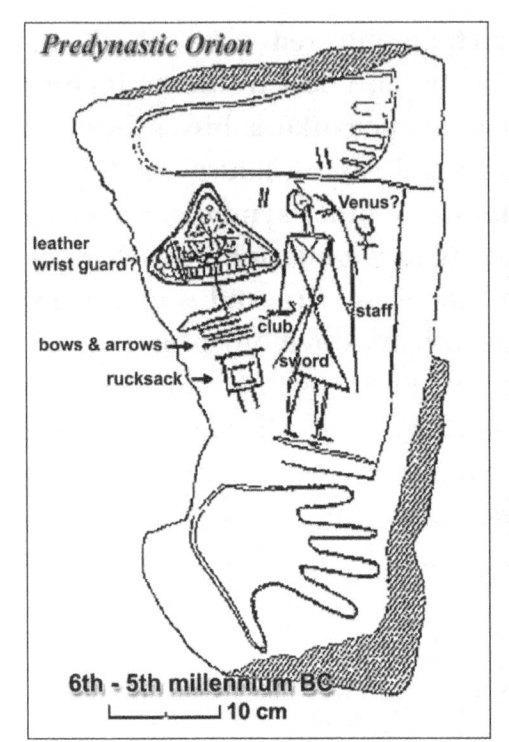

Left: petroglyph, Nephthys Hill, Dakhla Oasis, about 225 miles west of Karnak. Herodotus called it one of the "Isles of the Blessed."[24] Top and bottom show footprint and handprint, perhaps those of the slab's carver. The human's hourglass torso is possibly one of the earliest depictions of Orion. In his right hand is a club; in his left is perhaps a stalk of barley. The Egyptians knew one form of Orion as "Smati-Osiris, the Barley God."[25] On the left are a backpack and bow-and-arrows, which Orion is sometimes conceptualized as using. The triangular shape above them has been interpreted as a wristguard. However, it may instead represent either a *yardang*, which is a natural, pyramid-shaped hill, or an actual pyramid. Right: Dogon *kanaga* mask with hourglass. It symbolizes both the static nature of the creator-god Amma and his kinetic descent to Earth in order to reorganize the world's chaos.

# Chapter 13
## *Cosmic Double Take*

### Labrys' Labyrinth[1]

This chapter continues our examination of the geometric dyad. Sometimes the two opposing triangles are not part of a torso but are either merely an hourglass by itself or a double ax. Author Joscelyn Godwin describes the various cultural significances.

> "...the double-headed ax is one of the most venerable symbolic arms, found where the Aryan race has spread, from Tibet to Scandinavia. It refers to the duality of constructive and destructive forces (both of which the ax can serve) that govern the manifested world. Then it is equivalent to the thunderbolt (resembling in shape the Indian *vajra* or Tibetan *dorje*) which is peculiarly the attribute of cosmic or sky gods. Ancient people recognized the lightning-stroke as a life-bringing force, and modern scientists have expressed the same idea in their fantasies about the origins of organic compounds from the action of lightning on some primeval molecular 'broth'."[2]

Potent symbols, however, frequently span the gamut. Lithuanian-American archaeologist Marija Gimbutas has a diametrically opposed interpretation of the dual triangle motif. "The hourglass form symbolizes the subterranean or subaqueous life force of the Goddess and imminent rebirth."³ She also claims that the geometric shape is frequently associated with both vulvas/seeds and snakes.

With imagery going back to about 5000 BC, the hourglass anthropomorphs sometimes have bird wings or claws. "Bird claws identify the hourglass figures with the Vulture, Owl, and other Bird of Prey Goddesses, who, as we know, is the Goddess of Death and Rebirth. The main component of her image—the triangle (vulva)—secures regeneration. A related image is the butterfly and 'double axe' (a horizontal hourglass), also an epiphany of the same Goddess."⁴ (We recall from p. 187 the pictographs of bird-human therianthropes from Tamil Nadu, India.)

Gimbutas goes on to remark: "The double axe of the Bronze Age was originally an hourglass-shaped Goddess of Death and Regeneration. Epiphany of the Goddess in her aspect of emergent life, the butterfly rises from the body or skull of the sacrificed bull in a tableau symbolic of both seasonal fertility and fructifying waters. The butterfly is, in short, the embodiment of the principle of Transformation."⁵

Frank Waters claims that the Hopi Butterfly Clan is symbolized by a stylized double-delta.⁶ The Hopi generally associate butterflies with fecundity—rain, pollen, and the squash blossom. These insects are the "pets" of the underworld germination god Muy'ingwa, or Alosaka⁷ (discussed in my book *Journey of the Serpent People*). The supreme emblem of maidenhood is the butterfly whorl hairdo (*poli'ini*), which resembles the hourglass shape.

| Letter M for Mu,→ Mother continent, 10 tribes. | | | ←Hopi maiden, photo Edward Curtis. |
|---|---|---|---|

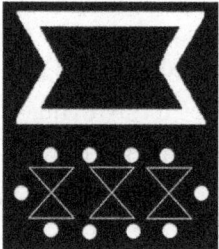

Another permutation of the hourglass figure is the Old Norse rune called *dagaz*. The key words of this rune are: transformation, breakthrough, day, God's light, prosperity, and fruitfulness.[8] "Dagaz is the rune of day, meaning the period from sunrise to sunset and sunset to sunrise. It can also represent the god Dagr, who is the embodiment of day and light. Dagaz is the cyclical process of time and life—we are born and eventually pass away into a new beginning."[9] By extension the rune is associated with the summer solstice when the sun's strength is greatest.

St. Andrew's cross is a modified hourglass with two ends open. We find this manifested in the crossed-arm pose of the pharaohs, holding a crook and a flail, symbols of dominion and power. Two crossed thighbones beneath a human skull is, of course, associated with death and piracy.

**Left: Sarcophagus of Tutankhamun (Tut-ankh-amun) with cross and flail. Right: Logo of Skull and Bones, a secret society at Yale University. The number 322 (BC) may refer to the death-date of Greek statesman Demosthenes, one year after Alexander's death.**

By visualizing an Egyptian style pyramid from a vantage directly above its apex, we find the four sloping sides of the three dimensional pyramid become an X-shaped St. Andrew's cross in two dimensions.

**Overview of the Giza Plateau, top is north. Upper-right/Khufu (Great Pyramid), middle/Khaufre, lower-left/Menkaure. Image courtesy of DigitalGlobe, satellite altitude 450 kilometers.**

This type of cross is also frequently found in the New World. Graham Hancock found the top of the Mayan "Magician's Pyramid" at Uxmal covered with them. He recalls finding them as well at the Andean site of Tiawanaku and at the Olmec center of La Venta.[10] The scholar Karl W. Luckert, who has studied in depth both the Olmecs and the Hopi, finds a similar commonality: "The so-called St. Andrew's Cross, which can be seen on numerous Olmec statues, appears again in the Hopi sand altar [in the Antelope *kiva* during the Snake Ceremony]. Apparently it has been derived from the diamond pattern on the backs of rattlesnakes."[11] Jesse Walter Fewkes also comments on the celestial significance of St. Andrew's cross:

> "These crosses, like that with four arms representing the Sky god in modern Hopi symbolism, probably represent the Heart of the Sky. A similar cross is figured on paraphernalia used in modern Hopi rites or on altar slabs; when it is represented by a wooden frame, it is called *tokpela* [literally, "sky"], and hangs before the altar. The same object is sometimes attached horizontally to the top of the helmet of the personification of the Sky god."[12]

Hence, we see that this type of cross is associated with both the serpent and the celestial ream.

Megalith and rock art investigator Julie Ryder notes that Navajo shaman Leon Sacatero has called the hourglass motif a "Changing of the World Symbol." Ryder observes:

> "Changing of the World Symbol is an hourglass type symbol that represents a wormhole/torus/tunnel between dimensions in time and space. This symbol is found throughout the ancient world and more recently discovered in crop circles and cymatic symbols. Changing of the World Symbol is a hypothetical topological feature that would fundamentally be a shortcut through

spacetime. A wormhole is much like a tunnel with two ends, each in separate points in spacetime."[13]

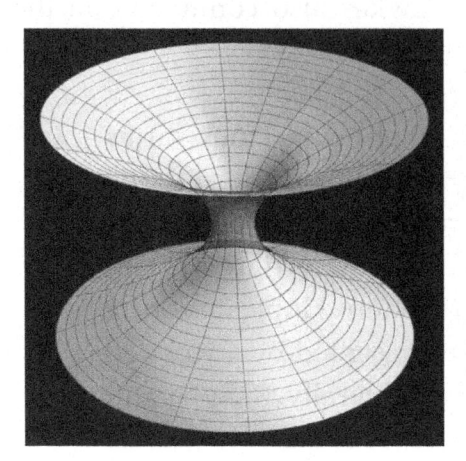

Left: Artistic conception of a Schwarzschild wormhole or Einstein-Rosen bridge. Right: Crop circle, June 25, 2013, Silbury Hill, England.

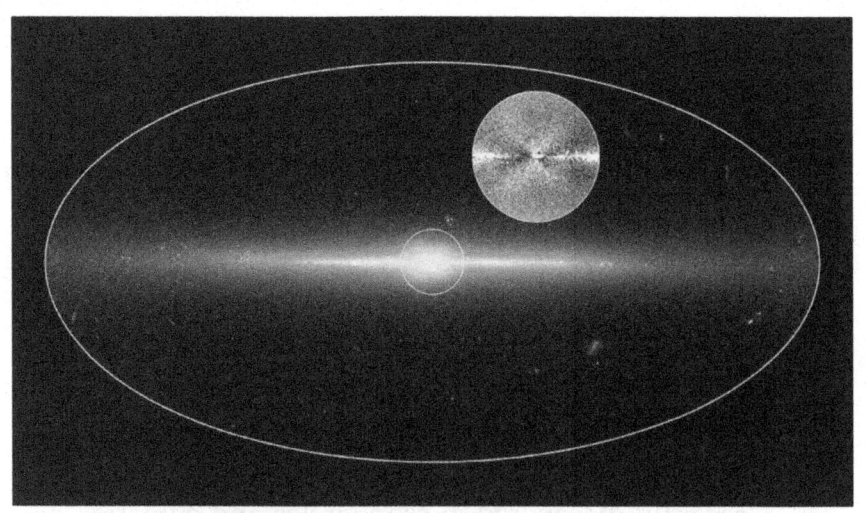

X or hourglass shape at the central bulge of the Milky Way, NASA's Wide-field Infrared Survey Explorer (WISE space telescope), 2010.[14]

Jain mandala of Mount Meru, sacred center of the universe in Hindu cosmology (Mount Sumeru in Buddhist cosmology). Its terrestrial manifestation is Mount Kailas in the Himalayas, which is the abode of Lord Siva.

Southern face of Mount Kailas, elevation 21,778 feet.

The late researcher of esoterica Colin Wilson describes the majesty and sanctity of Mount Kailas (or Kailash).

> "With its four facades facing north, east, south, and west, Mount Kailas looks like an enormous diamond. Seventy-five percent as high as Mount Everest, the mountain is one of the tallest peaks in the Himalayas. Nearby is the source of the Indus, Sutlej, and Brahmaputra Rivers. The source of the Ganges is not far away. On its southern face, a vertical gash crosses horizontal layers, creating the image of a swastika. The word comes from svastika, Sanskrit for well-being and good fortune. Buddhists regard the mountain as a mandala—the sacred circle from which the sacred rivers flow like the spokes of the eternal wheel."[15]

Below: Hourglass Meru with golden city on top, Turkestan painting. Right: Siva and his family on Mount Kailas.

Buddhist pilgrims, who call Mount Kailas *Kang Rinpoche,* or "Precious Snow Mountain," customarily circle clockwise around the sacred peak—an arduous 50-kilometer (31-mile) route, which takes over three days. If they prostrate themselves along the way, it may take even longer. As many as 13 circuits are sometimes made. Adherents of the pre-Buddhist Bön religon of Tibet circumambulate it counterclockwise, and call it the "Nine-Story Swastika Mountain."[16] Meru is clearly an *axis mundi* that reaches to the heavens. According to historian of religion Mircea Eliade, "In Indian cosmology Mount Meru rises at the 'Center of the World' and above it shines the Pole Star."[17] Of course, the North Star in whatever age has traditionally been linked to the swastika.

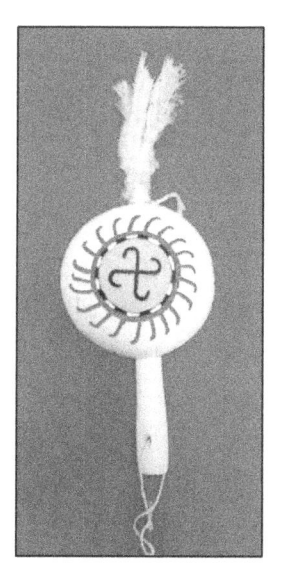

**Left: Hopi *Aya*, or "moisture rattle" with swastika, the late Grandfather Martin Gashweseoma, Hotevilla, Arizona. Photo courtesy of Kymberlee Ruff. Right: Ursa Major (in Hopi, *Sookuyapi*, or "star-ladle"), revolving counter-clockwise through the seasons, forms a swastika centered upon the Pole Star.**

As the photo on p. 199 shows, Mount Kailas is shaped somewhat like a pyramid. It is perhaps more than a coincidence, then, that the promontory is 1° 5′ 15″ north of the Great Pyramid—a difference in latitude of only 75 miles, even though Kailas and Khufu are 2,955 miles apart.

## *Linga* Lingo

Mount Meru/Mount Kailas is also considered a macrocosmic Siva *lingam*. Early 19th century mythologist Godfrey Higgins claims that the legend of Jason and the Argonauts, and his quest for the Golden Fleece of the Ram, originated not in Greece but in India. He bases this notion on the fact that the steersman Canopus is an eponym of the second brightest star in the heavens, and this star cannot be seen from Grecian latitudes. The Siva-Sakti (or *lingam-yoni*) duality is symbolized by the respective mast and hull of the Greek ship Argo, or in Hindu terms, the *Argha*.

> "The mystic Ocean in which the ship Argha floated, is the ethereal space or fluid, called firmament in Gen. i 7, in which the bodies of the planetary system revolve. The Ark or Argha, the ship with its mount Meru in the center by way of mast, may be seen in every temple of India, and requires no explanation. It is the Omphale [*Omphalos*] of Delphi. The Earth was often called Arga: this was imitated by the mystic Meru. The north pole was the Linga, surrounded by seven dwips or zones rising one above another, and seven seas, or rivers, or waters, and an outward one called Oceanus. In

this Oceanus the whole floated. Thus the earth, mother Eartha, became the Argha or Ione, and Meru the pole, the Linga."[18]

Higgins further comments on the suspended Hindu copper vessel containing water that trickles down upon the *lingam*, which was noted on p. 185. "The Argha is represented by a vessel of copper, by the Brahmins in their sacred rites. It is intended to be a symbol or hieroglyphic of the universal mother. It is very often in the form of an elliptic boat or canoe, having both ends similarly pointed, or biprora, as its name was. In the center of it is an oval rising, embossed, which represents the Linga."[19]

The Siva complex is basically a syncretism of stasis and dynamism, a dialectic of introverted meditation and extroverted manifestation. Scholar of Eastern Religions R. C. Zaehner comments: "…Śiva is both the great ascetic and the ithyphallic god who delights in the worship of his *lingam* or phallus. As ascetic he is eternally at rest, 'isolated', and rapt in the contemplation of his own unfathomable Being, while in his phallic capacity he is eternally productive of forms. In him the finite and the infinite meet, and in him all opposites are reconciled."[20] A. L. Basham continues in the same vein:

> "Though in this aspect Śiva is continually wrapped in meditation, he can, in his divine power, divide his personality. Not only is he the god of mystical stillness, but also the Lord of the Dance (*Natarāja*). This aspect of Śiva is specially popular in the Tamil country, where religious dancing was part of the earliest known Tamil tradition. In his heavenly palace of Mount Kailāsa, or in his southern home, the

temple of Cidambaram or Tillai (near the seacoast about 50 miles south of Pondicherry), mystically identified with Kailāsa, Śiva dances. He has invented no less than 108 different dances, some calm and gentle, others fierce, orgiastic and terrible. Of the latter the most famous is the *tandāva*, in which the angry god, surrounded by his drunken attendants (*ganas*), beats out a wild rhythm which destroys the world at the end of the cosmic cycle."[21]

Siva *Natarāja*, 10th century bronze Tamil sculpture. Upper-right hand holds a *damaru* (hourglass drum), upper-left hand holds flames, his aloof face acts as a pivot, and his foot crushes a demon. A cobra wreathes lower-right arm.

The *Trimūrti*, or Trinity, of the main Hindu deities is comprised of Brahma the Creator, Vishnu the Preserver, and Siva the Destroyer. Unlike the apocalyptic eschatology of Judaism, Christianity, and Islam, Hinduism sees the "Destroyer" Siva as more of a "Re-Creator" or transformer.[22] In other words, both the microcosmic individual life via the doctrine of transmigration of souls (i.e., reincarnation) and the macrocosmic physical universe (i.e., serial cosmogony) are reborn/renewed. Death does not lead to non-existence but to revivification. This concept of cyclical time is shared by the Hopi, Maya, and Aztecs of the New World. Physicist Fritjof Capra underscores the hermetic-cum-quantum implications of the Cosmic Dancer.

> "For the modern physicists, then, Shiva's dance is the dance of subatomic matter. As in Hindu mythology, it is a continual dance of creation and destruction involving the whole cosmos; the basis of all existence and of all natural phenomena. Hundreds of years ago, Indian artists created visual images of dancing Shivas in a beautiful series of bronzes. In our time, physicists have used the most advanced technology to portray the patterns of the cosmic dance. The bubble-chamber photographs of interacting particles, which bear testimony to the continual rhythm of creations and destruction in the universe, are visual images of the dance of Shiva equaling those of the Indian artists in beauty and profound significance. The metaphor of the cosmic dance thus unifies ancient mythology, religious art, and modern physics."[23]

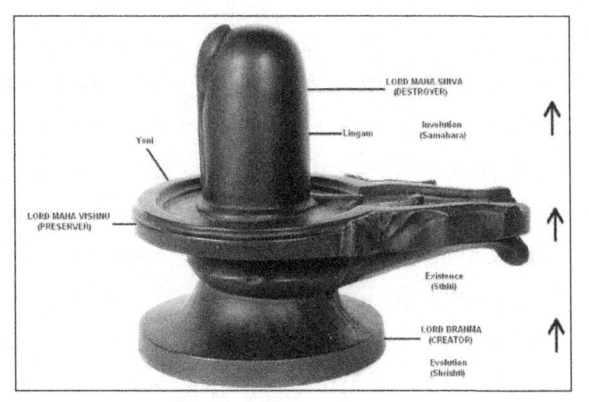

Siva *lingam* manifests the *Trimūrti* (Brahma, Vishnu, Siva). A modified hourglass supports the basin, i.e., *yoni* (vulva) and the rounded cylinder, i.e., *lingam* (phallus).

Above: Aladdin's "magic lamp," a form of the Siva *lingam*.

Hourglass painted on ceramic mug, Black-on-White, Mesa Verde, Ancestral Puebloan, 1200 – 1300 AD. Dots represent raindrops, or perhaps grains *of sand*.

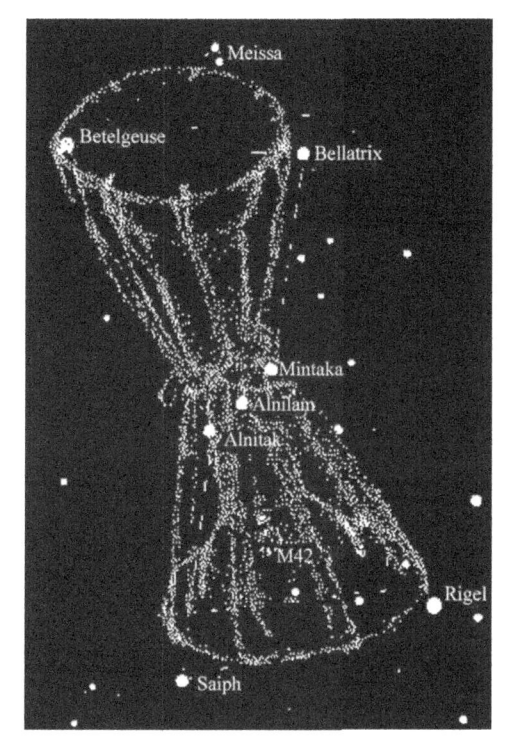

**Left:** Japanese Orion, *mitsu boshi* ("three stars"), or *tsuzumi boshi*, "drum." (*Tsu* is Hopi for "rattlesnake.")[24] **Right:** Replica of onyx chalice, Basilica of San Isidoro, León, Spain. Some believe that the goblet, which belonged to 11th century Queen Urraca, is the veritable Holy Grail.

Another manifestation of the hourglass motif is the legendary Holy Grail, the chalice reputedly used at the Last Supper and the vessel that collected Christ's blood at the Cruxifixion. If viewed in conjunction with the Serpent, an archetypal dynamism results: *lingam-yoni*, yang-yin, *yab-yum*, phallus-uterus, Father Sky–Mother Earth, pestle-mortar, alembic-retort (alchemical), snake-egg (Gnostic), etc. In their book *The Serpent Grail*, co-authors Philip Gardiner and Gary Osborn discuss the Greek sky god's relationship to ophiolatry, temporality, and immortality.

"Although Zeus, the universal Aether and father of the Greek pantheon, is never depicted with serpents, as the Olympian Zeus Meilichios he takes on the form of a serpent to attend the spring rites of the Mother Goddess, Earth. This shape-shifting ability – an ability attributed to shamans – would be only natural if he personified those able to control the serpent energy of the cosmos. As we further discovered, Zeus took the form of the serpent Ophion to avoid the ravages of his father, Chronos, the god of time, from whom we derive the word 'chronology'. (In Rome, Chronos is equated with Saturn.) Zeus thus avoided the two things we all fear the most: time catching up with us, and death itself. But even Zeus, the greatest of all Greek gods, needed to take on the form of the serpent in order to gain immortal life."[25]

←Hopi sky god Sotuknang, *katsina* doll with hourglass symbols, Heard Museum, Phoenix.

Are we running out of time?

**Middle: symbol of Extinction Rebellion, a nonviolent movement protesting climate chaos. Right: nuclear reactor.**

# Chapter 14
## *Celestial Birdman of Antiquity*

**Wings Over the World**

Many ancient cultures around the world have legends of the Birdman, which describe in various forms a half-human, half-avian creature. These tales are possibly connected to our universal psychological yearnings for flight. In liturgical literature and visual art, for instance, the appearance of angels, or simply humans with wings, may be the result of our innate desire to soar above the Earth into the realm of God. The soul itself is sometimes portrayed as winging up to heaven. More archaic traditions conceptualize the bird as a psychopomp, carrying the soul to the underworld. The proto-surrealist painter Hieronymus Bosch may have been considering this darker role in his early 16$^{th}$ century "Garden of Earthly Delights." His triptych shows the "Prince of Hell" as a Birdman with a chamber pot for a crown, who devours human corpses and excretes them on his "throne."

The Birdman is a particular type of therianthrope, a word that literally means "beast-man." Myths of this cryptocreature are not confined to any one continent but are found in Egypt, Mesopotamia, India, China, Africa, North and South America, and Australia. Many people with even a casual interest in Egyptology are familiar with the falcon-headed solar god Horus, son of Osiris and Isis. Each pharaoh became the manifestation of this protector deity in life and Osiris/Orion in death. In addition, the ancient Egyptians recognized ibis-headed Thoth as the god of knowledge, writing, magic, and science. The *Ba*, or "soul," was depicted with a bird body and a human head. "The Egyptians, like the Greeks, the Babylonians, and many other peoples, saw manifestations of the dead in birdlike apparitions, with thin piping voices, fluttering through the air near their former haunts."[1]

**Hieronymous Bosch, detail from "Garden of Earthly Delights," circa 1500.**

**Below: human-headed *Ba* with entheogenic blue lotuses, Kalabsha Temple, Nubia. Right: Ibis-headed Thoth, Temple of Ramesses II, Abydos.**

*Tragically, Nimrud was destroyed by Islamic State militants in early 2015.

Left: falcon-headed Horus. Right: eagle-headed deity anointing the World Tree, neo-Assyrian, 9th century BC.

The Birdman also played a key role in Mesopotamia. At the Assyrian city of Nimrud,* bas-relief sculptures were found of a winged, eagle-headed genie that protected the people from diseases and evil forces. In his right hand he carried a pinecone sprinkler; in his left either a purifying water vessel or a shaman's purse. He wore a feather robe, thong sandals, and a dagger in his belt.

The half-eagle, half-man entity from India was called Garuda, who also had the head and wings of a bird and the body of a human. He was king of the feathered tribes and adversary of the serpent race.[2] The Chinese version of Birdman was a storm god named Lei Kung, who had a human body but the head and claws of a rooster. He carried a hammer in one hand and a chisel in the other, with which he produced thunder and lightning.[3] In Hindu and Buddhist mythologies the male *kinnara* and the female *kinnaris* are half-bird, half-human creatures that were paradigmatic lovers that reveled in poetry, song, and dance.[4]

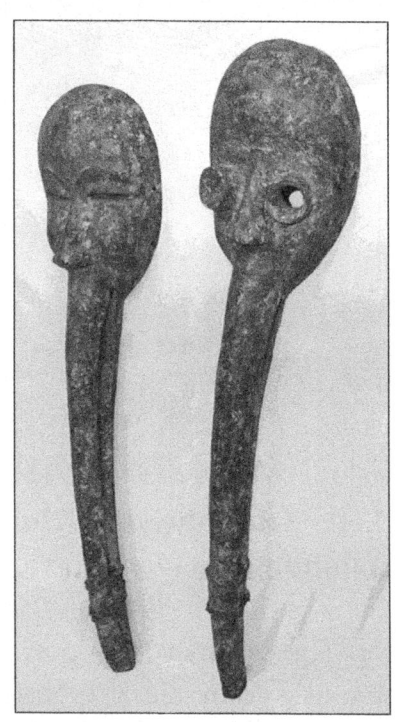

**Left: Garuda statue, National Museum, Delhi, photo courtesy of Hyougushi. (See Birdmen pictographs from Tamil Nadu, India, p. 187.) Right: Wooden masks of Birdman, Dan tribe, Poro Society, Ivory Coast, 8" by 33".**

Members of the Dan tribe that inhabited Côte d'Ivoire in Africa were conceptualized as Bird-men. These beings with human bodies and birds-of-prey heads reputedly bequeathed all the arts and sciences of civilization to the native people of West Africa. Scholar Andrew Collins speculates that the Danite Bird-men may actually have been connected to the biblical Watchers, or fallen angels, who by their astral flights engaged in bird shamanism.

> "The idea of bird-men acting as bringers of knowledge and wisdom to mortal kind is not unique to the Middle East. An African tribe called Dan, who live close to the village of Man on the Ivory Coast, say that at the beginning of time, in the days of their first ancestors, a race of 'attractive human birds appeared, possessing all the sciences which they handed on to mankind'. Even today the tribal artists make copper representations of these bird-men, who are shown with human bodies and heads supporting long beaks, like those of birds of prey."[5]

A similar creature with bird-head and human frame was worshipped by the bird cult on Easter Island (Rapa Nui). Atop a high precipice at the lip of the Rano Kao volcano on the southwestern tip of the island, hundreds of petroglyphs of therianthropes, depicted in profile with arched backs and curved beaks, have been carved in bas-relief into the rocks. Over 50 semi-subterranean stone chambers, mostly oval-shaped, were used to house the Bird-men, who were called *tangata manu* (literally, "man-bird"; note tan-/Dan similarity) as they waited for the return of the sooty tern (*Sterna fuscata*) to a tiny island a short distance off the coast. Graham Hancock claims that the Easter Island name for the sooty tern is *manu-tera*, literally "bird-sun," suggesting the primordial egg of the phoenix in Heliopolis. He furthermore states that the word *tangata-manu* (he spells it *tangatu*) actually means "learned man of the sacred bird" and refers to ibis-headed Thoth with his long, curved beak.⁶

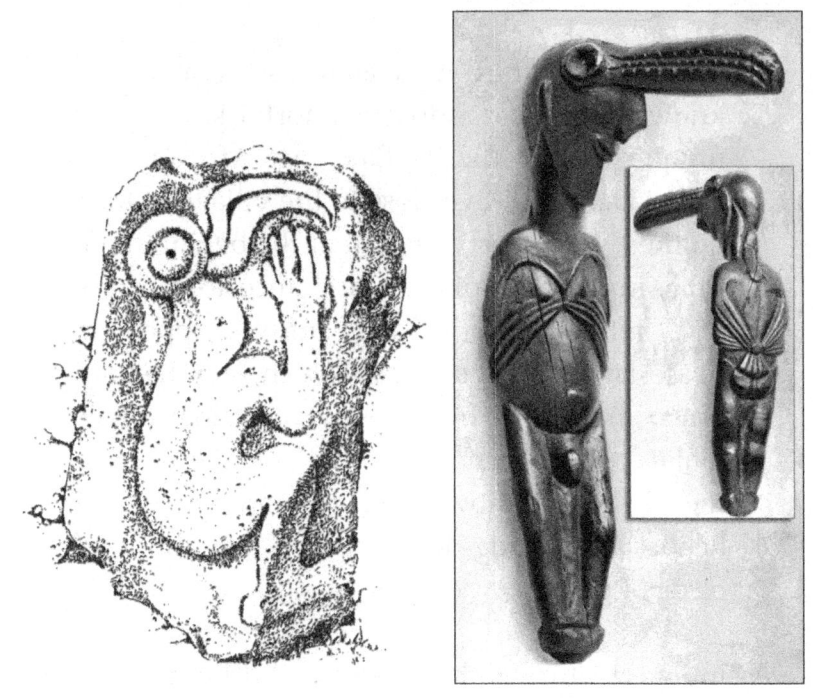

**Left: Birdman, bas-relief petroglyph, Orongo, Rapa Nui.
Right: Wooden statue of Birdman, 10.3", British Museum.**

The Maya manifested a seated Birdman in the form of the nocturnal Yucatan Screech Owl (*Otus choliba thompsoni*), or "moan-bird," an evil therianthrope whose mournful, quavering cry signified death and drought.⁷ The Hopi of northern Arizona conversely portray the Eagle Kachina (or *katsina*, i.e., a spirit messenger) as a benevolent figure that assisted with the burgeoning of the agricultural cycle. In addition, the Mimbres tribe of southwestern New Mexico painted on a ceramic bowl one long beaked aquatic Birdman holding a string of large fish.

Mayan Birdman, Yucatan Screech Owl.
1 & 3 from Dresden Codex, 2 from the Tro-Cortesianus.

Artifacts found at Cahokia near present-day Saint Louis, Missouri, and Etowah Indian Mounds in Georgia prove that the Birdman played a significant role for the Mound Builder cultures. During the mid-1st millennium AD in northern Peru, the Moche human sacrifice ceremony featured a Birdman figure as well. Equally brutal, the Aztecs also employed the motif.

Left: Mimbres water birdman on ceramic bowl, circa 1000 AD, southwestern New Mexico. Right: Maya winged ballplayer with purse, Young Museum, Texas.

Left: Hopi *Kwaahu* (Eagle) *Katsina* (Kachina) dancer.
Right: Birdman Tablet, sandstone, Cahokia, circa 1200 AD.

Previous page, bottom-left: "A Zuñi House Shrine," photo by Edward S. Curtis, 1925. "Knife Wing," flint knife feathers and tail, original war god whose guardian is the Mountain Lion of the north, weapons of flint knife, rainbow, and lightning. **Bottom-right:** Rogan Plate, dancing Birdman, copper, Etowah, Georgia.

Moche Warrior Priest hands a goblet
to the Bird Priest, northern Peru.

Bird-men, Nazca culture, 1-500 AD, textile, Peru.
Did these Bird-men survey the Nazca Lines from above?

**Left: Aztec Eagle Man, clay statue, Field Museum, Chicago.
Right: Olmec birdman, courtesy of The Young Museum.**

The continent of Australia is apparently replete with the Birdman figures, usually depicted as petroglyphs. Rock art researcher Rex Gilroy states in this regard:

> "Carved into a large boulder at one end is a strange symbol: a human-bodied, winged, bird-headed figure. Similar winged, human-bodied figures are commonplace at open, flat summits of hills lying among the old terraced Uruan structures standing southwest of Sydney, in the Campbelltown district, and upon clifftops and high tabletop areas throughout the nearby Blue Mountains. They also occur upon tabletop summits of hills and

mountains across the Australian continent, including Tasmania. They are images of the 'Bird-Men' of Uru, the first humans to begin the conquest of the skies. Some Blue Mountains rock art shows there were 'Bird-women' too. These rock engravings show that, over 15,000 years ago, employing the simplest materials, the Blue Mountains Uru had taken to the air in the earliest hang gliders built on earth. It is significant that traditions of these 'birdmen and women' are preserved by Aboriginal tribes with Uru-sounding names Australia-wide."

**Left: Petroglyph of a Bird-woman with pendulous breasts, Sydney area, Australia, photo by Angel John Gallard, courtesy of Evan Strong.[9] Right: Hopi Birdman, Fred Kabotie, Kiva Room, Desertview Tower, Grand Canyon, AZ.**

Anthropo-avian representations were occasionally gender-equal as well. As "Queen of the Night," this nude birdwoman is flanked by a pair of owls and stands upon a pair of male lions. Babylonian terracotta plaque, 1800 BC – 1750 BC, 15" X 20", British Museum. She possibly represents either Ishtar, goddess of fertility, love, and war or Ereshkigal (Inanna), goddess of the underworld and death, or even a female demon called *lilitu*, in Hebrew "Lilith."[10] The rod-and-ring held in each hand resembles the Egyptian *shen* symbol, which signifies "eternal protection." The Egyptian word *shen* means "to hover over, to alight" (written with a bird hieroglyph). The word *shenu* means both "circle, circuit, to surround" and "endless time, eternity, 10,000,000 years," but also "lake, Nile flood," and "vases, vessels," and "court nobleman."[11]

# Chapter 15
## *The Orion Mind in the Cave*

### The Birdman of Lascaux

In this chapter I'd like to go out on a limb with a very old Birdman—perhaps the world's oldest. In the Vézère Valley of the Dordogne region of southwestern France near the village of Montignac, three teenage boys as recently as 1940 discovered the incredible cave system known as Lascaux. This subterranean wonder was dubbed the "Sistine Chapel of Prehistory" and subsequently became a UNESCO World Heritage site. The 2,000 or so figures exquisitely rendered in mineral pigments of red hematite, yellow goethite, and black manganese oxide were painted by Cro-Magnon artists on the calcite walls and ceiling in the Upper Paleolithic as much as 20,000 years ago. Animal pictographs included aurochs (*Bos Primigenius*), bison, equines, felines, ibexes, reindeer, a bear, a bird, and a woolly rhinoceros. Geometric iconography includes dots, hooks, crosses, and squares as well as rectilinear and nested figures.[1]

In the deepest part of the cave, a single human form haunts the walls of a roughly oval section known as the Shaft. In fact, it is the only anthropomorph depicted in the whole cave complex. This grotto was probably considered as a sort of *sanctum sanctorum*. Initiates would descend vertically about 16 feet by rope into this narrow cleft in order to take part in divine rituals that most likely involved the underworld spirits, who undoubtedly guided the painters as they co-created this cosmic tableau. In his book *The Mind In the Cave*, David Lewis-Williams, Professor Emeritus and Senior Mentor in the Rock Art Research Institute at the

University of Witswatersrand, Johannesburg, describes the *mysterium tremendum* that the participants must have experienced—as vital and spirtually transformative as the Eleusinian Mysteries of Greece or the Mithraic rites of Rome.

> "It is highly probable that, as in many shamanistic societies, the metaphors of transformation into a shaman would have been woven into a myth or series of myths. But it would be naïve to assume that the images in the Shaft merely 'illustrate' a myth, as pictures in a child's book may illustrate events in a fairy tale. Rather, the metaphors and images that lay at the heart of Lascaux shamanism and that structured the people's thinking were expressed in different contexts—myth and art, and probably dance and music as well. Those who descended the Shaft did not simply view pictures: they saw real things, real spirit animals and beings, real transformations. In short, they saw through the membrane [of the rock surface] and participated in the events of the spirit realm. The paintings in the Shaft capture the essence of Lascaux shamanism in a compaction of its complex metaphors."[2]

Indeed, the living lithic panel was a liminal membrane or mystical veil, a dual passageway to the realm of both the clan ancestors and totemic forebears of a psychically therianthropic people who hunted and fought, danced and loved, gave birth and died as immanent entities walking through their inscrutable world wrapped in sunshine and starlight.

**Birdman, bird-on-a-staff, bison, and rhino in the Shaft.**

In general, anthropomorphic figures are quite rare in Upper Paleolithic cave art. This naked, stick-like figure (as opposed to the naturalistic bison) reclines at an angle of about 45 degrees. He is called the Birdman because of his bird beak, although he has no wings. He does, however, have four fingers on each hand, which parallels the four claws of a bird. As we shall see, the relationship between this human figure and the bull are proportional to that of the constellations Orion and Taurus respectively.[3]

Some have also called this humanoid figure the "Wounded Man" ("Wounded Healer"?) or even the "Dead Man." Admittedly, the figure certainly seems intimidated by the bull, although the latter's entrails appear to be dangling down, so perhaps it was wounded in the confrontation. The figure also is ithyphallic, although it is difficult to understand how a person in this state could have an erect phallus. Maybe the rigors of mortis have something to do with it. But seriously, male arousal is commonly found in dreaming and altered states of consciousness, so the erection may signify the shaman's ecstatic journey to the spirit world rather than mere physical virility or fertility. Also, his rigid penis is pointing to the heart of the bull—a sort of interspecies mating of the minds.

The extended left arm of Birdman is pointing to the lowered left horn of Bull, who appears to be preparing to charge with hackles raised, despite his potentially mortal wound. An oblique shaft at the upper right transects both his anus and the area of his genital potency—his symbolic raison d'etre—coming (no pun intended) to rest both at his hooves and at Birdman's oddly pointed feet. What is perhaps a barbed weapon with a cross stave lies below. Birdman's bent right arm points to Perched Bird on a vertical pole, whose head points in the same direction as both Big Bull and Retreating Rhino. The latter creature, not fully executed in the painting, indeed appears to be departing the scene. The painting's interactive imagery plays out its holistic drama on a curving lithic canvas, so to speak, which is about six-and-a-half-feet tall.

The cognitive archaeologist Lewis-Williams rejects the notion that the panel is merely a description of a hunting scene created for the purpose of sympathetic magic. "So what we have in the Shaft is not a hunting disaster; far too many points count against so simple an interpretation. Rather, we have transformation by death: the 'death' of the man paralleling the 'death' of the eviscerated bison. As both 'die', the man fuses with one of his spirit helpers, a bird."[4]

Sharing Lewis-Williams' non-hunting interpretation but for a different reason, Dr. Michael Rappenglück of Munich University claims that the images on the panel represent the constellations forming the Summer Triangle. Specifically, the avian-humanoid inclined at approximately a 45-degree angle of corresponds to Deneb in Cygnus, the bird on a stick corresponds to Altair in Aquila, and the bull corresponds to Vega in Lyra. However, in another section near the cave's mouth, a bovine with six dots over its shoulder had been painted, clearly depicting Taurus and the Pleiades.[5] If one accepts Rappenglück's theory, it would mean that a bull in one place in the complex represents Taurus, while in another place in the same cave it represents the tiny and decidedly unbull-like constellation of Lyra. Were the traditional shamanic astronomers really that inconsistent?

Since the auroch in the painting on the next page most likely represents Taurus with the Pleiades hovering above his right shoulder, I would like to propose an alternative celestial scenario to Rappenglück's constellations for the figures in the Shaft.

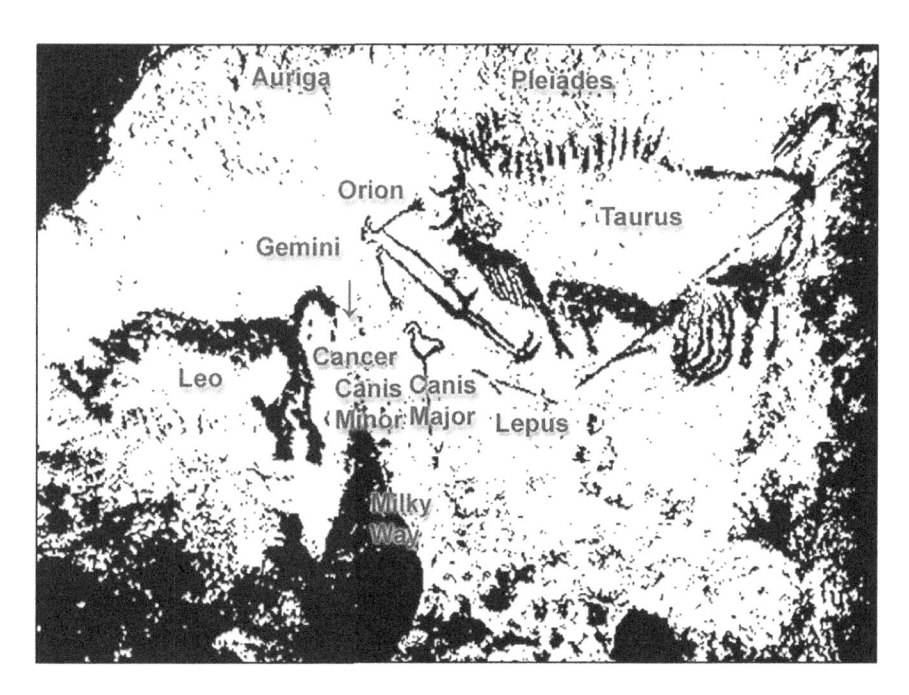

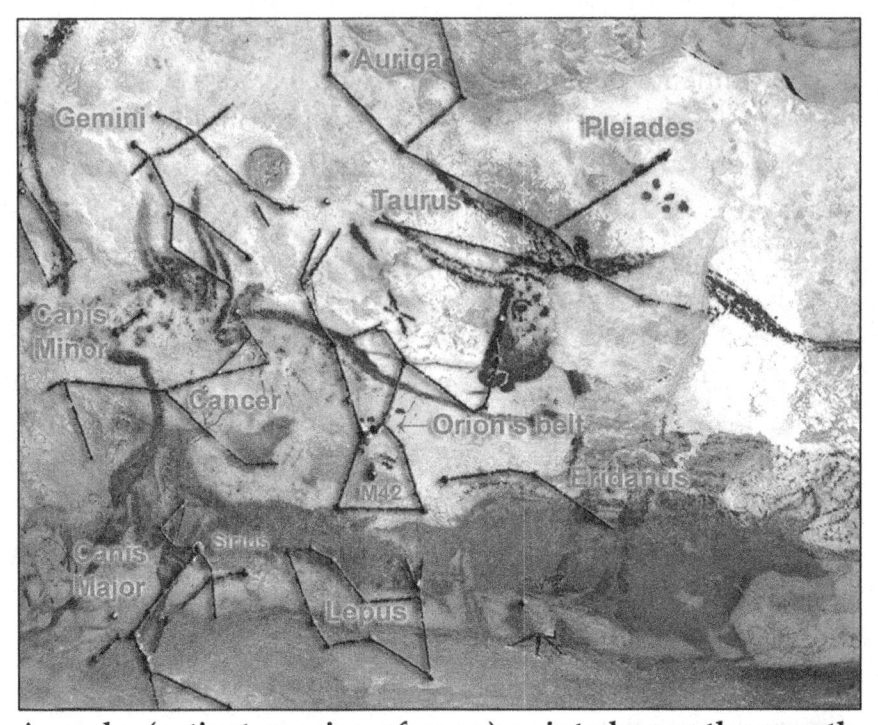

Aurochs (extinct species of oxen) painted near the mouth of Lascaux Cave with superimposed constellations. Horns of the male auroch on the right correspond to the horns of Taurus. Six dots above its shoulder correspond to the visible stars of the Pleiades. The dots below and to the left of this auroch's nose correspond to Orion's belt. This bull is staring at the X-shape near Orion's head (Meissa). The wedge between its lower horn (Zeta Tauri) and Orion's upraised right hand may correspond to the two equinox points where the celestial equator crosses the ecliptic. The horns of the other auroch on the center-left correspond to Gemini, its eye to Canis Minor, its chest to Monoceros, and its left foreleg to Canis Major. The natural formation directly adjacent to Gemini may represent the full moon on the ecliptic. The hind end of Canis Major rests on the floor of the cave, which represents the horizon. The bison at the bottom-right (Eridanus) is more recent.

As previously hinted, Birdman and adjacent Big Bull in the Shaft may have been an attempt to bring the deific dominion of the rising constellations Orion and Taurus into the realm of the subterranean grotto. If so, this cosmographic construction project was aimed to fuse the ever-after world of Above to the ever-before world of Below.

The woolly rhinoceros at the left (the only such animal depicted in the cave) may represent Leo—the raised tail corresponding to the curved neck of the "Lion." The finial bird on a vertical staff, which may be a capercaillie, or black grouse with a *red* crescent above each eye, represents Canis Major on the southern horizon, with Sirius being the bird, and the stick being the backbone of the "Great Dog." Ptolemy, Cicero, Horace, and Seneca all described Sirius as a *red* star, especially during its heliacal rising and setting. Mircea Eliade comments on the perched bird motif.

> "Because shamans can change themselves into 'birds,' that is, because they enjoy the 'spirit' condition, they are able to fly to the World Tree to bring back 'soul-birds.' The bird perched on a stick is a frequent symbol in shamanic circles. It is found, for example, on the tombs of Yakut shamans. A Hungarian *táltos* 'had a stick or post before his hut and perched on the stick was a bird. He sent the bird wherever he would have to go.' The bird perched on a post is already found in the celebrated relief at Lascaux (bird-headed man) in which Horst Kirchner has seen a representation of a shamanic trance. However this may be, it is certain that the motif 'bird perched on a post' is extremely archaic."[6]

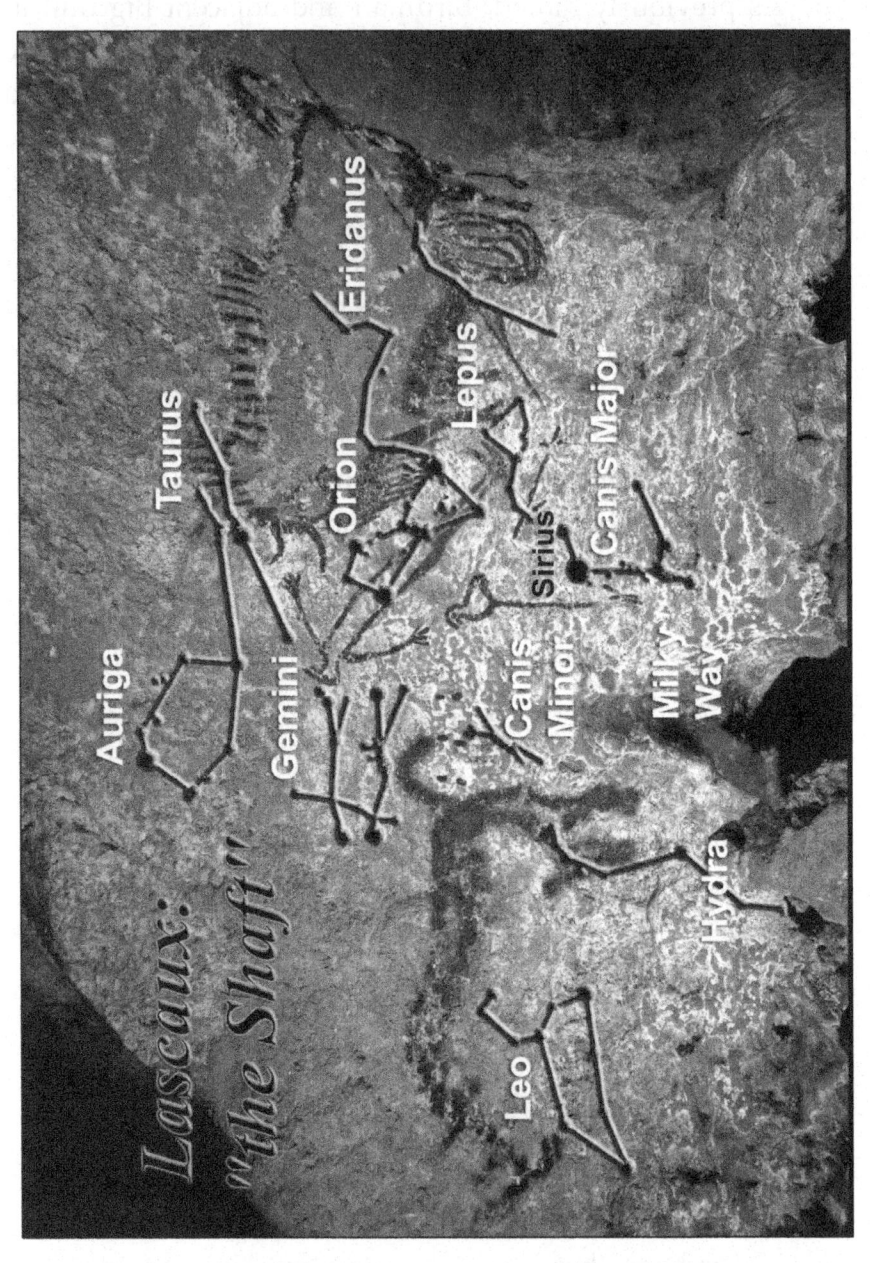

The primary figures in this archaic spiritual psychodrama
echo the template of the constellations.

Less certain are the representations for the three pairs of black vertical dots at the hind end of the rhino. These dots grouped in a rectangle might correspond to Gemini: the twins Castor and Pollux on the left, Mebsuta and Mekbuda in the middle, and Propus and Alhena on the right. Alternately, the two dots on the right possibly correspond to Canis Minor (Gomeisa and its brightest star Procyon), the two in the middle may be a couple stars in the constellation Cancer and/or the star cluster M 44, while the two on the left may be two planets on the ecliptic. (On the other hand, the six marks might merely be rhino poop, which is as good a guess as any when it comes to rock art interpretation.) The atlatl-like weapon lying at the foot of Birdman may correspond to the constellation Lepus. The two dots on the upper left at the top of the panel perhaps correlate to Capella and Minkalinan in the constellation Auriga. The oblique line at the hind end of the bull also suggests the celestial equator.

The roughly circular well of the Shaft must have functioned somewhat like the very much later round *kivas* of the Hopi—i.e., a physical descent signifying a temporal retrograde to the realm of the ancestor therianthropes, or, as Eliade has said, the "eternal return." The main "scene" of Birdman, Bull, and Rhino are located on the north wall of the chamber. Thus, the two beasts and the bird on the staff are pointed toward the west, whereas Birdman is facing east. One other figure, however, appears on the opposite (southeast) wall: a lone black horse appears with its head likewise pointed west. If in our chthonic planetarium, Birdman indeed correlates to Orion, Bull to Taurus, and Rhino to Leo, then Horse might also correlate to either Aquarius or the wingéd horse Pegasus on the opposite horizon.

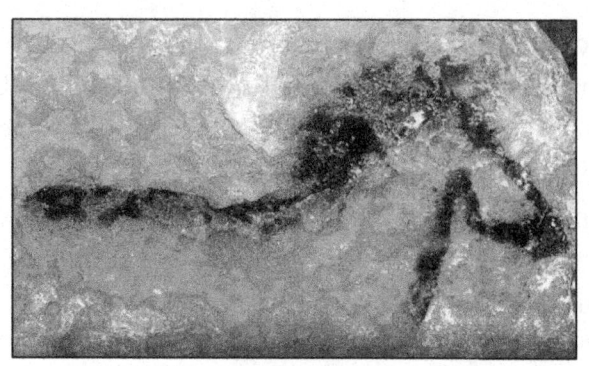

**Horse on the wall opposite the thaumaturgic scene.**

In addition, white calcite crystals have formed, both undernearth (before) and on top of (after) the painting. Thus, it appears that Birdman/Orion is floating upon the starry bed of the Milky Way, whereas the hide of the bison is highlighted by the natural ocher hue of the limestone.

In his multi-genre book *Juniper Fuse: Upper Paleolithic Imagination & the Construction of the Underworld*, poet Clayton Eshleman speculates on the role of the rising Birdman vis-à-vis the Bull.

> "...one may interpret one aspect of the 'scene' as involving a bird shaman who has sacrificed, or envisioned the sacrifice of, a bison. If ethnographical parallels are deemed acceptable for any Upper Paleolithic shamanic interpretations, there is solid evidence to suggest that this bird-headed figure is at some stage of bringing a bison's soul to a Magdalenian celestial realm. To put it this way does not presume some God or Supreme Being as being the recipient of such a gift. Nearly all shamanistic lore posits an ur-shaman who once spoke with animals and had direct access to all

realms as the overseer and/or goal of any later shaman's journey. It does not seem farfetched to me to propose that this bird-headed man, in a magical, not religious, sense, lifting up from the depths of Lascaux's Shaft, is reestablishing a communication between earth and some 'height' that his prowess and paraphenalia symbolize his potential access to. He may be spreading his arms in imitation of the flight of the bird designated by his mask and staff. Or it also seems possible that with his outspread left hand he is 'directing' the strangely pivoting bison head, and with his outspread right hand inducting power from the bird-staff below it."[7]

Mythologist Joseph Campbell also comments on the vertical ascension of the shaman's airy (aerie) spirit from the aqueous underground subconscious through the sun-baked terrestrial plane of overt action to the fiery celestial supraconscious.

"And so it is, I believe, that we can say that in the mythogenetic zone of the Franco-Cantabrian caves the rendition in art of the mythological realm itself was achieved for the first time in the history of the world. All cathedrals, all temples since—which are not mere meeting houses but manifestations to the mind of the magical space of God—derive from these caves. And I would say, also, that we have here our first certain sign of the operation of the fertilized masculine spirit, the upbeat to *La Divina Commedia* and to all those magical temples of the Orient wherein the heart and mind are winged away from earth and reach first the heavens of the stars, but then beyond."[8]

But when, exactly, was this "first certain sign"?

## World Enough and Time

In 2004 Rappenglück noted the following: "The 14C-date of 18,600 ± 160 BP indicates that the cave had been visited as early as the end of the Badegoulian (18,500 – 17,000 BP)."[9] The official archaeological website of the French government states that Solutreans, not the Magdalenian, were the probable creators of this Upper Paleolithic, parietal ideogrammic-mythographic complex.[10]

> "In 1998, and then in 2002, two radiocarbon analyses carried out on fragments of a reindeer antler baton, unearthed by Henri Breuil and Séverin Blanc [the initial excavators of Lascaux], tended to push back the former estimates to between 18,600 and 18,900 BP, at the boundary between the upper Solutrean and the Badegoulian [earliest phase of Magdalenian culture]. A formal analysis of the figures at Lascaux leads one to think that the art belongs to a Solutrean tradition. Clearly, they are more reminiscent of the works at the well-dated sites of Fourneau-du-Diable or Roc-de-Sers, than of any Magdalenian example."[11]

British independent researcher Andrew Collins, who agrees with Rappenglück's Birdman-Cygnus interpretation, also believes that the Solutreans were responsible for the iconography of the subterranean gallery. "Radiocarbon testing of organic material removed from the Shaft of the Dead Man at Lascaux has provided dates in the region of 16,500 to 15,000 BCE. Thus it seems likely that the cosmic bird in question is the constellation Cygnus, which coincided with the northern celestial pole circa 15,750 to 12,750 BCE (and arguably for 1,000 years or so before this time). Since a time frame of 16,500 to 15,000 BCE hints strongly at the fact that Solutreans were responsible for this cave art, this tells us that these cosmological notions almost certainly featured in their beliefs and practices."[12]

The oldest radiocarbon dates on the reindeer antler baton are 16,950 – 16,650 BC (18,900 – 18,600 BP). In the Birdman-Orion scenario, during this time we see Orion arcing across the *southern* sky, appearing to transit the vertical band of the Milky Way in the same manner that Birdman appears to be issuing from the dark cleft in the lower part of the panel. That the depiction is on the *northern* wall of the Shaft may have to do with the underworld being conceptualized as the cosmological reverse of the earth plane.[13] Above and to the right of Orion are Taurus and the Pleiades, painted as a dying Bull. To the left is Leo, rendered as the retreating Rhino. In 16,950 BC, Sirius had been seen as a recognizable bird-on-the-staff, hovering 3° above the horizon at 180° azimuth. Three centuries later in 16,650 BC, it had sunk to 1° above the horizon. For thousands of years Sirius' meridian passage had been gradually descending. In time the fiery Bird would disappear altogether. Instead of solitary Cygnus as Birdman at the North Pole, the Lascaux tableau seems more likely to be a gestalt of these contiguous constellations.

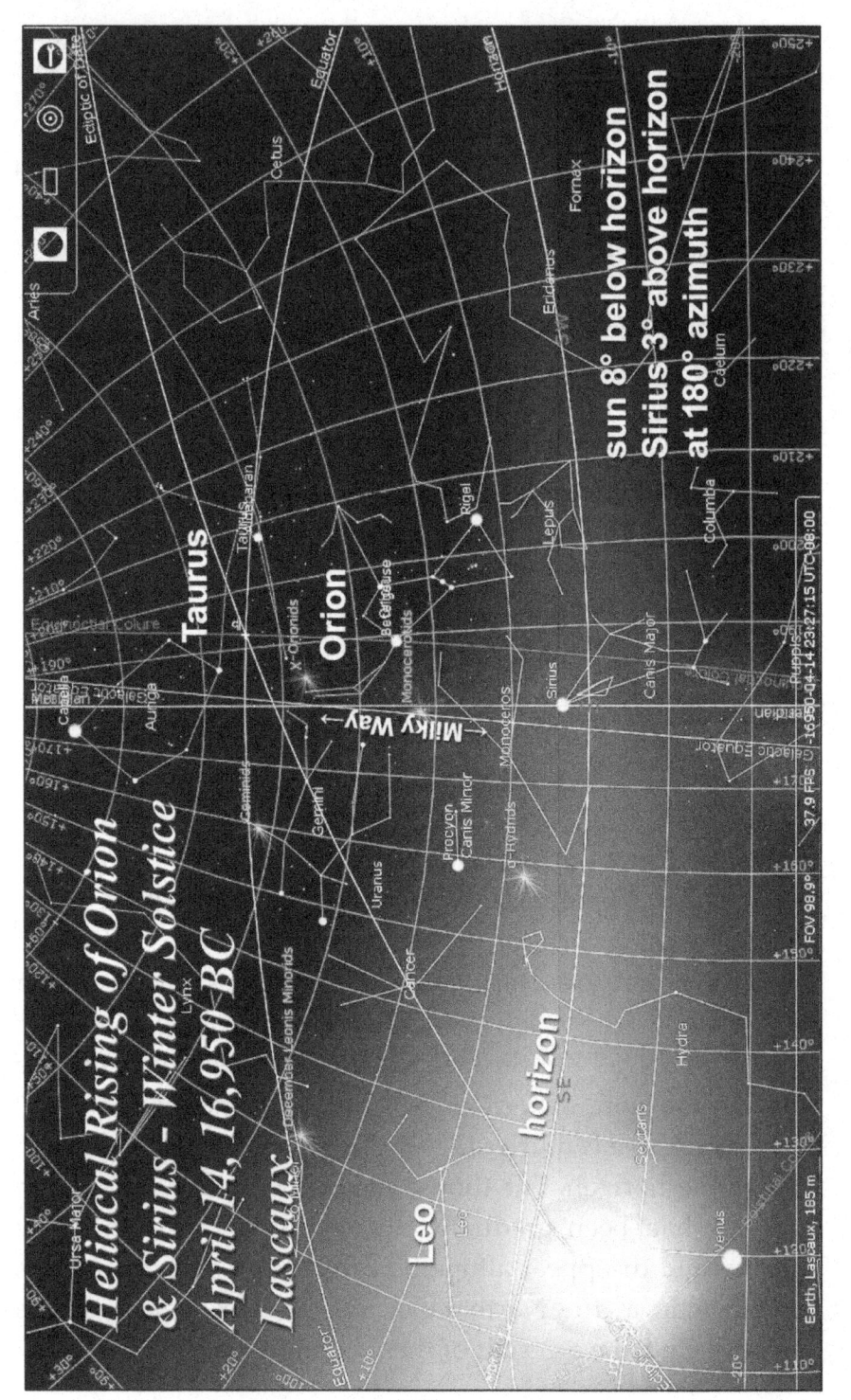

*Heliacal Rising of Orion & Sirius – Winter Solstice April 14, 16,950 BC Lascaux*

sun 8° below horizon
Sirius 3° above horizon
at 180° azimuth

## The Magic Lamp of Lascaux

Known as *Le Brûloir de Lascaux*, this exquisitely carved and polished oil lamp of red sandstone was discovered at the foot of the Shaft panel near the rhino's tail. It measures 8¾ inches long, 4³/₁₆ inches wide, and 1¼ inches thick.

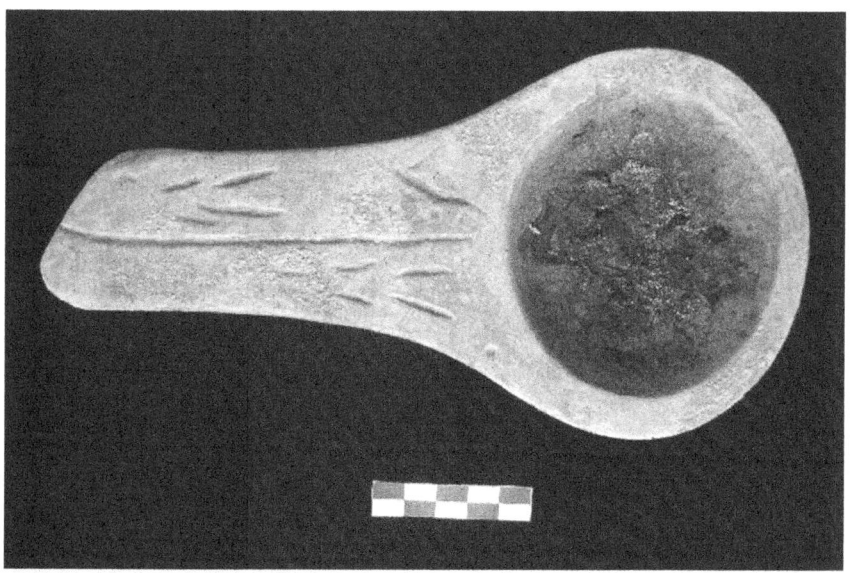

**Photo shows lamp just before it was cleaned of its carbon residue. Musée National de Préhistoire, Les Eyzies-de-Tayac. This photo and the one below courtesy of Don Hitchcock.[14]**

The organic material from the lamp has been radiocarbon dated to 17,500 ± 900 BP, or *approximately* 15,550 BC.[15] If we assume the oldest date of this burnt "juniper fuse" dipped in animal fat, it brings us to 18,400 BP, or 16,450 BC; the youngest date for this artifact is 16,600 BP, or 14,650 BC. Given the two dated artifacts—namely, the reindeer antler (discussed above) and the lamp—the possible range of the Shaft scene is between 16,950 BC and 14,650 BC, with a median date of 15,800 BC.

In 16,450 BC (oldest 14C-date of the lamp), Sirius was seen precisely perched upon the horizon at 0°. But by 15,800 BC the star-bird was -3°, and by 14,650 BC (youngest date) it was nearly 9° below the horizon—deep in the underworld. If the bird-on-a-standard really does correspond to Sirius, then either the dating of Lascaux painting in the Shaft is inaccurate (viz., older) or the memories of its artists were very long. But perhaps the Solutrean/Magdalenian artists did indeed remember intergenerational stories of the brightest bird in the sky that had hovered over the Earth Mother for millennia, and then, inexplicably, flew into the subterranean realm beyond visibility.

However, a newer technique for dating called uranium-series disequalibrium was recently used on 50 paintings in 11 different Upper Paleolithc caves in northern Spain, including the World Heritage site of Altamira. Uranium isotopes were measured in the thin calcite layers that began to form above the paintings—the same sort of encrustation noted above.The tests determined the ages to be 5,000 to 10,000 years *earlier* than previously thought. According to team leader Dr Alistair Pike of the University of Bristol in the UK, this opens up the possibility that the artwork may have been executed not by Cro-Magnons (i.e., European Early Modern Humans) but by Neanderthals! "Evidence for modern humans in Northern Spain dates back to 41,500 years ago, and before them were Neanderthals. Our results show that either modern humans arrived with painting already part of their cultural activity or it developed very shortly after, perhaps in response to competition with—or perhaps the art is Neanderthal art."[16] It might even have been a Neanderthal-human hybrid creation.

If this earlier dating is possible for the Paleolithic caves of Spain, the same might hold true for Lascaux in France, in which case Sirius as the bird on the staff would have been certainly visible on the southern horizon. Neanderthals had undoubtedly inhabited the Vézère Valley for a very, very long time. According to researcher Alistair Coombs, "At Regourdow Cave, which is located only 800m away from Lascaux, are the remains of a man-bear burial where a Neanderthal man and brown bear were buried in deliberate proximity about 80,000 years ago."[17]

Putting aside the issue of exact age, let's look at the lamp itself. We are intuitively drawn to its geometric perfection, its smooth shape, its simple markings on the handle incised in a pattern that some have identified as chevrons. This lamp cries out for an interpretation that is beyond the utilitarian. With its wavering, sooty illumination reflected upon the enigma of those parietal paintings at Lascaux from 17 millennia ago, what is this artifact trying to tell us?

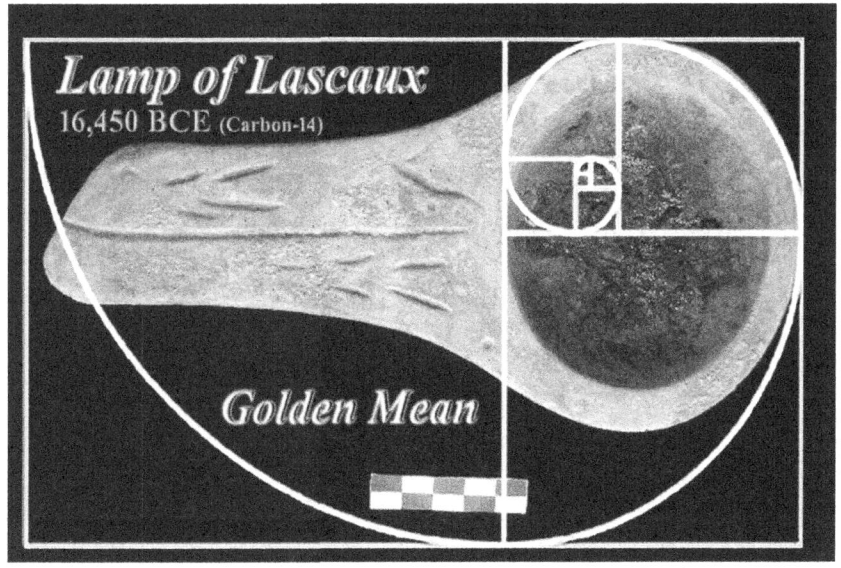

**The Golden Mean spiral is a measure of the ancient craftperson's precision and artistic sensibility. But is there more to it than just pure aesthetics?**

*Heliacal setting of Orion, Taurus & Pegasus - Summer Solstice October 13, 16,450 BC Lascaux*

My work has never been criticized for being speculatively too cautious. After all, I have not been trained as a scientist, nor do I claim to be an anthropologist, an archaeologist, or even an archaeo-astronomer, though some have variously labeled me with such vocations. No, I am simply a wayward poet who has strayed into these intriguing realms of epistemological hermeneutics. So, why not shed some light on the Lascaux Lamp?

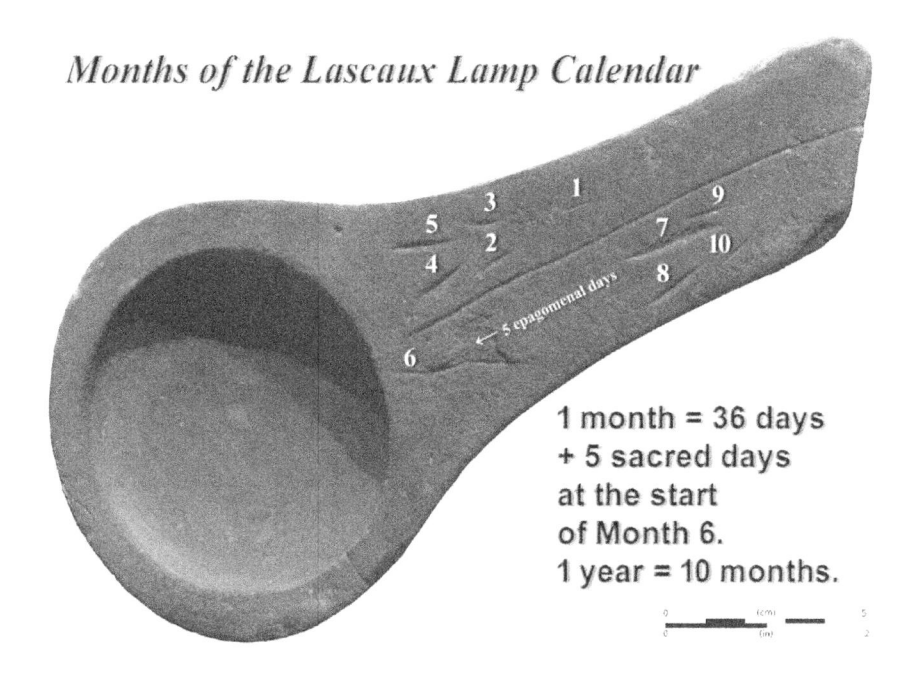

*Months of the Lascaux Lamp Calendar*

1 month = 36 days
+ 5 sacred days
at the start
of Month 6.
1 year = 10 months.

I would like to suggest that this artifact, beyond its pragmatic function as fire-bearer inside the cave, is in fact a calendar consisting of 10 months. The first month starts with the winter solstice, represented by the shortest line. Due to the precession of the equinoxes, about 18,000 years ago the first day of winter was in the constellation Leo—rather than in Capricorn, as it is today. As we saw, the former star pattern was depicted as a rhinoceros in the Shaft tableau. As the length of daylight increases throughout the year, the lines (i.e., months) get increasingly longer until the sixth month is reached at the summer solstice—located in the constellation Aquarius (instead of in Cancer). Aquarius visually corresponds to the horse on the opposite wall.

At that annual point the five so-called epagomenal days were celebrated, probably with various religious and social ceremonies during the longest days of summer. In this regard author Robert Temple explains the calendrical reckoning of the Akkadian and Egyptian systems. "No doubt the five 'epagomenal' days left over in order to fill out this resulting 360-day year to a 365-day year are referred to in the line: 'After defining the days of the years of (heavenly) figures,' which is again identical with the Egyptian tradition where the five left-over days are each assigned to five different gods or heavenly figures [namely, constellations] and thus defined. In Egypt these five left-over days are called 'the days upon the year.' These five days are also extremely important in Maya astronomy."[18] These sacred days "outside of time" were the high point of the year when solar potency was pronounced, fecundity of plants, animals, and humans was prodigious, and mundane existence was propitious. The late British archaeologist Brian M. Fagan describes this particular period of the calendar.

> "The masterpieces of Altamira and Lascaux, of Niaux and Trois Frères, tempt us to think of the Cro-Magnon societies of southwestern France and northern Spain as exceptually rich and unusual. But, judging from clear signs of anatomical stress in a few Cro-Magnon burials, life was not always easy, and the threat of starvation was never far away. The Cro-

Magnons enjoyed a richly symbolic social and ceremonial life during those special weeks of the year when shamans sang and danced, when age-old rituals sanctified human and animal fertility, the close relationship that always existed between Ice Age peoples and their environment."[19]

After these sacred days the year proceeds on the other side of the long line parallel to the handle, decreasing in daylight, which is represented by increasingly shorter lines. I should add that seventeen millennia ago the autumnal equinox was in Taurus, which, of course, corresponds to the painted Bull, and the vernal equinox was in Scorpius with its brightest star Antares. I previously posited that the perched Bird on a staff represents Sirius, which is on the opposite side of the Milky Way from Scorpius. In some ancient cultures, however, these two stars are related. As scholar George E. Lankford has stated: "The Cherokee, as might be expected of the Southeastern representatives of the Iroquoian peoples, were participants in the Path of Souls mythology. [S.] Hagar identified two 'dog stars,' Sirius and Antares, as guards of the two 'opposite points of the sky, where the Milky Way touches the horizon.'"[20] In another volume, Lankford says: "[Hagar in 1906] identified them as dogs who greet the souls at the beginning and end of the Path of Souls, the Milky Way."[21] (See Chapter 16.)

You might be asking whether or not the Upper Paleolithic people had a numerical system or any kind of rudimentary arithmetic. In fact, numbers were not necessarily needed in constructing a calendar. One 20th century American journalist-turned-paleontologist thought so when he proposed a theory for a lunar calendar. (Continued on p. 243.)

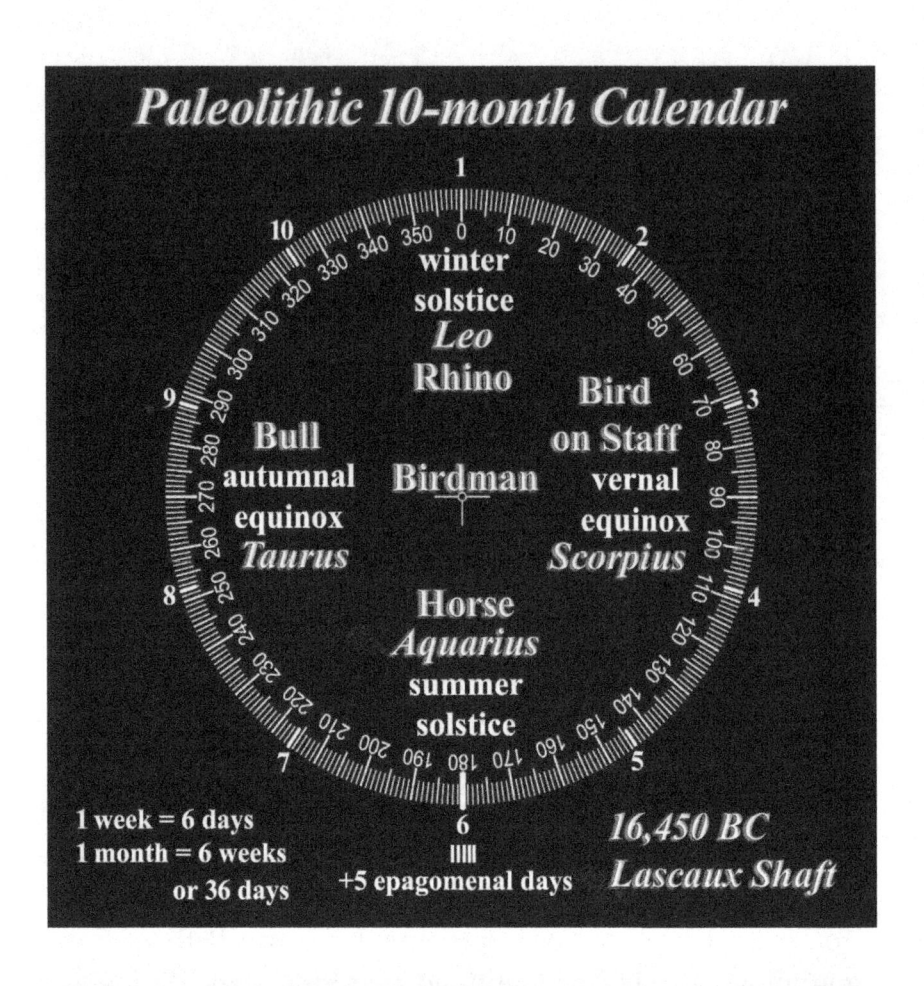

### Paleolithic 10-month Calendar

- winter solstice — *Leo* — Rhino
- Bird on Staff — vernal equinox — *Scorpius*
- Horse — *Aquarius* — summer solstice
- Bull — autumnal equinox — *Taurus*
- Birdman (center)

1 week = 6 days
1 month = 6 weeks or 36 days
6 ||||| +5 epagomenal days

**16,450 BC**
**Lascaux Shaft**

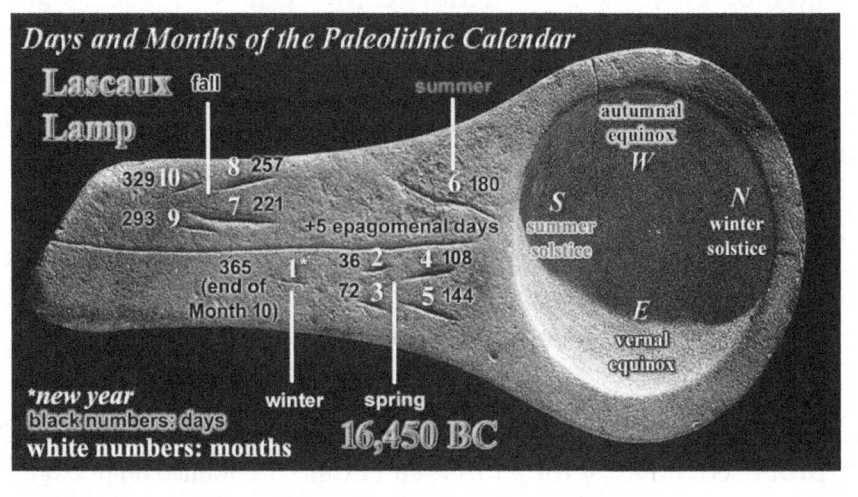

### Days and Months of the Paleolithic Calendar

**Lascaux Lamp**

- fall
- summer
- 329 10
- 293 9
- 8 257
- 7 221
- 6 180
- +5 epagomenal days
- 365 (end of Month 10) 1*
- 36 2
- 72 3
- 4 108
- 5 144
- winter
- spring

autumnal equinox — W
summer solstice — S
winter solstice — N
vernal equinox — E

*new year
black numbers: days
white numbers: months

**16,450 BC**

Alexander Marshack initially looked at an artifact from the Congo dated circa 8500 BP. Oxford-trained scholar Richard Rudgley summarizes this finding that eventually led to Marshack's influential oeuvre. "On a hunch he felt that this modest artifact from the Stone Age might be 'time-factored'; he compared the groupings of marks on the bone with the lunar phases and found them to be a pretty good match. He soon realized that this bone artifact could be evidence for a lunar notation that was non-arithmetical, in that the days were not counted and calculated arithmetically but were recognized by their positioning into sets with breaks or special markings which indicated phases of the lunar cycle."[22]

By the same token, the Lascaux lamp can be considered a 10-month calendar if cheirometrics (Greek *cheiro-* "hand," Greek *metron*, "measure") are taken into account. In other words, we return to the theme I will deal with exclusively in the next chapter: using 10 fingers to figure out a problem. I am assuming that the artists were predominantly left-handed (and right-brained), so we start with this hand.

*Reckoning Days in One Month:* Each week begins and ends with the same digit except on opposite hands. In addition, the first and last weeks have the same configuration of digits. Thus, each month has 6 X 6 days = 36 days.

*Reckoning Ten Months:* Similar to lunar waxing and waning throughout a month, there is also a solar waxing and waning (length of daylight) throughout the year. The first month begins with the winter solstice (shortest day); thereafter the days lengthen until the summer solstice (longest day), when daylight again starts to decrease. However, the five sacred days "out of time" are set aside for religious rituals and/or weddings. 10 months, 36 days each = 360 + 5 = 365 days = 1 year.

## *Cheirometrics of Reckoning 36 Days = One Month*

*Week One*
    Start with left hand: thumb-index-middle-ring-pinkie,
        continue with right hand: thumb.
*Week Two*
    Start with right hand: index-middle-ring-pinkie,
        continue with left hand: thumb-index.
*Week Three*
    Start with left hand: middle-ring-pinkie,
        continue with right hand: thumb-index-middle.
*Week Four*
    Start with right hand: ring-pinkie,
        continue with left hand: thumb-index-middle-ring.
*Week Five*
Start with left hand: pinkie,
        continue with right hand: thumb-index-middle-ring-pinkie.
*Week Six*
    Start with left hand: thumb-index-middle-ring-pinkie,
        continue with right hand: thumb.

## *Cheirometrics of Reckoning Ten Months = One Year*

### Winter Phratry

*Month One*    Start with left hand: thumb (shortest digit—winter solstice).
*Month Two*    Continue with left hand: pinkie.
*Month Three* Continue with left hand: index (or ring—which ever is shorter).
*Month Four* Continue with left hand: ring (or index—which ever is longer).
*Month Five*    Continue with left hand middle.

### Summer Phratry

*Month Six*    Continue with right hand: middle (longest digit—summer solstice).

*+ Five Epagomenal Days*
   Right-hand metacarpal knuckles: middle-thumb-pinkie-index-ring.

*Month Seven* Continue with right hand: ring.
*Month Eight* Continue with right hand: index.
*Month Nine* Continue with right hand: pinkie.
*Month Ten*    Continue with right hand: thumb.

### Birdman or Minotaur?

As we saw in the previous chapter, the Birdman motif can have either a positive or a negative connotation, depending on the mythological traditions of the particular culture. In any case, it is a potent archetype throughout the world and in every period of history or prehistory. At Lascaux the ichthyphallic Birdman and the Bison may both be wounded, and as a result are in the process of jointly making their transition to the afterlife/celestial realm, assisted by the spirit-helper of the bird-on-the-staff. Bovine and bird could possibly signify the dual nature of life: physical and mental, body and soul, blind Eros and visionary Psyche. Despite the wounded state of the bull, it nonetheless has tremendous power over Birdman, who some have seen as fainting or falling. On the other hand, Birdman could more likely be conceptualized as *rising* from the cleft at the base of the tableau, draw by the stellar power of Bull, just like Orion rises from the underworld and becomes visible at the horizon after Taurus has ascended.

Some researchers of the Lascaux panel interpret the dual figures as the First Man and the Primordial Bull of the cosmogony. In the Zoroastrian tradition the deaths of both the Primal Man named Gayomart and the Primal Bull by the evil demiurge Ahriman assures the fertility of life on the earth.[23] According to esoteric author Barbara Hand Clow, "Many scholars believe that this painting is the death of the divine twin when the world was created… because twin kingship is a core shamanic archetype in world mythology."[24] In the first epoch as well as in all succeeding ones, "kingship" was considered to be kinship. However, in this case the twins were not two identical humans but a *twining* of two strands: Birdman and Bull. The Indo-

European peoples believed that in the Golden Age the divine regal twins were born.

The name of the supreme Persian ruler Yima (Sanskrit version = Yama and Norse version = Ymir) is derived from the word *yemo*, which literally means "twin." (As previously mentioned, a possible correlation to the constellation Gemini, the Twins, is located on the Lascaux panel.) According to the scholars Giorgio de Santillana and Hertha von Dechend, the ruler of the first peaceful age that the Persian *Avesta* identifies as Yima was also called Saturnus and Kronos in Latin and Greek respectively.[25] As previously noted, Francis Huxley in turn makes a direct correlation between Saturn and the constellation Orion. "For the Egyptians Orion was associated with Horus and the soul of Osiris; in the Hindu Brahmanas he is seen as Prajapati in the form of a stag; several nations in the Middle East refer to him as the Giant, or the hunter Nimrod mighty before the Lord; and he was Saturnus to the Romans."[26] In the Egyptian case, the soul of Osiris was located in Orion, and thus the former's son, the falcon-headed Horus, was also implicated in the genealogical lineage.

Yima was commanded by the supreme deity Ahura Mazda (or Ohrmazd, who was frequently depicted with wings and tail-feathers) to build a subterranean stronghold called a *var*. In some ways Yima parallels the biblical Noah, filling his underground fortress with sundry species of plants and animals. The threat, however, is not from flood but from "vehement destroying frost."[27] We recall that during the time the Lascaux paintings were created (circa 19,000 BP – 16,500 BP), much of the world was locked in the Last Glacial Maximum of the Ice Age. In essence, the underworld cavern system of Lascaux was a refuge from the harsh elements and a sanctuary that parallels the Persian *var*.

The late anthropologist Dr. Felicitas D. Goodman studied the ancient technique of assuming various physical postures in order to initiate a trance or altered state of consciousness. In one experiment she re-created (what she determined to be) the 37-degree angle of the Lascaux Birdman to generate physiological-psychological shamanic trances that led to an ecstatic transition from secular to sacred.

> "In other words, the posture prompted such excitation to arise that in the perception of the participants, a flow of energy was churned, the course of which then became controlled, converging on the genitals; hence, perhaps the erection of the Lascaux shaman. From there it started streaming up through the body and into the head, and then, as the astounded participants told so graphically, 'I was being squeezed out through my head,' or 'this thing was coming out as an exact duplicate of myself,' and "I came out, flying about in the blue.' The agreement with countless tales from around the world was evident. In fact, the conclusion was inescapable: We had rediscovered the ancient art of embarking on a spirit journey."[28]

This sounds very much like the serpentine *kundalini* energy piercing through successive chakras to exit the top of the skull and merge with the ultimate cosmic Source. (See Chapter 20, present volume.) In fact, Goodman suggests this precise possibility. "The bodily aspects correspond roughly to the thoracic, abdominal, and pelvic plexuses of Western anatomical science, together with the optic assemblage and the brain. I conjectured that perhaps by the postures, my subjects were activating various combinations of chakras, creating, in fact, a different altered state of consciousness for each posture."[29]

The specific angle of the Birdman apparently has universal significance. Ms. Clow goes on to describe Goodman's work as founder of the Cuyamungue Institute in Santa Fe, New Mexico.

> "Anthropologist Felicitas Goodman was intrigued by the angle of First Man as well as the odd position of his arms, and she thought it could be a ritual posture. She compared it with a similar Dynastic depiction of Osiris with the same angle and arm positions, which depicts Osiris rising toward the heavens, most likely to Orion. Goodman also links this painting with divine twinship mythology, and by linking the Lascaux painting with Dynastic Egypt through posture analysis, she spans *12,000 years and links the prediluvial* [i.e., antediluvian] *world with Dynastic Egypt.* Osiris was dismembered by his twin brother, Seth; he was put back together again by Isis so he could procreate and ascend; and his son, Horus, is bird-headed."[30]

The drawing on the next page shows ichthyphallic Osiris (Orion) reclining at an angle similar to that of the Lascaux Birdman. At the position where the Lascaux Taurus bull is located, we see in this case the sun-god Ra near the tip of the phallus, as well as the scarab that moves the sun across the sky on the ecliptic.

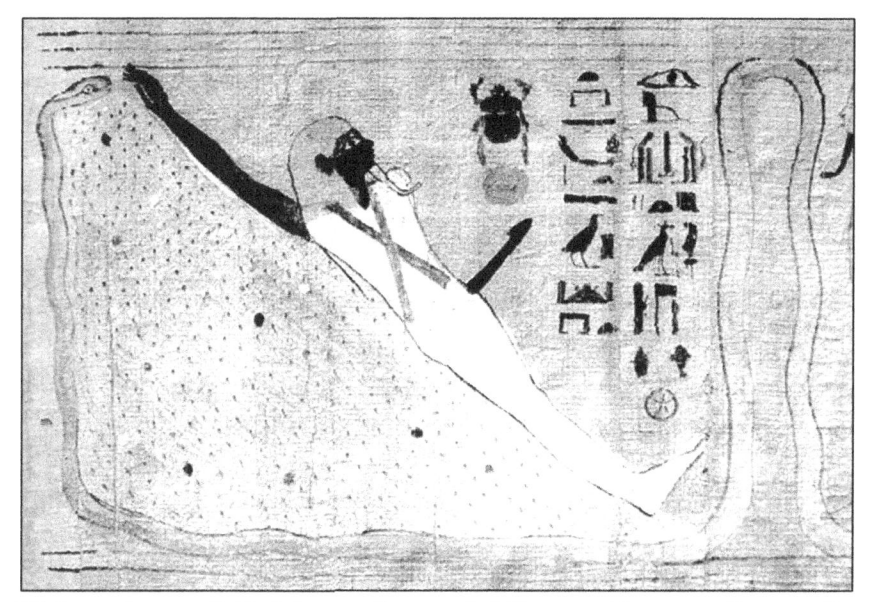

Either the god Osiris or the god Min, resting on the earth surrounded by a world-serpent, papyrus, Egyptian Museum, Cairo. It is also found in the tomb of Ramesses.

On the other hand, this figure may represent Min, the black deity of procreation in men, beasts, and plants. He was also god of rain, and was associated with the white bull—his shrine being crowned with bullhorns. The harvest festival, "Festival of the Stairs of Min," consecrated Min's center of creative power at the Primeval Mound, or the *axis mundi* of the cosmogony. This festival concluded with four birds being released to the cardinal directions. Min was thought to be the son of Osiris, thereby assuming an alternate of the falcon-headed Horus—analogue to the Shaft's bird-on-a-staff.[31]

In describing the Egyptian cosmology, Plutarch states: "...their souls shine in heaven as stars; and that of Isis so called by the Greeks the *Dog-star*, but by the Egyptians *Sothis*; that of Horus, Orion..."[32] Like father, like son.

Poet Clayton Eschleman, who experienced firsthand a number of the painted caves of the Dordogne region, writes about the somatic-psychic condition of their artists. "I felt I was witnessing the result of the crisis of paleolithic separating the animal out of their thus-to-be human heads, and that what we call 'the underworld' has, as its impulse, such a catastrophe behind it. Which is to say that Eden, which most people regard as the primordial image, from the viewpoint of the paleolithic art is the end of a truly primordial condition in which what is human and what is animal are bound together. It is possible to follow their separation as it is recorded in imagery."[33] In other words, paradise lost, which subsequently initiates the enduring human condition summed up by the title of Barbara Hand Clow's book, *Catastrophobia*. Thereafter, the therianthropes are severed: the *theri-* "beast" divided from the *anthrope* "human." In regard to the Lascaux panel, the human is removed from both the avian and the bovine.

Looking back 17 millennia or more, we are confronted with a numinous mindscape at the crucial point of this schism, or just before it. Joseph Campbell remarks on the non-naturalistic character of the animals that populate the labyrinthine passageways of the caverns—despite their anatomically correct renditions. "Such, then, were the animals selected by the Paleolithic master artists from the bounty of their environment for depiction in the galleries of their subterranean corridors and chambers, as being in some way significant of a *mystic dimension* [italics added] of their landscape perceived by the eye of the mind, not the eyes of the physical look of things." He concludes: "...the magnificently conceived grotto of Lascaux... is, namely, of an ordered system of metaphorical reflections preserved from an age beyond our horizon of time in the pictorial script of this truly amazing Stone Age testament. It is certainly not a mere mindless arrangement of accurately observed animal forms, expertly delineated by a school of accomplished artists striving for decorative optical effects. The sense of an intelligible metaphorical statement is incontestable."[34]

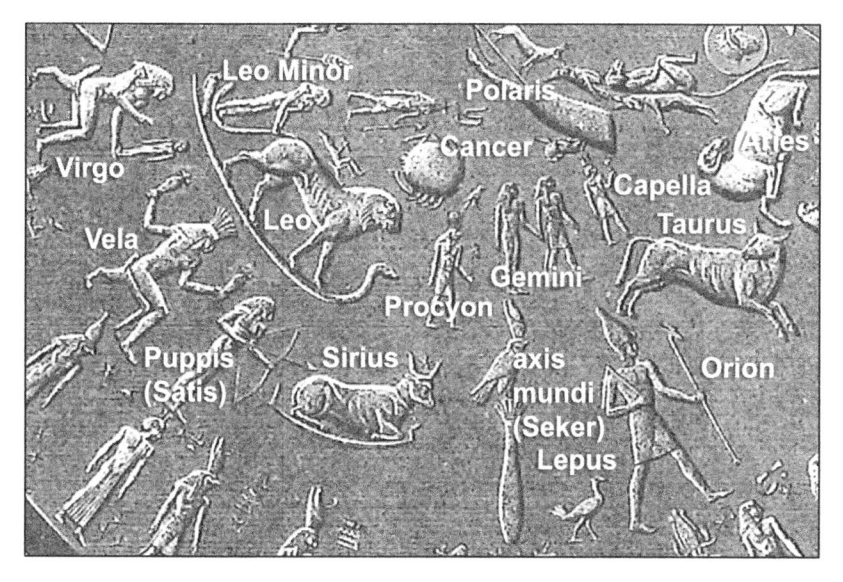

Drawing of a portion of the round Dendera Zodiac, circa 50 BC. Osiris/Orion holds a staff much like the one the Lascaux Birdman has dropped. The bird-on-the-staff is depicted as Horus, not Isis/Sirius, who is depicted as the cow Hathor behind the vertical *axis mundi*.

The bird-on-the staff in the Lascaux scenario is not only the Axis (see Chapter 9) but also the solar-crowned vernal equinox leading to the galactic center in Scorpius at the opposite end of the Path of Souls. In shamanistic terms, it is the Paleolithic magic wand that would later metamorphose into the wingéd caduceus of Hermes—his spiritual DNA.

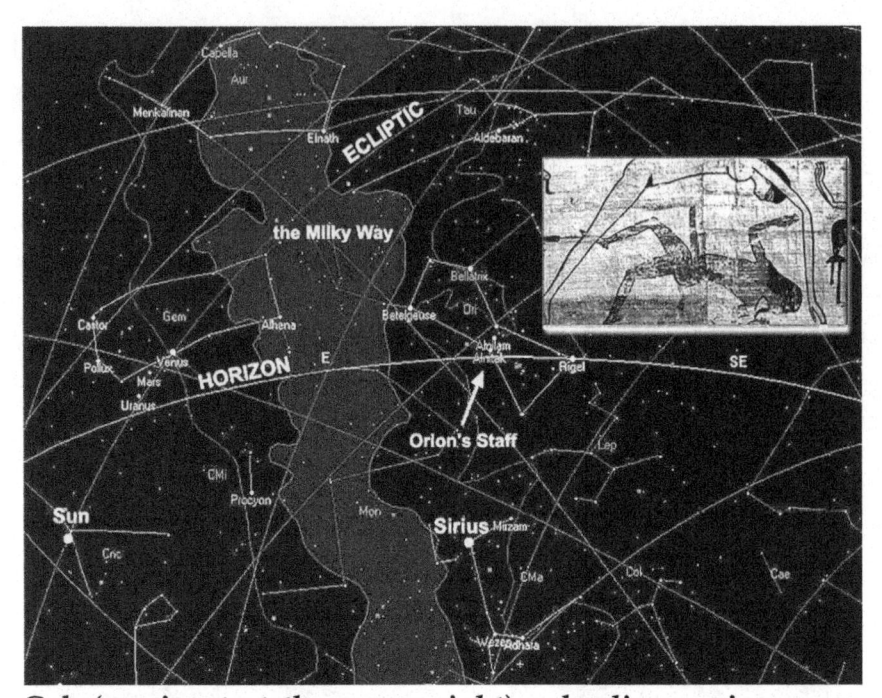

Geb (see inset at the upper-right), who lies supine upon the earth and whose green body represents vegetation, is also known as the father of the gods. He is usually portrayed as ithyphallic, while the goddess Nut—metaphorically, the Milky Way—arches above him with star-seed glistening on her breasts, belly, and thighs. The union of Geb and Nut, earth and sky, produces the brothers Osiris (Orion) and Seth, as well as the sisters/wives Isis and Nephthys. In this mythological nexus, Geb is conflated with Osiris, Nut with Isis. A celestial layer of further complexity shows Osiris associated with Sah/Orion and Isis with Sirius. Most appellations for Orion have a masculine connotation, and the three stars in a line are specifically called "Jacob's Rod," a reference to the virile forefather of the biblical twelve tribes of Israel. "Prepare a path for me, O you who are at peace; see, I enter into the Netherworld, I open up the beautiful West, I make firm the staff of Orion..."[35]

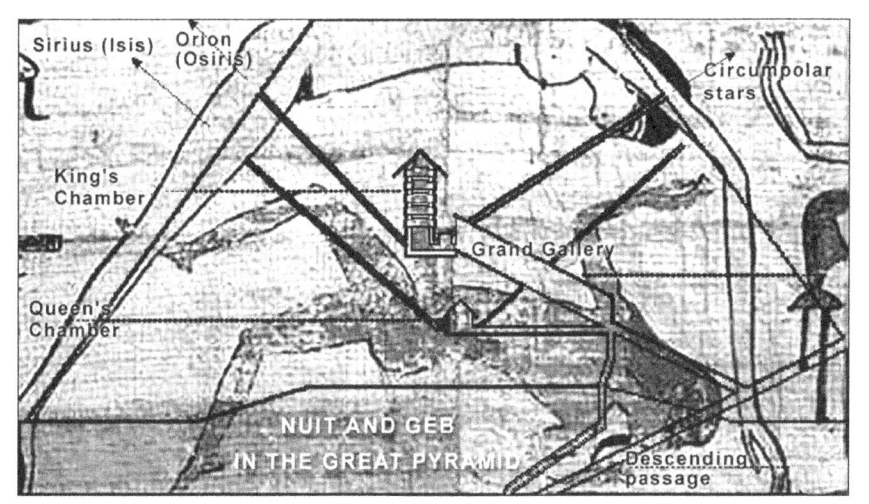

When superimposed upon Nut and Geb, the proportions of the Great Pyramid conform to the Sky-Earth mating.

This mystical dimension of which Campbell speaks undoubtedly included the sky realm with its myriad stellar portals and wormhole bridges. The Birdman of Lascaux, along with all the other Birdmen of the Earth's diverse cultures and histories, once served as shamanic intercessors between the chthonic, terrestrial, and celestial planes linked by the *axis mundi*, or vertical World Tree. As scholar Robert E. Ryan, Ph.D., eloquently and summarily tells us in regard to the shaman's staff:

> "Undertanding its relationship to the World Tree symbolism, we can see that it precisely complements the symbolism inhering in the structure of the cave as the portal to the Otherworld, expressed by the revelation of symbols of ascent paradoxically present in the cave depths. We can now perceive that all the symbols in the Shaft at Lascaux converge upon the bird-topped scepter, understood as the

symbolic equivalent to the World Tree; it is another incarnation of the archetypal revelation of symbols of trance ascent within the cave of initiation. The Shaft itself, the bird, soul flight or trance, the bird costume of the entranced shaman, his erect penis, the slain bison, and the 'animals of eternity' englobing the whole scene form a coherent grammar of universal symbols with which we are now familiar. Properly understood, they harmonize with and unify a larger context of Upper Paleolithic symbolism. We can see them as essential forms of the individual soul's expression of the cosmic source, encountered through its archetypal forms within the human mind. In this symbolism the heavens touch us from within, just as they have touched and awakened human beings since they first cast the forms of epiphany upon the blank walls of the Paleolithic caves."[36]

Now, for the most part, we can only gaze wistfully as skylark or vulture ascends to become a black dot in the infinite blue, while gravity and mortality intersect in the grave of our age. And Hieronymous Bosch's naked mansion glimpsed at the start of the preceding chapter is but a short subway stop from the blind ashes of our concentration camps' Holocaust. Again, the poet Clayton Eschleman:

> "Bird spirit flew into Apollo—
> animal spirit appeared in Dis.
> What was sky and earth became life and death,
> or hell on earth and psychic depth,
> and I wonder: how has Hades been affected by Dachau?

In the cold of deepest bowels, does a stained
fluid drip? Does pure loss now have an odor
of cremation, a fleshy hollow feel
of human soul infiltrating those realms
Hades had reserved for animals?
Are there archai, still spotted with
this evening's russets, stringing and quartering
an anthrobestial compost? Or are there zeros,
of which we are increasingly composed,
folding out the quick of animal life?
Is that why these outlines, these Hadic kin,
take on mountainous strength,
moving through the shadows of these days?"[37]

Movie poster for "Birdman," 2014, Michael Keaton.

# *Part III*
# The Mudras[1] of Immortality

# Chapter 16
## *Grasping the Hand Constellation of the Mississippians*

**High Five**

One of the most humiliating memories from my early childhood involved first grade arithmetics class, when the teacher asked me what the sum of 9 + 8 was. I had neglected to memorize my addition tables, so I began to count via my digits. The whole class erupted: "Miss Pacek, he's using his fingers!" Apparently the only right answer would have been in my head.

Yet what a miraculous appendage is the hand! It allowed us as hominins to descend from the forest and range across the savanna in search of prey, and in the process discover distant vistas to explore. It allowed for the production and manipulation of tools, which guaranteed our survival as a species. With this most primitive of computers we could calculate the number of various objects or people, which ultimately led to the invention of the decimal and (using our feet) vigesimal numeral systems in the physical world. In more metaphysical realms the science of yogic *mudras* seeks to understand how spiritual energy and consciousness is directed within the body.

Even the most basic semiotics of the hand are manifold. The open palm of an upraised arm can signal a greeting, yet an open hand on an outstretched arm means "Stop!" Two upraised hands can signify prayer or supplication or surrender—the latter either to an enemy or to God. An extended open palm suggests something a person wants to show or reveal. A closed fist, of course, is shorthand for resistance or violence but two raised fists may point to victory. The unmistakable middle finger salute needs no explanation, whereas the partially closed fist with the index and pinkie fingers extended is universally beloved by heavy metal rockers as the "horns of the Devil." The hippies believed that the index and middle fingers splayed would bring world peace, while the same two fingers slightly curved traditionally signified a blessing, as seen in Leonardo da Vinci's painting "Salvator Mundi." A thumb stuck between the forefinger and middle finger with the other fingers closed is called a *figga* or *fico* and is said to represent male genitalia, but the icon of an upraised thumb and closed fingers is simply "okay." To give someone a hand may mean either applause or help. And who can forget Mr. Spock's "Live long and prosper" hand signal?

Many cultures across the globe have incorporated this simple yet potent sigil in their legends, iconography, and artifacts. According to the esteemed scholar E. A. Wallis Budge: "In all ages and among all peoples, the hand has been a symbol of strength and power, and a picture of it has been regarded as a representation of God. In the Egyptian text of the *Book of Gates* on the alabaster coffin of Seti I… the 'Great Hand' means the supreme Power which rules heaven and earth."[1] Puerto Rican author Migene González-Wippler additionally comments on the Western history of the hand: "One of the most miraculous prayers of the Catholic Church is dedicated to the All Powerful Hand, which is depicted as a gigantic hand in the clouds. Raising the hand is regarded as an invocation to God, and is commonly used as an oath in Europe and in the United States. During court procedures and during investiture ceremonies, one hand is placed on the Bible, while the other is raised in oath. This custom originated in Western Asia."[2]

In my previous book *Journey of the Serpent People*, I mentioned the hand-eye motif found in the Berber culture of North Africa—the so-called *hamsa* (or *khamsa*) amulet, also known as the "Hand of Fatima," daughter of the Prophet Muhammud. Author Linda Heaphy describes its historical roots.

> "The first known use of the symbol can be traced to the civilization of Phoenicia that spread across the Mediterranean between 1550 – 330 BCE. The Phoenicians used an image of the hand to represent Tanit, patron goddess of their capital city Carthage and controller of the lunar cycle. With time, her hand became a protective amulet in its own right and was used to ward off the evil eye, one of the oldest manifestations of human fear. The symbol was adopted by the ancient Sephardic Jewish community of the Iberian Peninsula, who named it the Hand of Miriam after the sister of the biblical Moses and Aaron and associated it with the number five (*hamesh* in Hebrew) to represent the five books of the Torah. It also symbolizes the fifth letter of the Hebrew alphabet, 'Het', which represents one of God's holy names, and further reminds Jews to use their five senses when praising God."[3]

My book also referenced the Mississippian culture of southeastern United States (1000 – 1400 AD) and its incisement of the all-seeing Eye-in-the-Hand into a slate palette at Moundville, Alabama.[4] Many of the artifacts unearthed at this site also depict this symbology.

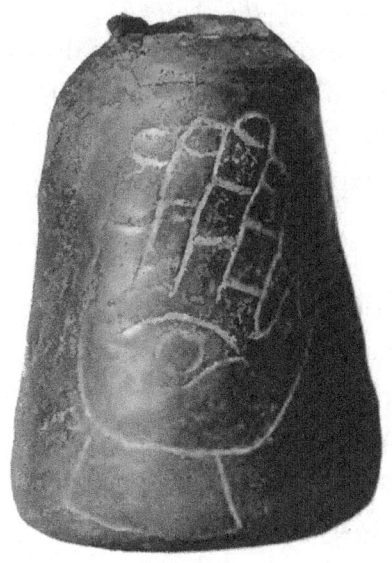

FIG. 173.—Vessel No. 2. Field west of Mound R. (Diameter 3.75 inches.)

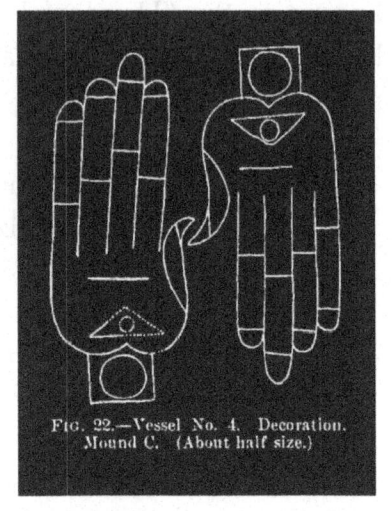

FIG. 22.—Vessel No. 4. Decoration. Mound C. (About half size.)

**Left: Ceramic pot (top broken off). Right: Eye in a pyramid.**

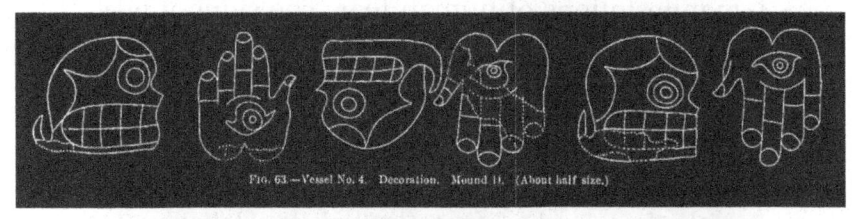

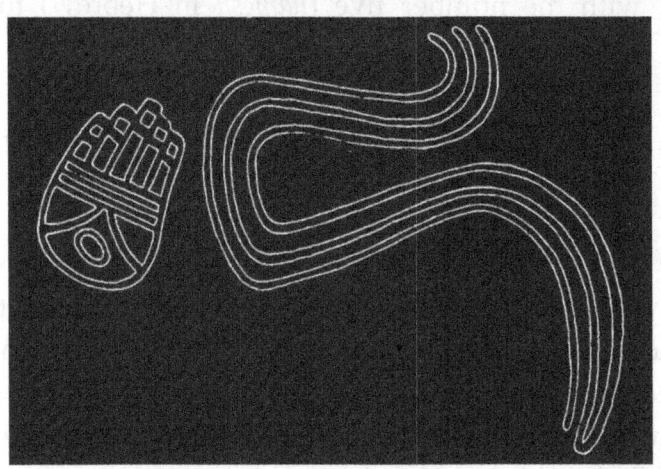

FIG. 63.—Vessel No. 4. Decoration. Mound H. (About half size.)

**Stylized hand-eye (or -ogee) motif on ceramic vessel.**

262

Left: Chimerical bird. Right: two hand-eyes and spindle
(or UFO?). Center: Twisted *axis mundi* with two skulls.

FIG. 152.—Vessel No. 17. Decoration. Ridge north of Mound R. (About half size.)

Plumed and horned rattlesnake with forked eye, like the Hopi
and the Maya. It possibly represents the constellation Scorpius.[5]

FIG. 9.—Vessel No. 71. Ground south of Mound D. (Height 6.7 inches.)

FIG. 86.—Eagle's head, from pipe, as it would appear on a flat surface. (Full size.)

Above: Ceramic bottle, hand-eye, eagle's head with forked eye, Moundville, Alabama.

Below: Clarence B. Moore: "Several experts who have charge of eagles in captivity inform us that under certain circumstances the "hump" on the tongue is visible on the living bird. Possibly the aboriginal artist at Moundville was familiar with the characteristics of eagles through the possession there of captive birds—a custom observed among the Zuñi of New Mexico at the present time."[6] This custom is also still followed by the Hopi to this day.

Among the ancient tribes of the Southeast, the Ohio Valley, and the Great Plains, the iconography of the hand-eye motif evinced a remarkable continuity of meaning. The various accounts collectively conceptualize this symbol as a doorway or portal in the heavens. However, it is an inter-dimensional passageway that no physical being may access. The hand-eye is frequently found in a funereal context with burial accouterments or artifacts (such as the ones on the preceeding two pages), so we may assume that a journey of the soul through the afterlife realm is involved. Moreover, the specific celestial location is consistently identified in most legends as the constellation Orion.

In his most recent book *America Before*, Graham Hancock has written extensively about the hand-eye motif in connection with the Moundville site. "There are in fact dozens of such accounts specifically referencing an ancient Native American constellation in which the stars of Orion's belt form the wrist of the hand—sometimes said to belong to a great warrior chieftain and sometimes to a malevolent celestial being called 'Long Arm,' who used it in an attempt to block a portal between earth and sky but lost the hand when it was chopped off by a human hero."[7]

In their 2014 book *Path of Souls—The Native American Death Journey*, Gregory Little and Andrew Collins describe the scenario of the soul's journey to the spirit world via Orion and the ghost road of the Milky Way. Collins from his Foreward:

> "Among a large number of Native American tribes Orion was seen as a severed hand (the constellation's three belt stars symbolizing the severed wrist), hanging downward, with what looks like an eye symbol in its palm. Through

this eye, which is in fact an ogee (a split or opening in the fabric of physical reality), the soul of the deceased was able to gain access to the Milky Way after an initial journey that took it west to the edge of the earth's disk. Here it waited until a specific moment when the 'Hand' was seen low in the western sky before dawn. The soul then must make a leap of faith to a star portal symbolized by the ogee in the hand constellation, identified with the fuzzy nebula called Messier 42 (M42) located in the 'sword' of Orion. Once on the Milky Way, the soul uses it like a celestial highway to reach its place of destination in the afterlife."[8]

Little further explains:

"As the Hand constellation sets into the horizon in the winter, the Milky Way is seen as a horizontal wall that falls below the horizon in the west not long after the Hand disappears. The belief was that if the soul made the leap to the portal successfully, it would then transition to the falling Milky Way to start its journey on the Path of Souls. The movement from the ogee to the Path occurred because the Milky Way sank below the horizon immediately after the Hand. Once a soul had successfully entered the ogee in the sky and safely reached the Milky Way, it could remain on the 'path' during the trip through the underworld to the south."[9]

In their legend "The Chief Who Lost His Arm," the Lakota (Sioux) also recognized Orion as the severed hand constellation they called *Nape*. This tribe's territory once included western South Dakota, southwestern North Dakota, southeastern Montana, eastern Wyoming, and northwestern Nebraska—the Sacred Center of which was the Black Hills, known as the "Heart of Everything That Is" (*Wamaka Ognaka y Cante*). Because the chief refused to engage in the traditional self-sacrifice of blood during the annual Sun Dance ceremony held during the summer solstice, the avian *Wakinyans*, or Thunder Bird, Thunder Beings (celestially represented by the circumpolar constellation Draco), tore off his arm and hid it. According to the late Ronald Goodman, professor at Sinte Gleska College on the Rosebud Reservation:

> "The Lakota undertand the stars to be 'the holy breath of God,' the *woniya* of *Wakan Tanka*. Thus, the Lakota constellations in the night sky represent sacred utterances—holy speech, whose specific meanings are transmitted through stories and ceremonies in the oral tradition. The Lakota interpret the annual disappearance from the night sky of the Hand constellation in the spring as a divine signal of the impending loss of fertility. Therefore, the disappearance of 'the Hand' (which represents the arm of the chief in this story) is also a summons to the whole Lakota nation. In the context of Lakota culture it means a willing sacrifice of blood is necessary. The annual Sun Dance ritual, where Lakota men and women shed their blood, enables the Lakota to

participate in the cosmic renewal of life; their generosity stands in contrast to that of the Chief's selfishness."[10]

The Lakota phrase *Wangi Ta Cangu*, literally "the road of the spirits," refers to the Milky Way—the Path of Souls.[11] As Graham Hancock observes: "The Milky Way, the connection with Orion, the perilous afterlife journey of the soul, and the notion of creating an image or copy of the realm of the dead on the ground were all genuinely present in the Mississippian religion, just as they were in the ancient Egyptian religion. No one familiar with with the Pyramid Texts and the Book of the Dead could fail to notice those obvious resemblances."[12] For comparisons between the two cultures and cosmologies, I refer the reader to his book cited above, which profusely details the parallels. George E. Lankford, Ethnohistorian and Professor Emeritus at Lyon College, likewise finds correlations between the New World and the Old, as he stresses the underlying teleology in archaeoastronomy.

> "The Path of Souls concept, however, is much more important than a mere astronomical image or label, for any such designation immediately opens the door to the crucial human category of mortuary beliefs. No society is cavalier about the fate of souls after death, and any cultural identification of the Milky Way as the path they walk should be taken as a serious statement. It may be that such a belief is the basis of a complex guidebook similar to the Egyptian "Book of the Dead." Native Americans, like the Egyptians,

needed to talk about their mortuary beliefs in order to prepare everyone for the inevitable journey, and the Path of Souls would have to be an important part of such a body of lore."[13]

Across the spectrum of Native American legends, Orion is portrayed as a selfish chief who betrays the traditional norms, responsibilities, and duties of his tribe, thereby losing a limb in the process. This is in keeping with Orion's global character: fierce, brutal, impious, ruthless, etc. Per example, we need only to remember the Greek myth regarding his rape of Merope, daughter of King Oenopion of Chios. For this misdeed the king got him drunk and had him blinded.[14] However, in the Native American version, Orion's hand reappears in the firmament with the surreal ability of vision. But this Eye in the Sky is also a window through which the soul must pass in order to attain the Trail of Wraiths in its afterlife journey southward toward the center of the galaxy.

**Ceramic bottle with ogee, or inter-dimensional portal.**[15]

This pendant discovered at a Moundville, Alabama burial site represents a celestial symbology in keeping with much Mississippian mythic lore.[16] At its bottom we see the hand-eye motif, which has been interpreted as the nebula in Orion (with its black hole), and the wrist of the severed hand as the constellation's belt. Author Gregory Little speculates that the split is the Dark Rift in the Milky Way, and the six-pointed star and ogee are Deneb in Cygnus.[17] However, if this were the case, the star would actually be located next to the hand and the split would be at the top, the way these stellar objects are distributed along the Milky Way. I contend the star instead represents either Antares in Scorpius or the black hole at the galactic core.[18] The text to the right from the Egyptian Book of the Dead, "Spell for fetching a ferry boat in the sky," identifies the avian theme.

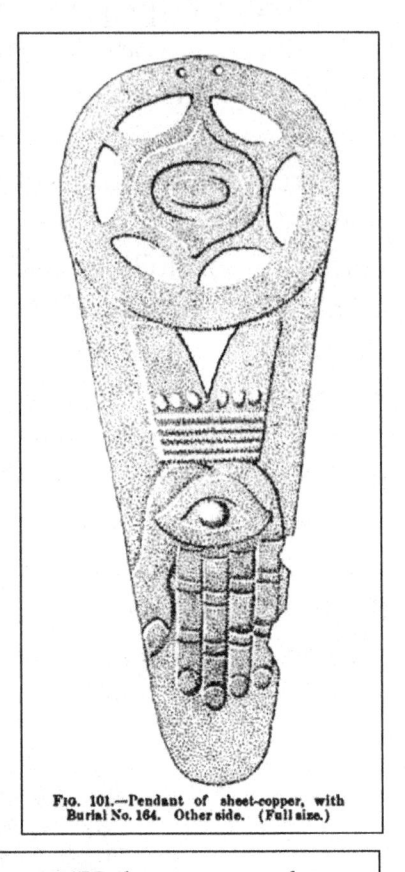

FIG. 101.—Pendant of sheet-copper, with Burial No. 164. Other side. (Full size.)

"Hail to you, you plateau which is in the sky north of the Great Waterway [the Milky Way], for whoever sees it will not die. I stand upon you, I appear as a god, I have seen you and I will not die. I stand upon you, I appear as a god, I cackle as a goose [of the north], I fly up as a falcon [of the south] upon the branches."[19]

## The Great Reed and Three Beads on a String

Like the ancient Egyptians, the Ancestral Puebloans, of which the Hopi are direct descendants, most likely saw the Milky Way as a pathway to the spirit world. 20th century ethnographer Florence Hawley Ellis comments: "The Galaxy or Milky Way is revered by all the Pueblos. On Zuni and Acoma masks and altars it is represented by a white band or a band of black and white squares or a ladder, for like the rainbow it was believed to provide a bridge from earth into the heavens, but the occasional addition of eyes and mouth indicates that it was personified like the stars as a whole which are spoken of as Night People, 'our fathers and mothers,' and 'little priests.'"[20] The checkerboard pattern is considered to be one of celestial roadways of the Hopi Warrior Twins.[21] By using a planisphere, one can see the nightly and seasonal revolving of the Milky Way around the polar axis like a vinyl record turning around a spindle.

Timing is everything. The Hopi consider of utmost importance the period between the winter solstice and the month after the summer solstice. This ceremonially is designated as the *katsina* season. The first spirit messengers signal the beginning of the new year upon their arrival in December from the San Francisco Peaks—highest mountains in Arizona—to the Hopi Mesas. Previous to this time the *taawamongwi*, or sun-watcher, has been gauging the rising and setting sun upon the horizons. The sun god *Taawa* at last reaches his Winter House located at the farthest southern position. As I have written in previous books, the conclusion of *Soyal*, the nine-day winter solstice ceremony, begins as Orion is viewed shortly after midnight on December 21st in the overhead hatchway of the semi-subterranean *kiva* (communal prayer chamber). Thus, this solar ritual is synchronized by *Hotòmqam*, literally "strung-up" or "beads on a string,"[22]—either the belt stars or Betelguese, Alnilam, and Rigel—in what the Hopi consider as their most significant constellation. In fact, the Hopi recognize very few constellations in the night sky. In this regard Richard Maitland Bradfield, scholar of the Hopi, writes about remarks made by early 20th century ethnographer A. L. Kroeber: "The Milky Way (*soñwuka*, in Hopi) crosses the meridian about an hour behind Orion, and is the only constellation (galaxy), apart from Orion and the Pleiades, named by the Hopi."[23] Archaeo-astronomer Ray A. Williamson confirms Orion's paramount psycho-spiritual connotation. "A very important winter constellation for the historic Pueblo, Orion was very likely important for the Anasazi [Ancestral Puebloans] as well. Because it is an easily recognizable winter constellation, it today serves as a timing device for winter kiva ceremonies. When it appears above the eastern horizon, when it is overhead, and when it sets are all important milestones in the course of Hopi kiva celebrations."[24]

The three temporal positions of Orion in the heavens frame the *katsina* season: (1) midnight on winter solstice with the constellation directly overhead, (2) the heliacal setting of the stars in late spring when they descend to the underworld for a period of about 2 ½ months , and (3) the heliacal rising of the stars a few weeks after summer solstice when they remerge from the underworld and again become visible with increasing prominence as autumn progresses. According to Alph H. Secakuku, a Second Mesa Hopi of the Snake Clan, "The *katsinam* [plural of *katsina*, or kachina] are the benevolent spirit beings who live among the Hopi for a six-month period each year. They first arrive during *Soyalwimi* in December and begin to appear in great number during the *Powanmuya* ceremonial season (in February), and return to their spirit world after the Niman ceremony (in July)."[25] During the non-*katsina* season no masked dances are held, though other ceremonies occupy the ritual calendar.

In addition to the black hole at the center of the galaxy located at a distance of 26,000 light years, scientists have also recently found a probable black hole 200 times the mass of our sun in the Trapizium, four bright stars at the center of the Orion Nebula Cluster—a mere 1,300 light years away.[26] These dual black holes corroborate the theory of the early 5th century Roman philosopher Macrobius, who stated that souls ascend through the "Gate of Capricorn" to transcend the physical plane and descend to be reincarnated through the "Gate of Cancer." Because of the precession of the equinoxes caused by the slight wobble of the Earth's axis, the former gate is currently located between Scorpius and Sagittarius on one end of the Milky Way (the southern "stargate" near the galactic center), while the latter gate is found between Taurus and Gemini near Orion on the opposite end (the northern "stargate" near the galactic anticenter).

Again, the crucial time for the soul of the deceased to gain access to the galactic tunnel (the "Great Reed," as the Hopi conceive of it) is from the period after the December solstice, when Orion is at a midnight meridian, until late spring, when Orion disappears on the western horizon at sunset as he descends to the underworld. There he will reign until early July, when he reappears on earth at the eastern horizon.

The optimum window (or doorway) of opportunity for the soul is that brief period just before Orion sets, with the path of the Milky Way hovering above it and parallel to the horizon. Lankford comments:

"The portal in the Hand must be entered at the optimum time, which is a ten-minute window which occurs once each night from November 29, when the Hand vanishes into the water in the west at dawn, to April 25, when the hand sinks at dusk and is not seen again for six months. During that winter period the portal is on the horizon for a breathless few minutes each night, and the free-soul must enter at that time or be lost. Free-souls who do not make the transition remain in the west and can eventually become unhappy threats to the realm of the living."[27]

Actually, Orion is currently visible in July at dawn during its heliacal rising.[28] With the stars rising four minutes earlier each day, by the time late autumn rolls around, the rising constellation is visible in the evening, while its setting occurs just before dawn.

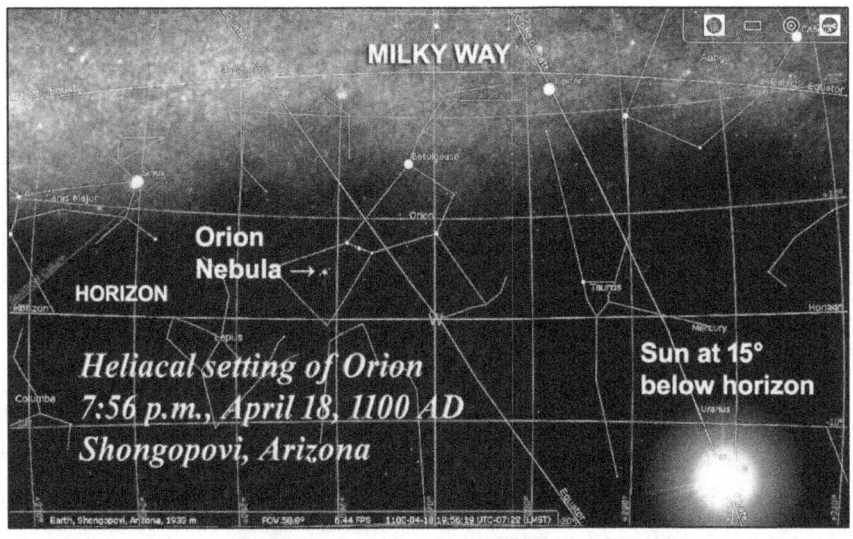

**Milky Way (emphasized) setting parallel to the horizon.**

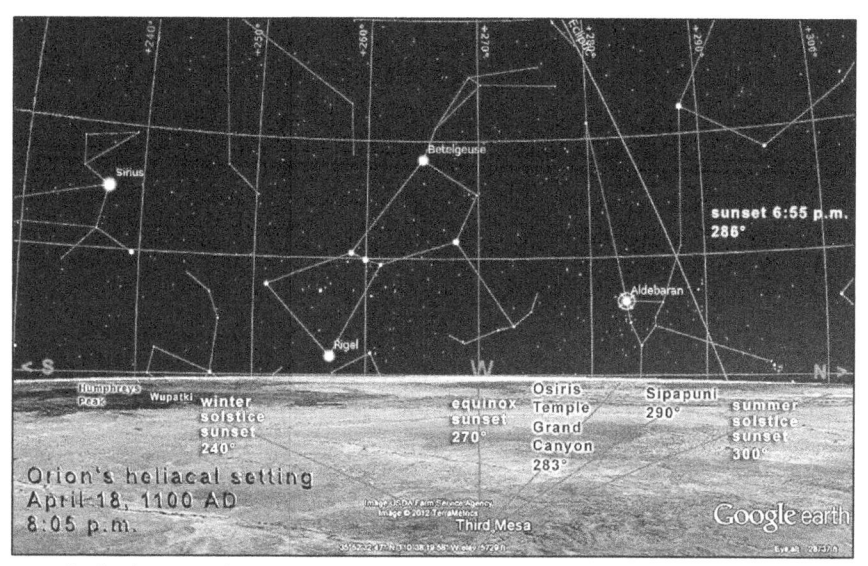

Solstice and equinox points on the western horizon.

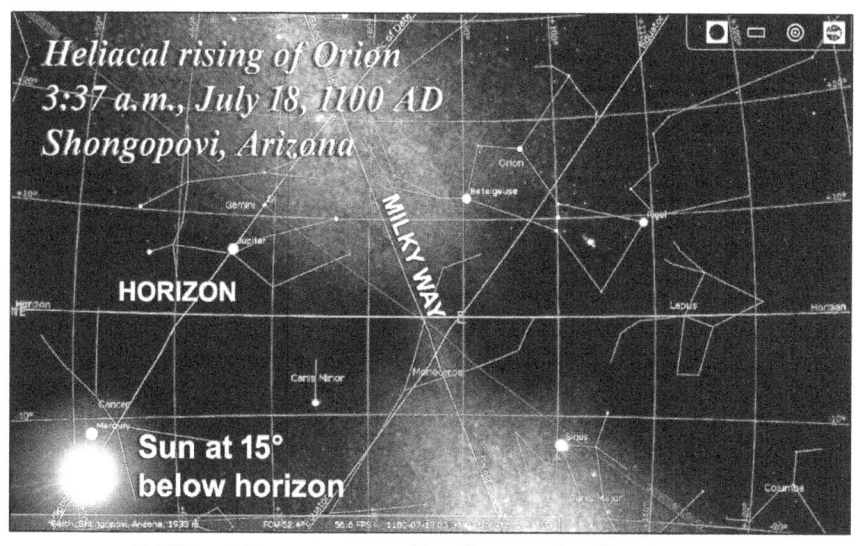

Milky Way perpendicular to the horizon.

The following chapter peers into the gloomy, chthonic-plutonic realm found in Hopi legends and shamanic experience in order to chart the native soul's afterlife fate.

# Chapter 17
# *The Hopi Underworld Journey*

### Travels and Travails in *Maski*

The Hopi term *Maski* means "the Underworld, world of the dead," literally "corpse-home" or "gray-home."[1] The god of nether realm is called Màasaw, whose name is formed by the prefix *mas-*. As I've pointed out in previous books, his skin is known to be corpse-like and gray, and his skull and facial features greatly resemble those of an extraterrestrial Grey. Be that as it may, the Hopi oral tradition is filled with accounts of a young individual, pensive and curious, who wonders what the afterlife is like. He actually makes a journey there to find out and returns to describe his harrowing experience. Variations of the legend tell of the Warrior Twins' journey to the land of the dead, and in one case an ill Hopi man has an NDE (Near Death Experience). Furthermore, these accounts parallel those of the Mississippian and Great Plains cultures outlined by scholar George E. Lankford. The tribes include Ojibwa, Menomini, Miami, Potawatomi, Sauk, Fox, Shawnee, and various Algonkians. The common elements are as follows.

1. The soul moves westward.
2. The soul must jump to the other side of the sky vault through a portal, possibly the Orion Nebula.
   Failure to achieve this "leap of faith" results in the soul plunging into the waters below.
3. The soul finds itself on the route to the final home of the dead, i.e., on the Path of Souls, or the Milky Way.
4. The soul must cross a river or an abyss.

5. The soul may be attacked by one or more dogs.
6. The path splits; at this point there is a figure (an old man or woman) who judges the soul. Sometimes an eagle is located at this fork in the trail, possibly representing Deneb in Cygnus.
7. The soul continues to the south or southwest, where lies the village of the dead.
8. At the southern end of the path the soul encounters the guardian of the dead, sometimes a serpent.

Lankford sums up the religious schema. "All together, these belief statements form a composite account of a mortuary journey that is astounding in its scope, truly a saga of the soul. With this kind of complexity of the death process, it is small wonder that it constitutes a great part of Native American religious belief."[2]

The Hopi have multiple accounts of individuals' forays into the spirit world. Some accounts describe a certain "medicine" either eaten or rubbed upon the skin that causes unconsciousness, allowing the soul to be separated from its inert body.[3]

**1.**

- "At first the young man saw nothing. Everything was dark and silent as though he were truly dead. Then he found himself walking on a trail toward the west. He passed through a vast cactus field and came to a place where the trail ended at the edge of a steep bluff. He wondered how he could go on."[4]
- "After the young man had fallen asleep he saw a path leading westward. It was the road to the Skeleton house."[5]
- "From all appearances he was dead. He became aware of how his soul was departing from his body. Before long,

his soul had completely separated. He glanced back now and saw his body lying there. He looked at it for a long while, but went on his way, for surely there was someone out there waiting for him. Quickly he descended from his house and headed in a northwesterly direction. Weightless, he was able to move along rapidly."[6]

- "So the medicine man told him to lie down on his blanket, and he covered him with an ova [shroud, bridal robe] and rubbed some kind of medicine on him. After while that boy stopped breathing, just like he was dead. But his spirit, we call it breath [*hik'si*], got up and went out of the house and started walking west on the trail."[7]

## 2.

- What follows is a rather arresting image of a solid sky at the Sun's western portal, which opens and closes to squash like a bug any unworthy soul who tries to enter. "*Tok'pela pash ani huzru*, the sky is very hard, and the sides of this cañon are vertical (reaching to the Above infinitely) and they are constantly opening and closing, and would crush anyone (unauthorized) who attempted to pass through into the house of the Sun, and the other guards are angry... When the Twins reached close to the sky, the path lay along a narrow *tur'wi* (terrace or ledge) on one side of which was a *tuh'pela* (face of a vertical cliff, a wall) and on the other a precipice, which goes sheer to the Below, the Underworld."[8]
- "There I climbed a corn-meal path about halfway up a mountain and came upon a hole like a tunnel dimly lighted. I heard a voice on the right say, 'Don't be afraid. Walk right in.' Stepping in through a fog and past the little lights, I moved along swiftly, finally came out upon a flat mesa..."[9]

### 3.

- "There was a trail, still going west, and he went along that way. He began to see a lot of dead spirits walking along real slow."[10] Because of their iniquities on earth, these spirits progress very slowly, sometimes making just one step per year. Others are forced to carry heavy loads, such as manos and metates or burden baskets filled with pebbles—the strap thin as a bowstring cutting into their foreheads. Penitents pitifully plead for water along the path, and ask souls to spit into their mouths for relief. Men and women who had led licentious lives are forced to go naked and wear necklaces made of vulvas and penises respectively. Sorcerers, murderers, and rapists are pushed into burning pits where their incinerated bodies are transformed into black stinkbugs. (This infernal tormenting of sinners may be the result of a more recent Christian influence.)
- "From here the young man proceeded westward. The path led through large cactus and through many agave plants so that sometimes it could hardly be distinguished. He finally arrived at the rim of a steep bluff."[11] The thorns of the cacti may symbolize the glistening stars of the Milky Way.

### 4.

- The geography of the arid Hopi region requires that a canyon must be crossed, though sometimes reference is made to Grand Canyon with its Colorado River and Little Colorado River. A number of accounts mention a feather robe or ceremonial kilt spread out like a magic carpet, upon which the soul floats through the air across the chasm. "In time he reached the great gorge. He opened his bird cloth, laid it out on the ground and lay

down upon it. It rose into the air and carried him across the gorge, bringing him to earth on the other side."[12]
- "But hereupon the chief placed the young man's kilt on the ground, placed the young man on it, then lifted it up, and holding it over the precipice he threw it forward, whereupon the young man was slowly descending on the kilt as if he were flying with wings. When he had arrived on the ground below the bluff he put on his kilt again and proceeded."[13]
- "While he was standing there a kaletaka (warrior), an old man, a priest, came up and told him to take off his kilt and put it on the ground. He did that. The Kaletaka told him to stand on it, and he did that. Then the kilt just lifted up and floated over the canyon a ways and set him down at the bottom."[14]
- One version of the legend describes a "magic flier" as a sort of aerial craft that an *Aala* society member, or Two Horn priest, employs: "With that he too spread out something before them and instructed the boy. 'All right, climb on this thing with me. We'll use it to descend the cliff. There is no trail down to this place, so no one can go down without my aid,' he explained. The boy did as bidden and stepped on the thing after the Two Horn man. No sooner had the two climbed aboard that the thing rose off the ground. It first took them a little ways beyond the rim of the cliff, and then began its descent with both of them aboard. It was such a long cliff that it took a while to reach the ground below."[15]

## 5.

- Attack by canines does not appear to be part of the Hopi legends. One account does, however, feature a threatening human figure who attempts to thwart the soul as it passes on the road. "An old man *(wühtaka)* sat there with his back against the wall and his knees drawn up close to his chin, and when Püükoñ [Pokanghoya, the Elder Warrior Twin] was passing, the old man suddenly thrust his legs out, trying to knock him over the cliff. Püükoñ leaped backward and saved himself, and in reply to the protest of the Twins, Old Man said his legs were tired and he had thrust them out for relief."[16]

## 6.

- Most Hopi accounts record a fork or split in the Path of Souls, which may correspond to the Dark Rift in the Milky Way. "'Well, then,' two-horn priest said, 'stay for a while. You will come to understand about matters.' He pointed to where the trail divided. He said, 'One way, to the north, the trail goes to the Dark Canyon. That is where the evil ones live. There is no light there. It is always night. The other trail, to the west, is for people who have done no evil to others. Where that trail leads there is neither darkness nor sunlight, only a perpetual grayness like the first light of dawn. Go that way.'"[17]
- One of the versions takes up the Orpheus theme of a man following his deceased wife into the underworld. "The young man came to a fork in the trail. On one side, the trail led to a fiery pit, on the other side to a village. There were two guards standing at the fork. One wore a Kwakwan [One Horn] helmet, and the other wore an Aal [Two Horn] helmet with mountain sheep horns on it. They had sacred feathers hanging over their faces, and each one held a staff. They stopped the young man, said to him, 'Where are you going?' He said, 'I'm following my wife.'[18]

- "Then the boy came to the fork, and there was a One Horn and a Two Horn priest there. They saw he wasn't really dead and asked him what he wanted. He said he just wanted to see what it was like down there, to see if it was true. They said, 'No, you can't come down here till you die.' And the boy said, 'Well, as you can see, this isn't my real body, just the spirit. My real body is up at Oraibi [on Third Mesa].'"[19]
- "Together they went on and had not traveled very far when they came upon a fork in the road. There the Kwan [One Horn] man said, 'All right, this is as far as I can accompany you. But I will show you which road to choose. One of them leads directly to your destination, the other does not. Onto that road I usher all the evil ones. You must take the other road. Also, you will meet someone else who will lead you to your next station. Make sure you don't stray off this trail, though.' The Kwan man showed him the right trail to take and left him standing there."[20]
- Don Talayesva's mid-20th century autobiography states that during his Near Death Experience and subsequent shamanic journey through the underworld he climbed a large red stairway upon a promontory he calls "Mount Beautiful, the Judgment Seat" (actually named *Apòonivi*, "a sandstone crest on the southwesternmost tip of Third Mesa, also known as Oraibi Butte"). This reflects the reckoning aspect of this stage in the soul's journey. "As the ringing grew louder, I looked and saw a man climbing up the mountain from the west, dressed in a white buckskin, wearing a horn and holding a spear and a bell. It was Kwanitaka, a member of the Kwan [One Horn] or Warrior society, who watches the kivas during prayers and guards the village to keep out strangers and

let in the dead during the Wowochim [November *Wuwutsim*] ceremonies. He came up to me but did not shake hands, because he was a spirit god and doing police duty directing good people over the smooth highway and bad people over the rough road to the House of the Dead. He said, 'My boy, you are just in time, hurry! Look to the west and you will see two roads. You take the broad one, the narrow one is crooked and full of rocks, thorns, and thistles; those who take it have a hard journey. I have prepared the broad road for you. Now hurry and you will find someone to guide you."[21]

- The following account makes a distinction between the *Kwan*, or One Horn ("the strict one"), and the *Aal*, or Two Horn ("the lenient one"). The former tallies a soul's sins and condemns it, whereas the latter "…balances the good things they have done and asks for leniency." This is reminiscent of the judgement scene in the Egyptian Book of the Dead, where jackal-headed Anubis weighs the soul's heart against *Maat*, the feather of truth, after which Osiris, Lord of the Celestial *Duat* (Afterlife realm), makes the judgement. "'When they arrive here we decide which way they go. The trail to the right [viz., north] is the way to Dark Canyon and the deep pit of fire. The trail to the left [viz., south] goes to the village where the spirits live on. The Dark Canyon is without any bottom. The fires within it rage endlessly. It was from this burning pit that Masauwu [*Màasaw*] escaped in ancient times.'" As I have pointed out in my previous books, *Màasaw*, Hopi god of the dead and of fire, is analogous to the ancient Egyptian deity Osiris.[22]

- Again, from Don Talyesva's autobiographical NDE: "Somewhat frightened, I sped along to the left, reached the top of a steep mesa, and sort of floated down. Before me were the two trails passing westward through the gap of the mountains. On the right [north] was the rough narrow path, with the cactus and the coiled snakes, and filled with miserable Two-Hearts [i.e., equivocators or prevaricators] making very slow and painful progress. On the left [south] was the fine, smooth highway with no person in sight, since everyone had sped along so swiftly. I took it, passed many ruins and deserted houses, reached the mountain, entered a narrow valley, and crossed through a gap to the other side. Soon I came to a great canyon where my journey seemed to end; and I stood there on the rim wondering what to do. Peering deep into the canyon, I saw something shiny winding its way like a silver thread on the bottom; and I thought that it must be the Little Colorado River. On the walls across the canyon were the houses of our ancestors with smoke rising from the chimneys and people sitting out on the roofs."[23]

### 7.

- Many accounts of the Hopi journey to the underworld include the description of the idyllic village that the dead inhabit. If one has been righteous in his or her lifetime and has chosen the correct path on the galactic highway, then the soul will reach that blessed village. Here the souls exist in a geographic, architectural, and social scenario much like the one they previously knew in life. Outside of the spirits' village are fields burgeoning with bountiful crops. "Then, as the two [the soul and the One Horn] traveled on, they came upon a field in which were growing large amounts of many different plants. The boy had never seen any field quite like this before. Everything imaginable was growing there. He saw watermelons and muskmelons and their vines were spread out all around. There were also squashes growing there, their round shapes jutting up therough the vines. The stalks of corn stood tall, with tassels at their tops and long ears protruding from their leaves. Different kinds of beans, too, were there in large amounts. How he wanted to have such a marvelous field of his own! Surprisingly, there were no weeds visible among these plants. The field was so huge that it took them quite a while to traverse it. When they had, they came to a village."[24]

- "After that, they [the One Horn and the Two Horn priests] took the boy back to the fork and let him go on the other trail to the village where the dead sprits were living. He saw a bunch of kids on a rabbit hunt, but they were hunting grasshoppers and crickets and things like that. The saw him coming and began to yell, 'Look out, here comes a masawwu!' You see, they called him a dead spirit. They acted like they were alive and he were dead. They ran like anything. Well, he got to the village where the people were living. That village looked just like his own village, Oraibi. He even saw some old people he knew when they were alive. There were women and kids as well as men, but nobody paid any attention to him. He thought he would go on top of a roof and started to climb a ladder, but the steps, the rungs, just broke under him and he couldn't go up. Those steps were made out of cornstalks or sunflower stalks, and they wouldn't hold a live person. Only dead spirits could climb them."[25]
- It is interesting to realize that in Hopi culture the two realms—that of the living and that of the dead—function in a reciprocal relationship, unlike the modern, non-Indian world where life and afterlife are psychologically walled off from each other. The spirits speak thus to the

boy: "Some of us have only very few nakwákwosis left on our foreheads. They are worn out so we cannot see very well through them anymore. You must make many nakwákwosis and báhos [*nawakwusi*, prayer-feather on a cotton string; *paho*, prayer-feather on a stick][26] for us in the village and we shall also work for you here. You make prayer-offerings for us and we shall provide rain and crops and food for you. Thus we shall assist each other."[27]

## 8.

- The Hopi versions apparently do not display any confrontation with a great serpent, although threatening snakes are sometimes encountered along the way. It is possible that the guardian of the dead referred to in the Mississippian culture and Southeastern Ceremonial Complex could be construed in the Hopi context as the *Kwan*, or One Horn (Agave) members we have seen. According to mid-20th century anthropologist Mischa Titiev, "Of the four Tribal Initiation societies, the Kwan stands most apart; and the others are taught to regard it with awe and dread. This is due to its intimate association with Masau'u [*Màasaw*], god of death, and keeper of the home of the dead (Maski). Indeed, a Kwan is very commonly referred to not only as Kwanitaka (Kwan Man), but also as one of the Maskwakwantu (Masau'u's Kwan men)."[28]
- During the last part of his journey Talayesva is chased by *Màasaw* himself. "Now the canyon was full of smoke, and when I peered down I saw a gruesome creature in the shape of a man climbing the cliff. He was taking long strides with his shining black legs and big feet; an old tattered rag of a blanket was flying from his shoulder as

he approached swiftly with a club in his hand. It was big, black, bloody-headed Masua'u, the god of Death, coming to catch me. One of the Kwanitakas [Horns] pushed me and cried, 'Flee for your life and don't look back, for if Masau'u catches you, he will make you a prisoner in the House of the Dead!' I turned and ran eastward, while they pushed me along with their wands or spears so that I rose about six inches from the ground and flew faster than I had ever traveled before."[29]

- Note that Talayesva's soul is now advancing eastward, back toward Third Mesa. It is possible that this Hopi deity is fulfilling the role of "brain-smasher," or "brain-taker," frequently found in Eastern Woodlands mythology. This gruesome figure takes an unworthy soul's vitalizing force, or "brain," thereby annihilating him or her. "Maasaw always carries a drumstick-shaped club around with him to kill people. Actually, he does not really slay them but rather knocks them unconscious. Again, contrary to the norm, he carries the club in his left hand and strikes with that instead of with his right."[30] Lankford suggests that the "brain-taker" might be represented by the Raptor icon, which corresponds to the star Deneb in Cygnus and which guards the split in the path, i.e., the Great Rift in the Milky Way.[31] In this context it may be significant that soon after Orion departs from the upper world in late April and is invisible for a number of weeks, the Hopi men gather fledgling eagles in May to be kept on the village rooftops, tied by one leg to a beam or stone and fed rabbits or other small rodents. At the end of the *katsina* season in July they are ritually sacrificed with the utmost solemnity and reverence.[32]

- Scholar George Lankford recaps the details of the Missisippian and Southeastern Ceremonial Complex's

"Path of Souls" schema, which in many ways resembles the Hopi Journey to *Maski* detailed above. "The dead soul travels from its physical body in a western direction until it reaches the edge of the earth-disk. There it must wait until the Hand constellation descends to its proper place confronting the soul waiting on its bank. That place is precisely on the western horizon, and the Hand is visible at night, and therefore available for use, during the winter months. When the Hand reaches the level of the earth, the soul must make a leap for the portal during the few minutes before it continues beneath the water, with the Milky Way, like a wall, falling into the water behind the Hand."[33] In my previous book *Journey of the Serpent People*, I argued that the Hopi Snake Clan's legendary migration to the East allowed for a mixing of cultures and mythic streams, and perhaps even led to a shared construction of Ohio's Great Serpent Mound.[34] The notion of a similar chthonic journey mutually recognized by both the Hopi and the eastern tribes corroborates that diffusionist perspective.

**Hopi drawing of the sky god *Sotuknang* (nephew of *Taawa*, sun god) is associated with *Kwan* (the One Horn society). Members of this fierce paramilitary group act as village guardians, especially during the November *Wuwtsim* (New Fire) ceremony.**

# Chapter 18
# *Grasping the Hand Constellation of the Hopi*

### Spirit-Messengers of the Hand

This chapter will delineate the Hopi attributes of the Hand constellation (the Orion Dimension) as compared with those of their tribal brethren further east—*mano a mano*.

Found only on Third Mesa, the *Mastop Katsina* (Kachina) comes from the northwest—the direction of Grand Canyon's *Sipapuni* (Place of Emergence from the Third World into the Fourth World); hence he is associated with death. In fact, the translation of the name for this spirit-messenger is "Death Fly." Always arriving on the Hopi Mesas in pairs, he and his twin appear on the second to the last day of the *Soyal* (winter solstice) ceremony, a time of long nights and great darkness.

The bodies of the *Mastop katsinam* are painted black or dark brown, and they both wear a woman's old, discarded kilt or in former times a bobcat skin. Usually one white handprint (*maaveni*)[1] is painted on their chests, giving a rather arresting impression (at least to the contemporary eye), and other smaller handprints are painted on their legs and upper arms. They both carry a short black-and-white striped staff (à la Orion's club?) in their right hands with which to beat the dogs as they make their way through the village. Frantically leaping about, each *Mastop* dashes up to a crowd of females, grabs one of them by the shoulders from behind, and makes a series of short hops that simulate copulation. After this semi-humorous pantomime, they rush to the Chief Kiva in order to confer with the priests in disguised voices. Then they suddenly run back to the cluster of females, repeating this serious fertility ritual (despite the antics) until all of them have been approached in a similar manner.

The celestial connection of *Mastop* is made apparent when viewing his black, cylindrical helmet with a rounded crown. On each side of the mask is painted a grouping of white dots representing stars. One author claims that the right side is the Pleiades and the left side is the Great Bear. However, the V-shaped configuration just as easily could represent Orion's belt together with his sword, the latter containing Iota Orionis and the fertile star-seeds of the Great Nebula, M42 and M43. Given the virile aspect of *Mastop*, Orion's phallic sword is an appropriate mask decoration. However, Harold S. Colton, former Director Emeritus of the Museum of Northern Arizona, claimed that this *katsina* is also associated with *Màasaw*, thus stressing the dual aspects of fertility and death.[2] (The word *màasa-* + *wu'y* literally means "death spirit."[3] *Màasaw* is the deity most closely related in Hopi cosmology to the constellation Orion. The term *màasaki* means "hand gesture, whereas *masa'y* means "wing.[4] The late author Frank Waters comments on this awesome—in the original sense of the word—spirit entity. "The Mastop Kachina appears the following day [of the winter solstice ceremony], a frightening figure in his black mask, his body painted black, with the imprints of human hands in white, a wild animal's pelt worn for a kilt, and his feet covered with wildcat skins. He has come a long, long way. His black helmet mask suggests the interstellar space he has traveled, the three white stars on each side of his head being the three stars in Orion's belt."[5]

Photo of a Hopi mask of a *Mastop katsina*.

Left: *Mastop katsina*, painting, Cliff Bahnimptewa, Oraibi.
Right: *Mastop katsina* doll, Museum of Northern Arizona.

# *Plexus of Cognates from Separate Continents*

## Hopi of North America

– *Mastop*, Orion's phallic sword is an appropriate mask decoration.
– This *katsina* is also associated with *Màasaw*, god of death and underworld.
– *màasaki* means "hand gesture, *masa'y* means "wing."
– *maa'at* means "hand"
– *màata* means "show, be revealed,"
*maataq* means "become visible"

## Ancient Egyptian of North Africa

– *maa-t* meant "sight, vision, something seen, tableau"
– Maa-t was the goddess of law, rule, truth, order, righteousness, justice
– *shespit* meant "hand"
– Shespit was "one of the seven stars of Orion. Its god was [hieroglyphic of falcon and a quincunx of stars]."[6]

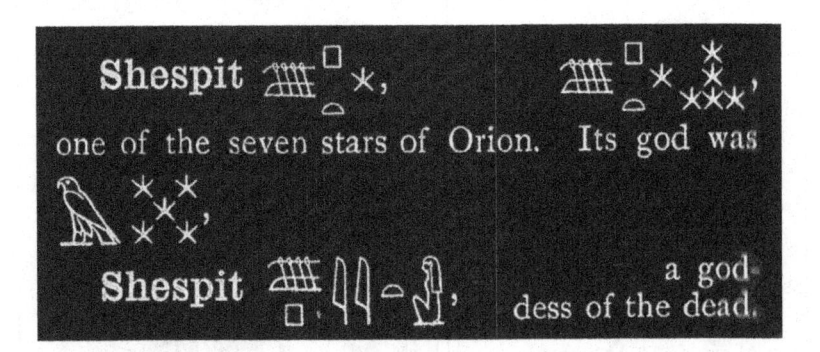

Shespit ⋯, ⋯, one of the seven stars of Orion. Its god was ⋯, Shespit ⋯, a goddess of the dead.

Another *katsina* with a handprint either on his mask or both on his mask and chest is called *Malatsvetaqa*. This is a Racer, or Runner, *katsina*, who uses soot mixed with grease to put handprints upon the backs of his opponents.[7] The term *malats* actually means "fingers."[8] This *katsina* is particularly active at the footraces held in the village plaza against the men and boys. These take place in April (*Kwiyamuya*, "windbreak moon"), when sweetcorn (*tawaktsi*) is planted, which will be harvested around the time of the *Niman* (Home Dance) ceremony in July.[9] (Again, we see the seasonal framework of April-July, when Orion is in the underworld.) Also seen as a Zuni kachina, *Malatsvetaqa* is alternately called *Matya* (*Matia*, Hand *Katsina*) or a *Sivu'ikquitaka* (Pot Carrier *Katsina*), the latter followed by a woman named *Talakin* (*tal'a-* means "summer"), who stirs the pot on his back.[10] (The sexual connotation is obvious, as Bob Marley's song "Stir It Up" exemplifies. Not surprisingly, reggae is very popular on the modern Hopi reservation.)

**Matya (Hand *katsina*) or *Sivu'ikquitaka* (Pot Carrier), Hopi drawing, 1903.**

> Hand *katsina* doll, Heard Museum, Phoenix, Arizona. Photo by the author. *Nota bene*: White Bear Fredericks was author Frank Waters' primary informant for his *Book of the Hopi*.

Oswald "White Bear" Fredericks (1906-1996)
Sivu'ikwiwtaqa, c. 1959
Gift of Senator Barry M. Goldwater

Harold Colton notes the characteristics of this *katsina*: "Black case mask with a white hand outlined in red covering the case. Cloth or fox skin ruff. Kilt, sash, fox skin, hank of yarn over shoulder, and red moccasins. May wear white shirt or white body paint. Carries a pot on back, suspended by a tump line or from shoulders, and rattle. Appears in Mixed Kachina Dance and is said to be a Runner."[11]

Another *katsina* plays a significant role in the plaza races. This spirit-messanger, which probably originated at Zuni,[12] is a female version of Kokopelli, the fabled Humpback Flute Player. She (though impersonated by a male) is called

*Kokopölmana*, or "Robber (Asssasin) Fly Maiden,[13] and perhaps is similar to the *Mastop* "Death Fly" described above, since her mask is also black with a vertical white stripe down the center and a slender, pointed white snout painted with a black spiral. Scholar of the Hopi, Barton Wright describes her duties. "Very few of the racers are portrayed as women but one of the most avoided is Kokopell' Mana, the erotic counterpart of Kokopelli. Should the man that 'she' gets to race with her lose, she flings him to the ground and imitates copulation to the great delight of the audience. If she loses, which is not often as the better racers take this part, she pays with piki bread."[14] Thus, her feigning of copulation in order sympathetically to engender procreation and fertility is similar to that of *Mastop* previously mentioned.

We recall that Orion's belt was traditionally known as Jacob's Rod or Staff, and that that virile biblical patriarch had a dozen sons. (See p. 252.)

### Handprints—Terrestrial and Celestial

The handprint icon is ubiquitous in American Southwestern rock art, both painted and carved. In fact, it is found all over the world, including western Europe, southern Africa, Australia, and various locations. Many archaeologists speculate that it functions as a sort of signature of its maker in order to associate it with adjacent symbols. American rock art expert Polly Schaafsma explains:

> "The hand print, a universal symbol in primitive art and an important motif in Pueblo painting even today, has persisted from these earliest beginnings. Many Basketmaker caves

[1-700 AD] are filled with solid or patterned prints in several colors. The idea that these prints, usually made by pressing a painted-covered hand against the rock, served as a means of identification is supported by ethnographic information. Modern Pueblo Indians are reported to leave hand prints at sacred places where they may have prayed in order that the supernatural engaged will be able to identify the supplicant."[15]

The method Schaafsma describes produces what is called a positive handprint. A negative handprint is produced by placing the hand upon the rock surface and blowing dry pigment around the back of the hand and fingers.

**Both positive and negative handprints with Kokopelli on his back and snake, pictographs, Canyon de Chelly, Arizona. Photo by author.**

Another petroglyph-and-pictograph specialist, Campbell Grant, describes the handprints found in Canyon de Chelly, Arizona.

> "Sacred spots were sometimes marked by a handprint so that supernatural beings would know who had made the supplications and offerings. The handprints on the torsos of large human figures... might represent a similar wish for identification with the supernatural world. ...handprints are often an expression of sympathetic magic indicating the wish of the maker to bring forth whatever is depicted, such as clouds or deities. The red handprint is also a symbol for the elder war god [War Twin]. The Hopi had a Hand Kachina. There was a large red-and-white hand painted on the mask of this figure. The Zuni had a similar being [*Anahoho*]."[16]

**Tabirá (Salinas Region, New Mexico), Black-on-white potsherd. "The kachina shown, both in profile and full-face, was painted on a pitcher sherd. His distinguishing feature is a handprint on the face.** [continued on next page]

A pair of Zuni kachinas, Anahoho, wear white masks with red handprints on the cheeks rather than on the front— according to the myth acquired by dipping their hands in Navajo blood. Bloody Hand, a guard or side-dancer kachina at Cochiti [Pueblo, New Mexico] with similar markings, is probably the same character as Anahoho— and possibly is identified in the Las Humanas figure as well. The crucifix hanging from the neck of the latter is a touch seldom seen on modern kachinas."[17]

Five handprints (one upside down—death?), four stars, petroglyphs. Handprint on left has bird-tail feathers. Used as target practice by modern racist savages. Petroglyph National Monument, New Mexico. Photo by the author.

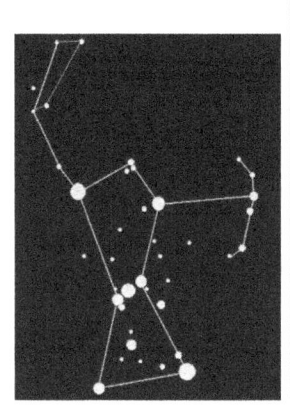

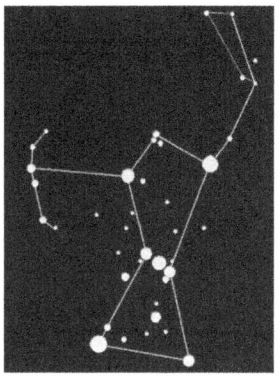

In the following thought experiment, we can see how the Ancients conceptualized rock art, not as a personal, individualized expression but as an interaction between the spirit world located on the opposite side of the vertical rock surface and the physical world from which the Ancients viewed the petroglyphs. The drawing on the left is the way we see Orion in the sky. The middle photo (taken by the author) is an example from Chevelon Canyon at Rock Art Ranch in Arizona. The figure raises his left hand in greeting. (To the viewer the upraised hand is on the right.) Incidentally, the Hopi traditionally saw the left hand as sacred, to be used for prayer-feather and corn meal offerings, whereas the right was the defiled "food hand," to be used for mundane eating.[18] The perspective of the spirit embodied in the petroglyph as he gazes toward the terrestrial plane is the same as the horizontally reversed version of Orion (on the right). In other words, the spirits' vantage from the other side of the stars looking toward the Earth is just like the spirits on the other side of the stone surface looking toward corporeal beings. Even though the latter executed the rock art, it was directed by the former.

The same perspective described in the Orion rendition at the right of the previous page, i.e., from beyond the fixed stars, is found in this drawing by Johannes Hevelius from his posthumous book *Prodromus Astronomia*, Vol. III: *Firmamentum Sobiescianum, sive Uranographia*, 1690.

In Chapter 16, we saw how the Mississippian, Southern Ceremonial Complex, and the Plains tribes conceptualized Orion as the Hand constellation, with its nebula (M42) as a portal to the underworld. This configuration of the Hand motif shows the belt as the severed wrist, which hangs down from the horizontal expansion of the Milky Way parallel to the western horizon, with the fingers pointed downward. (See sky chart on p. 274.) Rigel corresponds to the index finger, while the closest star in the River constellation Eridanus corresponds to the pinkie. The sword is comprised of the Great Orion Nebula as well as Theta Orionis (Trapezium) and Iota Orionis.

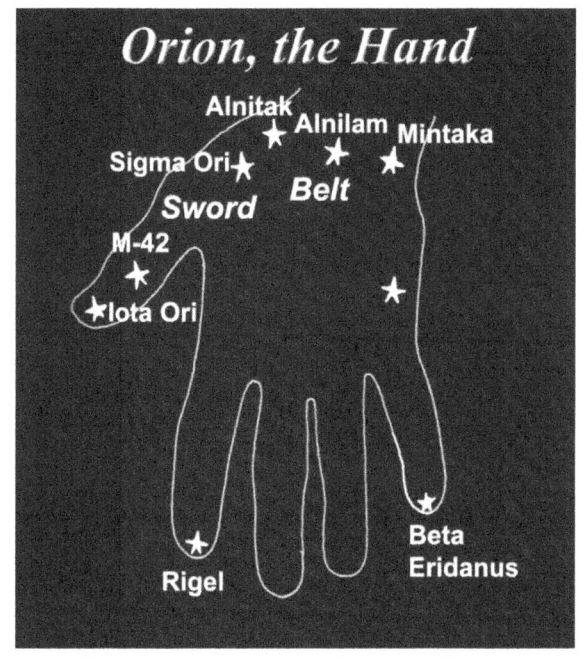

**Orion, the Hand**

Lakota (Sioux) Hand constellation.

However, it would make more sense if the so-called ogee (see p. 262) were located in the center of the palm, as the iconography suggests, rather than in the thumb. In the Hopi cosmology of the Orion Zone, which manifests the hermetic dictum "as above, so below," this seems to be the case. In addition, the orientation of the constellation is different than that of the cosmological configuration of Orion in the prehistoric Eastern U.S. This is due to the geographical and topological exigencies of the Southwestern landscape that the Hopi conceptualize by the phrase *Tutskwa I'qatsi*, "Land and Life"[19]—the inextricable web of life with its spiritual dimensions that cannot be separated from the tangible environment.

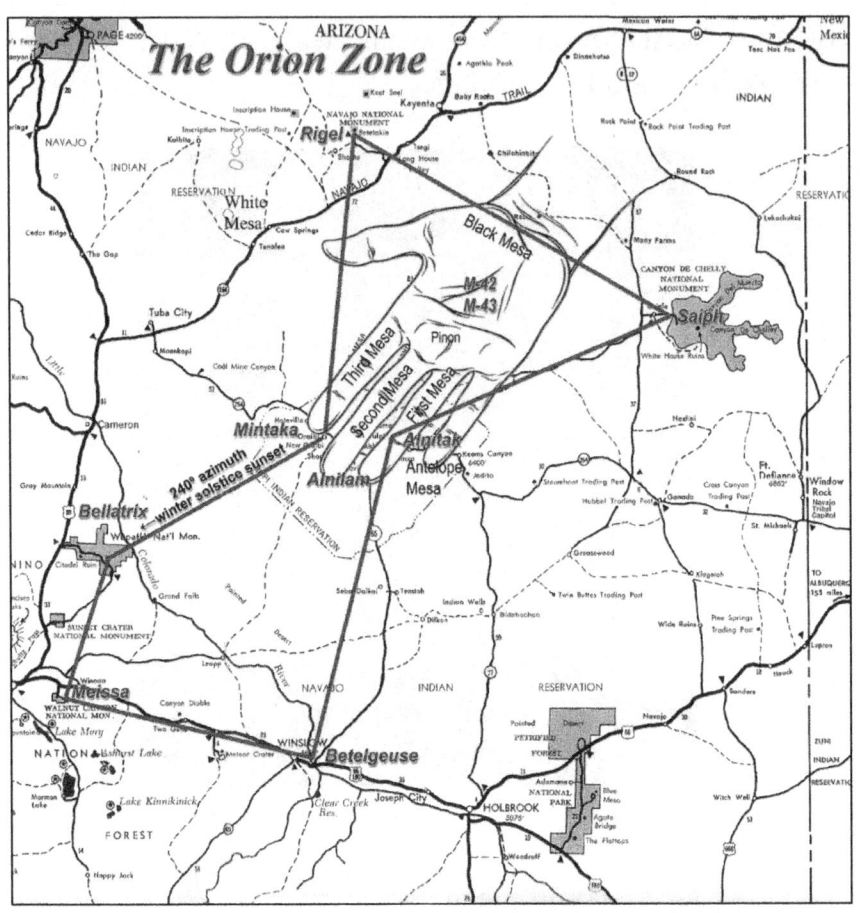

**Compare the Hopi Hand Constellation
with the Lakota Hand Constellation (above).**

The three Hopi Mesas range from northeast to southwest like fingers of rock extended from Black Mesa. The northern edge of Black Mesa from Tsegi Canyon (Navajo National Monument) to Canyon de Chelly (National Monument) forms the heel of the palm. The thumb points to White Mesa, while the pinkie points to Antelope Mesa, where the ruins of the extinct village of Awatovi are located. At the center of the palm, i.e., in the middle of Black Mesa, where the Hopi have traditionally mined coal, is the Navajo village of

Pinyon and the Hopi ruins called Burnt Corn. A Hopi-Tewa man named Albert Yava from First Mesa describes the site.

> "East of the trading post at Piñon there's an old ruins [sic] that belonged to the Kachina Clan. There were other clans living there, of course, but the Kachina Clan was the ruling group in that place. It's called Burnt Corn Ruins. The village was destroyed by fire, it seems. I went over there one time to look at it. The upper part of the walls has disappeared, but the foundations are visible, and if you dig around a little you can expose the storage rooms where they kept the corn. A lot of corn is still there, and it is burnt. Only the Kachina Clan has the details of what happened. They lived in that place before they came here to First Mesa."[20]

This ruin probably contained about one hundred rooms and was established about the same time as the villages farther south on the Hopi Mesas, or 1100 AD, though archaeologists believe it was abandoned circa 1250.[21] In the same vicinity near the head of Oraibi Wash at an elevation of 7,200 feet is *Kìisiwu*, one of the four major springs of the Hopi, "literally "Shadow Springs," representing the intercardinal direction of northeast.[22] This still is the traditional summer home of the *katsinam*, to which pilgrimages are made in order to obtain both the sacred water and Douglas fir (i.e., spruce) branches used in ceremonies.[23] Thus, from the winter solstice until mid-July the *katsinam* inhabit Black Mesa, blessing it with their beneficent presence. For the other half of the year, from July after the *Niman* (Home Dance) ceremony until the December solstice, the *katsinam* preside over the snowy San Francisco Peaks, or *Nuvatukya'ovi*, representing the inter-cardinal direction of southwest—their winter home.[24]

From the map on p. 302 we can see that the eye-in-the hand, or ogee, coincides with the summer home of the *katsinam*, where the power of *Taawa*, the Hopi sun god, is annually the strongest—in the northeast. In the celestial dimension this locus corresponds to the Great Orion Nebula (M42). Located at a distance of 1,300 light-years, this luminescent cloud of greenish gas and dust studded with stars emanating ultraviolet radiation is one of the largest emission nebulae in our galaxy—about 20 light-years in diameter.[25] In his classic, three-volume magnum opus, astronomer Robert Burnham, Jr. effuses:

> "The great flowing irregular cloud, shining by the gleaming light of the diamond-like stars entangled in it, makes a marvelous spectacle which is unequalled anywhere else in the sky. Barnard found it resembling a great ghostly bat as it came drifting into the field of the Yerkes telescope [the University of Chicago's 40-inch refractor in Williams Bay, Wisconsin], and spoke of a feeling of awe and surprise each time he saw it. To many others it creates, as does no other vista of the heavens, the single overpowering impression of primeval chaos, and transports the imaginative observer back to the days of creation. This irresistible impression is more than a poetic fancy, as modern astrophysics now confirms, for the Orion Nebula is undoubtedly one of the

regions in space where star formation is presently underway."[26]

Richard Grossinger, writer of creative nonfiction and publisher of North Atlantic Books, adds to the mysterium: "Today we know that M42, the Great Nebula of Orion, for instance, is a large, colorful gaseous cloud surrounding a potpourri of effects: nurseries of young stars, protoplanetary disks, brown dwarfs (unignitable substellar objects), and bright blue supersonic 'bullets' of molecular hydrogen (each ten times the diameter of Pluto's orbit)."[27] As mentiond above, astrophysicists in 2012 even discovered a black hole 200 times larger than the mass of our sun at the heart of the nebula.[28]

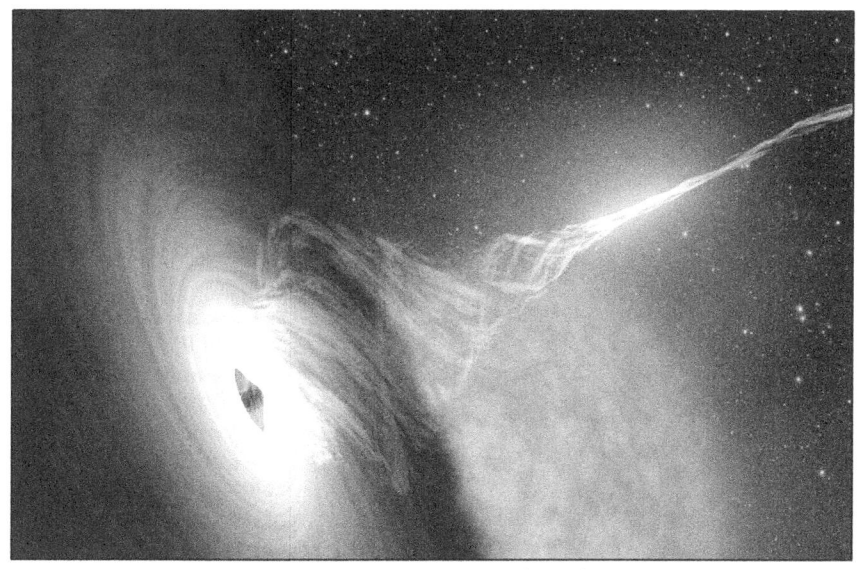

NASA artist's impression of a black hole
with ogee-like accretion disk and plasma jet.

BUREAU OF AMERICAN ETHNOLOGY                TWENTY-THIRD ANNUAL REPORT PL. CVII

*Zuni Petroglyph Map*

San Juan Mts. →
Utah mesas
Grand Canyon
Orion – Hopi Mesas ↓
Road of ← Plant Medicine
Canyon de Chelly
Road of Salt Woman →
Road of White People →
human →
Middle Place
Place of Mist
Pleiades?
cross ↓
Ursa Major or Hyades?

*I'tiwanna* – Middle Place: Zuni Pueblo

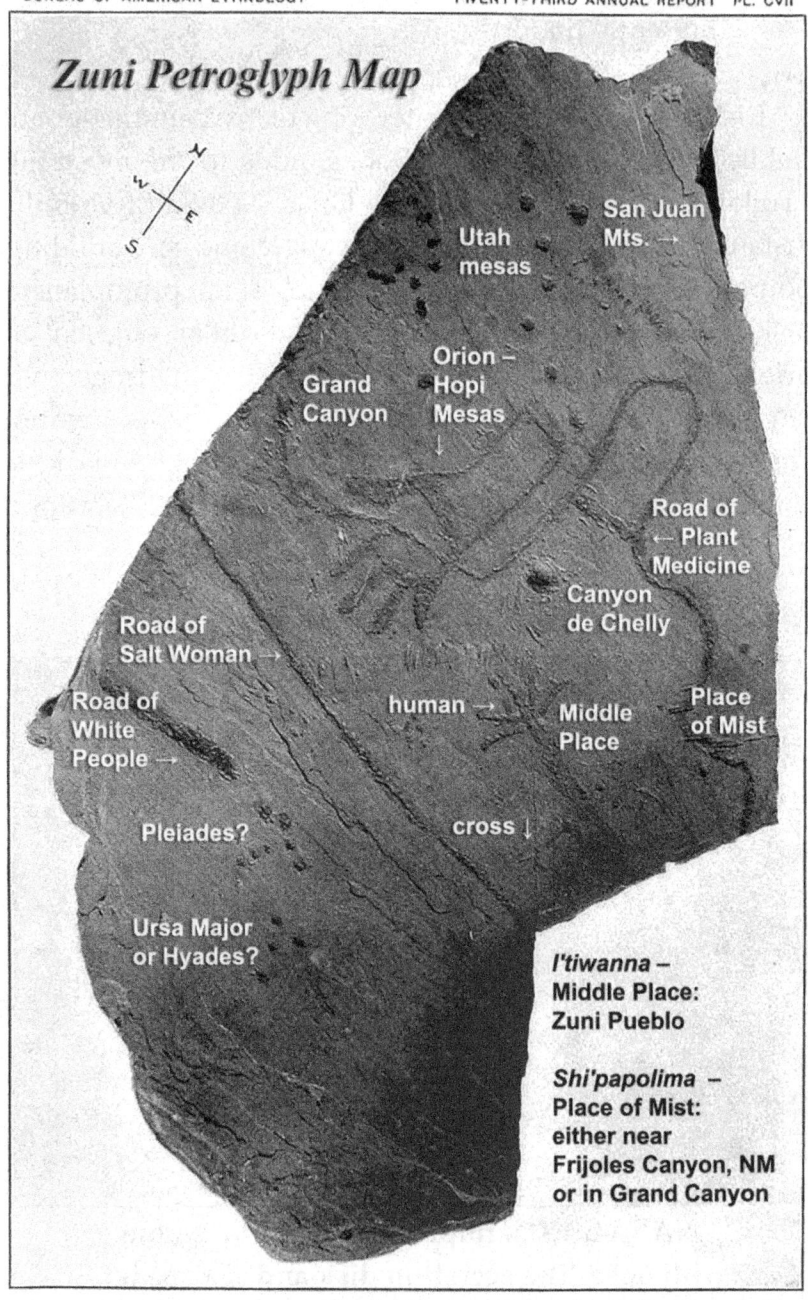

*Shi'papolima* – Place of Mist: either near Frijoles Canyon, NM or in Grand Canyon

MAP SHOWING ROUTE FOLLOWED BY 'HLE'WEKWE (WOOD FRATERNITY) IN QUEST OF THE MIDDLE PLACE

The previous page is a Bureau of American Ethnology photograph of a petroglyph map on sandstone found in the early 20th century about 1.5 miles southwest of Zuni Pueblo in New Mexico. Ethnographer Matilda Coxe Stevenson (1849 – 1915) summarily hacked off the slab and sent it to the Smithsonian Institution. Zuni culture and rituals are similar to those of the Hopi, although its language is completely different and unique. The description below provided by an "associate rain priest" (*A'shiwanni*) is tentative and my interpretation of the locations is speculative.

"This etching is believed by the Zuñis [A'shiwi] to have been made by the original director of the Hle'wekwe [Wood, or Sword Swallower] fraternity. The wavy line crossing the stone indicates the course of migration of the Hle'wekwe from Hän'lipĭnkĭa in the west to Shi'papolima in the east. After traveling a long distance northward, the Hle'wekwe turned south, and then proceeded to Shi'papolima ["Place of Mist"] in the east. The line crossing the bend in the road was followed by the fraternity to secure certain medicinal plants. They returned to the point whence they started for the plants and then resumed their journey. The pits north of the line of travel indicate mesas and mountain peaks. The significance of the hand symbol is not clear. The larger pit east of the hand is an extensive basin constantly filled with water from rains and snows. The dots surrounding the pit represent Ursa Minor. The short lines, no longer than an inch in the pictograph, indicate the number of years consumed by the Hle'wekwe in going from Hän'lipĭnkĭa to Shi'papolima and thence to I'tiwanna [the Middle Place], the site of the present Zuni. The human figure is an ancient Shi'wi before the tail and water moss had been removed and the webbed hands and feet cut. The dots about this figure denote hail, for the director of the Hle'wekwe fraternity desired much hail. The straight line extending east and west across the slab indicates the road leading from Hän'lipĭnkĭa to the Salt Mother before she left her home east of I'tiwanna. The cross near the east end of this line and south of it symbolizes the morning star. The group of seven dots denotes Ursa Major; the group of four, the Pleiades. The short heavy line implicates the road followed by the Kĭa'nakwe [White People] on their way to the place where they were found by the A'shiwi."[29]

# Chapter 19
# A Hopi-Dogon Divagation

## In the Loop

We saw in the preceding chapter how astronomer Robert Burnham, Jr. mentioned his esteemed predecessor in the field, E. E. Barnard (1857 – 1923). Among the latter's discoveries is the eponymous Barnard's Loop, which he photographed via long-exposure in 1894. "To my surprise these pictures showed an enormous curved nebulosity encircling the belt and the great nebula, and covering a large portion of the body of the giant."[1] This cloud is estimated to be up to 1,400 light years away (about the same distance as the belt) and at least 300 light years across.[2] According to science writer Deborah Byrd, "This area in general is called the Orion Molecular Cloud Complex. And its most spectacular area may be the great loop of stars surrounding Orion's three Belt stars. This great bubble in space is known as Barnard's Loop, and its exact origin is unknown. Bright young stars in Orion may have produced 'winds' that created it. Or long-gone supernovae may have blasted it out."[3]

My friend the scholar Laird Scranton has made some stunning discoveries himself vis-à-vis Barnard's Loop and both the ancient Egyptians and the Dogon tribe of Mali. He wondered whether the Egyptian cubit had any relationship to the stars of Orion, considering that the Great Pyramid measures 440 cubits per side and is 280 cubits tall. (The GP, according to author and Egyptologist Robert Bauval's well known theory, corresponds to Alnitak in the belt.) Laird writes: "Using an online search engine on my computer, I keyed the numbers 440 and 280 along with the word *Orion* and was pleasantly surprised to turn up references to an obscure, virtually invisible cosmic structure called Barnard's Loop, a structure that I had previously not know even to exist." He found that it actually had the dimensions of 440 by 280 light years—the same measurements in cubits as the Great Pyramid.[4] He then compared Dogon cosmology to this celestial Golden Mean spiral.

> "When we step back from the figure of Orion given above as part of the image of Barnard's Loop, we see that Barnard's Loop takes on the the appearance of the wheel of a chariot and gives the impression that Orion, the hunter, is actually standing in a chariot. It is to this resemblance that we credit the Dogon symbolic term for Barnard's Loop as the chariot of Orion. It is important to note that when modern-day Dogon priests diagram the concept of the chariot of Orion, they do so, at least publically, in relation to the visible stars in the constellation of Orion, which simply form a kind of parallelogram that surrounds the belt stars but bear no discernible resemblance either to a chariot or to the po pilu [Dogon "egg of the world," in the form of a spiral] as the Dogon priests insist they should. My contention is that the true symbolism of the term is to Barnard's Loop, an effectively invisible structure that is a near-exact conceptual counterpart to the po pilau and that the Dogon priests suggest will only be seen 'later.'"[5]

In regard to the unseen astronomical anomaly, suffice it to say that the Dogon, much like the Hopi, hint at a prophecy of the world being renewed as one World (Age) transitions to the next. In order to avoid becoming mired in the complexities of Dogon cosmology, however, I shall merely mention this tribe's conceptualization and ritualization of Orion and the Milky Way.[6]

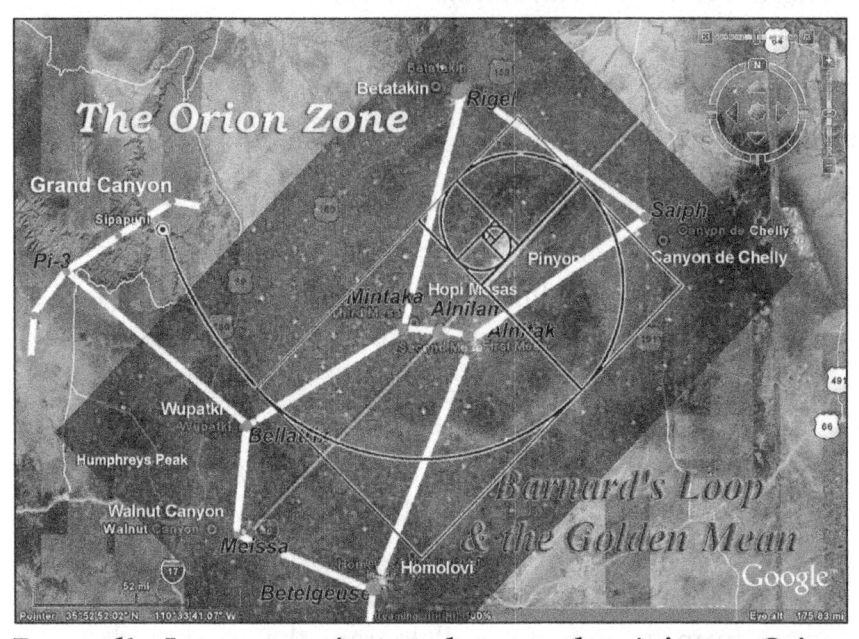

**Barnard's Loop superimposed upon the Arizona Orion Correlation. On the terrestrial plane the source of this Fibonacci spiral corresponds to village of Piñon (Pinyon) at the center of Black Mesa. (See pp. 14-15 and p. 303.)**

The four main stars of the "Chariot," which are arranged in a rectangle, are called the "navel of Amma," who is the immortal, omnipresent, and omnipotent Creator-God of the Dogon universe. They form a frame around Orion's belt and probably correspond to Betelgeuse, Bellatrix, Rigel, and Saiph—the shoulders and knees of our anthropomorphic constellation. These stars collectively make up Amma's foundation and the seat of the world. The Dogon represent them on the earth by four stone blocks, one at each corner of a rectangular field whose shorter sides face north and south and whose longer sides face east and west. At the center of the parallelogram is the "sign of Amma," which manifests as a chevron whose apex points south and whose two other points touch the eastern and western sides. Given the focus of their astro-spiritual ontology, the Dogon ultimately consider the source of all existence to be the belt stars of Orion, including its Great Nebula.[7]

The renowned French anthropologists Marcel Griaule (1898 – 1956) and Germaine Dieterlen (1903 – 1999), who published research on the Dogon for nearly a quarter century, describe this tribe's "Orion Zone," so to speak: "The stones placed at the field corners standing for the four stars of the Chariot also represent the 'four corners' of celestial space. Their different colors denote the four elements…[8] Thus, in stellar space, the Chariot is the symbol of Amma's seat; it surrounds *atanu*, the Belt, otherwise known as the three 'deputies.' It is related to the basic elements and to the cardinal directions, which presided during the realization of the universe that was 'thought' by the creator."[9]

In other words, "In the beginning was the Word, and the Word was with God, and the Word was God." (John 1:1 KJV)

Much like the Hopi *katsinam*, the Dogon also wear masks, one of which is called the *kanaga*—"Amma's hand." It embodies both the kinetic force of the supreme deity and the primordial energy of the whole universe.[10] Dieterlen comments: "The *kanaga* mask represents the movement imposed upon the universe by Amma. 'The trembling of its wearer's outstretched arm is the movement of Amma's hands creating the world.'"[11] During funeral ceremonies the top of the mask is touched to the ground in order to send the spirit of the dead to its celestial resting place.

Dogon *kanaga* masks. Inset (left): Figure with hand representing the transformation of celestial Ogo into the terrestrial "pale fox" (*Vulpes pallidus*) named Yuruga, a nocturnal trickster.

According to Robert Temple in his mythologically rich book *The Sirius Mystery*:

> "What Ogo the Fox seems to represent is man himself, an imperfect intelligent species who 'descended' or originated on this planet, which is the planet in our solar system to which the great umbilical cord is attached. Ogo is representative of ourselves, in all our cosmic impurity. It comes as a shock to realize that we

are Ogo, the imperfect, the meddler, the outcast. Ogo rebelled at his creation and remained unfinished. He is equavalent of Lucifer in our own tradition in the Christian West. And in order to atone for our impurity it is said over and over by the Dogon that the Nommo dies and is resurrected, acting as a sacrifice for us, to purify and cleanse the Earth. The parallels with Christ are extraordinary, even extending to Nommo being crucified on a tree, and forming a eucharistic meal for humanity and then being resurrected. We are told that the Nommo will come again. A certain 'star' in the sky will appear once more and will be a 'testament to the Nommo's resurrection.'"[12]

The Dogon also consider Orion's belt to be three Nommo: the twin sky Nommo, *nommo die* and *nommo titiyayne* (the left star Alnitak and the middle star Alnilam respectively), and *o nommo*, or the sacrificial Nommo (the offset right star Mintaka).[13] Incredible as it may sound, the Dogon claim that their civilization was founded by the Nommo, a group of amphibious creatures with fish tails and webbed fingers originating from the triple star system Sirius.[14] These celestial emissaries essentially assumed the role of "instructors" or "monitors" in order to civilize humanity and salvage the Earth made impure by the trickster figure of Yuruga. This tradition is similar to the one found in Babylonia or Sumeria with a semi-daemon called Oannes (also known as Enki or Ea), bringer of civilization to that region. Griaule's blind Dogon informant Ogotemmêli describes these entities:

"Water, which is the divine seed, was thus able to enter the womb of the earth and the normal reproductive cycle resulted in the birth of twins. Two beings were thus formed. God [Amma] created them like water. They were green in colour, half human beings and half serpents. Their red eyes were wide open like human eyes, and their tongues were forked like the tongues of reptiles. Their arms were flexible and without joints. Their bodies were green and sleek all over, shining like the surface of water, and covered with short green hairs, a presage of vegetation and germination."[15]

In regard to the anagogical conceptualization of the galactic plane, the Dogon view the Milky Way as the route of the blood flow caused by the third Nommo's sacrifice.

"The sacrifice of the Nommo is represented by a figure called 'drawing of the Nommo's slaughter and of his passage into the valley. It depicts an individual, the Nommo, on the left, whose curved arm recalls the leg of a crocodile. It ends in an oval representing the end of the blood flow, that is, in the image of the primoridial pond containing a dot: the rice. Another dot on the outside represents the millet. The *valu* is portrayed between the Nommo and the pond."[16]

It is noteworthy that the ancient Egyptian crocodile god Sobek was associated with Thuban (Alpha Draconis), the Pole Star in about 2830 BC.[17] The Dogon term *valu* refers to the horse-antelope, or roan antelope (*Hippotragus equinus*), one the largest and most aggressive of the species, with a mane, long legs, and long tail similar to those of horses. For the Dogon this bloody "Path of Souls" starts at the left (north), and passes by a "Two Horn" (see Hopi reference in Chapter 17). The mid-section possibly shows Cygnus. The road ends in the south at a cosmic pool—the Dark Rift with Altair in Aquila and Vega in Lyra, continuing on to a supermassive black hole at the galactic center near Sagittarius A.

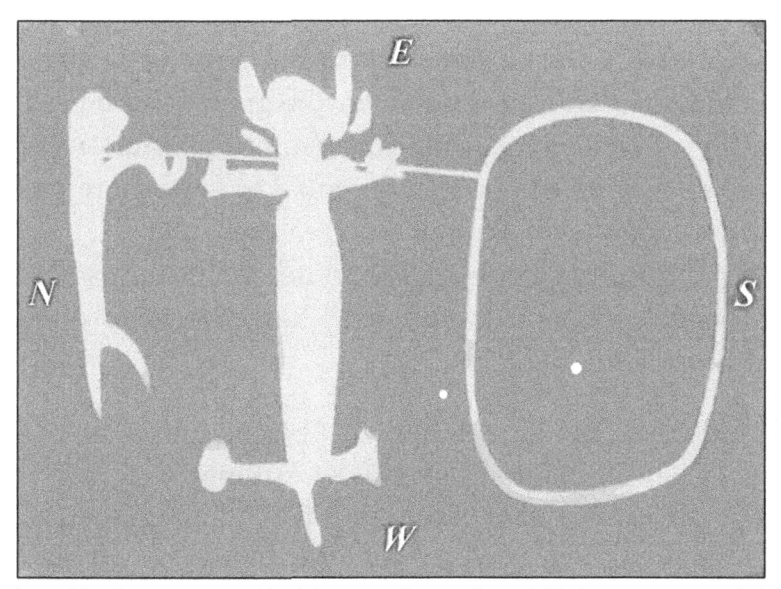

**Fish-tailed Nommo (left), antelope (middle), and pond (right).**

Griaule and Dieterlen continue their description of the Dogon "route of the blood": "Amma had followed the blood to its end before returning to divide up the body. The trace of blood flowing from the placenta formed a straight north-south line called *illi ozu*, 'path of the blood.' The track of Amma's walk parallel to it, called 'Amma's path,' is present in the sky. Together they make up the Milky Way, *yalu ulo*, 'bounds of space,' the evidence of which is the star *yalu ulo tolo*. Thus, the Milky Way has, ever since, been evidence in the sky of the discharge of the victim's blood."[18]

I should note here the similarity between the division of the Nommo's body and the dismemberment and dispersal of Osiris's body in Egyptian mythology. Also, the word "placenta" is conptualized in a specialized way. According to Robert Temple, "The placenta is used by the Dogon as a symbol of a 'system' of a group of stars or planets. Our own solar system seems to be referred to as 'Ogo's placenta', whereas the system of the star Sirius and its companion star and satellites, etc., is referred to as 'Nommo's placenta'. Nommo is the collective name for the great culture-hero and founder of civilization who came from the Sirius system to set up society on the Earth. Nommo – or to be more precise, the Nommos – were amphibious creatures..."[19]

Griaule and Dieterlen go on to describe what is possibly the Orion Nebula, or that which I have discussed above as the eye-in-hand motif.

> "...one draws in the *ginna* ['big house'] a *tonu* ['figure, diagram, schematic outline'[20]] of *yalu ulo tolo*, 'star of the Milky Way'. The funeral urn of the founder of the lineage, called 'bulging urn,' *bundo gwe*, represents this star. The opening of the container is surrounded by a bulge (*gwe*); 'the *bundo gwe* resembles *yalu ulo tolo*; the bulge of the *bundo* resembles the halo of *yalu ulo tolo*. During the consecration of the altar to the ancestors (*vague*), the picture of the

star is drawn under the urn which is placed first in line; those of the other deceased members of the lineage are all place in a spiral around it."[21]

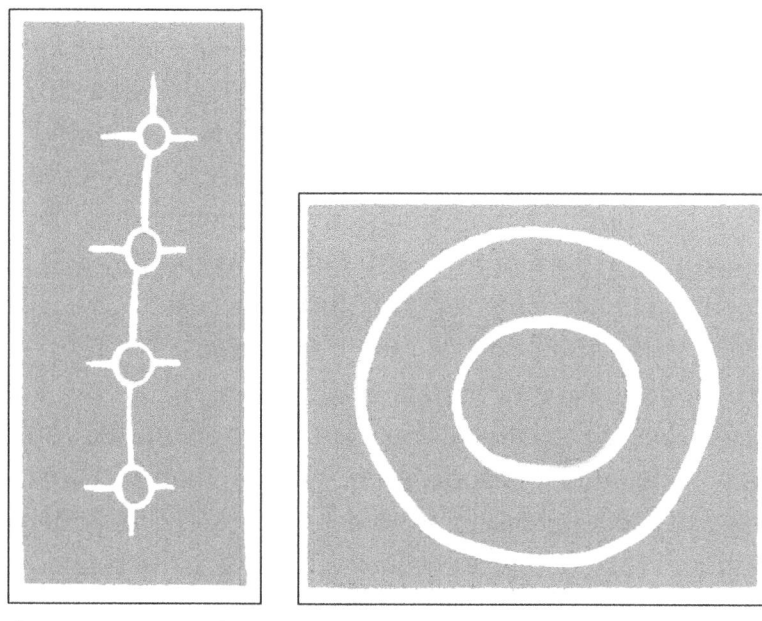

Left: "Drawing of the 'route of the blood' of the sacrificed *nommo* become stars,' i.e., the Milky Way.
Right: "*yalu ulo tolo* and it halo."

It is significant that the urn of the first ancestor is associated with this particular star in the Milky Way. The opening of the receptacle is perhaps related to the Mississippian ogee, or hand-in-eye, shown on pp. 262-264. This portal to the Afterlife, or M42, corresponds to Burnt Corn Ruins on Black Mesa in the Arizona Orion Correlation. (See map on p. 302.) "The figures representing *tolo dullogu* (that is, the two stars [Sigma Ori and Iota Ori] and the nebula of the Sword [M42] are oriented from northeast to southwest and symbolize ritual fields in the following order: *lebe, binu* and *vague* [ancestors of the various cults]."[22]

The co-authors speculate that the "halo" around the star of the Milky Way refers to the rings of Saturn, though they admit that more investigation needs to be done to confirm this. However, in his classic tome *Star Names: Their Lore and Meaning*, Richard Hinckley Allen suggests that Saturn, or the Roman god Saturnus (Greek Chronos), may actually be an alternate name for Orion: "**Saturnus** has been another title [of Orion], but its connection here I cannot learn, although I hazard the guess that as this divinity was the sun-god of the Phoenicians, his name might naturally be used for Uruanna-Orion, the sun-god of the Akkadians."[23] The direct correlation between Saturn and Orion made by Francis Huxley bears repeating. "He [Saturn] is also to be found in the constellation Orion, who wields that sickle-shaped sword called a falchion and which *farmers* [italics added] call a billhook.... For the Egyptians Orion was associated with Horus and the soul of Osiris; in the Hindu Brahmanas he is seen as Prajapati in the form of a stag; several nations in the Middle East refer to him as the Giant, or the hunter Nimrod mighty before the Lord; and he was Saturnus to the Romans."[24]

The consummate scholars Giorgio de Santillana and Hertha von Dechend add weight to the Saturn-Orion argument: "The Lord of the Mill is declared to be Saturn/Kronos, he whom his son Zeus dethroned by throwing him off his *chariot* [italics added], and banished in 'chains' to a blissful island, where he dwells in sleep, for being immortal he cannot die, but is thought to live a life-in-death, wrapped in funerary linen, until his time, some say, shall come to awaken again, and he will be reborn to us as a child."[25] Thus, Saturn-Orion is seen driving a chariot (namely, Barnard's Loop), similar to the Dogon cosmology. And, like the Dogon, this figure is directly connected with grain and agriculture.

For the Dogon, Orion's belt is associated with the south side of the four-sided celestial granary and essentially serves as the guardian of the grain. Again, Griaule and Dieterlen reinforce this idea: "The three stars of Orion's belt, oriented east-west, respectively represent *nommo die* [Alnitak], the *tityayne* [Alnilam], and the sacrificed Nommo [Mintaka], i.e., the guardians of the spiritual principle of the cereal grains that are entrusted to them between the harvest and the following sowing season. These are the stars that are therefore associated with the safekeeping of the grain seeds."[26] I might add that the ancient Egyptians knew Orion as Smati-Osiris, the Barley God.[27] Egyptologist Nicholas Grimal points out that Osiris compares with the Dogon ancestor Lebe, which, as we saw above, is associated with Orion's Sword with its nebula, and that the latter's resurrection echoes the regrowth of millet.[28]

One wonders if the Dogon have the same love of double entendres and puns that the ancient Egyptians apparently did. Case in point: the name of the triadic *Nommo* (that is, Orion's belt, sometimes spelled *Nummo*) is a near homonym of the Dogon word *numo*, or "hand," and *numi*, a "small round grindstone held in the hand with which one grinds (e.g. millet grain) on a large flat rock."[29] As previously stated, the Roman god Saturnus, patron of agriculture, had a Greek counterpoint in the titan Kronos, one homonym of which is *chronos*, denoting "time" but literally meaning "to grind." In this connection we are reminded of the rectangular grinding bins used by Hopi women (*nöma*, "wife"), together with their manos and metates.[30] In Hopi these domestic artifacts are called *matahki* and *mata* respectively.[31] As we saw above, *maa'at* means "hand" and *màata* means "be revealed." In order to achieve an increasingly finer corn meal, the bins were sometimes placed adjacent to each other in a row of three, indicating the triadic belt of the Hand constellation Orion.

**Hopi grinding bins, circa 1275 AD, Betatakin Ruin, Tsegi Canyon, Navajo National Monument, Arizona**

Chapters 16 and 18 discussed the Hand constellation of Orion and its portal to the Path of Souls as seen in a number of Native American traditions. The heliacal setting of Orion is the brief period when the spirit of the deceased may gain access to the Afterlife through the Great Nebula in the palm resting on the western horizon. Orion then departs for the underworld. Some weeks later he has his heliacal rising on the eastern horizon, the belt stars standing perpendicular to the horizon like the Tree of Life—known throughout history as the date palm (genus *Phoenix*). (See pp. 274-275.)

I shall close this chapter with a poem by Wallace Stevens, in which the phoenix sings.

>  The palm at the end of the mind,
>  Beyond the last thought, rises
>  In the bronze decor,

A gold-feathered bird
Sings in the palm, without human meaning,
Without human feeling, a foreign song.

You know then that it is not the reason
That makes us happy or unhappy.
The bird sings. Its feathers shine.

The palm stands on the edge of space.
The wind moves slowly in the branches.
The bird's fire-fangled feathers dangle down.[32]

# Chapter 20
# *Galaxias Ophis*

**The Sacred Way of the Serpent Fire**

As described in Chapter 1, the vital energy of individual consciousness in the chakra component of the Arizona Orion Correlation is projected from the Crown Chakra into the universal dimensions of the Absolute. In terrestrial terms, the Crown Chakra correlates to Tuzigoot and other Sinagua ruins in the Verde Valley. The resonant energy collected within the Orion configuration of ancient star villages is channeled southwest across the Sonoran Desert to the mouth of the Colorado River, after which it continues in the same vector across vast stretches of Pacific Ocean, traversing the equator and ultimately arriving at Te Hopai in the Bay of Plenty on New Zealand's North Island. The locus might have served as one "stepping stone" in the series of migrations of the *Patki* Clan (i.e., Water or Houseboat Clan) to their home in the Four Corners area of the U.S. This island and others in the region could even be the remnants of the primordial mother continent of Mu and the origin of the ancestral Hopi and other tribes.

Much like the anthropomorphic constellation Orion being turn "upside down" as we go "down under," we can also turn the Egyptian hermetic maxim on its head: "As below, so above." Likewise, "As within, so without." As George Harrison once sang: "And life flows on within you and without you." *Geo-divinicus, astro-divinicus. Homo divinicus.* In taxonomic terms, it is no longer enough to be doubly "wise," i.e., *Homo sapiens sapiens*. We are evolving— at least some of us.

The late Egyptologist and philosopher John Anthony West comments on the dual dimensions of the Serpent:

> "The serpent, seemingly a unity, is dual in expression—both verbal and sexual, dual and divisive by nature. But duality, and for that matter intellect, is not only a human but a cosmic function. There is a higher and a lower intellect. Thus, symbolically, there is the serpent that crawls, and the higher intellect, that which allows man to know God—the heavenly serpent, the serpent in the sky. The Egyptians knew perfectly well that snakes don't fly. But there is a deep meaning to their placing the serpent in the air under specific circumstances. The winged serpent, common to so many civilizations, was employed in Egypt as well and played a similar symbolic role."[1]

We need only to remember the plumed or feathered serpent Kukulkán and Quetzalcóatl of the Maya and Aztecs respectively. It is interesting to note additionally that the Hopi word *taawataho* (literally, "sun-whipsnake") denotes "…a fantastic snake that, when startled, flies away in the direction of the sun."[2]

It is obvious that much food for thought and extended exegeses over the centuries has been generated by Chapter 3 of the Book of Genesis, in which the "subtil" serpent entices Eve to eat from "a tree to be desired to make one wise." By the time we get to the New Testament, of course, Jesus admonishes his disciples to be "wise as serpents, and harmless as doves" (Matthew 10:16).

**Serpents among the stars, on the left with human limbs, on the right with wings. Temple of Hathor at Denderah, Egypt.**

Many North American tribes conceptualized the Milky Way as the "ghost road," stretching westward across the night sky. (See Chapter 16.) Either living shamans or souls of the recently deceased would tread upon this spirit-path, on their way to paradise. However, the galactic plane has been conceptualized not only as a "sky-way" but also as a cosmic serpent. Herman Bender, an independent researcher and archaeoastronomer with a background in geology, cultural landscape studies, and archaic shamanistic traditions, writes the following in this regard:

> "...the Lakota (Sioux) also viewed the Milky Way as 'the road of spirits', in their language *Wanagi Ta Canku*, the road that the *Wanagi*, i.e.

their soul or ghost travels to *Wanagi Yata* or 'the place of spirits' located somewhere in the southwestern sky world and thought to be at the end of the Milky Way... It was, however, not only a trail of light and ghost path for some tribes, but was also seen as a serpent and known as the serpent path, an idea that was shared by other cultures. The *Crooked Serpent* of the Bible (Book of Job, 26:13) may well have been the same as the Akkadian 'Great Serpent', the northern Hindu *Nagavithi* (meaning 'Path of the Snake') and the Viking or Norse *Midgardhsormr* or *Jormungand*, usually called the Midgard Serpent, all indicating Milky Way in form or shape with an association as a ghost or spirit path."[3]

Perhaps it is more than a coincidence that the Sanskrit word *naga* means "snake" and the Lakota word *nagi* means "soul."[4] The Hopi word for the Milky Way is *Soongwuqa*, literally "the big reed"—a morphologically serpent-like plant.[5] The related word *so'ngwamiq* means "towards the end, towards the source."[6] The related term *songowu* refers to the smaller reeds used to make a storage case (*songòosivu*) for a woman's wedding robe woven of white cotton that will be buried with her after her demise.[7] This tradition reflects the mythological significance of the hollow reed in the Hopi migration from the previous Third World to the present Fourth World, and the fact that reed boats were used to navigate to the west coast of North America. (See Chapter 4.)

Analyzing the composite phonemes, we find that *soo-* is the prefix of the Hopi word "star" (*soohu*) and *-ngwuvi* is a root that means "climb."[8] From this we can deduce that

*Soongwuqa* is the galactic tunnel through which the ancient Star People journeyed in order to descend to their terrestrial home.

**Got Milk?**

There are many great circles in the heavens (celestial equator, meridian, equinoctial and solstitial colures, etc.), but the two spiritually significant bands are the zodiac and the Milky Way. The word "zodiac" derives from the Greek *zodiakos kyklos*, or "circle of animals,[9] and denotes the path of the sun, moon, and planets along the ecliptic as they pass through each of the constellations represented by the familiar astrological signs.

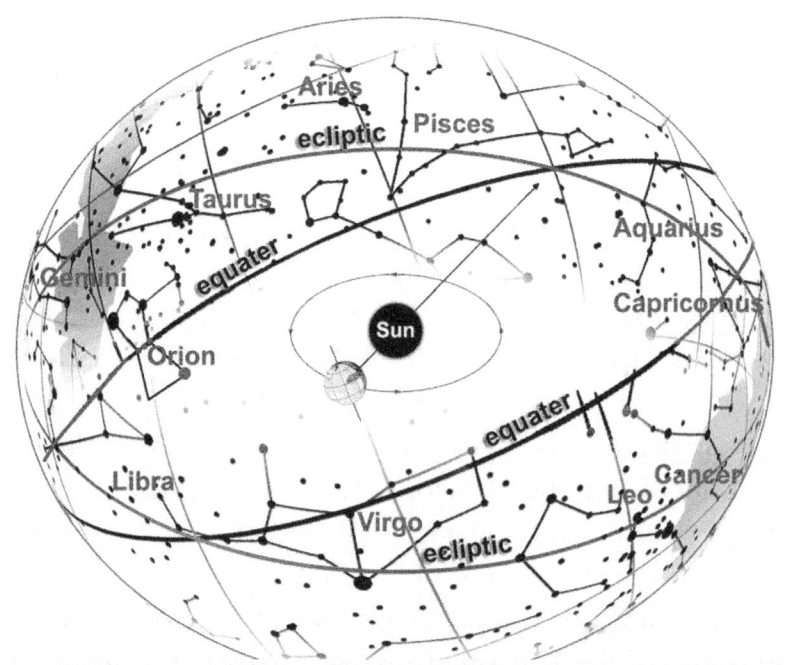

**The ecliptic path through the constellations of the zodiac.**

The phrase "Milky Way," our Galaxy, comes from the Greek *galaxias kyklos*, or "circle of milk."[10] "The main constellations through which the Milky Way passes are *Perseus, Cassiopeia, Cygnus, Aquila, Sagittarius*, Scorpius, Centaurus Vela, Puppis, Monoceros, *Orion, Taurus* and Auriga. [italics added, more on these below]"[11] On a macrocosmic level, this galactic belt is an *Ouroboros*—a stellar serpent swallowing her tail; on a microcosmic level, it is the ophidian phosphorescence of the *Kundalini*.

The Sanskrit word *kundalin* denotes "circular" and "having an annular form or shape," as well as "snake" and "peacock."[12] Regarding the first pair of meanings, we find a reference to the *ouroboros* in the *Yoga-Kundaly Upanishad*, dated from the early first millennium AD. "The auspicious power, Kundalini by name, which resembles the fine fibre of the lotus-stalk, having bitten the knot-like Muladhara [Root Chakra], with the top of its hood, as if it were the root of the lotus and *taken hold of its tail with its mouth* [italics added] reaches the Brahma-randhra."[13] This latter term refers to the the Crown Chakra, the Thousand-petaled Lotus, by which the soul may enter and exit the body. It is in the area of the soft spot in the skull of an infant, to which the Hopi refer to as the *kópavi*, "…the 'open door' through which he [the Hopi] received his life and communicated with his Creator."[14]

In regard to the second pair of meanings of the Sanskrit *kundalin*, the snake in syncretism with the peacock suggests the same ophidian-avian element as seen in the winged serpent panel at Denderah and in the specific Maya/Aztec deities previously mentioned. Arizona esoteric author Mark Amaru Pinkham describes the peacock's spiritual rainbow-rainment, after having experienced enthogenic revelations induced by ingesting the San Pedro cactus in Peru. He seemingly envisioned the Cosmic Peacock as the universe looking at itself via the myriad eyes in an infinite array of peacock feathers.

> "Having been deeply involved with the yoga path of India I naturally associated peacock feathers with Murugan or Sanat Kumara, the Son of Shiva and Parvati [the Mother Goddess, an aspect of Shakti], who was typically portrayed as riding on a peacock... Sanat Kumara is identified by his Hindu devotees at Kataragama [a temple in Sri Lanka] as Seyon, the Red One, as well as Agni, the Lord of Fire and the embodiment of the fiery Kundalini. Sanat Kumara's yanta or geometrical form body reveals his essential nature as the alchemical Kundalini force. The yantra of the Divine Son is the hexagram or six-pointed star, representing the alchemical union of the universal male-female polarity, Shiva and Shakti, that come together to produce the Serpent Power."[15]

Renowned psychologist Carl Gustav Jung elucidates the symbolism. "The peacock is an old emblem of rebirth and resurrection, quite frequently found on Christian sarcophagi. In the [alchemical] vessel standing beside the peacock the colours of the *cauda pavonis* ["tail of the peacock"] appear, as a sign that the transformation process is nearing its goal. In the alchemical process the *serpens mercurialis* ["mercurial serpent"], the dragon, is changed into the eagle, the peacock, the goose of Hermes, or the Phoenix."[16]

Finally, the eminent mythologist Joseph Campbell intuits the numinous iconography of the peacock's plumage. "The eyes in the tail plumes of the peacock suggest the opening from within of the eyes of the ground of being, to view the universe of its own body. They are the eyes (stars) of the night sky; the extended palms of the offered hands of the merciful Bodhisattva which may be likened to the wounds of Christ."[17](For the eye-in-the palm motif, see Chapter 16.)

This anomalous quality of omniscience brings to mind a Petrarchan sonnet by Austrian poet Rainer Maria Rilke called "Archaic Torso of Apollo" ("*Archaïscher Torso Apollos*"). The headless sculpture of the Greek god of poetry nonetheless retains its divine sovereignty.

> We cannot know his legendary head
> with eyes like ripening fruit. And yet his torso
> is still suffused with brilliance from inside,
> like a lamp, in which his gaze, now turned to low,
>
> gleams in all its power. Otherwise
> the curved breast could not dazzle you so, nor could
> a smile run through the placid hips and thighs
> to that dark center where procreation flared.
>
> Otherwise this stone would seem defaced
> beneath the translucent cascade of the shoulders
> and would not glisten like a wild beast's fur:
>
> would not, from all the borders of itself,
> burst like a star: for here there is no place
> that does not see you. You must change your life.[18]

YOU MUST CHANGE YOUR LIFE! Microcosm mirrors macrocosm, and vice versa. Your spinal column reflects Mount Meru,[19] gnomon on earth as Kailas.[20] Inflected "…in earth, as it is in heaven."[21] The chakra vector of the Ari-Zona Orion Correlation[22] enshrines the *Djed* pillar of Osiris.[23] Wheels within wheels, your chakras spin like "magic flying shields"—the Hopi name *paatuwvota*.²⁴ Earth dropped in the still waters of baptismal Space leadeth to annular rings of a vertebral World Tree, entwined by dual spirals of a Living Caduceus: sinister lunar *Ida* and dexter solar *Pingala*.²⁵ The pinions of Hermes (Thoth) be but a moth drawn to the rising Serpent Fire of *Kundalini*. Vortices in our Spinal Tunnel rack flashflood scintillations flocking to the raging roe of constellations—spirit-points of light Red Shifting on waves of dark energy in the Boat of Millions of Years.²⁶ Along the spectral Milky Way the Ur-Soul pierces storms of star-stuff from Gaia via the goddess Sothis/Isis, that is, Sirius to *Orion*→ *Taurus*→ *Perseus*→ *Cassiopeia*→ *Cygnus*→ *Aquila*→ *Sagittarius* to the black-holed Heart of *Galaxias maximus*: *Sah* to *Sahasrara*.²⁷

### Various Earth Chakras²⁸ (Dog)

> "The dog was one of the first animals that human beings domesticated, thousands of years before the written word, and was worshipped universally as a guardian, usually guarding the dead or taking dead souls back to their mother, the goddess. In early times, dogs in myth only accompanied the goddess [Isis, i.e., Sirius] and guarded the gates of death. The Egyptians called this guard or judge of the dead Anubis. In Christian mythology, he seems to have been represented by Saint Peter at the pearly gates of heaven, playing the same role as the dog—guarding, and sometimes judging who could pass through."²⁹

# Galactic Chakras

## 1. *Muladhara* – Base Chakra (Ant)

> "The seeming strength and desirability of the animal forces in man (*beautiful, blooming, strong, a mighty hunter*) and the apparent bondage of the individual to these forces ('Can'st thou . . . loose the bands of Orion?'). Man has a very dim comprehension that back of even his apparently animal forces and propensities that seem to bind him so tightly to the flesh there is something that is divine, there is some wonderful truth…"
>
> Yet, like the stars that represent truths apparently far beyond man's present conception, his inner forces and powers, with their origin and possibilities, are just beginning to be faintly understood by him."[30]
>
> "The Muladhara Chakra is the seat of the coiled Kundalini, the vital Shakti, or energy force. The Kundalini serpent is coiled around the Svayambhu Lingam. This foundation chakra is the root of all growth and awareness of the divinity of man."[31]

## 2. *Svadhisthana* – Sacral Chakra (Butterfly)

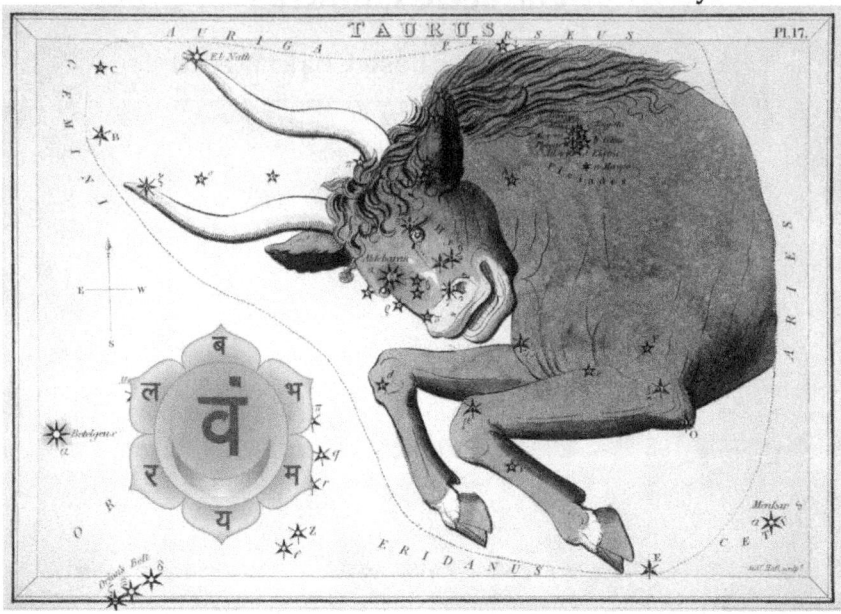

"After Aries, Taurus conserves the stuff that's left and grounds it in structure. Like the Pyramids of Egypt, the Bull makes a defiant stand: 'I am everything, I will last forever, without diminution or deterioration.'

The Bull is the creature who comes down to Earth and who makes himself a space here, a pasture, and who proceeds to ingest the materials of this Earth, to chew them, and in the process become one with Earth stuff, Earth substance. So the Bull is 'he who is here,' 'he who has arrived.'

The mystery of Taurus is that Taurus is not unto itself. Therefore getting lost in oneself in the center of springtime one gets lost in a dream. Taurus self-obsessed is a dream. It's a fantasy, an illusion. The whole nature of the sign of Taurus is the process of externalizing, of bringing forth the fruits, making things available, making them accessible, making them beautiful, making them present. Suddenly the whole manifest universe looms before us."[32]

"Thus the [Hopi] ceremony that is called the Butterfly Dance celebrates the flowering and fruition of all living things. In it the dancers wear elaborate and beautiful masks which portray clouds and falling rain and which include symbols of corn and of the sunflower."[33]   [continued on next page]

> "Svadhishthana Chakra encompasses the astral plane as well as the planes of entertainment, fantasy, nullity, jealousy, mercy, envy, and joy. The astral plane is the space between heaven and earth [i.e., star correlations]. Here the earth becomes a jewel and the heavens are within reach. Fantasy may be used to advantage through the crafts and fine arts."[34]

### 3. *Manipura* – Solar Plexus Chakra (Cobra)

*PERSEUS AND CAPUT MEDUSAE* — Pl. 6.

> "...Orion threatens undismayed the advancing Bull. Perseus, flying from his victory over the dread Medusa, slays the monster of the deep, and rescues fair Andromeda. This universal victory of humanity over the animal world, depicted in the constellations, is one of the chief features of these time-honoured configurations, and is clearly indicative of the fact that the ancient star groups are the product of design and not chance. Perseus, because of his gallantry, is known as 'the Knight Errant of Mythology.' The hero was the son of Jupiter and Danaë, and the favourite of the gods. His successful encounter with the Medusa rendered his name immortal, and at his death, it is said, he was transported to the starry skies, where he appears with upraised sword, holding the severed head of Medusa up to the gaze of all mankind, for all time."[35]

[continued on next page]

"A person dominated by the third chakra will strive for personal power and recognition, even to the detriment of family and friends… The plane of Manipura Chakra encompasses karma, charity, atonement for one's errors, good company, bad company, selfless service, sorrow, the plane of dharma and the celestial plane. Dharma is the timeless law of nature that interconnects all that exists."[36]

## 4. *Anahata* – Heart Chakra (Deer)

"Cassiopeia tips in her cradle across the axis of her plane, still whirling from the force with which Poseidon hurled her in her chair into the heavens. Once queen of Ethiopia, wife of Cepheus, she boasted recklessly of her own beauty and that of her daughter Andromeda, offending and later betraying the sea-god. Though her throne was exiled among the stars, she kept her glamor and pride: 'The longer you stare at Cassiopeia, the more beautiful she seems, despite her enormous, lonely distance. The stars of her chair range from fifty to about hundred ninety-eight light-years away…They shine there all night, year after year, backward and forward across the millennia. It glitters with some inescapable meaning.'"[37]

[continued on next page]

"The Arabs called these stars The Lady in a Chair, although earlier writings talk of them as The Hand Stained with Henna, i.e., the red hand. The Christians called her Mary Magdalene and at other time Deborah. The Egyptians placed the shape of the constellation, as well as the rest of the celestial royal family, on their seals. It would seem, therefore, that the major theme of this group of stars is one of female sovereignty, initially placed next to the king in balance but thrown into a state of punishment when the balance was lost."[38]

"Cepheus is an inconspicuous constellation, but evidently was highly regarded in early times as the father of the Royal Family, and his story well known in Greek literature of the 5th century before Christ. The name **Kepheus** [was] compared by [Robert Hewitt] Brown to **Khufu** of Great Pyramid fame... The later Hindus knew Cepheus as **Capuja**, adopted from Greece; but [James Francis] Hewitt claims that with their prehistoric ancestors it represented **Kapi**, the Ape-God [Hanuman], when its stars alpha (Alderamin) and gamma (Alrai) were respective pole-stars of 21,000 and 19,000 B.C."[39]

"It is in the heart chakra that Kundalini Shakti appears for the first time as a beautiful goddess. She sits in the lotus posture within a triangle. The triangle is pointed upward, showing the tendency of Shakti to move upward and carry the aspirant into the higher planes of existence... No longer is she personified as a destructive serpentine force, as is typified by the first chakra.

By evolving through the fourth chakra, one masters language, poetry, and all verbal endeavors, as well as his indriyas, or desires and physical functions. The person becomes master of his own self, gaining wisdom and inner strength. Male and female energy become balanced, and the resolution of the two energies interacting outside the body ceases to be a problem as all relationships become pure. The senses are controlled and the person flows freely, without hindrance from any external barrier...

The deer of Anahata Chakra runs swiftly, changing directions often, with an angular path. Similarly, a person in love may have the qualities and tendencies of a deer, such as dreamy eyes, restless wandering, and swift flight. When these come under control all emotional disturbances cease."[40]

## 5. *Vishuddha* – Throat Chakra (Peacock)

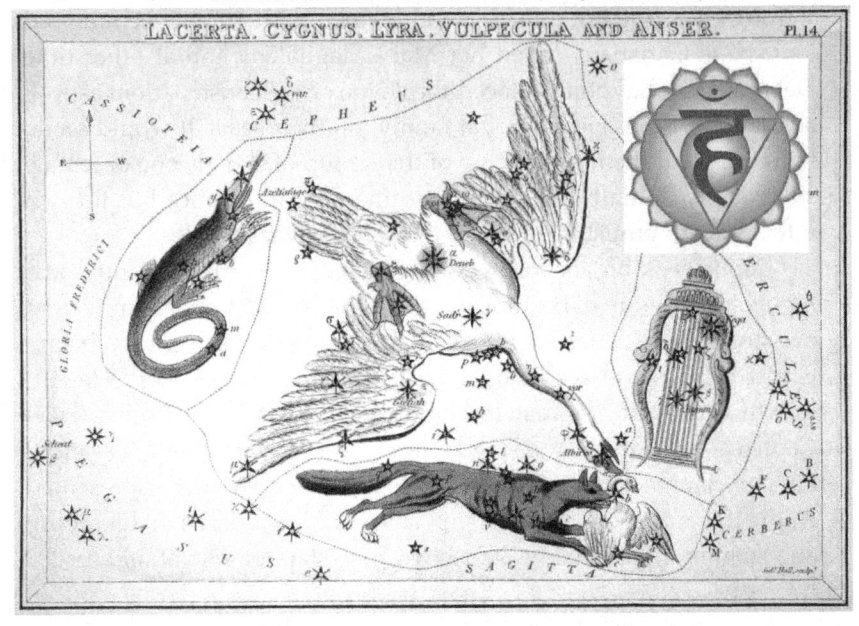

"In Taoism, however, the system is somewhat different, and instead of the main energy artery being solely up the spine [as in *kundalini*], it is in two halves. One, considered *yang* (male, active), flows from between the genitalia and anus around to the back, and then up the spine before going over the head to end at the upper lip. The other line, seen as *yin* (female), passive) flows from the same starting position, up over the front of the body to terminate on the lower lip. Thus a gap exists between the two lines where the mouth is, and only by the act of using the tongue to touch the upper palette behind the front teeth is the circuit, seen as a 'ring', made complete...

This enables the bringing together of the male and female energies, *yang* and *yin*, creating a perfect balance in both body and mind... Making the mouth and tongue of the *taiji quan* [Chinese *t'ai chi ch'uan*] practitioner synonymous with the Cygnus constellation allows us to perceive of it as the place from which the first word was spoken, as in the Logos or Word of God in Judeo-Christian tradition...

[continued on next page]

In other words the asterism becomes the source of the divine sound or vibration that brought the universe into manifestation, a concept met with previously in association with Egypt's Great Cackler, India's Swan-Goose of Eternity, and the Anfar [Peacock] of the Yezidi, which emites a loud cry that breaks the pearl and causes the formation of the primeval sea."[41]

"Meditation on the hollow space in the throat area gives calmness; serenity; purity; a melodious voice; command of speech and of mantras; and the ability to compose poetry, to interpret scriptures, and to understand the hidden messages in dreams. It also makes one youthful, radiant *(ojas)*, and a good teacher of spiritual sciences *(brahma-vidya)*... One who enters the plane of Vishuddha Chakra follows knowledge, the path that leads to man's true birth into the divine state... A person becomes *chitta*, free of the fetters of the world and the master of the total self. The Vishuddha Chakra embodies *chit*, or cosmic consciousness."[42]

## 6. *Ajna* – Third Eye Chakra (Swan)

[continued on next page]

"The eagle has always been associated with fire, lightning, and sun gods, so that the Greeks claiming this eagle as a form of Zeus, god of thunder and lightning, is in keeping with its mythology. It was a Roman custom to release eagles over the funeral pyres of emperors, for they believed the eagle would carry the soul of the warrior to the land of the immortals. The eagle was also the instrument for calling fire down from heaven to consume sacrifices made on the altar. Having passed through the sacrificial fire, the victims were borne away by the eagle or rose to heaven in the form of an eagle."[43]

"During the nine days of the Nima'n katçina festival [Home Dance], they are treated with special care and attention, then – early on the morning of the tenth day – all the birds in the [Hopi] village are ceremonially killed. The killing of the eagles is done in a special, prescribed manner; while one man holds the thong attached to the bird's leg, another throws a cloth or blanket over its head, pulls the bird to the ground and kills it by pressure exerted on the heart and throat. No eagle is killed by any other method; and each bird is killed in this way – 'that its breath may mount to Cloud with the Hopi prayers for rain, that its breath-body [*hik'si*] may return to its real home.'"[44]

"Our constellation is supposed to be represented by the bird figured on a Euphratean uranographic stone of about 1200 B.C., and known on the tablets as **Iduχu Zamama**, the Eagle, the Living Eye."[45]

"The Jaina of India pictured within part of Aquila a pikolan, or shoulder yoke (β-, α-, and γ-Aquila) with two baskets (σ-, μ-Aquilae). This type of yoke [i.e., *yoga*] and basket assembly was used to transport agricultural goods and other merchandise to and from market."[46]

"The third eye is the conscience. The two physical eyes see the past and the present, while the third eye reveals the insight of the future. All experience and ideas serves only to clarify one's perceptions in Ajna Chakra. The plane of neutrality (Sarasvati) appears as a balance between solar and lunar energy within the body... In Ajna Chakra the yogi himself becomes a divine manifestation. He embodies all elements in their purest form or essence. All external and internal changes cease to pose a problem. The mind reaches a state of undifferentiated cosmic awareness. All duality ceases... One who meditates on this chakra eradiates all sins or impurities and enters the seventh door, beyond Ajna Chakra."[47]

## 7. *Sahasrara* – Crown Chakra (supra-theriomorph)

"The sign of Sagittarius consists of what the ancient Greeks called a centaur—a composite creature, the lower half of whose body was in the form of a horse, while the upper half was human. The centaur is generally shown with a bow and arrow in his hands, aiming a shaft far off into the stars. Hence Sagittarius stands for two distinct principles: first, it represents the spiritual evolution of man, for the human form is rising from the body of the beast; secondly, it is the symbol of aspiration and ambition, for as the centaur aims his arrow at the stars, so every human creature aims at a higher mark than he can reach."[48]

"According to Subba Rao, this is a cosmic symbol expressive of the complete man—he who is at once animal, spiritual, and worthy of his divine origin. Man thus constitutes a link between heaven and earth, implying a state of tension which finds its symbolic expression in the arc (or rainbow). Sagittarius, the Centaur, or the Archer signifies this triple nature of the symbol; the horse symbolizes the instinctive organism, the human part denotes the three higher principles embracing the monad as expressed by the arrow. In the Babylonian epic of Gilgamesh, Sagittarius is represented by 'scorpion-men' who are 'no more than two-thirds divine'."[49]  [continued on next page]

"Another legend relates that Apollo urged the moon goddess Artemis to aim a shaft from her bow at a gleaming point on the horizon, which concealed Orion, the mighty hunter. Orion was thus unwittingly slain by Artemis. The constellation Orion is exactly in opposition to the so-called 'Bow stars' of Sagittarius, which accounts for this myth connecting the two constellations.

The legend is clearly astronomical in its significance, for in the variant form here depicted, Artemis is represented as sending a scorpion to sting Orion to death, and we find the stars marking the scorpion's sting in very close proximity to the Bow stars of Sagittarius."[50]

"The Sun passes through Sagittarius at the time of the hunt. Sagittarius has his arrow pointing to Antares, the heart of Scorpius, the Scorpion. Legend says that Sagittarius avenged Orion by slaying the Scorpion with one arrow shot. As a bull killer, we can follow Sagittarius in the sky around May or June. When the horntip of Taurus, the Bull, vanishes below the northwestern horizon, the first stars of Sagittarius come up in the southeast."[51]

"In any case, it is appropriate here to mention once again two valuable tool kits assembled by Franz Boll, who presents the whole tradition on the constellations 'Hades,' 'Acherusian lake,' 'ferryman,' with many more details than are needed now, as they have survived in astrological tradition. The topoi are found together around the southwestern crossroads of Galaxy [Milky Way] and ecliptic, between Scorpius and Sagittarius. Boll points out that, instead of Scorpion people, Virgil (*Aeneid* 6.286) and Dante posted centaurs at the entrance of the underworld, representing Sagittarius."[52]

"This chakra synchronizes all colours, encompasses all senses and all functions, and is all-pervading in its power. The form is the circle transcending various planes in ascending order, and finally, the ultimate state of Mahabindu, the supracosmic and metacosmic transcendental Void. The inverted lotus symbolizes the showering of the subtle body with cosmic radiations. The Sahasrara is the centre of quintessential consciousness, where integration of all polarities is experienced, and the paradoxical act of transcendence is accomplished in passing beyond ever-changing *samsara* and 'emerging from time and space.'"[53]    [continued on next page]

"Men's spirits were thought to dwell in the Milky Way between incarnations. This conception has been handed down as an Orphic and Pythagorean tradition fitting into the frame of the migration of the soul. Macrobius[54], who has provided the broadest report on the matter, has it that souls ascend by way of Capricorn and then, in order to be reborn, descend again through the 'Gate of Cancer.' Macrobius talks of *signs;* the constellations rising at the solstices in his time (and still in ours) were Gemini and Sagittarius: the 'Gate of Cancer' means Gemini. In fact, he states explicitly (*Commentary on the Dream of Scipio* 1.12.5) that this 'Gate' is 'where the Zodiac and the Milky Way intersect.' Far away, the Mangaians of old (Austral Islands, Polynesia), who kept the precessional clock running instead of switching over to 'signs,' claim that only at the evening of the solstitial days can spirits enter heaven, the inhabitants of the northern part of the island at one solstice, the dwellers in the south at the other. This information, giving precisely fixed dates, is more valuable than general statements to the effect that *the Polynesians regarded the Milky Way as 'the road of souls as they pass to the spirit world.'* [italics added] In Polynesian myth, too, souls are not permitted to stay unless they have reached a stage of unstained perfection, which is not likely to occur frequently. Polynesian souls have to return into bodies again, sooner or later."[55]

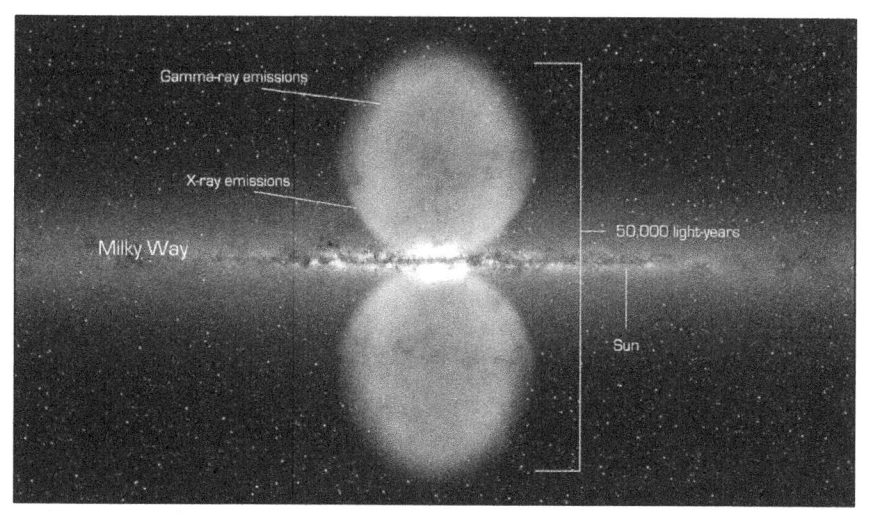

X-ray and Gamma-ray emissions form an infinity icon, or hourglass, issuing from the Galactic Center.

After the individual Ur-Soul, with its specific karmic requirements, receives the qualitatively distinct energies and benedictions of each Gaia chakra (or instead, merely those in particular that manifest the Soul's unique destiny in her current temporal incarnation), the Galactic Journey is undertaken. Isis as the Great Mother Sirius ushers us into the shadowy vestibule of the Afterlife, with psychopomp Anubis as famulus. Along the cosmic *Via Regia*[56] of the Milky Way, the constellations form a series of family houses in which the spiritual pilgrim temporarily rests, imbibing the essences of each holographic wavelength on the celestial spectrum in turn:

1. Base Chakra (*Muladhara*—the Alpha) – **Orion**: red/earth/smell/square; age 0 – 7 (first septennium)
2. Sacral Chakra (*Svadhisthana*) – **Taurus**: orange/water/taste/circle; age 8 – 14 (second septennium)
3. Solar Plexus Chakra (*Manipura*) – **Perseus**: yellow/fire/sight/triangle; age 15 – 21 (third septennium)
4. Heart Chakra (*Anahata*) – **Cassiopeia**: green/air/touch/hexagram
    with her consort Cepheus—their Cardiac dichotomy
    in a metempsychotic Arcadia;
    age 22 – 28 (fourth septennium)
5. Throat Chakra (*Vishuddha*) – **Cygnus**: blue/ether /sound/crescent; age 29 (Saturn return) – 35 (fifth septennium)
6. Third Eye Chakra (*Ajna*) – **Aquila**: indigo/astral/clairvoyance/torus; age 36 – 42 (sixth septennium)
7. Crown Chakra (*Sahasrasa*—the Omega) – **Sagittarius**:
    violet/superconsciousness/ Illumination/lemniscate-Mobius Strip;
    age 43 – 49 (seventh septennium)

Totemic analogues of meta-meat, i.e., the non-physiological chakra system, follow respectively: **1.** Ant **2.** Butterfly **3.** Cobra **4.** Deer **5.** Peacock and **6.** Swan—the 7th chakra being trans-theriomorphic.[57]

Near the end of the cosmic quest, the wreath of adjacent Corona Australis is visually emblematic of the Singularity's event horizon at the **Galactic Core**—the invisible wormhole of *Om-Uroboros*, the supra-supernova target at which the Archer's arrow points.

### Bardo[58] of the Kundalini Kosmos
by Gary David

**1.**
In her serpentine dream *Shakti*[59] sleeps,
an *Ur-Uroboros*[60] rapt
'round the *Lotos*[61] Root
of *Omphalos-cum-lingam*,[62]
as the etymon of macrophonic **Orion**
is microscopic *Morui*[63], antecedent to him,
like *hymenopteron* is to hymn.

**2.**
Bucrania of **Taurus** morphologize
the crucified ovaria of her sacred Sacrum's
eroticum, whilst his phallic caterpillar
transubstantiates the hookah crystal
chrysalis instar inside morphic
Strawberry Fields into
his Imago monarchy forever.

**3.**
Solar Plexus of **Perseus,** akin
the burgeoning brainstem
cobra's golden hoodie
as egoic Will to Power, glories
echoic in his karmic kingdom
for Ever and
a daydream still.

### 4.

Admixed mitochrondrial emotions
of the <u>Heart</u>'s flood, dear (deer) **Cassiopeia**, vain
Changing Woman,[64] mirrors your demotion
in the terra firmament—a circumpolar
-centrifugal fugue of bicameral sovereignty:
beatitude and solicitude vanquishing
celestial solitude.

### 5.

A *vajra*[65] avionics merger
of **Cygnus** & Aquila—AC/DC, Inc.— swaps
a Swan Lake swamp for his omnivident Peacock
rock fan, intuits a pituitary androgyne as psi
<u>Throat</u>-singer,[66] anodyne
with lunar larynx of Nyx,[67] *nada*[68] mother
of the vulgar boatman of Styx.[69]

### 6.

<u>Third Eye</u> of the finial pineal *Samadhi*,[70] sinless
Eleusinian Tripolemos[71] transported—serpent-borne—
via his wingéd chariot their ergot rot and smut
of Smati-Osiris,[72] with the tryptamine raptor
**Aquila** in the rafters of our skull, who shall soar
as seraph past our dolichocephalic fontenelle
to the Astral Aureole?

### 7.

O Chronos-wounded centaur
**Sagittarius,** who self-heals the thousand-tongued
*Logos*, Ophis inamorata, Ignis <u>Crown</u>ed
in the *Shiva*[73] sphere of *Sphota*,[74] your center
is everywhere and
your circumference is
the mandala to *Nirvana*.

345

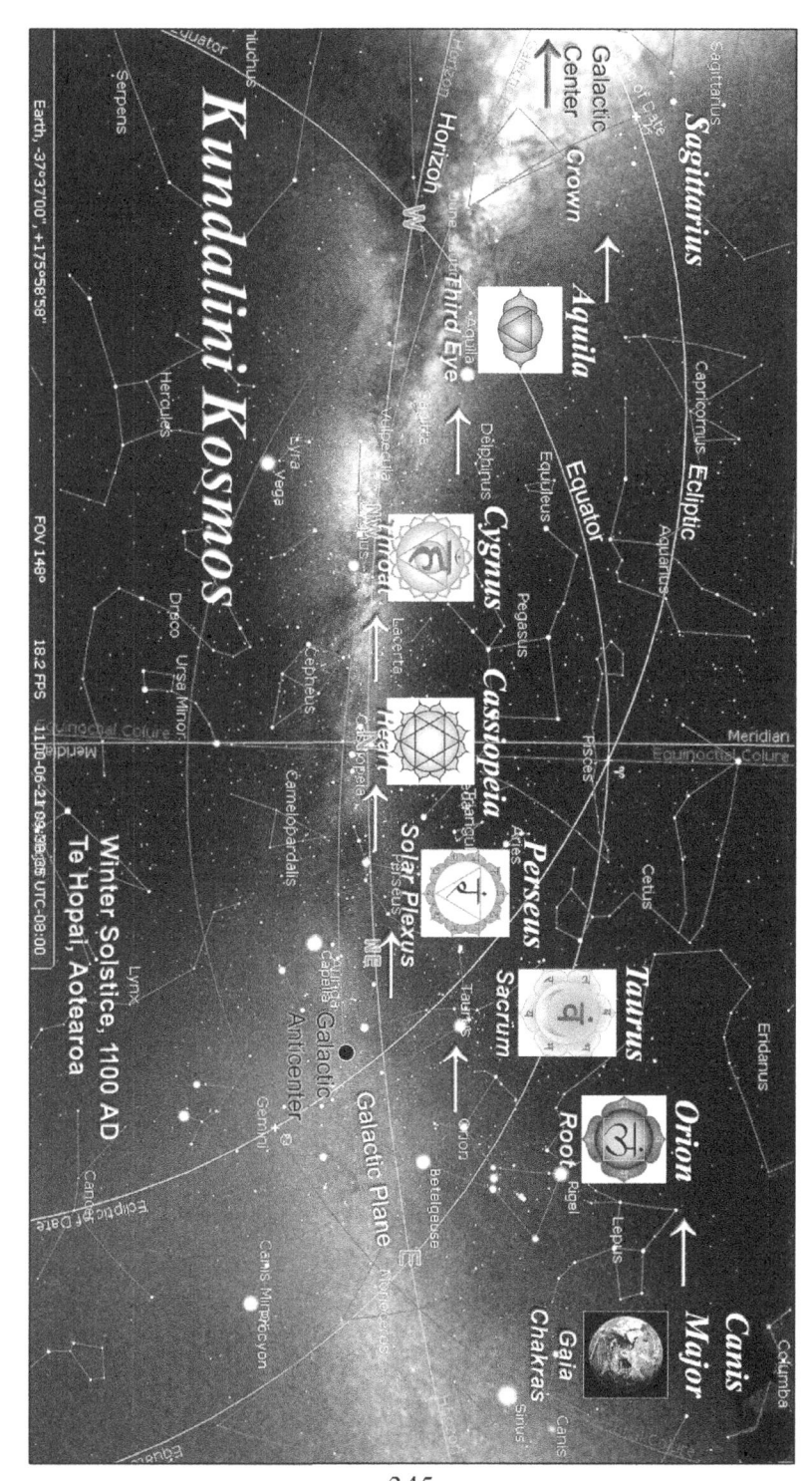

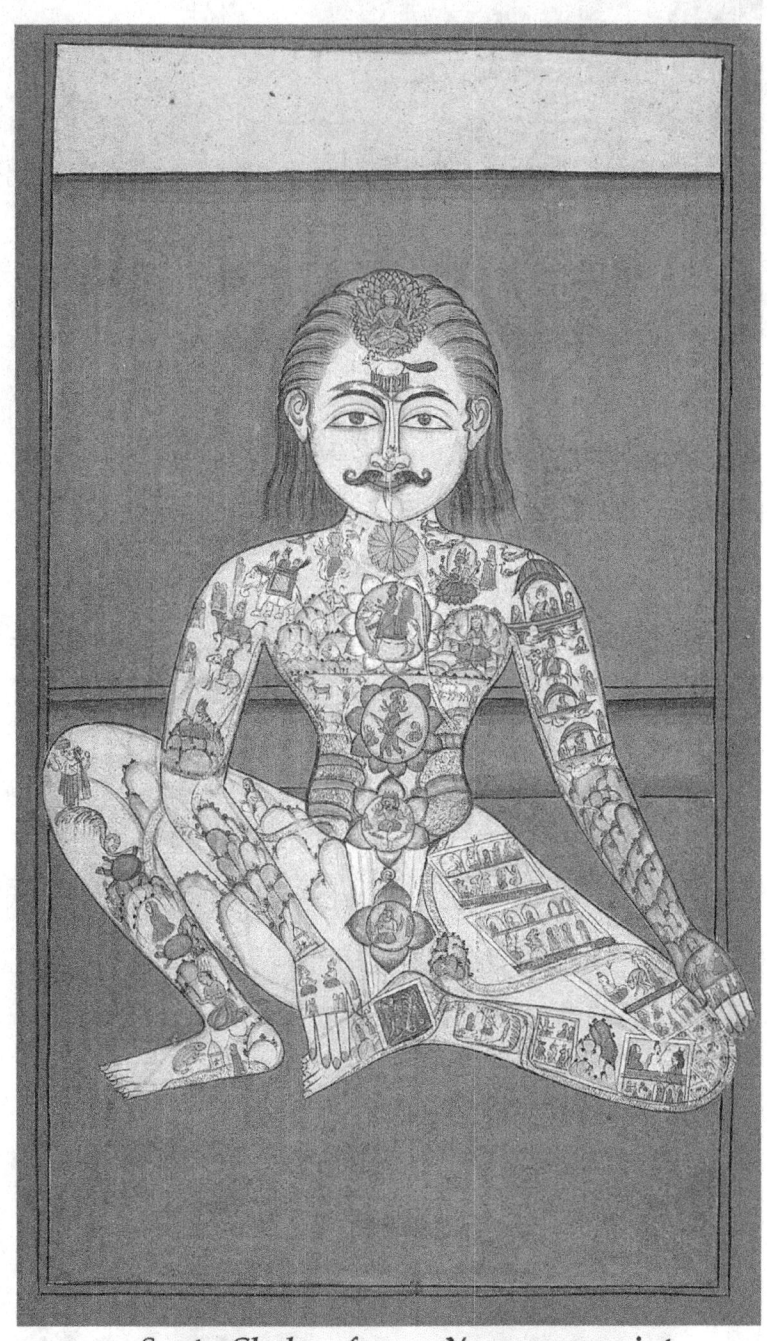

*Sapta Chakra*, from a Yoga manuscipt in Braj Bhasa language, 1899.

# Bibliography and Endnotes

## Copyright page

1. *Hopi-English Dictionary of the Third Mesa Dialect*, edited by Kenneth C. Hill, Emory Sekaquaptewa, Mary E. Black, and Ekkehart Malotki (Tucson: University of Arizona Press, 1998), p. 219.

## *Part I:* The Geodetics of Mythic Memory

1. Geodetics, pertaining to geodesy, "a branch of applied mathematics concerned with the determination of the size and shape of the earth and the exact positions of points on its surface," Merriam-Webster.

## Chapter 1  *The Chakras of Ari-Zona*

1. Janet Hizar Hansford, Ph.D., *Anthrogenesis: The Study of Humanity's Ancient Beginnings: Origins, Spirituality and Mythology* (Sedona, Arizona: Cities of Light Publishing, 2017, 2016), pp. 335-336.
2. John Michell, *The New View Over Atlantis* (San Francisco: Harper & Row, Publishers, 1983), p. 37.
3. Arthur Avalon (Sir John Woodroffe), *The Serpent Power: The Secrets of Tantric and Shaktic Yoga* (New York: Dover Publications, Inc., 1974, 1919), pp. 1-2, p. 8, p. 125; https://en.wikipedia.org/wiki/Chakra.
4. Harish Johari, *Chakras: Energy Centers of Transformation* (Rochester, Vermont: Destiny Books, 1987), p. 17.
5. Gary A. David, *The Orion Zone: Ancient Star Cities of the American Southwest* (Kempton, Illinois: Adventures Unlimited Press, 2006), pp. 131-135.
6. Frank Waters and Oswald White Bear Fredericks, *Book of the Hopi* (New York: Penguin Books, 1987, reprint 1963), pp. 9-11.
7. Dennis Slifer, *The Serpent and the Sacred Fire: Fertility Images in Southwest Rock Art* (Santa Fe: Museum of New Mexico Press, 2000), pp. 112-113.
8. Malotki et al., editors, *Hopi-English Dictionary*, op. cit., p. 694. See also, Gary A. David, *Journey of the Serpent People: Hopi Migrations and Star Correlations*, CreateSpace Independent Publishing Platform, 2017.

9. Gary A. David, *The Kivas of Heaven: Ancient Hopi Starlore* (Kempton, Illinois, Adventures Unlimited Press, 2010, see Chapter 5, pp. 82-98.
10. David, *The Orion Zone*, op. cit., pp. 63-65.
11. Will C. Barnes, *Arizona Place Names* (Tucson: The University of Arizona Press), 1997, 1988), p. 286.
12. David, *The Orion Zone*, op. cit., pp. 124-128.
13. Ibid., pp. 131-136.
14. "Aotearoa," native name of New Zealand.
15. Malotki et al., editors, *Hopi-English Dictionary*, op. cit., p. 678, p. 462; p. 150.
16. "**azimuth** The bearing of an object measured as an angle round the horizon easterwards starting from north as the zero point." Jacqueline Mitton, *The Penguin Dictionary of Astronomy* (London: Penguin Books Ltd, 1993, 1991), p. 41.
17. David, *The Orion Zone*, op. cit., p. 220.
18. David, *The Orion Zone*, op. cit., p. 226; see also, Chapter 9 of the current volume.
19. Alice A. Storey et al., "Radiocarbon and DNA evidence for a pre-Columbian introduction of Polynesian chickens to Chile," PNAS (Proceedings of the National Academy of Sciences), June 19, 2007, Vol. 104(25): 10335, https://www.ncbi.nlm.nih.gov/pmc/articles/PMC1965514. In addition, Lisa Matisoo-Smith, a biological anthropologist at the University of Otago in New Zealand, noticed in 2007 that some skulls found on Mocha Island (67 miles south of the El Arenal site) had characteristics that hinted at a Polynesian origin, such as a pentagonal shape when viewed from behind. Andrew Lawler, "Beyond Kon-Tiki: Did Polynesians Sail to South America?," *Science*, 328(5984), June 2010, p. 1344.
20. Edward Tregear, *The Maori-Polynesian Comparative Dictionary* (Ooosterhout N.B., The Netherlands: Anthropological Publications, 1969), p. 506.
21. The Maori word *whakaru*, "to stare," literally, "the open eye," Ibid., p. 607. The Whakaari volcano abruptly erupted in December of 2019, resulting in multiple fatalities.
22. Malotki et al., editors, *Hopi-English Dictionary*, op. cit., p. 41, p. 40.
23. Tregear, *The Maori-Polynesian Comparative Dictionary*, op. cit., p. 35.

# Chapter 2   *Hopi-Maori Cognation*

1. Philology, comparative and historical linguistics; peregrination, a voyage, especially a long, meandering journey.
2. https://www.merriam-webster.com/dictionary/cognate.
3. David, *Journey of the Serpent People*, op. cit., Chapter 2, Chapter 4, and Chapter 6.
4. Herbert John Davies, *A Tahitian and English Dictionary, with introductory remarks on the Polynesian language, and a short grammar of the Tahitian dialect: with an appendix containing a list of foreign words used in the Tahitian Bible, in commerce, etc., with the sources from whence they have been derived* (Tahiti: The London Missionary Society's Press, 1851), p. 108, p. 180; Malotki et al., editors, *Hopi-English Dictionary*, op. cit., p. 369.
5. Elsdon Best, *The Maori As He Was: A Brief Account of Maori Life As It Was in Pre-European Days* (Wellington, New Zealand: R. E. Owen Governement Printer, 1952, 1924), p. 33.
6. http://mymemory.translated.net/en/Maori/English/hopai; http://www.biblestudytools.com/dictionaries/eastons-bible-dictionary/shobai.html.
7. http://maoridictionary.co.nz/search?idiom=&phrase=&proverb=&loan=&histLoanWords=&keywords=hopi#; https://glosbe.com/mi/en/hop%C4%AB.
8. Tregear, *The Maori-Polynesian Comparative Dictionary*, op. cit., p. 81.
9. Malotki et al., editors, *Hopi-English Dictionary*, op. cit., p. 243.
10. Thomas Edwin Farish, *The History of Arizona*, Vol. VII (Phoenix: Arizona Board of Regents, 1918), p. 138, http://www.library.arizona.edu/exhibits/swetc/hav7/body.1_div.8.html.
11. Edward Tregear, *The Maori Race* (Wanganui, New Zealand: A. D. Willis, 1904), p. 121; A. W. Reed, *A Dictionary of Maori Place Names* (Auckland, New Zealand: Reed Book/Octopus Publishing Group, 1992, 1961), p. 61.
12. Gary A. David, *Eye of the Phoenix: Mysterioius Visions and Secrets of the American Southwest*, (Kempton, Illinois: Adventures Unlimited Press, 2008), Chapter 16, pp. 186-214.
13. Richard Maitland Bradfield, *An Interpretation of Hopi Culture* (Derby, England: self-published, 1995), p. 51.
14. https://glosbe.com/mi/en/hopi.

15. Thomas Kendall and Samuel Lee, *Grammar and Vocabulary of the Language of New Zealand* (London: Church Missionary Society, 1820), p. 154.

16. Jeremy Naydler, *Shamanic Wisdom in the Pyramid Texts: The Mystical Tradition of Ancient Egypt* (Rochester, Vermont: Inner Traditions, 2005), p. 261.

17. E. A. Wallis Budge, *An Egyptian Hieroglyphic Dictionary*, Vol. II (New York: Dover Publications, Inc., 1978, 1920), p. 782b, p. 791a.

18. Sir E. A. Wallis Budge, *Egyptian Language: Easy Lessons in Egyptian Hieroglyphics* (New York: Dover Publications, Inc. 1983, 1910), p. 60.

19. Dean Saxton, Lucille Saxton, Susie Enos, *Dictionary: Tohono O'odham/Pima to English* (Tucson: The University of Arizona Press, 1983), p. 29, p. 35, p. 34.

20. Jesse Walter Fewkes, *Tusayan Katcinas and Hopi Altars* (Albuquerque, New Mexico: Awanyu Publishing, Inc., 1990, reprint 1892), p. 265.

21. Charles E. Adams, *The Origin and Development of the Pueblo Katsina Cult* (Tucson, Arizona: The University of Arizona Press, 1991), p. 15.

22. Laird Scranton, *Decoding Maori Cosmology: The Ancient Origins of New Zealand's Indigenous Culture* (Rochester, Vermont: Inner Tradition, 2018), p. 38.

23. Malotki et al., editors, *Hopi-English Dictionary*, op. cit., p. 668, pp. 654-655.

24. Edward Tregear, *Maori-Polynesian Comparative Dictionary* (Wellington, New Zealand: Lyon and Blair, Lambton Quay, 1891), p. 542.

25. Malotki et al., editors, *Hopi-English Dictionary*, op. cit., p. 683.

26. Tregear, *Maori-Polynesian Comparative Dictionary*, op. cit., p. 81.

27. Ibid, p. 30.

28. Ibid., p. 342.

29. Malotki et al., editors, *Hopi-English Dictionary*, op. cit., p. 367.

30. Scranton, *Decoding Maori Cosmology*, op. cit., pp. 43-44.

31. Tregear, *Maori-Polynesian Comparative Dictionary*, op. cit., p. 342.

32. Ibid., 296.

33. Waters and Fredericks, *Book of the Hopi*, op. cit., p. 3.

34. Tregear, *The Maori Race*, op. cit., p. 458.

35. Malotki et al., editors, *Hopi-English Dictionary*, op. cit., p. 153.

36. Ibid., p. 471; Tregear, *Maori-Polynesian Comparative Dictionary*, op. cit., p. 152.

37. Budge, *An Egyptian Hieroglyphic Dictionary*, Vol. I, op. cit., p. 230b.

38. Best, *The Maori As He Was*, op. cit., pp. 36-37.

39. Malotki et al., editors, *Hopi-English Dictionary*, op. cit., p. 12.

40. Tregear, *Maori-Polynesian Comparative Dictionary*, op. cit., p. 28.
41. Davies, *A Tahitian and English Dictionary*, op. cit., p. 43.
42. Jane Ellen Harrison, *Prolegomena to the Study of Greek Religion* (London: Merlin Press, 1980, 1962), p. 272.
43. Ibid., p. 276.
44. Reed, *A Dictionary of Maori Place Names*, op. cit., p. 14.
45. Malotki et al., editors, *Hopi-English Dictionary*, op. cit., p. 13.
46. Tregear, *Maori-Polynesian Comparative Dictionary*, op. cit., p. 15.
47. Best, *The Maori As He Was*, op. cit., p. 46.
48. Barry Fell, *Saga America* (New York: Times Books, 1980), pp. 262-263, p. 294.
49. Malotki et al., editors, *Hopi-English Dictionary*, op. cit., p. 222.
50. Johari, *Chakras*, op. cit, pp. 26-27.
51. http://www.domainofman.com.
52. https://en.wikipedia.org/wiki/Torah. NB: A "scroll" is actually one form of a spiral; *The Compact Edition of the Oxford English Dictionary*, Vol. II, Oxford, England: Oxford University Press, 1981, 1971), p. 3355.
53. Malotki et al., editors, *Hopi-English Dictionary*, op. cit., p. 605.
54. Tregear, *Maori-Polynesian Comparative Dictionary*, op. cit., p. 480.
55. Tom Cryer, *Visual Testament and the Israelite Indian* (self-published, 1999), p. 203.
56. Tregear, *The Maori Race*, op. cit., p. 580.
57. https://www.britannica.com/art/haka.
58. Malotki et al., editors, *Hopi-English Dictionary*, op. cit., p. 67, p. 62.
59. Budge, *An Egyptian Hieroglyphic Dictionary*, Vol. I, op. cit., p. 515ab.
60. Tregear, *Maori-Polynesian Comparative Dictionary*, op. cit., p. 220.
61. Scranton, *Decoding Maori Cosmology*, op. cit., p. 118.
62. Malotki et al., editors, *Hopi-English Dictionary*, op. cit., p. 237.
63. Tregear, *Maori-Polynesian Comparative Dictionary*, op. cit., p. 478; Davies, *A Tahitian and English Dictionary*, op. cit., p. 253.
64. Malotki et al., editors, *Hopi-English Dictionary*, op. cit., p. 578.
65. Scranton, *Decoding Maori Cosmology*, op. cit., p. 81.
66. Tregear, *Maori-Polynesian Comparative Dictionary*, op. cit., p. 367, p. 299.
67. Malotki et al., editors, *Hopi-English Dictionary*, op. cit., p. 378.
68. https://www.encyclopedia.com/humanities/encyclopedias-almanacs-transcripts-and-maps/oraons.
69. J. F. Hewitt, *Primitive Traditional History: The Primitive History and Chronology of India, South-Eastern and South-Western Asia, Egypt, and*

*Europe, and the Colonies Thence Sent Forth*, Vol. II (London: James Parker and Co., 1907), pp. 870-871.
70. Malotki et al., editors, *Hopi-English Dictionary*, op. cit., p. 367, p. 58.
71. http://webapps.uni-koeln.de/tamil.
72. J. F. Hewitt, *The Ruling Races of Pre-historic Times in India, Southwestern Asia*, Vol. I (Westminster: Constable and Company, 1894), pp. 92-93.
73. James Churchward, *The Lost Continent of Mu* (Kempton, Illinois: Adventures Unlimited Press, 2007, 1926), pp. 46-48.
74. Swami Prabhavananda and Frederick Manchester, translators, *The Upanishads: The Breath of the Eternal*, (New York: The New American Library, Inc., 1957), p. 53.
75. Tregear, *Maori-Polynesian Comparative Dictionary*, op. cit., p. 257.
76. Scranton, *Decoding Maori Cosmology*, op. cit., p. 70.
77. Tregear, *Maori-Polynesian Comparative Dictionary*, op. cit., p. 257.
78. Tregear, *The Maori Race*, op. cit., p. 376; Tregear, *Maori-Polynesian Comparative Dictionary*, op. cit., p. 613.
79. Tregear, *The Maori Race*, op. cit., p. 471.
80. Kendall and Lee, *Grammar and Vocabulary of the Language of New Zealand*, op. cit., p. 183; see Chapter 4, David, *Journey of the Serpent People*, op. cit.
81. Malotki et al., editors, *Hopi-English Dictionary*, op. cit., p. 260, 262.
82. E. A. Wallis Budge, *An Egyptian Hieroglyphic Dictionary*, Vol. I (New York: Dover Publications, Inc., 1978, 1920), p. 293b.
83. Ibid., p. 294b, p. 295a.
84. Ibid., p. 295b.
85. E. A. Wallis Budge, *The Gods of the Egyptians*, Vol. II (New York: Dover Publications, Inc., 1969, reprint 1904), pp. 29-31.
86. Malotki et al., editors, *Hopi-English Dictionary*, op. cit., p. 368.
87. Tregear, *Maori-Polynesian Comparative Dictionary*, op. cit., p. 300.

# Chapter 3   *Cosmopolitan Polynesia*

1. https://www.merriam-webster.com/dictionary/cosmopolitan.
2. David Hatcher Childress, *The Lost World of Cham: the Transpacific Voyages of the Champa* (Kempton, Illinois: Adventures unlimited Press, 2017), p. 47.
3. Ibid., p. 12,
4. Ibid., pp. 56-57.

5. W. J. Perry, *The Children of the Sun: A Study of the Egyptian Settlement of the Pacific* (Kempton: Adventures Unlimited Press, 2004, 1923), p. 21.
6. Lewis Spence, *The Problem of Lemuria: The Sunken Continent of the Pacific* (Philadelphia: David McKay Company), 1933), pp. 73-74.
7. John Macmillan Brown, *The Riddle of the Pacific* (Kempton, Illinois: Adventures Unlimited Press, 2003, 1924), p. 236.
8. Tregear, *Maori-Polynesian Comparative Dictionary*, op. cit., p. 328.
9. http://humanorigins.si.edu/evidence/human-fossils/species/homo-floresiensis.
10. Susan B. Martinez, Ph.D., *The Lost Continent of Pan: The Oceanic Civilization at the Origin of World Culture* (Rochester, Vermont: Bear & Co., 2016), p. 81.
11. Davies, *A Tahitian and English Dictionary*, op. cit., p. 147.
12. S. Percy Smith, *Hawaiki: the Original Home of the Maori; With a Sketch of Polynesian History* (Wellington, New Zealand: Whitcombe and Tombs Limited, 1904), p. 39. Smith contends "that the Polynesians formed part of the very ancient 'Gangetic Race,' which had been in India from remote antiquity, but which became modified from time to time by contact with Tibetan, Semitic and other races. It would seem indeed, if we compare the Mythology of the Polynesians with those of the most ancient mythologies of the old world, that there are sufficient points of similarity to hazard the conjecture that the race is the remnant of one of the most ancient races of the world, who have retained in its primitive forms, much of the beliefs that gave origin to the mythology of Assyria." Ibid., p. 65.
13. Regarding Maori oral tradition and their astonishing memetic powers, S. Percy Smith expounds. "It is difficult for a civilized people which habitually uses writing in recording events, to conceive of the powers of memory possessed by people who have nothing but the memory to trust to. Some few instances of this may be mentioned: A Maori and his wife dictated to Mr. Elsdon Best, over 400 songs, and could generally tell the names of the composers and the incidents alluded to in them. Another Maori of mature age dictated to the writer 14 songs, etc. —and these were so impressed on his memory, that the quotation of one line was sufficient to recall the whole of the song at once. Another Maori wrote for the Polynesian Society 110 songs, and doubtless he knows many more, but the effort of writing wearied him. Again, another Maori has written 11 volumes of M.S. treating of the traditions, songs, customs, etc., of the Maori, and this, at a very advanced age, all of this matter having been retained in his mind, and including

hundreds of proper names. Two years ago the writer took down from the recital of an old Maori the genealogical descent of all the members of his tribe, involving the recollection of over 700 names, and going back for 34 generations. Each branch was followed out to the present day, and in most cases the reciter could supply the names of the husband or wife who did not come into the line of descent, and also
say what tribe they came from and give something of their history. Efforts of memory of this character are impossible with us, and are not known of, or not considered by the generality of writers on traditions, which are hence set aside for the fanciful creations of their own brains, after the manner of the German philosopher who was able to evolve the idea of a camel out of his inner consciousness!" Smith, *Hawaiki*, op. cit., pp. 20-21.

14. Tregear, *The Maori Race*, op. cit., p. 556, p. 557-558.
15. John MacMillan Brown quoted in Spence, *The Problem of Lemuria*, op. cit., pp. 70-71.
16. Malotki et al., editors, *Hopi-English Dictionary*, op. cit., p. 54, p. 167.
17. Ibid., p. 566, pp. 247-248.
18. Alexander M. Stephen and Elsie Clew Parsons, editor, *Hopi Journal*, Vol. II (New York: AMS Press, Inc., 1969, 1936), p. 849.
19. Malotki et al., editors, *Hopi-English Dictionary*, op. cit., p. 693.
20. Albert Yava, *Big Falling Snow: A Tewa-Hopi Indian's Life and Times and the History and Traditions of His People* (Albuquerque: University of New Mexico Press, 1982, 1978), pp. 61-62.
21. Malotki et al., editors, *Hopi-English Dictionary*, op. cit., p. 141; Yava, *Big Falling Snow*, op. cit., p. 46.
22. Yava, ibid., p. 70.
23. David, *Journey of the Serpent People*, op. cit., Chapter 4.
24. Bede Fahey, "The Asiatic Neolithic, the Southern Mongoloid Dispersal, and Their Possible Significance for the Americas," *Pre-Columbiana: A Journal of Long-Distance Contacts*, Vol. 2, No. 2 & 3, December 2000/June 2001, p. 181.
25. John D. Loftin, *Religion and Hopi Life in the Twentieth Century* (Bloomington: Indiana University Press, 1994, 1991), p. 66.
26. Yava, *Big Falling Snow*, op. cit., p. 36.
27. Lisa A. Mills, "Mitochondrial DNA analysis of the Ohio Hopewell of the Hopewell Mound Group," Ph.D. dissertation, Department of Anthropology, Ohio State University, 2003, p. 91, https://etd.ohiolink.edu/!etd.send_file?accession=osu1054605467&disposi

tion=inline; http://apps.ohiohistory.org/ohioarchaeology/ancient-dna-from-the-ohio-hopewell
28. David Lewis, *We, the Navigators: The Ancient Art of Landfinding in the Pacific* (Honolulu: The University Press of Hawaii, 1975, 1972), p. 15.
29. Carl L. Johannessen, *Pre-Columbian Sailors Changed World History* (privately printed, 2016), p. 35.
30. John L. Sorenson and Carl L. Johannessen, *World Trade and Biological Exchanges Before 1492* (KDP (Amazon), 2013), p. 280.
31. Best, *The Maori As He Was*, op. cit., pp. 134-135.
32. Ibid., pp. 184-185.
33. Nancy Red Star, *Star Ancestors: Extraterrestrial Contact in the Native American Tradition* (Rochester, Vermont: Bear & Company, 2012, 2000), p. xiii, p. xiv.

## Chapter 4    *Cayce and the Hopi Voyage from Mu*

1. Vada F. Carlson, *The Great Migration: Emergence of the Americas As Indicated in the Readings of Edgar Cayce*, (851-2) (Virginia Beach, Virginia: A.R.E. Press, 1970), p. 51.
2. Ibid., (1252-1), p. 53.
3. Ibid., (691-1), p. 52.
4. Carolyn Hatt, *The Maya, Based on the Edgar Cayce Readings*, (5750-1) (Virginia Beach, Virginia: A.R.E. Press, 1972), p. 42.
5. "Edgar Cayce – The Empire of Og," www.esoterism.ro/english/edgar-cayce-og.php.
6. Eric R., Wolf, *Sons of the Shaking Earth* (Chicago: University of Chicago Press, 1959), p. 119.
7. Séjourné, Laurette, *Burning Water: Thought and Religion in Ancient Mexico* (New York: Grove Press, Inc., Evergreen Paperbacks, 1960), p. 1.
8. Harold Courlander, *The Fourth World of the Hopis: the Epic Story of the Hopi Indians As Preserved In Their Legends and Traditions* (Albuquerque: University of New Mexico Press, 1991, 1971), p. 204, p. 56.
9. Malotki et al., editors, *Hopi-English Dictionary*, op. cit., p. 566, p. 247.
10. Ibid., p. 383.
11. Ibid., p. 369, p. 177.
12. Alexander M. Stephen, "Hopi Tales," *The Journal of American Folklore*, Vol. 42, No. 163, January/March, 1929, p 60.
13. Stephen and Parsons, *Hopi Journal*, Vol. I, op. cit., p. 54.

14. H. R. Voth, *The Traditions of the Hopi* (Chicago: Field Columbian Museum, Pub. 96, Anthropological Series, Vol. VIII, March, 1905), p. 53.
15. J. Walter Fewkes, "The New-Fire Ceremony At Walpi," *American Anthropologist*, Vol. 2 (new series), 1900 (New York: Kraus Reprint Corp., 1963), pp. 135-136.
16. Courlander, *The Fourth World of the Hopis*, op. cit., p. 64.
17. *Popol Vuh: The Mayan Book of the Dawn of Life*, translated by Dennis Tedlock (New York: Touchstone Book/ Simon & Schuster, Inc., 1886, 1985), pp. 84-85.

## Chapter 5   *Turtle Soup—Hopi "Red City" and Mayan "Black Rocks"*

1. Linton Satterthwaite, Jr., Mary Butler, and J. Alden Mason, PIEDRAS NEGRAS ARCHAEOLOGY, 1931-1939 PIEDRAS NEGRAS PRELIMINARY PAPERS, PIEDRAS NEGRAS ARCHAEOLOGY: ARCHITECTURE, edited by John M. Weeks, Jane Hill, and Charles Golden (Philadelphia, PA: University of Pennsylvania Museum of Archaeology and Anthropology), 2005, p. 1.
2. https://www.peabody.harvard.edu/cmhi/site.php?site=Piedras-Negras
3. Carlos Pallán Gayol, "The Classic Court of Itzam K'an Ahk of Piedras Negras: NewInformation On a Vessel from the Yaxche Phase with Hieroglyphic Dedicatory Formula," *The Pari Journal*, Volume X, No. 4, Spring 2010, p. 4,
http://www.mesoweb.com/pari/journal/archive/PARI1004.pdf.
4. Malotki et al., editors, *Hopi-English Dictionary*, op. cit., p. 781, p. 137.
5. Gregory L. Little, Ed.D., Lora Little, Ed.D., and John Van Auken, *Edgar Cayce's Atlantis* (Virginia Beach, Virginia: A.R.E. Press, 2008, 2006), pp. 185-186.
6. Ibid., p. 182.
7. David Stuart, "More On the Paddler Gods," University of Texas, Austin, July 28, 2016,
https://decipherment.wordpress.com/2016/07/28/more-on-the-paddler-gods/.
13.0.0.0.0 4 Ahau 8 Cumkuis variously construed as August 11th, or 12th, or 13th, 3114 BC. "This correlation between the Olmec/Maya calendar and our own was first worked out by American John Goodman in 1905, who fixed it at August 11th; in 1926 the Mexican astronomer Juan Martínez Hernández corrected it to August 12th, and a year later Englishman John

Eric Sydney Thompson refined it further and settled for August 13th. (Thompson, 1927.) As a result, it is only fitting that we define it by using all three of their names, calling it the Goodman-Martínez-Thompson correlation." Vincent H. Malmström, "The Astronomical Insignificance of Maya Date 13.0.0.0.," https://www.dartmouth.edu/~izapa/M-32.pdf.
8. Mark Pitts, *A Brief History of Piedras Negras As Told by the Ancient Maya: History Revealed in Maya Glyphs*, The Aid and Education Project, Inc., 2011, p. 12, p.14,
http://www.famsi.org/research/pitts/pitts_piedras_negras_history.pdf.
9. http://folkstudioin.blogspot.com/2013/12/blog-post.html#!/2013/12/blog-post.html.
10. Tedlock, *Popol Vuh*, op. cit., pp. 63-64.
11. John Major Jenkins, *The 2012 Story: The Myths, Fallacies, and Truth Behind the Most Intriguing Date in History* (New York: Tarcher/Penguin, 2009), p. 137.
12. J. Eric S. Thompson, *Maya Hieroglyphic Writing: An Introduction* (Norman: University of Oklahoma Press, 1971, 1960), p. 118; Patricia Turner and Charles Russell Coulter, *Dictionary of Ancient Deities*, http://book.google.com.
13. David Freidel, Linda Schele, and Joy Parker, *Maya Cosmos: Three Thousand Years on the Shaman's Path* (New York: William Morrow and Company, Inc., 1993), p. 94.
14. Yava, *Big Snow Falling*, op. cit., p. 44.
15. Alfonso Ortiz, *The Tewa World: Space, Time, Being, and Becoming In the Pueblo World* (Chicago: The University of Chicago Press, 1969), p. 75.
16. Freidel, Schele, and Parker, *Maya Cosmos*, op. cit., pp. 80-5.
17. J. Eric S Thompson, *The Rise and Fall of Maya Civilization* (Norman: University of Oklahoma Press, 1970, 1954), p. 218.
18. Barton Wright, *Hopi Kachinas: The Complete Guide to Collecting Kachina Dolls* (Flagstaff, Arizona: Northland Publishing, 1988, 1977), pp. 110-2.
19. Malotki et al., editors, *Hopi-English Dictionary*, op. cit., p. 788.
20. http://www.mesoweb.com/encyc/index.asp?passcall=sitenosearch&password=turtle-shell%20signs&passwordAND; http://research.famsi.org/mdp/mdp_list.php?letterSearch=M.
21. Budge, *The Gods of the Egyptians*, Vol. II, op. cit., p. 153, p. 154.
22. Malotki et al., *Hopi-English Dictionary*, op. cit., p. 36.
23. Budge, *An Egyptian Hieroglyphic Dictionary*, Vol. I, op. cit., p. 233a; Vol. II, p. 778b.
24. Ibid., p. 118b, p. 119b.

25. Budge, *The Gods of the Egyptians*, Vol. II, p. 376.
26. Charlotte A. Black Elk, "Black Hills Sacred Ceremonies of Spring," in Ronald Goodman, *Lakota Star Knowledge: Studies In Lakota Stellar Theology* (Rosebud, South Dakota: Sinte Gleska College, 1990, p. 51.
27. Daniel G. Brinton, *The Walam Olum: Excerpt from The Lenâpé and Their Legends*, 1885, http://www.sacred-texts.com.
28. Frank Russell, *The Pima Indians* (Tucson:The University of Arizona Press, 1980, 1975), p. 306.
29. James George Frazier, *The Golden Bough: A Study in Magic and Religion*, abridged edition (New York: The Macmillan Company, 1940, 1922), pp. 502-504.
30. Mark Amaru Pinkham, *Guardians of the Holy Grail: The Knights Templar, John the Baptist, and The Water of Life* (Kempton, Illinois: Adventures Unlimited Press, 2004), pp. 52-54; Pinkham, "Nicholas Roerich and Chintamani Stone," *Four Corners Magazine*, December 13, 2015, http://sirius-star.ro/roerich-chintamani-stone.
31. https://www.culturalindia.net/indian-history/akbar.html.

# Chapter 6  *Palatkwapi—the Case for Piedras Negras*

1. "Piedras Negras Ruler A," http://mesoweb.com.
2. John Van Auken and Lora Little, Ed.D., *The Lost Hall of Records: Edgar Cayce's Forgotten Record of Human History in the Ancient Yucatan* (Memphis, Tennessee: Eagle Wing Books, Inc., 2000), pp. 182-184.
3. Satterthwaite, Butler, and Mason, PIEDRAS NEGRAS ARCHAEOLOGY, op. cit., p. 18.
4. J. E. Cirlot, *A Dictionary of Symbols* (New York: Philosophical Library, 1971, 1962), p. 306.
5. Van Auken and Little, *The Lost Hall of Records*, op. cit., p. 98.
6. http://www.domainofman.com/book/cover.html.
7. Malotki et al., editors, *Hopi-English Dictionary*, op. cit., p. 605.
8. Alex Patterson, *Hopi Pottery Symbols* (Boulder Colorado: Johnson Books, 1994), p. 28.
9. Van Auken and Little, *The Lost Hall of Records*, op. cit., p. 101.
10. Waters and Fredericks, *Book of the Hopi*, op. cit, pp. 67-68.
11. Satterthwaite et al., PIEDRAS NEGRAS ARCHAEOLOGY, op. cit., p. 349.

12. http://www.famsi.org/reports/02055/section05.htm.
13. Ignatius Donnelly, *Atlantis: The Antediluvian World* (New York: Dover Publications, Inc., 1976, reprint 1882), p. 167.
14. https://howtoperu.com/tawantinsuyu-and-the-frontiers-of-the-inca-empire/.
15. J. M. Allen, *Atlantis: the Andes Solution* (Gloucestershire, England: The Windrush Press, 1998), p. 14.
16. Malotki et al., *Hopi-English Dictionary*, op. cit., p. 498, p. 382.
17. Waters and Fredericks, *Book of the Hopi*, op. cit., p. 17.
18. Homer, *The Odyssey*, Book XI, lines 572-675, translated by Richard Lattimore (New York: Harper & Row, 1967).
19. http://www.was-this-atlantis.info/cayce/10.html.
20. Waters and Fredericks, *Book of the Hopi*, op. cit., pp. 67-68.
21. Stephen and Parsons, *Hopi Journal*, Vol. II, p. 1162.
22. Zach Zorich, "Defending a Jungle Kingdom," *Archaeology*, Vol. 64 No. 5, Sept./Oct. 2011, https://archive.archaeology.org/1109/features/maya_warfare_yaxchilan_piedras_negras.html.
23. David, *The Kivas of Heaven*, op. cit., pp. 320-324.
24. "The Yucatan Hall of Records - The Atlantis Connection," YouTube, https://www.youtube.com/watch?v=AbJ3RVb-HS0&list=PLIkmcTo_EHdONM5R4EDixw_TiGQJn0cPA&index=10 .
25. Stephen D. Houston, Héctor Escobedo, Perry Hardin, Richard Terry, David Webster, Mark Child, Charles Golden, Kitty Emery, and David Stuart, "Between Mountains and Sea: Investigations at Piedras Negras, Guatemala," *Investigations at Piedras Negras, Guatemala: 1998 Field Season*, FAMSI, 1999, p. 7.
http://www.famsi.org/reports/97006/97006Houston01.pdf.
26. Waters and Fredericks, *Book of the Hopi*, op. cit., pp. 70-71.

# Chapter 7    *Cayce's Tuaoi Stone*

1. Little, Little, and Auken, *Edgar Cayce's Atlantis*, op. cit., p. 45.
2. Ibid., p. 46.
3. http://huttoncommentaries.com/article.php?a_id=69#Footnotes.
4. Van Auken and Little, *The Lost Hall of Records*, op. cit., p. 180.
5. Ibid., p. 15.
6. Malotki et al., editors, *Hopi-English Dictionary*, op. cit., pp. 654-655.
7. Ibid., p. 683, p. 355.

8. Ibid., pp.717-718.
9. http://huttoncommentaries.com/article.php?a_id=69#Footnotes.
10. Waters and Fredericks, *Book of the Hopi*, op. cit., p. 150.
11. Malotki et al., editors, *Hopi-English Dictionary*, pp. 222-223.
12. Michael Haederle, "Mystery of Ancient Pueblo Jars Is Solved," New York Times, February 3, 2009, http://www.nytimes.com/2009/02/04/us/04cocoa.html?_r=1; http://www.nps.gov/chcu/planyourvisit/upload/Cacao-Site-Bulletin-jan-2011.pdf.
13. Little, Little, and Van Auken, *Edgar Cayce's Atlantis*, op. cit. pp. 116-117, pp. 140-147.
14. Malotki et al., editors, *Hopi-English Dictionary*, p. 99.

## Chapter 8  *Geodesy of the Four Corners Odyssey*

1. Manly P. Hall, *The Secret Teachings of All Ages: An Encyclopedic Outline of Masonic, Hermetic, Qabbalistic and Rosicrucian Symbolical Philosophy* (New York: Jeremy P. Tarcher/Penguin, 2003, 1928), p. 217.
2. Freddy Silva, *The Divine Blueprint: Temples, Power Places and the Global Plan to Shape the Human Soul* (Portland, Maine, Invisible Temple, 2016, 2012), pp. 33-41, p. 47, p. 62.
3. Norman T. Oppelt, *Guide to Prehistoric Ruins in the Southwest* (Boulder, Colorado: Pruett Publishing Company, 1989, 1981), pp. 125-126.
4. Oppelt, *Guide to Prehistoric Ruins*, op. cit. pp. 102-104; David, *The Orion Zone*, op. cit. pp. 73-79.
5. See David, *The Kivas of Heaven*, op. cit., Chapter 5 for discussion of the "Sun Temple" (really, an Orion temple), which is in proximity to Cliff Place ruin.
6. Robin Heath, *Sun, Moon and Earth* (New York, New York: Walker Publishing Co., Inc., 2001, 1999), p. 50.
7. Robin Heath and John Mitchell, *The Lost Science of Measuring the Earth: Discovering the Sacred Geometry of the Ancients* (Kempton, Illinois: Adventures Unlimited Press, 2006), p. 40.
8. Ibid., pp. 45-47.
9. https://en.wikipedia.org/wiki/Annwn#cite_note-2.
10. Budge, *An Egyptian Hieroglyphic Dictionary*, Vol. II, op. cit., p. 958b.
11. https://en.wikipedia.org/wiki/Heliopolis_(ancient_Egypt). It may be just a linguistic coincidence that the Tewa tribes of New Mexico refer to the mythical plumed or horned serpent as *Awanyu*.

12. E. O. James, *The Ancient Gods: The History and Diffusion of Religion in the Ancient Near East and the Eastern Mediterranean* (Edison, New Jersey: Castle Books, 2004, 1960), p. 73.
13. Heath and Mitchell, op. cit., p. 73.
14. Ibid., p. 54.
15. Sarah Steele, "The Myths, Legends and Controversy Behind the Preseli Bluestone," The Gemmological Association of Great Britain, https://gem-a.com/news-publications/news-blogs/from-the-archives/from/stonehenge-preseli-bluestone-ancient-stone.

# Chapter 9  *The Meridian Connection — Hopiland and Easter Island*

1. Lyrics from "Axis, Bold As Love," by Jimi Hendrix.
2. Graham Hancock, *Fingerprints of the Gods: the Evidence of Earth's Lost Civilization* (New York: Crown Trade Paperbacks, 1995), pp. 28-29.
3. https://www2.kenyon.edu/Depts/Religion/Fac/Adler/Reln101/Otto.htm.
4. Stephen H. Lekson, *The Chaco Meridian: Centers of Political Powere in the Ancient Southwest* (Walnut Creek, California: Altamira Press, 1999), pp. 167-168.
5. Sergei Rjabchikov, "The Ancient Astronomy of Easter Island: The Mamari Tablet Tells (Part 3)," May 3, 2017, https://arxiv.org/ftp/arxiv/papers/1705/1705.01218.pdf.
6. Malotki et al., editors, *Hopi-English Dictionary*, op. cit., p. 587.
7. https://en.wikipedia.org/wiki/Ahu_Akivi#CITEREFMaras2010; http://www.osterinsel.de/05-ahu-akivi.htm.
8. E. R. Edwards, J. A Belmonte, "Megalithic astronomy of Easter Island: a reassessment," *Journal for the History of Astronomy*, Vol. 35, Part 4, No. 121, 2004, pp.442-427, http://articles.adsabs.harvard.edu//full/2004JHA....35..421E/0000421.000.html.
9. Graham Hancock, *Heaven's Mirror: Quest For the Lost Civilization* (New York: Crown Publishers, Inc., 1998, p. 224.
10. Ibid., p. 247.

# Chapter 10   *Rongorongo and Mohenjo Daro*

1. http://www.csgnetwork.com/degreelenllavcalc.html.
2. In my book *The Orion Zone*, op. cit., p. 226, I observed that Canyon de Chelly in Arizona and Easter Island are both on the same longitude line: 109° 22' W. Reseacher John Patrick Hill, a "beautiful mind" of Barstow, California, has subsequently noted this fact. He also somehow associates the Barringer Meteor Crater in Arizona with Stonehenge. "The diameter of Barringer Crater is 0.72 miles (1.16 kilometers) across, east to west. That measure, multiplied with the numbers of the 5/12/13 Pacific Triangle theory [sic—It is in Britain.] began to set something amazing ablaze. At first it was the 8.64 of the 0.72 x 12 that resulted in the find of Mummy Cave 8.64 miles (13.9 kilometers) above Spider Rock. [correct] Thereafter it was the 3.60 [feet?] of the 0.72 x 5 that pointed to the diameter of the outer ring at Stonehenge. [sic—The actual diameter of the outer ditch is 320 feet.] The sum of 9.36 (13 x 0.72) was the last gift and sent this whole world toward the Solfeggio frequencies of the Benedictine monk, Guido of Arezzo. [sic—The actual solfeggio frequency is 396 Hz.] Solfeggio frequencies make up the ancient 6-tone scale thought to have been used in sacred music, including the Gregorian Chants and it is purported to bring about spiritual healing." In his article Hill wrongly cites my book *The Orion Zone* as "*The Orion Code.*" https://members.ancient-origins.net/articles/can-ancient-mathematics-avert-meteor-strikes-and-hopi-prophecy-fiery-cataclysm
3. Igor Witkowski, *Axis of the World: The Search for the Oldest American Civilization* (Kempton: Illinois: Adventures Unlimited Press, 2008, p. 49.
4. https://en.wikipedia.org/wiki/Rongorongo#cite_note-def-3.
5. Alfred Métraux, translated from the French by Michael Bullock, *Easter Island* (Geneva, Switzerland: Editions Ferni, 1978, 1941), pp. 246-247; "…most of such ceremonies have been performed on the occasion of burials. Here it seems fairly sure that the recitations of the *rongorongo* men from their wooden tablets referred to conjurations for rebirth. As the pictographs on the statues as well as on the small wooden images represented a rebirth symbolism, it seems very probable that the glyphs originally served in general for this purpose, as was the case with the glyphs of the civilizations of the Old Orient, and with the runes of Nordic peoples. Hence the tablets probably were originally tablets of the dead, and there might have been a time when the wooden tablets with their inscriptions formed the walls of a coffin, as in the death cult of Old

Egypt.... Thus the tablets of Easter island seem to be grouped around the subject of death, being either maledictions on death or conjurations against death. As it is told of the belief of the Egyptians as well as of the Mayans, the origin of hieroglyphics was in Hades where the hieroglyphics served as a conjuration for rebirth; this was probably also the case in Easter island." Werner Wolff, "The Mystery of the Easter Island Script: Probable Causes of the Disappearance of the Hieroglyphic System," *Journal of the Polynesian Society*, Vol. 54, No. 1, 1945, pp. 1-38.

6. Egbert Richter-Ushanas, "Two Systems of Symbolic Writing - The Indus Script and the Rongorongo Script of Easter Island," https://web.archive.org/web/20080417162754/http://www-user.uni-bremen.de/~ushanas/#introduction.

7. https://en.wikipedia.org/wiki/Indus_script; Asko Parpola, "Deciphering the Indus script, https://www.harappa.com/script/parpola0.html.

8. Richter-Ushanas, op. cit.

9. Rainbow Warrior (pseudonym), "Rongorongo and the Indus Script," https://www.academia.edu/2384225/Rongorongo_and_the_Indus_Script?auto=download.

10. T. L. Subash Chandira Bose and Anitha Kumar, *Ancient Thamizh: The Falculty of Harappan Symbols and Scripts* (Tiruchirapalli, Tamil Nadu, India: A Center for Ultimate Studies, 2018), p. 44, p. 58.

11. https://www.sanskrit-lexicon.uni-koeln.de/monier.

12. Malotki et al., editors, *Hopi-English Dictionary*, op. cit., p. 367.

13. Bose and Kumar, *Ancient Thamizh*, op. cit. p. 2, p. 82.

14. Ibid., p. 45.

15. Lokmanya Bal Gandgadhar Tilak, *Orion: A Search into the Ancientness of Aryan-Vedic Culture* (Delhi, India: Vijay Goel, 2005), pp. 70-71.

16. Richard Hinckley Allen, *Star Names: Their Lore and Meaning* (New York: Dover Publications, Inc., 1963, reprint 1899), pp. 309-310.

17. https://www.sanskrit-lexicon.uni-koeln.de/monier.

18. See Chapter 17, David, *Journey of the Serpent People*, op. cit.

19. Dr. B. R. Kishore, *Atharvaveda*, New Delhi, India, Diamond Pocket Books Pvt. Ltd., no publication date, p. 118.

20. The equinoctial colure is the great circle derived from the meridian that passes through both celestial poles and the two points of the equinox, vernal and autumnal; likewise, the solstitial colure is the circle that passes through the poles and the two points of the solstice, summer and winter.

21. Santillana and Dechend, *Hamlet's Mill*, op. cit., p. 233.

22. Kishore, *Atharvaveda*, op. cit., pp. 118-119; Ralph T. H. Griffith, *Hymns of the Atharva Veda*, 1895, http://www.sacred-texts.com/hin/av/av10008.htm.

23. Bose and Kumar, *Ancient Thamizh*, op. cit. p. 44, p. 53; T. L.Subash Chandira Bose, M. Pandurangan and Anitha Kumar, "The Indus Seal M-304 reveals Lord Siva is the father all beings," http://harappansymbolsandscripts.blogspot.com/2018/05/the-indus-seal-m-304-reveals-lord-siva.html#!/2018/05/the-indus-seal-m-304-reveals-lord-siva.html.

24. Warrior, op. cit., https://www.academia.edu/2384225/Rongorongo_and_the_Indus_Script?auto=download.

25. It is interesting to note that the ancient Egyptian conception of Heka connoted magic, incantation, etc., or "the god who utters words of power..." E. A. Wallis Budge, *The Book of the Dead: The Hieroglyphic Transcript and Translation into English of the Ancient Egyptian Papyrus of Ani* (New York: Gramercy Books, 1999, 1960, 1895), p. 134.

26. See Chapter 8 and Chapter 9, David, *Journey of the Serpent People*, op. cit.

27. One scholar of the Indus River Valley script also shows the main figure of the Proto-Shiva seal depicting Orion, although some of the other constellations are identified differently. Jeyakumar, "Indus Seals portray Star constellations," https://sites.google.com/site/induscivilizationsite/book-published-ii/indus-symbols-page-2.

28. Sindhology is the study of the Sindh, a province of Pakistan, which includes the Indus River civilization. Asko Parpola, "Religion reflected in the iconic signs of the Indus script: penetrating into long-forgotten picto+graphic messages," *Visible Religion 6*, 1988, pp. 114-135, https://www.harappa.com/script/parpola7.html.

29. Ibid.; https://en.wikipedia.org/wiki/Amri,_Sindh.

30. Original German: "Der große Hai ist eines der Zeichen für die Milchstraße in Rongorongo. Das Fischzeichen ist ein anderes für unsere Galaxie. Aber am Himmel in der Nacht über dem Stillen Ozean gab es viel verschiedene Fische als Einzelsterne oder Sternbilder..."
Michael H. Dietrich, "Rongorongo ist entzifferbar," "Rongorongo is decipherable," https://www.rongorongo-script.de/Rongorongo/Rongorongo-Script/1/goto=11

31. In May of 2017 I guided Graham and his wife, the photographer Santha Faiia, on a ten-day tour of various Ancestor Puebloan sites in the Southwest, which ended a day or two before his massive, amnesiac seizure episode in New Mexico described in his book. Graham Hancock, *America Before: The Key to Earth's Lost Civilization* (New York: St. Martin's Press, 2019), p. 466.

## *Part II:* The Semiotics of Synchronicity

1. Semiotics, "a general philosophical theory of signs and symbols that deals especially with their function in both artificially constructed and natural languages and comprises syntactics, semantics, and pragmatics"; synchronicity, "the coincidental occurrence of events and especially psychic events (such as similar thoughts in widely separated persons or a mental image of an unexpected event before it happens) that seem related but are not explained by conventional mechanisms of causality —used especially in the psychology of C. G. Jung," Meriam-Webster.

## Chapter 11   *The ABCs of Orion— Ants, Bulls, and Copper*

1. Waters and Fredericks, *Book of the Hopi*, p. 343.
2. http://www.theorionzone.com/maps.htm.
3. Joseph T. Shipley, *Origin of English Words: A Discursive Dictionary of Indo-European Roots*, pp. 256-258.
4. Malotki et al., editors, *Hopi-English Dictionary*, op. cit., p. 143.
5. Ibid., p. 137.
6. David P. Seaman, *Hopi Dictionary* (Flagstaff, Arizona: Northern Arizona University Anthropological Paper No. 2, 1996, reprint 1985), p. 53.
7. Gene D. Matlock, B.A., M.A., "Is the Hopi Deity Kokopelli an Ancient Hindu God?", www.viewzone.com/kokopeli.html; http://dictionary.tamilcube.com/sanskrit-dictionary.aspx.
8. James, *The Ancient Gods*, op. cit., pp. 80-81.
9. Andrew Collins, *From the Ashes of Angels: the Forbidden Legacy of a Fallen Race* (Rochester, Vermont: Bear & Company, 2001, 1996), p. 290.
10. Malotki et al., editors, *Hopi-English Dictionary*, op. cit., p. 728.

11. Gene D. Matlock, personal email communication with the author, January 3, 2002.
12. Waters and Fredericks, *Book of the Hopi*, pp. 13-16.
13. Elsie Clews, Parsons, *Pueblo Indian Religion*, Vol. 1 (Lincoln, Nebraska: University of Nebraska Press, 1996, 1939), p. 236.
14. Voth, *The Traditions of the Hopi*, op. cit., p. 239.
15. Hamilton A., Tyler, *Pueblo Gods and Myths* (Norman, Oklahoma: University of Oklahoma Press, 1964), pp. 129-130.
16. Mischa Titiev, *Old Oraibi: A Study of the Hopi Indians of Third Mesa* (Albuquerque, New Mexico: University of New Mexico Press, 1992, reprint 1944), p. 116.
17. Malotki et al., editors, *Hopi-English Dictionary*, op. cit., p. 31, p. 288.
18. James, *The Ancient Gods*, op. cit., p. 73.
19. http://www.britannia.com/celtic/gods/don.html.
20. Robert Bauval, *Secret Chamber Revisited: The Quest for the Lost Knowledge of Ancient Egypt* (Rochester, Vermont: Bear & Company, 2014, 2000, 1999, pp. 133-136.
21. E. A. Wallis Budge, *An Egyptian Hieroglyphic Dictionary*, Vol. I & Vol. II (New York: Dover Publications, Inc., 1978, 1920), p. 958a, p. 56b.
22. Malotki et al., editors, *Hopi-English Dictionary*, op. cit., pp. 103-104.
23. Waters and Fredericks, *Book of the Hopi*, p. 158.
24. http://sesotho.blogspot.com/2005/01/morui.html.
25. "Orion the Hunter: Greek myth born in Syrian Mountain," Global Arab Network, February 1, 2011, http://www.english.globalarabnetwork.com/201102018849/Travel/archaeologists-orion-the-hunter-greek-myth-born-in-syrian-mountain.html.
26. *New Larousse Encyclopedia of Mythology* (London: The Hamlyn Publishing Group Limited, 1972, reprint 1959), p. 144; http://en.wikipedia.org/wiki/Hyria_(Boeotia).
27. http://en.wikipedia.org/wiki/Pissant.
28. Malotki et al., editors, *Hopi-English Dictionary*, op. cit., p. 508.
29. Sanford Holst, "Sea Peoples and the Phoenicians: a Critical Turning Point in History," http://www.phoenician.org/sea_peoples.htm#_ednref17.
30. Frank Joseph, *Survivors of Atlantis: Their Impact on World Culture* (Rochester, Vermont: Bear & Co., 2004), p. 5.
31. Cf. David, *The Kivas of Heaven*, op. cit.
32. Plato, Critias, translated by Benjamin Jowett, http://classics.mit.edu/Plato/critias.html.

33. John Lemprière, *A Classical Dictionary: Containing a Copious Account of All the Proper Names Mentioned in Ancient Authors*, 1809, http://books.google.com.
34. Waters and Fredericks, *Book of the Hopi*, op. cit., pp. 17-20; Malotki et al., editors, *Hopi Dictionary*, op. cit., p. 383.
35. David Grant Noble, *Ancient Ruins of the Southwest: An Archaeological Guide* (Flagstaff, Arizona: Northland Publishing, 1991, 1981), p. 22.
36. *The Compact Edition of the Oxford English Dictionary*, Oxford, England: Oxford University Press, 1981, 1971, Vol. II, **Zone**, *zona*, 3c., p. 3871.
37. Prash Trivedi, *The 27 Celestial Portals* (Twin Lakes, Wisconsin: Lotus Press, 2005), p. 97, http://books.google.com.
38. "Sanskrit, Tamil and Pahlavi Dictionaries," http://webapps.uni-koeln.de/tamil.
39. S. Kalyanaraman, "Who invented the oxhide shape? Meluha artisans. An archaemetallurgical journey along the Maritime Tin Route," http://bharatkalyan97.blogspot.com/2017/04/who-invented-oxhide-ingot-shape-meluhha.html?view=classic.
40. Hugh Fox, *Home of the Gods* (Lakeville, MN: Galde Press, Inc., 2005), p. 70.
41. Jim Bailey, *Sailing to Paradise: The Discovery of the Americas By 7000 B.C.* (New York: Simon & Schuster, 1994), p. 284.
42. Catherine Acholonu, *The Lost Testament of the Ancestors of Adam* (Wuse Abuja, Nigeria: CARC Publications, 2010), p. 49.
43. Santillana and Dechend, *Hamlet's Mill*, op. cit., p. 210.

# Chapter 12   *Orion's Hourglass Archetype*

1. Cirlot, *A Dictionary of Symbols*, op. cit., p. 145.
2. Francis Huxley, *The Way of the Sacred: The Rites and Symbols, Beliefs and Tabus, That Men Have Held in Awe and Wonder Through the Ages* (New York: Dell Publishing Co., Inc., Laurel Edition, 1976, 1974), p. 212.
3. Tilak, *Orion*, op. cit., p. 90. The period of Orion, which the Hindu author Tilak states is 4000 – 2500 BC, may be similar to the Western astrology's Age of Taurus, approximately 4000–2000 BC.
4. Hancock, *Fingerprints of the Gods*, op. cit., p. 262.
5. LanVan Martineau, *The Rocks Begin To Speak* (Las Vegas: KC Publications, Inc., 1973), pp. 105-106.

6. Polly Schaafsma, *Indian Rock Art of the Southwest* (Santa Fe and Albuquerque, New Mexico: School of American Research and University of New Mexico Press, 1995, 1980), pp. 315-331.
7. *New Larousse Encyclopedia of Mythology*, op. cit., p. 144; http://en.wikipedia.org/wiki/Hyria_(Boeotia).
8. Waters and Fredericks, *Book of the Hopi*, op. cit., p. 343; Courlander, *The Fourth World of the Hopis*, op. cit., p. 236; Malotki et al., editors, *Hopi-English Dictionary*, op. cit., p. 354.
9. K. Balakrishnan, Dr. P. Thamizhagan, Dr. V. Ramkumar, T. L. Subash Chandira Bose, "Papers from the 19th Congress of the Rock Art Society of India, Pondicherry, December 4-6, 2014" (Tiruchirapalli, India: Arivom Arivippom Centre, 2014), unpaginated.
10. Shipley, *The Origins of English Words*, op. cit, pp. 256-258.
11. Allen, *Star Names*, op. cit., p. 306; William Smith, LL.D., *Smith's Bible Dictionary* (New York: Family Library, 1973), p. 474.
12. John Lemprière, *A Classical Dictionary: Containing a Copious Account of All the Proper Names Mentioned in Ancient Authors* (New York: Evert Duyckinck, & Co., 1825), p. 501, http://books.goggle.com.
13. Waters and Frederick, *Book of the Hopi*, op. cit., pp. 17-20; Malotki et al., editors, *Hopi-English Dictionary*, op. cit., p. 383.
14. David Grant Noble, *Ancient Ruins of the Southwest: An Archaeological Guide* (Flagstaff, Arizona: Northland Publishing, 1981), p. 22.
15. "Sanskrit, Tamil and Pahlavi Dictionaries," http://webapps.uni-koeln.de/tamil.
16. See Chapter 5, David, *Mirrors of Orion*, op. cit.
17. "Sanskrit, Tamil and Pahlavi Dictionaries," op. cit.
18. T. L. Subash Chandira Bose, "Papers from the 19th Congress of the Rock Art Society of India, "op. cit., unpaginated.
19. T. L. Subash Chandira Bose, TM R. Veerasekaran, M. Lakshmanaperumal, Ph.D., *The Kizhvalai Rock Art* (Tiruchirapalli, India: A Center For Ultimate Studies, 2016), p. 59.

The following is from"Cosmic Symbolism Found at Various Rock Art Sites in Tamil Nadu," The 19th Congress of Rock Art Society of India, held at Pondicherry. (December 4th - 6th, 2014) Papers presented by K. Balakrishnan.

"The Cosmos is a complex and orderly system, such as our universe. The sky watchers identified the Star or Group of Stars as Constellations in the shapes of their own imagination and also comparing with the earthly beings and non-beings. Biman Basu* said: 'They also named those constellations after Mythological Gods, Heroes, Living Creatures or Common objects.' (*The joy of Star Watching, National Book Trust, India, p. 13.)

"The ancient sky watchers lived in a land presently known as Tamil Nadu, registered their observation of those constellations as Rock Arts. Among those 'the Milky Way Galaxy and the Orion Constellation' are to be noted.

## Orion

"Orion is a prominent Constellation located in the celestial equator and visible in the entire world. It is one of the most commonly visible and recognizable Constellations.

"The distinctive pattern of Orion has been recognized in numerous cultures around the world, and many myths have been associated with it. It has also been used as a symbol in the modern world.

"At Narthamalai there is a Pictograph of a Hunter, and other Pictographs of three different human figures as single group are drawn in white color. It is drawn on celling of the Shelter, which is underneath of a hill known as Aalurutimalai.

## The Milky Way Galaxy

"The Milky Way galaxy is drawn in the form of Petroglyph at Yerbet, Nilgiri District, and Tamil Nadu in India. This site was found by Mr. K. T. Gandhirajan and others. 'This Petroglyph consists of symbols such as a Serpent, a Human like figure and also a Scorpio like figures. Almost similar Rock Art without Scorpius is also found in Wardaman painting in Australia,* in which [there are] a human figure said to be the Sky Boss and the Serpent at the bottom said to be the Milky Way. (Thanks to Bill Yidumduma Harney for the picture).* Ray P.Norris and Duane W. Hamacher, Astronomical symbolism in Australian Aboriginal Rock Art, accepted in "Rock Art Research" (2010), p. 2.

"During December and January months the Milky Way Galaxy can be seen at the tail side of the Scorpius Constellation. In this Petroglyph the Milky Way is drawn like a Serpent below Scorpio."

Gary A. David's contribution:

"I am the author of *The Orion Zone* and five other books on Archaeo-Astronomy, concentrating on the southwestern area of the United States.

I have also have been featured on international radio interviews and on U.S. television programs.

"Since 1997, I have studied Orion and various man-made structures and rock art that represent this constellation. All over the globe, the Orion-pattern in the sky is frequently reproduced by certain megalithic constructions on the ground. (Mega- means 'large' and lithic means 'stone.') In essence, the earth structures mirror the pattern in the sky. In addition, the rising and setting of Orion's stars are sometimes lined up with certain astronomical markers. Various cultural sites in Peru, Mesoamerica, North America, Great Britain, Ireland, Europe, Africa, and Egypt, along with other locations across the world, concentrate on this particular constellation with an archetypal intensity.

"Now we have a solid proof of the 'Orion archetype' found in the pictographs (rock paintings) of Narthamalai, Tamil Nadu, India, dated to 1500 BC or earlier. Painted in white, a human figure is seen with the typical upraised right arm as well as the left arm holding either a shield or club or spear. Associated with this figure is a representation of two triangles with their apexes touching.

"This type of figure is also found in rock art of the Americas and Africa. In North America it signifies warfare between Native American tribes. For the Igbo tribe of Nigeria it signifies the Great Mother Goddess called Mbari. In India this double-triangle may represent the Female-Male complex. It may also represent the 'hourglass drum'or 'dumroo', a two-headed sacred drum of Lord Shiva.

"Shree T. L. Subash Chandira Bose – Archaeo-Symbolist, K. Balakrishnan and V. Kannan have discovered a number of important rock paintings with a great astronomical, mythological, and spiritual significance. It is my wish and hope that in the future the cultural heritage of India and the world be further explored and documented."

To read full article:
https://arivomarivippom.blogspot.com/2015/04/?m=1&fbclid=IwAR37yrpc38OhhDZ7e1UqAsjiTisgytYAumYPkuvGwA7qMym8owfubyW9tWo
20. See Chapter 13, David, *Eye of the Phoenix*, op. cit.
21. Hermann Oldenberg, *The Religion of the Veda: Samkhya and Yoga Systems of Religious Thought* (Motilal Banarsidass Publishing, 1988, 1894), p. 112.
22. Robert Bauval and Thomas Brophy, Ph.D., *Black Genesis: The Prehistoric Origins of Ancient Egypt* (Rochester, Vermont: Bear & Company, 2011), p. 210.

23. Robert Hewitt Brown, *Stellar Theology and Masonic Astronomy, or the Origin and Meaning of Ancient and Modern Mysteries Explained* (Kessinger Publishing, reprint of 1882), p. 86.
24. Garrick Mallery, *Picture-Writing of the American Indians*, Vol. II (New York: Dover Publications, Inc., 1972, 1893), p. 662; Budge, *An Egyptian Hieroglyphic Dictionary*, Vol. I, op. cit., p. 317b, p. 485b.
25. Herodotus, *The History*, 3:26, (Chicago: University of Chicago Press, 1987), p. 222.
26. Allen, *Star Names*, op. cit., p. 308.

# Chapter 13    *Cosmic Double Take*

1. "labrys," a ritualistic, double-headed ax, https://www.ancient-symbols.com/symbols-directory/labrys.html.
2. Joscelyn Godwin, *Mystery Religions In the Ancient World* (San Francsico/London: Harper & Row, Publishers/Thames and Hudson Ltd., 1981), p. 154.
3. Marija Gimbutas, *The Language of the Goddess: Unearthing the Hidden Symbols of Western Civilization* (San Francisco: HarperCollins Publishers, 1991, 1989), p. 239.
4. Ibid., p. 245.
5. Ibid., p. 273.
6. Waters and Fredericks, *Book of the Hopi*, op. cit., pp. 50-51.
7. Bradfield, *An Interpretation of Hopi Culture*, op. cit., p. 237.
8. Ralph Blum, *The Book of Runes* (New York: St. Martin's Press, 1982), pp. 111-112.
9. Faolchú Ifreann and Tyrsoak Josephsson, *Odin's Chosen: A Handbook of Ásatrú* (Hubbardston, Massachusetts: Asphodel Press, 2016), p. 67.
10. Hancock, *Fingerprints of the Gods*, op. cit., p. 154.
11. Karl W. Luckert, *Olmec Religion: Key to Middle America and Beyond* (Norman: University of Oklahoma Press, 1976), pp. 154-155.
12. Jesse Walter Fewkes, *Prehistoric Pottery Designs* (New York: Dover Publications, Inc., 1973, reprint of *Seventeenth Annual Report to the Bureau of American Ethnology*, 1898; and *Thirty-Third Annual Report to the Bureau of American Ethnology*, 1919). p. 155-156.
13. Julie Ryder, Galacticfacets, http://www.galacticfacets.com/ancient-pictographs.html.
14. http://www.huffingtonpost.com/entry/x-structure-milky-way_us_57914045e4b0bdddc4d3db54

15. Colin Wilson, *The Atlas of Holy Places & Sacred Sites*, (New York: DK Publishing, Inc., 1996), p. 119.

16. Ken Zafren, "Pigrimages in the High Himalayas," *Travel Medicine: Tales Behind the Science*, edited by Annelies Wilder-Smith, Marc Shaw, Dr. Eli Schwartz, (Oxford, United Kingdom: Elsevier Ltd., 2007), p. 280.

17. Mircea Eliade, *Shamanism: Archaic Techniques of Ecstasy* (Princeton, New Jersey: Princeton University Press/Bollingen Series LXXVI, 1974, 1951), pp. 266-267.

18. Godfrey Higgins, *Anacalypsis: An Attempt To Draw Aside the Veil of the Saitic Isis or An Inquiry Into the Origin of Languages, Nations, and Religions*, Vol. I (Brooklyn, New York: A & B Books Publishers, 1992, 1836), p. 335.

19. Ibid., p. 336.

20. R. C. Zaehner, *Hinduism* (London: Oxford University Press, 1968, 1962), p. 82.

21. A. L. Basham, *The Wonder That Was India: A Survey of the Culture of the Indian Sub-Continent Before the Coming of the Muslims* (New York: Grove Press, Inc., 1959, 1954), pp. 307-308.

22. W. J. Wilkins, *Hindu Mythology: Vedic and Puranic* (Calcutta: Rupa & Co., 1991, 1882), p. 263.

23. Fritjof Capra, *The Tao of Physics: An Exploration of the Parallels Between Modern Physics and Eastern Mysticism* (New York: Bantam Books, 1975), p. 233.

24. Steve Renshaw and Saori Ihara, "*Yowatashi Boshi*; Stars that Pass in the Night—Japan's Cultural Heritage Reflected in the Star Lore of Orion," *Griffith Observer*, Vol. 63, No.10, October, 1999, pp. 2-17, http://www.renshaworks.com/jastro/orion.htm; Malotki et al., editors, *Hopi-English Dictionary*, op. cit., p. 649.

25. Philip Gardiner and Gary Osborn, *The Serpent Grail: The Truth Behind the Holy Grail, the Philosoper's Stone and the Elixir of Life*, (London: Watkins Publishing, 2005), pp. 129-130.

# Chapter 14   *Celestial Birdman of Antiquity*

1. Henri Frankfort, *Ancient Egyptian Religion: An Interpretation* (New York: Columbia University Press, 1948), p. 97. In addition: "To that part of man which beyond all doubt was believed to enjoy an eternal existence after the death of the body, the Egyptians gave the name BA, a word which has been thought to mean something like 'sublime,' 'noble,' and which has always hitherto been translated by 'soul,' or 'heart-soul

[i.e., *ab-ba*]. It was closely associated with the Ka and the Åb, or heart, and it was one of the principles of life in man. In form it is depicted as a human-headed hawk, and in nature and substance it is stated to be exceedingly refined or ethereal. It revisited the body in the tomb and re-animated it, and conversed with it; it could take upon itself any shape that it pleased; and it had the power of passing into heaven and of dwelling with the perfected souls there. It was eternal." Budge, *The Book of the Dead*, op. cit., p. 76.
2. W. J. Wilkins, *Hindu Mythology* (New Delhi: Rupa & Co., 1991, 1882, pp. 449-456.
3. E. T. C. Werner, *Myths and Legends of China* (London: George G. Harrap & Co. Ltd, 1992), p. 20; http://www.gutenberg.org/files/15250/15250-h/15250-h.htm.
4. http://en.wikipedia.org/wiki/Kinnara.
5. Andrew Collins, *From the Ashes of Angels: The Forbidden Legacy of a Fallen Race* (Rochester, Vermont: Bear & Company, 2001, 1996), p. 58.
6. Hancock, *Heaven's Mirror*, op. cit., pp. 243-244.
7. Herbert J. Spinden, *A Study of Maya Art: Its Subject Matter and Historical Development* (New York: Dover Publications, Inc., 1975), pp. 79-80; Alfred M. Tozzer, Ph.D and Glover M. Allen, Ph.D., *Animal Figures in the Maya Codices*, Papers Vol. IV, No. 3 (Cambridge, Massachusetts: Peabody Museum of American Archaeology and Ethnology, Harvard University, 1910), pp. 337-340, http://www.gutenberg.org/files/19042/19042-h/19042-h.htm#image03.
8. Rex Gilroy, "Australian UFOs Through the Window of Tine," http://www.mysteriousaustralia.com/rexufo/bird-mystery.shtml.
9. http://forgottenorigin.com.
10. https://en.wikipedia.org/wiki/Burney_Relief
11. Budge, *An Egyptian Hieroglyphic* Dictionary, Vol. II, op. cit., p. 743a, p. 743b, p. 744a.

# Chapter 15    *The Orion Mind in the Cave*

1. Take a fantastic video tour: http://www.lascaux.culture.fr/.
2. David Lewis-Williams, *The Mind In the Cave: Consciousness and the Origins of Art* (London: Thames & Hudson, 2002), pp. 265- 266.
3. Alternative researcher Wayne Herschel has made a similar observation, http://www.thehiddenrecords.com/lascaux_cave_france.

Truth be known, a few years ago Herschel stole a photograph I had taken of a petroglyph panel at Homolovi State Park in Arizona and photoshopped in order to corroborate his pet "Sol Star" theory. What he marks as Orion's Belt is clearly three bulletholes. I have spent all day during multiple summer solstices at the site, whereas I doubt whether Hershel has ever set foot in Arizona. If he has, he certainly did not visit this petroglyph panel, which is obscure and not publically marked, but merely opined and spun his fuzzy-headed yarn from afar in South Africa. He then goes on to smear my Arizona Orion Correlation theory, and even cites the professional hyperskeptic and archeo-troll Jason Colavito to back him up. You decide (see under HOMOLOVI STATE PARK PETROGLYPH section): http://thehiddenrecords.com/chaco-canyon.php. One thing I will say for Herschel: he's got some slick web graphics.

4. Lewis-Williams, *The Mind In the Cave*, op. cit., p. 265.

5. Dr. Michael A Rappenglück, "A Paleolithic Planetarium Underground – The Cave of Lascaux (Part I)," *Migration & Diffusion: an International Journal*, Vol. 5, No. 18, April-June, 2004, pp. 93-119, https://www.academia.edu/2548536/A_Palaeolithic_Planetarium_Underground_-_The_Cave_of_Lascaux_Part_1; M.A, David Whitehouse, "Ice Age star map discovered," BBC News, August 9, 2000, http://news.bbc.co.uk/2/hi/871930.stm.

6. Sirius is usually designated today as blue-white in color, even though the star appears to display multi-colored scintillations on the horizon. However, some ancient cultures designated it as *rubra canicula*, referring to its ruddy or fiery red hue. D. C. B. Whittet, "A physical interpretation of the 'red Sirius' anomaly," *Mon. Not. R. Astron. Soc.*, 310, 1999, pp. 355-359, http://mnras.oxfordjournals.org/content/310/2/355.full.pdf; Eliade, *Shamanism*, op. cit., p. 481.

7. Clayton Eshleman, *Juniper Fuse: Upper Paleolithic Imagination & the Construction of the Underworld* (Middletown, Connecticut: Wesleyan University Press, 2003), pp. 183-184.

8. Joseph Campbell, *The Masks of God: Primitive Mythology* (New York: Arkan/Penguin Books Ltd, 1991, 1959), p. 398.

9. Rappenglück, "A Paleolithic Planetarium Underground," op. cit., p. 113.

10. David, *Journey of the Serpent People*, op. cit., see Chapter 12.

11. http://archeologie.culture.fr/lascaux/en/dating-figures-lascaux.

12. Andrew Collins and Gregory L. Little, *Denisovan Origins: Hybrid Humans, Göbekli Tepe, and the Genesis of the Giants of Ancient America* (Rochester, Vermont: Bear & Company, 2019), p. 83.
13. Gary A. David, *Star Shrines and Earthworks of the Desert Southwest* (Kempton, Illinois: Adventures Unlimited Press, 2012), p. 104, graphic re. Hopi Cosmology: "The horizontal plane of the earth's surface bisects the sphere. The underworld is a mirror image of the upperworld. North and south in the two hemispheres are opposite of each other. The summer solstice sunset in the upper world becomes the winter solstice sunrise in the lower world, etc."
14. https://www.donsmaps.com/lascauxlamp.html.
15. Lewis-Williams, *The Mind In the Cave*, op. cit., p. 263.
16. http://www.sciencedaily.com/releases/2012/06/120614142840.htm; http://news.sciencemag.org/2012/06/did-neandertals-paint-early-cave-art.
17. Alistair Coombs, "Zoos and Zodiacs: The Lascaux Shaft Scene," https://alistaircoombs.com/2018/08/24/the-lascaux-shaft-scene/.
18. Robert K. G. Temple, *The Sirius Mystery* (Rochester, Vermont: Destiny Books, 1987, 1976), pp. 116-117.
19. Brian M. Fagan, *The Journey From Eden: The Peopling of Our World* (New York: Thames and Hudson, Inc., 1990), p. 175. Incidentally, on this same page is a drawing of a painted pebble from Mâs d' Azil in Ariège in the French Pyrenees that clearly resembles an Egyptian *ankh*, although the author does not care to comment on it.
20. George E. Lankford, "The 'Path of Souls': Some Death Imagery in the Southeastern Ceremonial Complex," *Ancient Objects and Sacred Realms: Interpretations of Mississippian Iconography*, edited by F. Kent Reilly III and James F. Garber (Austin: University of Texas Press, 2007), p. 190.
21. George E. Lankford, *Reachable Stars: Patterns in the Ethnoastronomy of Eastern North America* (Tuscaloosa: University of Alabama Press, 2007), p. 32.
22. Richard Rudgley, *The Lost Civilizations of the Stone Age* (New York: Touchstone/Simon & Schuster, Inc., 1999), pp. 101-102.
23. http://www.themystica.org/mythical-folk/~articles/g/gayomart_the_myth_of%20.html.
24. Barbara Hand Clow, *Catastrophobia: The Truth Behind Earth Changes* (Rochester, Vermont: Bear & Co., 2001), p. 89.
25. Santillana and Dechend, *Hamlet's Mill*, op. cit., p. 146.
26. Huxley, *The Way of the Sacred*, op. cit., p. 212.
27. Collins, *From the Ashes of Angels*, op. cit., pp. 289-290.

28. Felicitas D. Goodman, *Where the Spirits Ride the Wind: Trance Journeys and Other Ecstatic Experiences* (Bloomington: Indiana University Press, 1990), p. 23.
29. Ibid, p. 24.
30. Clow, *Catastrophobia*, op. cit., p. 90; http://www.cuyamungueinstitute.com.
31. Henri Frankfort, *Kingship and the Gods: A Study of Ancient Near Eastern Religion as the Integration of Society and Nature* (Chicago: University of Chicago Press/Oriental Institute Essays, 1978, 1948), pp. 188-189.
32. Plutarch, *Plutarch's Morals: Theosophical Essays on Isis and Osiris*, translated by Charles William King, 1908, http://www.sacred-texts.com/cla/plu/pte/pte04.htm.
33. Clayton Eschleman, Preface, *Hades In Manganese* (Santa Barbara, California: Black Sparrow Press, 1981), p. 11.
34. Joseph Campbell, *Historical Atlas of World Mythology/Way of the Animal Powers: Mythologies of the Great Hunt*, Vol. I, Part 2 (New York: Harper & Row, Publishers, 1988), p. viii.
35. R. O. Faulkner, "Spell 180," *The Ancient Egyptian Book of the Dead*, (Austin: University of Texas Press, 1990), p. 17.
36. Robert E. Ryan, Ph.D., *The Strong Eye of Shamanism: A Journey Into the Caves of Consciousness* (Rochester, Vermont: Inner Traditions, 1999), p. 240.
37. Eschleman, title poem, *Hades In Manganese*, op. cit., p. 40.
From an article recently published in *Nature*, "Earliest hunting scene in prehistoric art," Maxime Aubert et al., December 11, 2019: "Here we describe an elaborate rock art [pictopgraph, or rock paintings] panel from the limestone cave of Leang Bulu' Sipong (Sulawesi, Indonesia) that portrays several figures that appear to represent therianthropes hunting wild pigs and dwarf bovids; this painting has been dated to at least 43.9ka on the basis of uranium-series analysis of overlying speleothems… Although the meanings of the imagery are uncertain and likely to remain so, this rock art scene may be regarded not only as the earliest dated figurative art in the world but also as the oldest evidence for the communication of a narrative in Palaeolithic art. This is noteworthy, given that the ability to invent fictional stories may have been the last and most crucial stage in the evolutionary history of human language and the development of modern-like patterns of cognition. The figures that we interpret as therianthropes are also the earliest images of this kind yet discovered. These figures are perhaps twice as old as the 'birdman' in the much-discussed shaft scene at Lascaux, and at least

several millennia older than the iconic lion-headed figurine from Aurignacian Germany. Our findings therefore further suggest that the first known indication of religious-like thinking—the ability to conceive of non-real entities such as therianthropes—comes not from Europe as has long been assumed, but occurs at least 43.9 ka in Sulawesi. The conspicuousness of therianthropes in the oldest recorded hunting scenes also offers hints at the deeply rooted symbolism of the human–animal bond and predator–prey relationships in the spiritual beliefs, narrative traditions and image-making practices of our species."

## *Part III: The Mudras of Immortality*

1. Mudra, "one of the symbolic hand gestures used in religious ceremonies and dances of India and in yoga," Merriam-Webster.

# Chapter 16 *Grasping the Hand Constellation of the Mississippians*

1. Sir E. A. Wallis Budge, *Amulets and Talismans* (New York: Collier Books, 1970, 1930), p. 467.
2. Migene González-Wippler, *The Complete Book of Amulets & Talismans* (Woodbury, Minnesota: Llewellyn Worldwide, LTD, 1991), p. 174.
3. Linda Heaphy, "The Hamsa (Khamsa)," Kashgar blog, April 28, 2017, https://kashgar.com.au/blogs/ritual-objects/the-hamsa-khamsa.
4. David, *Journey of the Serpent People*, op. cit., pp. 310-311. "Certainly, the result of the construction of New Cahokia [near East St. Louis, Illinois] was the beginning of what archaeologists today call Mississippian culture, which spread in one form or another across eastern North America from Minnesota's lakes to Louisiana's swamps and from the eastern Plains to the Atlantic. New towns were founded shortly thereafter [i.e., circa 1050 AD], populated by people who grew corn, built rectangular pyramidal and flat plazas, and crafted or decorated objects with images of sky and earth gods and godlike ancestors." Timothy R. Pauketat, *Cahokia: Anceint America's Great City on the Mississippi* (New York: Penguin, 2010, 2009), pp. 23-24.
5. Graphics on this and the preceeding page from Clarence B. Moore, *Certain Aboriginal Remains of the Black Warror River* (Philadelphia: "The Journal of the Academy of Natural Sciences," Vol. XIII, reprint, 1905).

6. Clarence Bloomfield Moore, *Moundville revisited* (Philadelphia: Reprint from the Journal of the Academy of Natural Sciences of Philadelphia, Vol. XIII, 1907), p. 390.
7. Hancock, *America Before*, op. cit., p. 309.
8. Gregory Little, foreward and afterward by Andrew Collins, *Path of Souls—The Native American Death Journey: Cygnus, Orion, the Milky Way, Giant Skeletons in Mounds, & the Smithsonian* (Memphis, Tennesse: ATA-Archetype Books, 2014), p. 2. An "ogee" is an architectural term used to describe a pointed arch comprised of two gentle S-shaped curves.
9. Ibid., p. 155.
10. Ronald Goodman, *Lakota Star Knowledge: Studies in Lakota Stellar Theology* (Rosebud, South Dakota: Sinte Gleska University, 1992), pp. 25-27.
11. Ibid., pp. 56-57. For a discussion of Lakota cosmology, see David, *Star Shrines and Earthworks of the Desert Southwest*, op. cit., pp. 40-45.
12. Hancock, *America Before*, op. cit., p. 310.
13. Lankford, *Reachable Stars*, op. cit., p. 204.
14. Robert Graves, *The Greek Myths* (Mt. Kisco, New York: Moyer Bell Limited, 1988, 1955, p. 151.
15. Moore, *Moundville revisited*. op. cit., p. 367.
16. Ibid., p. 400.
17. Little and Collins, *Path of Souls*, op. cit. p. 131.
18. For a discussion of the dual "stargates," each located at opposite ends of the Milky Way, see Chapter 2, David, *The Kivas of Heaven*, op. cit.
19. Spell 98, *The Ancient Egyptian Book of the Dead*, translated by Raymond O. Faulkner (Austin: University of Texas Press), 1990, 1985, 1972), p. 89.
20. Florence Hawley Ellis, "A Thousand years of the Pueblo Sun-Moon-Star Calendar," *Foundations of New World Cultural Astronomy*, edited by Anthony Aveni (Boulder: The University Press of Colorado, 2008), p. 665.
21. James R. Cunkle and Markus A. Jacquemain, *Stone Magic: Petroglyphs, Shamanic Shrine Sites, Ancient Rituals* (Phoenix, Arizona: Golden West Publishing, Inc., 1996, 1995), p. 167.
22. Malotki et al., editors, *Hopi-English Dictionary*, op. cit., p. 104.
23. Bradfield, *An Interpretation of Hopi Culture*, op. cit., p. 440. Actually, the Hopi acknowledge winter constellations other than Orion, such as Taurus, Canis Major, and Auriga.
24. Ray A. Williamson, *Living the Sky: The Cosmos of the American Indian* (Boston: Houghton Mifflin Company, 1984), pp. 142-143.

25. Alph H. Secakuku, *Following the Sun and Moon: Hopi Kachina Tradition* (Flagstaff, Arizona: Northland Publishing in cooperation with the Heard Museum, 1998, 1995), p. 3.
26. https://earthsky.org/space/a-black-hole-in-the-orion-nebula; https://www.skyandtelescope.com/astronomy-news/a-black-hole-in-orion.
27. Lankford, "The 'Path of Souls'," *Ancient Objects and Sacred Realms*, op. cit., p. 177.
28. In Dynastic Egypt the heliacal rising of Sirius in Canis Major, which is adjacent to Orion, coincided with the summer solstice and the flooding of the Nile. "The ancient skywatcher could also use the first appearance, after a seasonal absence, of a bright star rising just before sunrise, the 'helical rising' of the star. This, too, would mark the passage of a year. Additionally, it has seemed reasonable to conjecture the use of key heliacal risings to signal an approaching equinox or solstice 'benchmark' on the path of the solar disk. I am also suggesting that the stellar appearance was of an earlier importance than that of the positions of the sun." Jane B. Sellers, *The Death of Gods in Ancient Egypt: an Essay on Egyptian Religion and the Frame of Time* (London: Penguins Books, 1992), p. 27.

# Chapter 17    *The Hopi Underworld Journey*

1. Malotki et al., editors, *Hopi-English Dictionary*, op. cit., p. 234.
2. Lankford, *Reachable Stars*, op. cit., pp. 213-215.
3. The "medicine" mentioned in some of these account may have been Sacred Datura, or jimsonweed (*Datura wrightii*). See Chapter 12, David, *The Kivas of Heaven*, op. cit., especially pp. 240-246.
4. Courlander, *The Fourth World of the Hopis*, op. cit., p. 103.
5. Voth, *The Traditions of the Hopi*, op. cit., p. 115.
6. Ekkehart Malotki and Ken Gary, *Hopi Stories of Witchcraft, Shamanism, and Magic* (Lincoln: University of Nebraska Press, 2001, pp. 74-75.
7. Harold Courlander, *Hopi Voices: Recollections, Traditions, and Narratives of the Hopi Indians* (Albuquerque: University of New Mexico Press, 1982), p. 102.
8. Stephen, "Hopi Tales," *The Journal of American Folklore*, op. cit., pp. 18-19.

9. Don Talayesva, edited by Leo W. Simmons, *Sun Chief: An Autobiography of a Hopi Indian* (New Haven: Yale University Press, 1974, 1942), pp. 121-122.
10. Courlander, *Hopi Voices*, op. cit., p. 102.
11. Voth, *The Traditions of the Hopi*, op. cit., p. 115.
12. Harold Courlander, *People of the Blue Corn: Tales and Legends of the Hopi Indians* (New York: Henry Holt and Company, 1996, 1970), p. 130.
13. Voth, *The Traditions of the Hopi*, op. cit., pp. 115-116.
14. Courlander, *Hopi Voices*, op. cit., p. 102.
15. Malotki and Gary, *Hopi Stories of Witchcraft, Shamanism, and Magic*, op. cit., p. 79.
16. Stephen, "Hopi Tales," *The Journal of American Folklore*, op. cit., p. 19.
17. Courlander, *People of the Blue Corn*, op. cit. p. 134. The Tibetan Book of the Dead describes a similar color in the afterlife Bardo state. "All the time there will be a grey haze like the grey light of an autumn dawn, neither day nor night. This kind of bardo state will last for one, two, three, four, five, six, or seven weeks, up to forty-nine days." *The Tibetan Book of the Dead: The Great Liberation through Hearing in the Bardo* translated by Francesca Fremantle and Chögyam Trungpa (Boston: Shambala, 1987), pp. 74-75.
18. Yava, *Big Falling Snow*, op. cit., p. 102.
19. Courlander, *Hopi Voices*, op. cit., pp. 102-103.
20. Malotki and Gary, *Hopi Stories of Witchcraft, Shamanism, and Magic*, op. cit., p. 80.
21. Malotki et al., editors, *Hopi-English Dictionary*, op. cit., p. 32; Talayesva, *Sun Chief*, op. cit. p. 123. "The One Horn Society is the most powerful of all Hopi sacred societies or fraternities and is regarded with great awe by the Hopi, for it is the duty of these priests to look after the dead. They are in charge of the spirit upon its journey from this world into Muski [*Maski*], the underworld or spirit world of the Hopi. These priests serve Mui-aingwa [*Muy'ingwa*], the Germ God, owner of the underworld, and Masauwu [*Màasaw*], God of the earth and of death. When they die, their spirits cannot return to visit the living in the form of white clouds as is the privilege of most spirits, but must forever remain in the underworld." Edmund Nequatewa, *Truth of a Hopi: Stories Relating to the Origin, Myths and Clan Histories of the Hopi* (Flagstaff, Arizona: Museum of Northern Arizona, 1967, 1936), p. 126.
22. Courlander, *The Fourth World of the Hopis*, op. cit., p. 105.
23. Talayesva, *Sun Chief*, op. cit. p. 124.

24. Malotki and Gary, *Hopi Stories of Witchcraft, Shamanism, and Magic*, op. cit., p. 83.
25. Courlander, *Hopi Voices*, op. cit., pp. 103-104.
26. Malotki et al., editors, *Hopi-English Dictionary*, op. cit., p. 288, p. 379.
27. Voth, *The Traditions of the Hopi*, op. cit., p. 119.
28. Titiev, *Old Oraibi*, op. cit., p. 134.
29. Talayesva, *Sun Chief*, op. cit. p. 126.
30. Ekkehart Malotki and Michael Lomatuway'ma, *Stories of Maasaw*, a *Hopi God* (Lincoln, Nebraska: University of Nebraska Press, 1987), p. 33.
31. Lankford, "The 'Path of Souls'," *Ancient Objects and Sacred Realms*, op. cit., pp. 208-209.
32. See Bradfield, *An Interpretation of Hopi Culture*, op. cit., pp. 255-256. Because of the sensitivity of this subject, some Hopi have attempted to underscore the sacred nature of this ceremony. For instance, "The Hopi believe that anything young, like eaglets, is innocent and pure of heart, thus possessing the greatest spiritual powers. Treated the same as newborn Hopi children, the eaglets receive ritual blessings, have their 'hair' washed, and are given a Hopi *tungni* (surname). The name they receive will be in accordance with the clan that adopts them. The eaglets remain within the village to live with and observe the people of the village." Secakuku, *Following the Sun and Moon*, op. cit., p. 70.
33. Lankford, "The 'Path of Souls,' *Ancient Objects and Sacred Realms*, op. cit., p. 203.
34. See Chapters 7, 8, and 9 of David, *Journey of the Serpent People*, op. cit.

# Chapter 18   Grasping the Hand Constellation of the Hopi

1. Malotki et al., editors, *Hopi-English* Dictionary, op. cit., p. 222.
2. Harold S. Colton, *Hopi Kachina Dolls with a Key to their Identification* (Albuquerque: University of New Mexico Press, 1990, 1949), pp. 21-22.
3. Malotki et al., editors, *Hopi-English Dictionary*, op. cit., p. 219.
4. Ibid., p. 219, p. 232.
5. Waters and Fredericks, *Book of the Hopi*, op. cit., p. 155.
6. Malotki et al., editors, *Hopi-English Dictionary*, op. cit., pp. 220-221; Budge, *An Egyptian Hieroglyphic Dictionary*, Vol. I and II, op. cit., p. 266b, p. 271b, p. 752b.
7. Secakuku, *Following the Sun and Moon*, op. cit., p. 68.

8. Malotki et al., editors, *Hopi-English Dictionary*, op. cit., p. 225.
9. Secakuku, *Following the Sun and Moon*, op. cit., p. 64.
10. Jesse Walter Fewkes, *Hopi Katcinas* (New York: Dover Publications, Inc., 1985, reprint of *Twenty-First Annual Report to the Bureau of American Ethnology*, 1903), p. 104; Malotki et al., editors, *Hopi-English Dictionary*, op. cit., p. 569.
11. Harold S. Colton, *Hopi Kachina Dolls with a Key to their Identification* (Albuquerque: University of New Mexico Press, 1990, 1949), p. 46.
12. Fewkes, *Hopi Katcinas*, op. cit., p. 125.
13. Malotki et al., editors, *Hopi-English Dictionary*, op. cit., p. 146.
14. Wright, *Hopi Kachinas*, op. cit., p. 76.
15. Schaafsma, *Indian Rock Art of the Southwest*, op. cit., p. 119.
16. Campbell Grant, *Canyon de Chelly: Its People and Rock Art* (Tucson, Arizona: The University of Arizona Press, 1984, 1978), pp. 169-170.
17. Alden C. Hayes, Jon Nathan Young, A. H. Warren "Excavation of Mound 7, Gran Quivira National Monument, New Mexico," (Washington, DC: U.S. Government Printing Office, National Park Service/U.S. Department of the Interior, 1981), p. 89.
18. Alex Patterson, *A Field Guide To Rock Art Symbols of the Greater Southwest* (Boulder, Colorado: Johnson Books, 1992), p. 108.
19. Malotki et al., editors, *Hopi-English Dictionary*, op. cit., p. 678, p. 462.
20. Yava, *Big Falling Snow*, op. cit., p. 97.
21. Michael A. Adler, editor, *The Prehistoric Pueblo World, A.D. 1150-1350* (Tucson, Arizona: The University of Arizona Press, 1996), p. 259.
22. Malotki et al., editors, *Hopi-English Dictionary*, op. cit., p. 139.
23. Bradfield, *An Interpretation of Hopi Culture*, op. cit., p. 207; Armin W., Geertz and Michael Lomatuway'ma, *Children of the Cottonwood: Piety and Ceremonialism in Hopi Indian Puppetry* (Lincoln: University of Nebraska, 1987), p. 102.
24. Malotki et al., editors, *Hopi-English Dictionary*, op. cit., p. 345.
25. Mitton, *The Penguin Dictionary of Astronomy*, op. cit., pp. 284-285; Michael Zeilik, *Astronomy: The Evolving Universe* (New York: Harper & Row, Publishers, 1985), p. 276.
26. Robert Burnham, Jr., *Burnham's Celestial Handbook: An Observer's Guide to the Universe Beyond the Solar System*, Vol. 2 (New York: Dover Publications, Inc., 1978, reprint, 1966), p. 1317.
27. Richard Grossinger, *The Night Sky: Soul and Cosmos* (Berkeley, California: North Atlantic Books, 2014, 1988, 1982), p. 150. In the same volume, see pp. 30-31 for Grossinger's description of the Arizona Orion Correlation.

28. Deborah Byrd, "A Black Hole In the Orion Nebula?", Earthsky, November 5, 2012, http://earthsky.org/space/a-black-hole-in-the-orion-nebula.

29. Matilda Coxe Stevenson, " The Zuñi Indians: Their Mythology, Esoteric Studies, and Ceremonies," *Bureau of American Ethnology, 23rd Annual Report to the Secretary of the Smithsonian Institution, 1901-1902*, J. W. Powell, Director (Washinton, D.C.: Government Printing Office, 1904), p. 444. There is some confusion about the location of the "Place of Mist," or *Shi'papolima*. Stevenson writes that the entrance to this region is "…on the summit of a mountain about 10 miles from the pueblo of Cochiti, N. Mexico. Two crouching lions, or cougars, of massive stone in bas-relief upon the solid formation of the mountain top guard the sacred spot. The heads of the animals are to the east. A stone wall some 4 feet high forms an inclosure 18 feet in diameter for the cougars. Additional stone walls, also about 4 feet in height and 14 feet in length, mark a passageway 3 feet wide from the inclosure. A monument of stone stands 12 feet before the middle of the entrance, which faces east or a little south of east." Stevenson, who visited the spot (now within the boundaries of Bandelier National Monument) in 1904, claims that the local tribes have no legends about the sculptures other than that they were turned to stone when a great conflagration swept the earth. Ibid., p. 408. (See also, David, *Star Shrines and Earthworks of the Desert Southwest*, pp. 107-108.) However, my Zuni friend Clifford Mahooty, of the Galaxy Medicine Society (*Ne'wekwe*), says that the *Shi'papolima* is the same as the Hopi *Sipapuni* on the north bank of the Little Colorado River at the bottom of Grand Canyon, whence the people emerged from the underworld. Also, a discrepancy exists between "Hän'lipĭnkĭa in the west"and Hardscrabble Canyon in eastern Arizona that is the shrine and petroglyph site where the clans were once named. "The relationship between visual forms and traditional narratives is not one-sided; narratives can evoke the image of a visual form. For example, the mention of a place name in reciting a portion of the Zuni origin myth can evoke an image of the place named, both as an important point in the ancestors' quest for the Center and also as a known place in the physical world. Hanlhibinkya [Hän'lipĭnkĭa], where the clans were named, not only has mythic existence in the past but physical existence in the present as a specific place in Arizona to which Zunis make periodic pilgrimages. Thus, past and present coexist; the time of the myth is one with everyday existence." M. Jane Young, *Signs From the Ancestors: Zuni*

*Cultural Symbolism and Perceptions of Rock Art* (Albuquerque: University of New Mexico Press, 1990, 1988), p. 150.

## Chapter 19 *A Hopi-Dogon Divagation*

1. E. E. Barnard, "The Great Photographic Nebula of Orion, Encircling the Belt and Theta Nebula,"*Popular Astronomy*, Vol. 2, No. 14, 1894, pp.151-154, http://articles.adsabs.harvard.edu/cgi-bin/nph-iarticle_query?1894PA......2..151B&data_type=PDF_HIGH&whole_paper=YES&type=PRINTER&filetype=.pdf.
2. https://en.wikipedia.org/wiki/Barnard%27s_Loop.
3. Deborah Byrd, "Barnard's Loop and More," EarthSky, February 24, 2015, https://earthsky.org/todays-image/barnards-loop-and-more-in-orion.
4. Laird Scranton, *The Cosmological Origins of Myth and Symbol: From the Dogon and Ancient Egypt to India, Tibet, and China* (Rochester, Vermont: Inner Traditions, 2010, pp. 165-166.
5. Ibid., pp. 168-169.
6. The Dogon have received the most recent attention vis-à-vis the star Sirius and its two invisible companions, which I discuss in my book: Gary A. David, *Mirrors of Orion: Star Knowledge of the Ancient World* (CreateSpace, 2014), pp. 135-150. *Nota bene*: Dogon cosmology recognizes the following stars: Sirius (*sigi tolo*) and its first and second satellites (*po tolo* and *emme ya tolo*), Orion's belt (*atanu tolo*), his sword (*tolo dullogu*) and the four stars (i.e., Betelgeuse, Bellatrix, Rigel, and Saiph) of the "Chariot"(*amma bogu tolo*), the Polestar (*aduno giru*) and the Southern Cross (*aduno giru ley* ), Procyon in Canis Minor (*tara tolo*), the Pleiades (*tolo duno*), Sheratan in Aries (*yara tolo*), and the Milky Way (*yalu ulo*). Apparently the Dogon do not recognize the constellation Cygnus.
7. Marcel Griaule and Germaine Dieterlen, translated from the French by Stephen C. Infantino, Ph.D., *The Pale Fox* (Chino Valley, Arizona: Continuum Foundation, 1986, 1965), pp. 502-504. The Dogon god Amma may be related to the Egyptian creator-god Amun (also Amon, Amen, and later, Amun-Ra).
8. Northwest: white & air; Northeast: mottled (yellow?) & earth; Southeast: black & water; Southwest: red & fire.
9. Griaule and Dieterlen, *The Pale Fox*, op. cit., pp. 503-504.
10. Ibid., pp. 194-197. See also David, *Star Shrines and Earthworks of the Desert Southwest*, op. cit., p. 338.

11. Germaine Dieterlen, "Masks and Mythology Among the Dogon," *African Arts*, UCLA, Vol. XXII, No. 3, May 1989, p. 35.
12. Temple, *The Sirius Mystery*, op. cit., pp. 76-77.
13. Griaule and Dieterlen, *The Pale Fox*, op. cit., p. 360, Pl. XVIII.
14. D. Benest and J. L. Duvent, "Is Sirius a Triple Star?," *Astronomy and Astrophysics*, 299, 1995, pp. 621-628, http://www.bibliotecapleyades.net/archivos_pdf/sirius_triple_star.pdf.
15. Marcel Griaule, *Conversations with Ogotemmêli: An Introduction to Dogon Religious Ideas* (London: Oxford University Press, 1970, 1965), p. 18.
16. Griaule and Dieterlen, *The Pale Fox*, op. cit., p. 313.
17. Iona Miller, "Sobek: Wild Psyche," https://ionamiller2017.weebly.com/sobek---wild-psyche.html; David, *Journey of the Serpent People*, op. cit., pp. 129-130, p. 174; https://www.whiteoakwildlife.org/animal-programs/roan-antelope.
18. Griaule and Dieterlen, *The Pale Fox*, op. cit., pp. 313-314.
19. Temple, *The Sirius Mystery*, op. cit., p. 75.
20. Griaule and Dieterlen, *The Pale Fox*, op. cit., pp. 41-42, p. 543.
21. Ibid, pp. 314-315.
22. Ibid., p. 363.
23. Allen, *Star Names*, op. cit., p. 308.
24. Huxley, *The Way of the Sacred*, op. cit, p. 212.
25. Santillana and Dechend, *Hamlet's Mill*, op. cit, p. 148.
26. Griaule and Dieterlen, *The Pale Fox*, op. cit., p. 360.
27. Allen, *Star Names*, op. cit., p. 308. See also Chapter 3, David, *Star Shrines and Earthworks of the Desert Southwest*, op. cit.
28. Nicholas Grimal, *A History of Egypt* (Malden, Massachusetts: Blackwell Publishers, Inc. 1998, 1988), p. 45.
29. James Back, *A Dogon-English Dictionary* (Charleston, South Carolina: CreateSpace Independent Publishing Platform, 2016), p. 232, p. 236, p. 235.
30. Malotki et al., editors, *Hopi-English Dictionary*, op. cit., p. 331.
31. Ibid., p. 237.
32. Wallace Stevens, "Of Mere Being," *The Palm at the End of the Mind: Selected Poems and a Play by Wallace Stevens* (New York: Alfred A. Knopf, 1971), https://www.poetryfoundation.org/poems/57671/of-mere-being.

# Chapter 20   *Galaxias Ophis*

1. John Anthony West, *The Serpent In the Sky: The High Wisdom of Ancient Egypt* (New York: The Julian Press, 1987, 1979), p. 71.
2. Malotki et al., editors, *Hopi Dictionary*, op. cit., p. 568.
3. Herman Bender, "The Serpent's Tale: the Milky Way," 2017, https://www.academia.edu/37653209/A_Serpents_Tale_the_Milky_Way. Similar to the Akkadian term mentioned in the quotation, the Assyrian name referring to the Milky Way is *Nahru tsiri*, which means the "River-of-the-Snake." Allen, *Star Names*, op. cit., p. 475. The word *tsiri* is possibly an onomatopoetic suggestion of hissing, similar to the Hopi word *tsu*, which means "rattlesnake." Malotki et al., editors, *Hopi Dictionary*, op. cit., p. 649.
4. http://spokensanskrit.org/index.php?mode=3&script=hk&tran_input=naga&direct=se&anz=100.
5. Malotki et al., *Hopi Dictionary*, op. cit., p. 521.
6. P. David Seaman, *Hopi Dictionary* (Flagstaff, Arizona: Northern Arizona University Anthropological Paper No. 2, 1996, reprint 1985), p. 44.
7. Malotki et al., editors, *Hopi Dictionary*, op. cit., p. 520.
8. Ibid., p. 521, p. 324.
9. https://www.etymonline.com/word/zodiac.
10. Emily Upton, "How the Milky Way Got Its Name (and What Other Languages Call It)," Gizmodo, 8/26/13, https://gizmodo.com/how-the-milky-way-got-its-name-and-what-other-language-1201204037.
11. Jacqueline Mitton, *Dictionary of Astronomy*, op. cit., p. 254.
12. http://spokensanskrit.org/index.php?mode=3&script=hk&tran_input=kundalin&direct=au&anz=100.
13. *The Yoga Upanishad-s*, translated by T. R. S'rinivasa Aasyangar, B. A., L.T. (Madras, India: The Adyar Library, 1938), pp. 263-264, https://ia800304.us.archive.org/5/items/TheYogaUpanishads/TheYogaUpanisadsSanskritEngish1938.pdf.
14. Waters, *Book of the Hopi*, op. cit., pp. 9-10.
15. Mark Amaru Pinkham, *Sedona: City of the Star People* (Kempton, Illinois: Adventures Unlimited Press, 2015), p. 117, pp. 112-117, p. 130.

16. C. G. Jung, *The Archetypes and the Collective Unconscious*, translated by R. F. C. Hull (Princeton, New Jersey: Princeton University Press, 1990, 1969), pp. 375-376.
17. Joseph Campbell, *The Masks of God: Creative Mythology* (New York: Penguin Books, 1976, 1968), p. 503.
18. Rainer Maria Rilke, "Archaic Torso of Apollo," translated by Stephen Mitchell, *Ahead of All Parting: Selected Poetry and Prose of Rainer Maria Rilke* (New York: Modern Library, 1995.)
"…one of the basic tenets of Hindu religion and the archstone of the science of yoga is the belief, emphatically upheld by almost every scripture, that by properly directed effort it is possible for a man to complete the evolutionary cycle of human existence in one life and blossom into a *transfigured adept* [italics added] in tune with the infinite Reality beyond the phenomenal world, forever released from the otherwise endless chain of births and deaths." Gopi Krishna, *Kundalini: The Evolutionary Energy In Man* (Boston: Shambala, 1985, 1967), p. 123.
19. For more on Mount Kailas, see Chapter 13 of the present volume, pp. 199-202.
20. "The universe consists of a *Mahabrahmanda*, or grand Kosmos, and of numerous *Brihatbrahmanda*, or macrocosms evolved from it. As is said by the Nirvana Tantra, all which is in the first is in the second. In the latter are heavenly bodies and beings, which are microcosms reflecting on a minor scale the greater worlds which evolved them. 'As above, so below.' This mystical maxim of the West is stated in the Vishvasara Tantra as follows: 'What is here is elsewhere; what is not here is nowhere.'" Arthur Avalon, *Tantra of the Great Liberation (Mahanirvana Tantra)* (New York: Dover Publications, Inc., 1972, 1913), p. xlv.
21. Matthew 6:10, KJV.
22. According to the *Oxford English Dictionary*, a 1599 reference for the word "zone" from T. Hill's Schoole of Skil has the following meaning: "The constellation named Zone or the gyrdle of Orion." In other words, a constellation within the larger constellation, or his belt. Following Aristotle's usage, the Latin poet Ovid refers to "*Zona*" specifically as the three central stars of Orion. Allen, *Star Names*, op. cit., p. 315.
23. "**s-aha Tet** [or *Djed*], to set up the Tet, or backbone of Osiris." Budge, *An Egyptian Hieroglyphic Dictionary*, Vol. II, op. cit., p. 591b.  The *djed* pillar's "…status as either lying horizontally on the ground or standing upright is an allusion to Osiris's condition as on the one hand 'asleep' (i.e. , dead) or on the other hand 'awake' (i.e., reborn as Horus). The fact that the raising of the *djed* was a ritual probably enacted at the end of the

Sed festival to symbolize the regeneration of Osiris and his rebirth as Horus reinforces the likelihood of a Sed festival background to this utterance [Pyramid Texts, 271]. The raising of the *djed* may have also been the preliminary to the king's ascent to the sky, for it also symbolized the world pillar or pillars that, once raised, support the sky." Naydler, *Shamanic Wisdom in the Pyramid Texts*, op. cit. p. 266.

24. Malotki et al., *Hopi Dictionary*, op. cit., p. 376. *Pa*, "indication of wonder, awe, surprise, doubt, depending on what precedes," and *-pa*, "water." Ibid., p. 367.

25. *"Ida"* and *"Pingala,"* in the *Kundalini* chakra system, the dual *nadis*, or subtle channels, that spiral around the *Sushumna*, or central channel along the spinal column. They permit the flow of *prana*, "breath," or life-force.

26. "Entrance to the Boat of Millions of Years was likewise obtained by the knowledge of magical words and formulae, and of the secret names of the great gods, but the food on which lived the beatified souls who succeeded in securing a place in the Boat consisted of the emanations of the god Ra, or, according to the priests of Amen, Amen-Ra. In other words, the beatified souls in the Boat became beings formed of the light of Ra, on which they subsisted." E. A. Wallace Budge, *The Egyptian Heaven and Hell*, Vol. III (Mineola, New York: Dover Publications, Inc., 1996, 1905), p. 20.

27. *Sah*, "Orion, one of the 36 Dekans." Budge, *An Egyptian Hieroglyphic Dictionary*, Vol. II, op. cit., p. 638b; *Sahasrara* , the Crown Chakra, "thousand-spoked, thousand-rayed," and a"kind of cavity to be found in the top of the head and to resemble a lotus revered."
http://spokensanskrit.org/index.php?mode=3&script=hk&tran_input=Sahasrara&direct=se&anz=100.

28. Gaia Chakras: (1) Base – Mt. Shasta, California. (2) Sacral – Lake Titicaca, Peru and Bolivia. (3) Solar Plexus – Uluru (Ayers Rock) and Katatjuta, Australia (4) Heart – Glastonbury and Shaftesbury, England, (5) Throat – Great Pyramid and Sphinx, Mt. Sinai, Egypt, and Mount of Olives, Jerusalem. (6) Third Eye (Aeon Activation Center, mobile — moves west 1/12th of the Earth's circumference with each astrological Age ) – currently Western Europe. (7) Mt. Kailas, Tibet (see pp. 199-202). http://earthchakras.org/Locations.php.

29. Bernadette Brady, *Brady's Book of Fixed s* (York Beach, Maine: Samuel Weiser, Inc. 1998), p. 80.

30. Charles Fillmore, *Metaphysical Bible Dictionary* (Unity Village, Missouri: Unity School of Christianity, 1931), p. 496. For the concept of Ant = Orion, see p. 153.
31. Johari, *Chakras*, p. cit., p. 53.
32. Ellias Lonsdale quoted in Grossinger, *The Night Sky*, op. cit., p. 574. Lonsdale gave a lecture on astrology in 1975 at Goddard College for Grossinger's students.
33. Walter Collins O'Kane, *Sun in the Sky: The Hopi Indians of the Arizona Mesa Lands* (Norman: University of Oklahoma Press, 1970, 1950), p. 217. "Song of the Butterfly Dance," translated by Albert Yava: *"The earth with its blue, red, white and yellow / And all things that are sung about, to bear fruit— / as your butterfly maidens, corn maidens and other maidens, / Life will go on forever."* Ibid., p. 219. *Nota bene*: In the Orion Zone Chakra system, the Hopi Mesas correspond to the Sacral Chakra. See p. 13.
34. Johari, *Chakras*, op. cit., p. 58.
35. William Tyler Olcott, *Star Lore: Myths, Legends, and Facts* (Mineola, New York: Dover Publications, Inc., 2004, 1911), pp. 301-302.
36. Johari, *Chakras*, op. cit., p. 62.
37. Grossinger, *The Night Sky*, op. cit., p. 22, and quoting Dana Wilde, *Nebulae: a Backyard Cosmography*, 2012.
38. Brady, *Brady's Book of Fixed Stars*, op. cit., p. 93.
39. Allen, *Star Names*, op. cit., p. 156.
40. Johari, *Chakras*, op. cit., pp. 68-69.
41. Andrew Collins, *The Cygnus Mystery: Unlocking the Ancient Secret of Life's Origins in the Cosmos* (London: Watkins Publishing, 20060, pp. 199-201. According to a Chinese legend, every magpie in the land comes together each year to form a celestial bridge over the Milky Way called *Tianjin,* or "heavenly ford," which, Collins claims, is identified with the constellation Cygnus. However, other sources assert that this bird-bridge over the galactic plane is not Cygnus but the adjacent constellation Aquila. "This constellation [Aquila] and Lyra are associated with the curious Chinese legend of the Spinning Damsel and the Magpie Bridge, a legend current in Korea also. It is as follows: A cowherd fell in love with the spinning damsel. Her father in anger banished them both to the sky, where the cowhere became $\alpha$, $\beta$, and $\gamma$ Aquila, and the spinning damsel the constellation Lyra. The father decreed that they should meet once a year, if they could contrive to cross the river (the Milky Way). This they were enabled to do by their friends the magpies, who still once a year, the seventh night of the seventh moon, congregate at the crossing point, and form a bridge for them to pass over." Olcott, *Star Lore*, op. cit., p. 48.

42. Johari, *Chakras*, op. cit., pp. 74-75.
43. Brady, *Brady's Book of Fixed Stars*, op. cit., p. 57.
44. Bradfield, *An Interpretation of Hopi Culture*, op. cit., pp. 255-256.
45. Allen, *Star Names*, op. cit., p. 56.
46. Julius D. W. Staal, *The New Patterns in the Sky: Myths and Legends of the Stars* (Blacksburg, Virginia: The McDonald and Woodward Publishing Company, 1988), p. 180.
47. Johari, *Chakras*, op. cit., pp. 79-80.
48. Hall, *The Secret Teachings of All Ages*, op. cit., p. 159.
49. Cirlot, *A Dictionary of Symbols*, op. cit., pp. 264-265.
50. Olcott, *Star Lore*, op. cit., p. 317.
51. Staal, *The New Patterns in the Sky*, op. cit., p. 213.
52. Santillana and Dechend, *Hamlet's Mill*, op. cit., p. 296.
53. Ajit Mookerjee, *Kundalini: The Arousal of the Inner Energy* (Rochester, Vermont: Destiny Books, 1986, 1982), p. 44.
54. See Chapter 16, present volume, p. 273.
55. Santillana and Dechend, *Hamlet's Mill*, op. cit., pp. 242-243.
56. *Via Regia*, "Royal Road."
57. Johari, *Chakras*, op. cit., p. 92.
58. *Bardo*, in Tibetan cosmology, the intermediate realm between physical incarnations. Some distinguish six different types of the *Bardo*: 1. The 49 days of the realm between the end of one life and the beginning of the next, detailed in The Tibetan Book of the Dead 2. the "natural *Bardo*" of corporeal existence 3. the *Bardo* of dreaming 4. the *Bardo* of meditation 5. the *Bardo* of dying and 6. the *Bardo* of Clear Light and visions.
59. *Shakti*, personification of the dynamic female serpent energy.
60. *Ur-Uroboros*, the snake swallowing its tail at the Base Chakra, *Yoga Kundalini Upanishad*, 1.82; see also, p. 327, present volume.
61. *Lotos*, i.e., *Lotophagi*, or eaters of the hallucinogenic blue lotus.
62. *Omphalos-cum-lingam*, *Omphalos*, literally, "navel," the geodetic oracular stone located at Delphi in Greece; *lingam*, Sanskrit, "phallus" (exoteric), the male principle (esoteric).
63. *Morui*, Indo-European "ant"; see also, p. 163.
64. Changing Woman, Navajo goddess, their most revered deity. "The name Estsánatlehi is derived by syncopation from etsán, woman, and natléhi, to change or transform. She is so called because, it is supposed, she never remains in one condition, but that she grows to be an old woman, and in the course of time becomes a young girl again, and so passes through an endless course of lives, changing but never dying. It is probable that she is the apotheosis of Nature, or of the changing year."

Washington Matthews, *Navaho Legends* (Salt Lake City: University of Utah Press, 1994), p. 34.

65. *vajra,* Sanskrit, a weapon-like ritual artifact that symbolizes both the thunderbolt or lightning and the diamond.

66. Throat-singer, one who used the Tibetan Buddhist technique of overtone chanting.

67. Nyx, Greek goddess of night, darkness, chaos.

68. *nada,* Sanskrit, "…cosmic sound approaching manifestation. Anahata nad is the 'unstruck' sound experienced in Sushumna [central subtle channel],"Mookerjee, *Kundalini,* op. cit., p. 106.

69. "boatman of Styx," the infernal ferryman; also, the 1979 song "Boat on the River" by the rock group Styx.

70. *Samadhi,* "…enstasis, a trance-like state in which the fluctuation of the mind ceases; the last stage of yoga in which the final identification is reached." Mookerjee, *Kundalini,* op. cit., p. 107.

71."It was Triptolemos who first sowed grain for cultivation, travelling throughout the world in a flying chariot drawn by serpents. His gospel was the reborn seed, the barley or *alphi,* a word that can be traced to a formulaic conjunction in Indo-European for the food from cultivation as opposed to the natural food, *meli* or honey. The barley for the Eleusinian ceremonies was specifically grown in the Rarian plain and threshed upon the floor of Triptolemus. Together with water and *glechon* [pennyroyal (*Mentha palegium*), an aphrodisiac and possibly a psychotomimetic] it was an ingredient of the sacred potion." Gordon Wasson, Carl P. Ruck, and Albert Hoffman, *The Road to Eleusis: Unveiling the Secret of the Mysteries* (New York: Harcourt, Brace & Jovanovich, Inc., 1978), p. 100. If improperly grown, barley sometimes reverts to its more primitive form called *aira,* or darnel (*Lolium temulentum*), which is commonly infested with the parasitic fungus ergot, the sclerotium of *Cleviceps purpurea* or "rust." Ibid., p. 115. The authors claim that the hallucinogenic alkaloid ergot of barley, which is chemically similar to LSD, was a primary ingredient in the Eleusinian elixir. See also, David, *Star Shrines and Earthworks of the Desert Southwest,* op. cit., pp. 72-74.

72. Smati-Osiris, the Egyptian Barley God, Allen, *Star Names,* op. cit., p. 308.

73. *Shiva,* personified god of Pure Consciousness, transcendent divine principle, Lord of the Dance, and consort of Shakti.

74. *Sphota,* "…the eternal sound element, pure and unmanifested, the creative principle of the universe." Mookerjee, *Kundalini,* op. cit., p. 107.

Made in the USA
Coppell, TX
23 April 2024